ACCLAIM FOR STUART DIAMOND AND
HIS NEGOTIATION CLASSES

"If I had spent my entire tuition at USC to take only your course, it would have been well worth it—the most valuable class ever, including the U of Chicago, Skidmore, and UCLA."

—Beth S. Brandegee, MBA, USC

"The best class at Wharton; it changed my life."

—Jim Vopelius, Vice President and CFO, Trident Risk Management

"There isn't an hour that goes by in my personal and professional lives when I *don't* use what I learned from your class."

—Bill Ruhl, Director, National Customer Service Operations, Verizon

"I am living proof that this course does pay! I saved $245 million for my company."

—Richard T. Morena, CFO, Asbury Park Press

"The best class ever at Google—it should be required for all salespeople. I know I will use all of my newly realized tools for the rest of my life."

—Patrick Grandinetti, Senior Manager, Google

"I have found the lessons I learned at Wharton from Stuart Diamond invaluable to helping me achieve my goals, whether on the field, in the office, or at home with my five children."

—Anthony Noto, CFO, National Football League

"I would rate this course as the crown jewel. It fundamentally changed my way of thinking."

—Ravi Radhakrishnan, Senior Manager, Accenture

"In the years since I graduated, it has become clear that there is one class that has paid for my entire education—negotiation. I was able to sell an asset that I purchased for $1 to a public company for $450,000. It was a direct result of what I learned in the class."

—Bradford S. Oberwager, CEO, Sundia Corporation

"There have been hundreds and hundreds of situations where what I learned has made the difference."

—Robert Silver, Executive Director, UBS

GETTING
MORE

How to Negotiate to Achieve
Your Goals in the Real World

Stuart Diamond

CROWN
BUSINESS
NEW YORK

Published in the United States by Crown Business, an imprint of the Crown Publishing Group,
a division of Random House, Inc., New York.
www.crownpublishing.com

CROWN BUSINESS is a trademark and CROWN and the Rising Sun colophon are registered
trademarks of Random House, Inc.

Crown Business books are available at special discounts for bulk purchases for sales promotions or
corporate use. Special editions, including personalized covers, excerpts of existing books, or books
with corporate logos, can be created in large quantities for special needs. For more information,
contact Premium Sales at (212) 572-2232 or e-mail specialmarkets@randomhouse.com.

Library of Congress Cataloging-in-Publication Data

Diamond, Stuart.
Getting more : how to negotiate to achieve your goals in the real world / Stuart Diamond.—1st ed.
p. cm.
1. Negotiation. I. Title.
BF637.N4D53 2010
302.3—dc22   2010017638

ISBN 978-0-307-71689-7
eISBN 978-0-307-71691-0

Printed in the United States of America

Book design by Helene Berinsky

10 9 8 7 6 5 4 3

For Kimberly and Alexander

Contents

Preface

This is an optimistic book, intended to make your life better. It starts with the principle that you can get more. No matter who you are, no matter what your personality, you can learn to be a better negotiator. You can get more.

In the twenty-plus years I have been teaching, I have had the palpable experience of watching people become better negotiators before my eyes. They became more aware of themselves and particularly others in their quest to get more in their lives through negotiation.

A lot of the tools that they learn in my class and use in their lives challenge the conventional wisdom. Many seem counterintuitive at first. But the success of my students' day-to-day experiences, and their personal growth, are the markers of a new way of looking at human interactions. The *Getting More* process presented in this book redefines negotiation theory: simplifying it, eliminating the jargon, and providing a more practical, realistic, and effective way of dealing with others.

You will see how the conventional concepts of rationality, power, walking out, and "win-win" actually don't work very well much of the time. Instead, strategies like emotional sensitivity, relationships, clear goals, being incremental, and viewing each situation as different are much more persuasive.

My students learn to get more by communicating even in the face of hostility, and by valuing the other side's perceptions no matter what they are. They learn about the loss of profit from confrontation and "us versus them" tactics, and gain much more value by constantly pushing for collaboration. And they learn to handle hard bargainers by using their words against them in the least combative way. They offer trust but insist on commitments in return. They are not patsies. They meet their goals.

As mentioned throughout, the title of this book is *Getting More*, not *Getting Everything*. The book is intended to significantly improve the life of anyone who reads it and embraces its tools and strategies. Some elements will work sometimes; some will work better than others. It will teach you to determine what works best for you and train you to make those tools your own.

At the end of the day, *Getting More* is not about learning how to negotiate; it is about becoming a negotiator to your core, so these tools become as much a part of you as your personality. Once the tools are internalized, virtually every interaction you have will improve.

Not everything in this book will apply to you. Some of you don't have children, and others are uninterested in public issues. But in writing this book I tried to communicate advice that touches a very broad audience. Something that you already know may be very fresh to someone else, and vice versa. The point is to identify what you can use, now and throughout your life, and key on it. Look for the things that can help you, that can add value to your life and the lives of others.

All of the material, whether applicable to you or not, is presented through the stories of my students and my own experiences, in the hope that their successes—and failures—will be interesting to you even as you are learning the tools.

Unless you practice with these tools, however, they will remain words on a page. You must see them work for you to own them.

You may think that some of the negotiation tools in this book cannot possibly work. But everything has been tested and tested again. They do work; often they tap into fundamental tenets of human psychology. If you're skeptical, try them in nonrisky environments, and incrementally, and see what happens. You're likely to be pleasantly surprised. Don't do everything at once. Try something, feel it out, improve it for yourself, and then add something else. You have a lifetime to do this.

Finally, let me know how you are doing. I'm a teacher at heart. I want to know how my students are doing, and anyone else who addresses the material. Write me at www.gettingmore.com. This book is intended to begin a dialogue among those who have looked around at the world we live in, and decided it's time to get more.

Haverford, Pennsylvania, August 12, 2010

GETTING
MORE

1

Thinking Differently

My run slowed to a jog as we approached the gate for our flight to Paris. The plane was still there, but the door to the Jetway was shut. The gate agents were quietly sorting tickets. They had already retracted the hood connecting the Jetway to the airplane door.

"Hi, we're on this flight!" I panted.

"Sorry," said the agent. "We're done boarding."

"But our connecting flight landed just ten minutes ago. They promised us they would call ahead to the gate."

"Sorry, we can't board anyone after they've closed the door."

My boyfriend and I walked to the window in disbelief. Our long weekend was about to fall to pieces. The plane waited right before our eyes. The sun had set, and the pilots' downturned faces were bathed in the glow of their instrument panel. The whine of the engines intensified and a guy with lighted batons sauntered onto the tarmac.

I thought for a few seconds. Then I led my boyfriend to the center of the window right in front of the cockpit. We stood there, in plain sight, my entire being focused on the pilot, hoping to catch his eye.

One of the pilots looked up. He saw us standing forlornly in the window. I looked him in the eye, plaintively, pleadingly. I let my bags slump by my feet. We stood there for what seemed an eternity. Finally, the pilot's lips moved and the other pilot looked up. I caught his eye, as well, and he nodded.

The engine whine softened and we heard the gate agent's phone ring. She turned to us, wide-eyed. "Grab your stuff!" she said. "The pilot said

to let you on!" Our vacation restored, we clutched each other joyously,
snatched our bags, waved to the pilots, and tumbled down the Jetway to
our plane.

—RAYENNE CHEN, Wharton Business School, Class of 2001

The story above, told to me by a student in my negotiation course, was
clearly an account of a negotiation. Completely nonverbal, to be sure. But
it was done in a conscious, structured, and highly effective way. And it used
six separate negotiation tools that I teach that are, in practice, invisible to
almost everyone.

What are they? First, be dispassionate; emotion destroys negotiations.
You must force yourself to be calm.

Second, prepare, even for five seconds. Collect your thoughts.

Third, find the decision-maker. Here, it was the pilot. There was not a
second to waste on the gate agent, who was not about to change company
policy.

Fourth, focus on your goals, not on who is right. It didn't matter if the
connecting airline was late, or wrong in not calling ahead to the gate. The
goal was to get on the plane to Paris.

Fifth, make human contact. People are almost everything in a negotiation.

And finally, acknowledge the other party's position and power, valuing
them. If you do, they will often use their authority to help you achieve your
goals.

These tools are often very subtle. But they are not magic. They helped
this young couple in a way they will remember for a lifetime. And they
help to bring about successful negotiations, day in and day out, for those
who have learned these tools from my courses. From getting a job to getting a raise, from dealing with kids to dealing with colleagues, the kind of
negotiation practiced here has given upwards of thirty thousand people
more power and control over their lives.

My goal with this book is to re-create my course on the page, making it available to readers everywhere. It offers a set of strategies, models,
and tools that together will change the way you view and conduct virtually
every human interaction. These teachings are *very* different from what you
have read or studied about negotiation. Based on psychology, they don't
depend on "win-win" or "win-lose." They don't depend on being a "hard"
or "soft" bargainer. They don't depend on a rational world, on who has
the most power, or on phrases that make much of negotiation seem inac-

cessible and impractical. Instead, they are based on how people perceive, think, feel, and live in the real world. And they will help *anyone* do what this book suggests: get more.

And that's one of those instinctive human desires, isn't it? More. Whenever you do almost anything, don't you wonder if there's more? It doesn't have to mean more for me and less for you. It just has to be, well, more. And it doesn't necessarily mean more money. It means more of whatever you value: more money, more time, more food, more love, more travel, more responsibility, more basketball, more TV, more music.

This book is about more: how you define it, how you get it, how you keep it. Whoever you are, wherever you are, the ideas and tools in this book were meant for you.

The world is full of negotiation books telling you how to get to yes, get past no, win, gain an advantage, close the deal, get leverage, influence or persuade others, be nice, be tough, and so forth.

But of those who finish reading them, few can go out and do it. Besides, sometimes you may *want* to get to no. Or you want to get to maybe. Or you just want to delay things. But, instinctively, you always want to get more of what you want.

In *Getting More*, I present this information in such a way that you will actually be able to use it—immediately—whether ordering a pizza or negotiating a billion-dollar deal or asking for a discount on a blouse or a pair of pants. This is what people who take my course are *required* to do. I tell them to use the strategies the same day, write them down in their journals, practice them, and use them again.

WHY IS THIS SO IMPORTANT?

Negotiation is at the heart of human interaction. Every time people interact, there is negotiation going on: verbally or nonverbally, consciously or unconsciously. Driving, talking to your kids, doing errands. You can't get away from it. You can only do it well or badly.

That doesn't mean you have to actively negotiate everything in your life all the time. But it does mean that those who are more conscious of the interactions around them get more of what they want in life.

There is an old maxim about the difference between expert and nonexpert knowledge. A nonexpert looks at a field and sees flat land. An expert looks at the same field and sees small peaks and valleys. It takes no more time and energy for the expert to collect the greater amount of information from that landscape. But the expert can make much better use of that information to pursue opportunities or minimize risks.

What we are talking about in *Getting More* is learning better negotiation tools so that you become exquisitely more conscious of the topography of your dealings with others.

Like Rayenne Chen at the opening of the book, most of those who have taken my course are ordinary people. But they have learned to achieve extraordinary results by negotiating with greater confidence and skill. More than one woman from India in my class, using tools from the course, persuaded her parents to let her out of her own arranged marriage. My advice on the negotiation process helped to end the 2008 Writers Guild strike. It is the same kind of advice taught in my classes and outlined in Chapter 2.

A business student who hadn't made it past the first-round interview with eighteen firms took the course, applied my negotiation tools, and got twelve consecutive final-round interviews and the job of his choice. Parents get their young children to brush their teeth without complaint.

We added up the money made and saved by students using these tools: $7 here, $132 there, $1 million or more in some cases. The total exceeded $3 billion for about a third of the stories we have collected. And that doesn't count the marriages saved, the jobs obtained, the deals concluded, the parents who were persuaded to go to the doctor, the kids who did just what they were asked.

Most of the more than 400 anecdotes in this book use the actual names of the people involved. They will tell you how they got a raise, achieved satisfaction after buying defective merchandise, got out of a speeding ticket, got their kids to do their homework, closed a deal—how, in a million ways, their lives became better. How they got more.

For me and the tens of thousands of people I've taught, unless these tools work in real life, we're not interested.

Who are these people? They come from all walks of life, and myriad cultures. Senior executives of billion-dollar companies, housewives, students in school, salespeople, administrative assistants, executives, managers, lawyers, engineers, stockbrokers, truckers, union workers, artists—you name it. And they come from around the world: the United States, Japan, China, Russia, Colombia, Bolivia, South Africa, Kuwait, Jordan, Israel, Germany, France, England, Brazil, India, Vietnam, and so forth.

These tools work for all of them. And they will work for you, too.

Like Ben Friedman, who almost always asks the companies whose services he uses if new customers are treated better than existing, loyal customers like himself—for example, with discounts or other promotions. By asking that question one day, Ben got 33 percent off his existing *New York Times* subscription.

Or Soo Jin Kim, who looks for connections everywhere. One day she saved $200 a year for her daughter's after-school French program. How? Before asking for a discount, she made a human connection with the school's manager, talking about her trips to France. These strategies will save you a little here, a little there. But it can add up to many thousands of dollars a year.

Some make millions at the start. Paul Thurman, a management consultant in New York, reduced a large client's expenses by 35 percent, an "incredible" twenty points more than he had been able to do before the course. He used standards, persistence, better questions, relationships, and being incremental, as learned in the course. The first-year savings was $34 million; by now it's over $300 million, he said. "I have a major advantage in the marketplace," he said.

Richard Morena, then the chief financial officer of the *Asbury Park Press*, got $245 million more for the company in its sale, and $1 million more for himself, by using standards, framing, and other course tools. "I'll keep practicing," he said. To benefit from the strategies in the book, as Richard did, you have to think differently about how you deal with others.

HOW THIS BOOK IS DIFFERENT

Below are the twelve major strategies that together make *Getting More* very different from what most people think negotiation is all about. These strategies will be expanded throughout the book, including the tools that support them and the perspectives that go with them. The strategies will be followed by chapters on how they are used in specific familiar applications, such as parenting, travel, and jobs.

The strategies together amount to a different way of thinking about negotiation. It's the difference between saying "I play football" and "I play professional football." The two are barely even the same game.

1. Goals Are Paramount.

Goals are what you want at the end of the negotiation that you don't have at the beginning. Clearly, you should negotiate to meet your goals.

Many, if not most, people take actions contrary to their goals because they are focused on something else. They get mad in a store or relationship. They attack the wrong people. In a negotiation, you should not pursue relationships, interests, win-win, or anything else just because you think it's an effective tool. Anything you do in a negotiation should *explicitly* bring you closer to your goals for that particular negotiation. Otherwise, it is irrelevant or damaging to you.

2. It's About Them.

You can't persuade people of anything unless you know the pictures in their heads: their perceptions, sensibilities, needs, how they make commitments, whether they are trustworthy. Find out what third parties they respect and who can help you. How do they form relationships? Without this information, you won't even know where to start. Think of yourself as the least important person in the negotiation. You must do role reversal, putting yourself in their shoes and trying to put them in yours. Using power or leverage can ultimately destroy relationships and cause retaliation. To be ultimately more effective (and persuasive), you have to get people to *want* to do things.

3. Make Emotional Payments.

The world is irrational. And the more important a negotiation is to an individual, the more irrational he or she often becomes: whether in world peace or a billion-dollar deal, or when your child wants an ice-cream cone. When people are irrational, they are emotional. When they are emotional, they can't listen. When they can't listen, they can't be persuaded. So your words are useless, especially those arguments intended for rational or reasonable people, like "win-win." You need to tap into the other person's emotional psyche with empathy, apologies if necessary, by valuing them or offering them other things that get them to think more clearly.

4. Every Situation Is Different.

In a negotiation, there is no one-size-fits-all. Even having the same people on different days in the same negotiation can be a different situation. You must analyze every situation on its own. Averages, trends, statistics, or past problems don't matter much if you want to get more today and tomorrow with the people in front of you. Blanket rules on how to negotiate with the Japanese or Muslims, or that state you should never make the first offer, are simply wrong. There are too many differences among people and situations to be so rigid in your thinking. The right answer to the statement "I hate you" is "Tell me more." You learn what they are thinking or feeling, so that you can better persuade them.

5. Incremental Is Best.

People often fail because they ask for too much all at once. They take steps that are too big. This scares people, makes the negotiation seem riskier, and magnifies differences. Take small steps, whether you are trying for raises or treaties. Lead people from the pictures in their heads to your goals, from the familiar to the unfamiliar, a step at a time. If there is little trust, it's even more important to be incremental. Test each step. If there are big differences between parties, move slowly toward each other, narrowing the gap incrementally.

6. Trade Things You Value Unequally.

All people value things unequally. First find out what each party cares and doesn't care about, big and small, tangible and intangible, in the deal or outside the deal, rational and emotional. Then trade off items that one party values but the other party doesn't. Trade holiday work for more vacation, TV time for more homework, a lower price for more referrals. This strategy is much broader than "interests" or "needs," in that it uses all the experiences and synapses of people's lives. And it greatly expands the pie, creating more opportunities, at home as well as the office. It is rarely done the way it should be.

7. Find Their Standards.

What are their policies, exceptions to policies, precedents, past statements, ways they make decisions? Use these to get more. Name their bad behavior when they are not consistent with their policies. Did they ever allow late hotel checkout? Will they agree that no one should interrupt anyone else? Should innocent people be harmed? Isn't high customer service part of their promise? This is especially effective in dealing with hard bargainers.

8. Be Transparent and Constructive, Not Manipulative.

This is one of the biggest differences between *Getting More* and the conventional wisdom. Don't deceive people. They will find out and the long-term payoff is poor. Be yourself. Stop trying to be tougher, nicer, or something you're not. People can detect fakers. Being real is highly credible, and credibility is your biggest asset. If you're in a bad mood or too aggressive, or don't know something, say so. It will help take the issue away. Your approach and your attitude are critical. This does *not* mean being a patsy or disclosing everything up front. It does mean being honest, being real.

9. Always Communicate, State the Obvious, Frame the Vision.

Most failed negotiations are caused by bad communication, or none at all. Don't walk away from a negotiation unless all parties agree to take a break—or unless you want to end the negotiation. Not communicating means not getting information. Threatening or blaming the other party just results in their responding in kind: valuing them gets more. The best negotiators state the obvious. They will say, "We don't seem to be getting along." Package what's going on in a few words to give them a vision of where you want them to go: "Is it your goal to make your customers happy?"

10. Find the Real Problem and Make It an Opportunity.

Few people find or fix the real, underlying problem in negotiations. Ask, "What is *really* preventing me from meeting my goals?" To find the real problem, you have to find out *why* the other party is acting the way they are. It may not be obvious at first. You have to probe until you find it. You have to get into their shoes. A dispute over a child's curfew or a business valuation may really be a problem of trust and an opportunity for a better relationship. And problems are only the start of the analysis. They usually can be turned into negotiation opportunities. View problems as such.

11. Embrace Differences.

Most people think different is worse, risky, annoying, uncomfortable. But different is actually demonstrably better: more profitable, more creative. It leads to more perceptions, more ideas, more options, better negotiations, better results. Asking a few more questions about differences will produce more trust and better agreements. Companies, countries, and civilizations have shown repeatedly by their actions how they hate differences, despite their public relations statements. Great negotiators love differences.

12. Prepare—Make a List and Practice with It.

These strategies are the start of a List, which is the entire collection of negotiation strategies, tools, and models. The List is like a pantry, from which you choose items for every meal. From the List, you would choose specific items to help you in an individual negotiation based on the specific situation. One is a tool: that is, a specific action to implement a strategy. Apologies and concessions are tools to help you implement the emotional payments strategy. Strategies and tools in this book are organized into a *Getting More* Model for easy reference. The list is on my website, www .gettingmore.com. You should make your own List. If you don't have a List, you aren't prepared. If you aren't prepared, you won't do as well. Even spending a few minutes with the List produces better results. Keep pursuing the List—be persistent—until you meet your goals. That means you need to practice with these strategies and tools and review them after each negotiation.

The effectiveness of these models and strategies, and of the individual tools that support them, have been confirmed by the 30,000 students and professionals from dozens of countries I have taught. Their experiences are documented in more than 100,000 journals, emails, and notes they have written, as well as in countless interviews and conversations over more than twenty years.

All of that is backed by further research and consultation, and my own practical experience over forty years as a teacher, researcher, journalist, lawyer, business executive, and negotiation practitioner. Much of what this book discusses will seem counterintuitive. But it works, in the real world, immediately. In *Getting More*, you will see exactly how.

INVISIBILITY

Two things are evident about these strategies and many of the tools presented here. First, they are not rocket science. Second, unless you already know what they are, they are invisible, buried in ordinary language.

"I started to realize," said Eric Stark, an MBA student at the University of Southern California, "that the people I was negotiating with had no idea what I was doing. They had *no idea.*" Now a telecommunications and Internet expert, he says that this is still true, fifteen years after the class.

My most common opening in a negotiation is "What's going on?" Seems like an ordinary question. But there are at least four tools folded into that question. First, it helps to establish a relationship with the other person—you start out informal and chatty. Second, it is a question—questions are a great way to collect information. Third, it focuses first on the other party and their feelings and perceptions, instead of on "the deal." Fourth, it consists of small talk to establish a comfort level between us.

Unless you explicitly know what the tools are, you can't replicate them effectively from situation to situation. You just keep going on instinct. And you can't get much better at negotiating that way.

A few years ago I was negotiating with someone on a very snowy day. I started the negotiation by saying with some frustration, "How about this snow?" To which the other person replied, "Actually, I love the snow. I love to ski." So then I said, "Well, how do you feel about the heat?"

Why did I say that? Unless you can identify the exact negotiation tool used, you can't do much better, because you can't consciously replicate it in future negotiations. I was trying to find a common enemy. Common enemies bring parties closer together and make the negotiation easier. That's why people complain about the weather; it establishes a human connection, and a shared vantage point. People complain half-jokingly about attorneys, or traffic, or bureaucracy for exactly that reason.

Most people are unaware of the "common enemies" tool. It is invisible to you. You can't make it visible unless someone tells you about it. Mutual needs are also good (although with less psychological impact) if you can find them at the start of negotiations.

These strategies and tools are also invisible because they are relatively new, at least in how they are used. The modern field of negotiation, created by lawyers around 1980, focused on resolving conflicts. This was good but incomplete. It protected the downside of a negotiation, but didn't focus as much on the upside. Economists got more involved in the negotiation field in the 1990s and developed more strategies to make money and gain opportunity. But this was also incomplete, because it relied on people being rational.

Getting More accounts for these factors, of course, but it also focuses on the psychology of the people involved. This is what most of negotiation should be about: the pictures in people's heads. You can't discover the opportunity or the resolution of conflict unless you think hard about the psychology of the other person.

WHAT THIS BOOK IS NOT

Getting More is not a manifesto to gain power over people in order to force your will on them. "Power," or "leverage," is greatly overrated as a negotiation device. Most negotiation teaching, as well as portrayals of negotiation in movies and TV, urges people to gain advantage over the other party so you can force them to do what you want. This has many problems.

First, the moment you use raw power over someone, the relationship is usually over. People don't want relationships with those who try to force them to do things against their will. Second, it sends the wrong message— one of tension, struggle, and conflict. This is less profitable because people use their energy to defend themselves instead of building something. Third, the raw use of power prompts retribution, whether now or later, whether "malicious obedience" at work, or suicide bombers worldwide. Fourth, using power over reluctant subjects is expensive, as will be seen below. Finally, if it's overused, you will often lose your power when others see it expressed.

Power must be used gingerly, tactfully, with the approval of others (in the military or courts, for example), and for fairness. One should know about the power balance in order to understand how to promote fairness in a negotiation and meet your goals. And these strategies give you power; it's the application, how you use them, that matters. Inherently, they are morally neutral: they can be used for good or ill, like science or kitchen knives. It is okay to increase your power with hard bargainers who are acting unfairly or trying to hurt you with *their* power. It is, for example, a great tool for beleaguered consumers to use with unfair companies. It is okay to seek other options if your counterpart is unfairly pressing you. But you always have to be conscious and careful of its abuse.

As seen below, use of power or leverage is a form of negotiation; it's usually just not a very good one. It's more expensive and less self-enforcing. If I persuade you to willingly do something, it's usually not very expensive. If I can't do that, I might have to turn to an outside party, such as an attorney, to negotiate for me. If the attorney can't persuade you, then the attorney will turn to another outsider, such as a judge or jury. The attorney then negotiates with that outsider, who can then force you to do what you don't want to do. As you can see, there is still negotiation going on, but the more parties and force I add, the more expensive it becomes. As a last resort it may be needed, but not as an early choice, and certainly not as a knee-jerk one. It is a premise of this book that by using better negotiation skills, you can persuade more people, by yourself, to do things willingly.

The invisible strategies stated above can be a major source of competitive advantage. Nonetheless, you should share them with the other side. This way, they won't feel manipulated, and you will get more over the long term.

This book is also not about "best alternative to a negotiated agreement"—BATNA—or other acronyms that seem handy. In reality, they cause people to focus more on walking away than on working out something better with the other party. I often say, "Let's assume everyone can walk away and do fine. Given that, can we get more in negotiating with each other?"

"Bargaining range" is another item less useful than many people think. You might know the monetary bargaining range: the highest the buyer will pay and the lowest the seller will accept. But you can change the bargaining range by adding other elements to a negotiation, such as by trading items of unequal value. So the more creative you are, the less useful bargaining range, BATNA, and its various cousins are.

After all is said and done, there may be a better alternative to the option you finally develop. And you should explore your options. But first you should find out what you can do with the people in front of you, as creatively as possible. And if you use your options to beat up the other party, it's like going on a date and mentioning all the other people you could go out with. The relationship will probably not get far. I will return repeatedly in *Getting More* to the problems with power. It's easy to fall back into old habits, as in, let's make them do it. I want to make sure this doesn't happen.

A NEW DEFINITION OF NEGOTIATION

Let's start our journey with a new definition of what negotiation is. First, done right, there is no difference between "negotiation," "persuasion," "communication," or "selling." They all should have the same process. That is, they should start with goals, focus on people, and be situational.

Let's dispense with negotiating phrases such as making a "series of mutual concessions" or "finding a positive settlement range." And it's not true that people are either "cooperative" or "competitive." How they behave often depends on the situation. People and situations don't fit into neat little boxes.

Instead, let's define negotiation in ways that will help you organize what you actually need to do, and give you a better window into the process. This definition of negotiation has four levels, beginning with the most superficial.

Negotiation is the process of:

1. *Forcing People to Do What You Will Them to Do.* This involves threats, violence, take-it-or-leave-it demands, the use of raw power. Of course this is negotiation—you've persuaded people that unless they do it your way, at least for the time being, you will beat them black and blue. And sometimes it works: battles and wars have been won. Aggression has sometimes carried the day.

The main problem with force is not that it doesn't work. With $20 trillion, the United States can probably do whatever it wants in the Middle East for the foreseeable future. With virtually unlimited resources, the United States could probably do whatever it wanted in Afghanistan or anywhere else. The problem is that force is very expensive, is not reinforcing, and as such takes a long time, if not forever, for continued compliance. So the questions to ask include: Is force the best use of my resources? Is this the easiest way to meet our goals over time? For example, if you use violence and don't wipe out the other side, they will probably keep fighting. If you threaten them, they will find a way to get back at you. Mostly, you've persuaded them not to fight back *today.*

In limited, specific situations, raw power might be justified. But to watch TV or the movies, or listen to many leaders, you'd think it is the human behavior of choice. In fact, it is the most suboptimal choice. Overall, it's not as profitable or effective as other choices. Look how expensive it is to fight someone in court.

2. *Getting People to Think What You Want Them to Think.* This second level is better: getting people to see the rational benefit in your idea. This is what has been called "interest-based negotiation," and popularized in many negotiation books. However, it depends on people being rational.

But in the real world, it usually doesn't carry the day by itself. Most important negotiations have a big emotional component. There is often a lot of irrational behavior. The more important the negotiation is to the other party, the less interest-based negotiation works. A family quarrel over where to go on vacation, or a workplace argument over who gets what office, is hard to settle with interest-based negotiation alone. It's not enough to focus on what rational or reasonable people think might work well.

And that brings us to what is really effective in negotiation, persuasion, and communication. This is where the real success in dealing with others begins.

3. *Getting People to Perceive What You Want Them to Perceive.* Now you are looking at the world the way the other side does. And you are thinking of ways to change their perceptions. You are starting with the pictures in their heads. This is the right place to begin in order to persuade them.

Misperception, often from communication failures, causes conflict and negotiation breakdowns everywhere, every day. Understanding others' perceptions is essential to successful negotiation. You then change their perceptions incrementally. It will actually make the negotiation shorter, more self-enforcing, and easier.

4. *Getting People to Feel What You Want Them to Feel.* This approach is totally self-enforcing. You are tapping into their emotions, their "irrationality," if you will. Almost everyone views the world through their own feelings and perceptions. When the pressure is on, when the stakes are high, their feelings usually take over—whether evident or not. A negotiation that considers feelings is much broader than "interests." And it includes all needs—the entire menu of what people want—from the reasonable to the crazy. When the other party realizes you care about their feelings, they will listen more, making them more persuadable.

In my experiance, few people acknowledge or use this in negotiations. Imagine opposing attorneys, or sports owners with striking players, or the United States with Iran, saying, "Before we sit down to formally talk about the issues, how do you guys feel? Are you happy? What is your favorite food? How's your family?" And yet this is what is *required* to get the best results. Throughout this book, you will see that people who did this negotiated better and got more.

All of this material—strategies, tools, models, attitudes—taken together is a negotiation *process.* It is a way of talking to others, a way of conducting yourself, a way that will help you get better results. Though a separate skill, it is intended to become part of you; effective negotiation becomes as natural as talking. It is not something done at a table or in a formal setting. It is your life.

The facts will change from situation to situation. But the process should not. Doing this well will enable you to negotiate anything, with anyone, anywhere, anytime.

Near the beginning of my courses I ask students, "Who negotiated something today?" It doesn't matter what the negotiation is about: a hot dog or a hot job. Each event can be broken down and deconstructed into its essential elements in the same way. These elements can then be examined, learned, and put back together again so you can negotiate at a higher level.

Think how much more effective you would be if you spent ten or fifteen minutes before a negotiation going down the List and asking how each strategy applies in this instance. Did you find out enough about the other party? Are your goals clearly defined? Are you being incremental enough? Afterward, you will assess how you did using the List, perhaps changing it a little, and learning for next time.

This is called an *inductive* process: starting from each situation and then figuring out the exact strategies and tools that are likely to be most effective. It's also knowledge you can then bring with you to the next negotiation. You might, for example, find that standards worked well in one situation, an appeal to relationships worked in another, and focusing on individual needs worked in a third.

Now let's start going over the List so that I can persuade you to think differently.

GOALS

This is one of the big differences between the advice in *Getting More* and what you've likely read elsewhere about negotiation. Goals are not just another negotiation tool to use. Goals are the be-all and end-all of negotiations. You negotiate to meet your goals. Everything else is subservient to that.

The goals are what you are trying to accomplish. Don't try to establish a relationship unless it brings you closer to your goals. Don't deal with others' interests or needs or feelings or anything else unless it brings you closer to your goals. Don't give or get information unless it brings you closer to your goals.

This is a really big point. People shouldn't negotiate to achieve "win-win" or to create a "relationship" or to get to "yes" unless it aligns with their goals. "Win-win" is overused; it sounds vaguely manipulative. When people say to me, "Let's go for a win-win," I think, "So they want something from me."

The point of negotiation is to *get what you want*. Why should you negotiate to create a relationship if it won't help you meet your goals? Why should you try for a win-win if others continue to try to hurt your career?

Maybe you actually want a "lose-win" outcome. You want to lose today, so they will give you more tomorrow. Maybe you want a "lose-lose," so you can both see how that feels. Maybe you want a "win-lose" outcome, in order to train them to act differently next time.

Don't get distracted and clouded with other stuff—being nice, being tough, being emotional, etc. Never take your eyes off the goal. It's what you want at the end of the process that you don't have now.

Much has been written about meeting goals. Studies show that goal-setting is one of the most important things someone can do for themselves. The mere act of setting a goal has been shown to increase performance by more than 25 percent.

What's invisible is not that no one knows they need to identify and meet their goals. What's invisible is that they *don't do it*! They don't do it because they don't focus on it. They don't do it because they get distracted. And then, if they finally start doing it, they don't complete it—they lose their way in the middle.

Some executives dismiss this advice with a wave of the hand. "We learned this stuff in business school," they say. Then why don't they *do* it?

It's important to execute things in a focused, ordered way. It's not enough to say, "Meet your goals." We need to know exactly how to do this. The first thing you need to do is decide what your goal is, explicitly, at the beginning and remind yourself often along the way.

What's your goal in going to the store? Knowing that in advance will stop you from wasting money on impulse buying. What's your goal in discussing vacation plans with your family? To prove who's right? To punish them for something else? Or to decide on a vacation you can take that will be nice for all of you?

How many times have you gone to a meeting and said to the people there, "What do you want at the end of this meeting that you don't have now?" If you haven't done this before, try it. It's very effective. Although people will sometimes lie or refuse to say, by and large people will tell you. And you will quickly find out whether everyone thinks they are at the same meeting with the same goals. Even a slight difference in goals can wind up as a mess in a negotiation.

Write down your goals and remind yourself. Have friends and colleagues remind you. Not just at the beginning of the process, but all along the way.

Not having a goal is like getting into the car without knowing where you are headed. And not checking your goals is like not checking the map along the way. People often get distracted in the middle of a meeting or a campaign. New information often emerges. Unless you check your goals at intervals, you are less likely to meet them. It doesn't matter how well you know the company or person.

I knew an executive who was hired as vice president for strategy at a leading U.S. firm. Just after she arrived, she wrote a note to the other twelve senior executives, inviting them to a meeting, asking them to bring their goals for the company.

After receiving the note, the company's CEO called her up and said, "Wait a minute. You just got here. We've been working here for years—we know our goals for the company."

"Fair enough," the new vice president said. "But you asked me to work on corporate strategy. I promise you that if you let the meeting happen, it will be worthwhile. And it won't take very long." The CEO said okay.

The other twelve senior executives came to the meeting with their goals for the company. The strategy vice president wrote them up on the board, one by one. At the end, the twelve executives saw that they actually had not one, or two, or three, or four goals. They had fourteen different goals. And most of these goals contradicted each other. "Oh," they said.

The more specific your goals, the better. "I'd like to go to Chicago" is better than "I'd like to go to Illinois." "Let's put a man on the moon" is better than "Let's explore space." "I want to graduate from college" is not as good as "I want to get at least Bs while I'm writing a book."

Too often, people think they can meet their goals only at the expense of others. You need to think about their goals as well as yours, or others will soon give you less. If you meet your goals today at the expense of the long term, you have served yourself poorly. *Getting More* means meeting your goals for all relevant people and periods.

Once you have identified your goals, it is important to keep asking, "Are my actions meeting my goals?" The world is full of people who fail to do this. They get emotional or distracted or are just not thinking this way. It goes for you, and it goes for others you care about.

Angela Arnold's father had a stroke. He wanted to leave the hospital before his rehab was complete. Angela, now a consultant, asked her father what he was most looking forward to at home. "Walking Ringo," his dog, Angela's father said. "Well," Angela said, "if you want to walk Ringo, and you leave the hospital now, you won't be able to walk Ringo." She said if he finished rehab, he'd be able to walk unassisted upon discharge. Then he could walk Ringo. Angela showed her father that his proposal would not have met his goals. Her father finished rehab.

Here's a new definition of competitiveness: your ability to meet your goals. This flies in the face of centuries of business thinking. Even today, the philosophy of Scottish economist Adam Smith (1723–1790) is predominant. Smith, widely cited as the father of modern economics, saw competitiveness as maximizing self-interest. It has been viewed since then as gaining power over opponents, winner takes all, taking no prisoners; some later called it economic Darwinism.

Today the most "competitive people" are replacing this with the thinking of John Nash, a Princeton University mathematician who won the 1994 Nobel Prize and was popularized in the movie *A Beautiful Mind.*

Nash proved mathematically the 1755 theory of Swiss philosopher Jean-Jacques Rousseau that when parties collaborate, the overall size of the pie almost always expands, so each party gets more than it could get alone. The typical example is that four hunters can each catch only one rabbit while acting alone, but they can catch a deer together.

Today, smart competitors collaborate whenever they can. Consider the PowerBook computer created among IBM, Apple, and Motorola. Or strategic alliances for research or marketing among pharmaceutical firms. Research shows that almost 90 percent of the time, people in cooperative environments perform better than people in traditional, "competitive," win-lose environments. In other words, performance contests in general don't enhance performance.

You might say, skeptically, that some pies can't be expanded, and that if one party wins, the other loses. If I ask for an example, the number-one answer people give is land. To which I reply, "Fine, if land is important to you, you take Congo, I'll take Japan." In other words, not all land is equal. There are lots of ways to compete. Don't get locked in to one dimension.

Again, write your goals down. Check them often.

YOU—YOUR ATTITUDE, CREDIBILITY, TRANSPARENCY

The attitude you bring to a negotiation has a direct impact on the result you get. If you come to a negotiation expecting a war, you will get one. And you will get less. Studies show that adversarial negotiators make about half as many deals as do more cooperative, problem-solving negotiators. And they get about half as much from the deals they do make. So if you are confrontational, expect about 25 percent of what's possible.

If you are in a lousy mood, it's not the right time to negotiate. Even if you are the company expert, you may not be the right person to negotiate if you can't connect with the other party.

This does *not* mean you should try to be someone else. Most people are bad at acting. People will detect it and you will lose your credibility. The most important asset you have in any human interaction is your credibility. If people don't believe you, it's hard to convince them of anything. Your credibility is more important than your expertise, connections, intelligence, assets, and looks.

Instead, you should use *Getting More* to learn how to *be yourself better*. There is no special way to talk. The strategies and tools in this book should become part of you, whoever you are.

People appreciate it when others are straight with them, no matter what "straight" is. This should lift the burden of having to be someone you are not.

This means, if you are very aggressive, warn people in the beginning. "If I get too aggressive, let me know." What does this do? First, it takes away the issue by resetting expectations. Second, it makes you more real; it increases your credibility. Third, it eliminates the need for you to do any sort of dance, to act in a way that is unnatural to you. Now you can focus on meeting your goals.

And if you are overly accommodating, let people know that you often give away too much and have to backtrack later. So they need to tell you if the deal is getting unfair. You give them the responsibility and give yourself an out if they try to take advantage of your generosity. Then you can be yourself.

When I go to another country and don't know the culture well, I will often apologize in advance. I will tell the other person, "I might accidentally say something inappropriate. I wish I knew your culture better. Every time I make a mistake, could you please advise me?" I've now turned every instance of potential conflict into an instance of collaboration, in which they are my advisors. And I have taken away the tension from cultural mistakes. I can be myself.

Great negotiators have a firm grasp of the obvious. If you are not getting along in a negotiation with the other party, you should say, "I don't think we're getting along here. Why not?" You might as well say it. The other party is thinking it. It's like an 800-pound gorilla in the room. It will prevent getting a decent agreement. If you are in a bad mood, tell the other side, "I'm in a bad mood." It will cause them to forgive some things they might not otherwise.

Transparency also means you should *share* these tools with the other side. The more people who know of these tools, the better the negotiation will be. Because this is not about getting the better of someone. This is about getting more. So give the List to your spouse, your kids, your friends, and your business associates.

This is counterintuitive to most people. Most negotiators think they should be anything but transparent. However, the result is a lack of trust. This doesn't mean you have to disclose everything. It does mean you should disclose as much as you can to meet your goals and make the other side comfortable. For the rest you can say, "I'm just not comfortable telling you this yet."

Effective negotiators are never satisfied with anything: their performance, results, process. This doesn't mean they are unhappy. It doesn't mean they are unsuccessful. It just means they continually try to figure out if they can get more.

Even as you are celebrating a successful deal, you should be saying to yourself: Was the relationship as good as it could have been? Did we do any cross-selling? Could we have done it faster or better? This is what pushes good negotiators to get even better.

My best students want to be criticized; they know that each mistake makes them stronger once they understand it. They are not likely to make that mistake again. I am always asking for criticism. You should, too.

SMALL STEPS

In our imaginations, big, bold moves produce big successes. In the real world, big, bold moves mostly scare people away: you are trying to go too far, too fast. Small, incremental steps accomplish more. This is especially true if two parties are far apart in a negotiation.

Incremental steps give other people a chance to catch their breath, look around, decide if the steps you've taken feel good, and then move on with confidence. Incremental steps anchor people to the step or steps they have already accepted. They reduce the perceived risk of moving forward.

An analogy: If you are a .280 hitter in baseball, and you get one extra hit every nine games, you become a .310 hitter in baseball. And that is worth a spot in the Baseball Hall of Fame, and $10 million more a year in compensation. All for one extra hit every thirty-six times at bat.

I'm not trying to hit home runs in negotiations. I'm trying to get one extra hit every nine games. It's a good lesson for negotiation, and a good lesson for life. A few incremental improvements and you will be fabulously more successful.

But let's not carry the sports analogy too far. In sports, the goal is for each side to win. Life is not a sports game. In sports, it is *expected* that one side will lose. There is a finite game, tournament, or season. In life, there is a tomorrow, and it is *expected* (at least normally) for people to all get something.

Even so, don't be greedy. It turns people off and causes them to distrust you and give you less. When you try to get a little more, you fall below most people's radar screens. Your proposal is digestible. You can always ask for more the next time. I tell my students, "Every ceiling is a new floor."

Jan Carlson, the legendary European SAS airline executive, once said, "The difference between success and failure is . . . two millimeters." In other words, it's something as seemingly insignificant as a turn of phrase. A look. A small gesture. The tools that work are very small, subtle, and yet very effective.

The title of this book is *Getting More,* not *Getting Everything.* No negotiation tools and strategies work all the time. *But they work more often than if you don't use them!* This is not intended to make you perfect. It is intended to make you better, every day.

Start with the easy things in a negotiation, and scale up from there. If you can increase your success by even a few percent in your negotiations with others, you will be fabulously more successful. Anyone who tells you that this or that strategy always works is blowing smoke at you. Again, all you're looking for is that one extra hit every nine games.

"Before this course, my tactics worked about fifty percent of the time; I thought I was a pretty good negotiator," said Gerald Singleton, a former student of mine at USC. "Now I use better tools and they work seventy-five percent of the time. For me, that's much better. And I have a framework to keep improving throughout my life."

EVERYTHING IS SITUATIONAL

Here is my entire negotiation course in three broad questions.

1. What are my goals?
2. Who are "they"?
3. What will it take to persuade them?

Every negotiation, every situation is different. That's because there are different people in the negotiation. Or the same people on different days. Or a different set of facts and circumstances. Or a different goal. So I need to ask these questions for every situation.

The third question depends on the answers to the first two. And this is why you need the List. You choose from the List, and from the various supporting individual tools, based on goals and people. You may act differently in two negotiations on the same subject, with the same facts. That's because either the goals or the people, or both, are different. There is no one-size-fits-all.

If anyone says to you, "Here's how you negotiate real estate deals," be skeptical. They may know various real estate tactics that work sometimes, or sort of. They may have real estate expertise. But until you define your goals and the people involved in that particular situation, you can't effectively decide what negotiation tools to use.

The people involved in a negotiation, and the process they use, comprise more than 90 percent of what is important in a negotiation. The substance, the facts, and the expertise make up less than 10 percent. This is quite counterintuitive for most people.

THE QUESTION OF POWER

Let's continue this conversation. First, let's define power as your ability to meet your goals over all relevant time frames. In other words, you need enough power to meet your goals, but not more. Power for its own sake is almost always useless; in fact, as I explained earlier, it can be harmful. Lessening the misuse of power by the other side is important only if it enhances your ability to meet your goals.

Although the tools in *Getting More* give you more power, they need to be used carefully. And raw power is much more fragile than usually assumed. If you overuse your power, for example, you can lose your power. If you are too extreme, you can seem unreasonable to others and lessen your ability to meet your goals. People hate it when others try to exert power over them. They then try to undermine you and change the power balance.

There is a relationship between power and negotiation skill. Consider this: women stereotypically tend to be better negotiators than men. First, women listen more. They collect more information. And more information leads to better persuasion and better results. Second, women try a lot harder than men to learn the tools in *Getting More*. That's because we still live in a male-dominated world. Women have less raw power, and this is too often used against them.

When you have a lot of raw power, your tool of choice is figuratively the baseball bat. As noted, this invites retaliation. When you have less power, you learn to use tools that are more subtle, less noticeable, even invisible to those with raw power. There is less risk of retaliation. Women comprise about 30 percent of the students who take my courses, but they get a much higher percentage of the highest grades. The subtler tools are ultimately more effective.

This is why small countries—Sweden, Switzerland, Malta—are more often thought of as better at conflict resolution than large countries. And it is why children are better negotiators than adults. And it's why children tend to lose those tools as they grow up and get a baseball bat—raw power. The better negotiators watch other parties carefully, focus on the other party, and ultimately meet their own goals more effectively. Studies show that less powerful parties tend to be more creative than more powerful ones.

As such, power is a complicated concept. People like to have power. So, by giving people power or validating their power, they feel good and will give things to you in return. We see this with children. The key is to be very sensitive to the implications, especially the long-term ones, of the use—and especially the misuse—of power.

IMPLEMENTING THE STRATEGIES AND TOOLS

It's not enough to know the negotiation strategies and tools in this book. You have to be able to use them in real time. If you can't, they are useless to you. This is a critical point. The world is full of great negotiation thinkers who have read books, have taken courses, and can have great discussions about negotiations. The world is not full of great negotiators who can execute successful negotiations in real time.

Let's say you are negotiating for a table at a crowded restaurant where you don't have a reservation. What do you do? How do you start with this particular maître d' in this particular situation?

Knowing the rules of negotiation doesn't mean that you can negotiate well—any more than you can beat a world-class tennis player because you have read forty-two books on tennis.

A main purpose of this book is to turn conceptual knowledge into operational knowledge, presenting step-by-step strategies with examples that, with practice, work in the real world. This book is like a first tennis lesson. To get better, you need to practice with these tools.

Rayenne Chen, the woman at the beginning of the book who got the pilots to bring back the plane, had a List. That was her starting point. But it wasn't enough. Her List was internalized through practice: *conscious practice.*

The same tools can be applied to widely different situations. So you don't have to practice on big things where there will be serious consequences if you make a mistake. Start with small things.

Go into a clothing store where things seem never to be on sale and ask the manager for a discount. They will probably say no. Ask if they have personal shoppers. Personal shoppers often work on commission—they make money only when you buy something. They are going to go out of their way to make a deal. Ask for their business card. Ask the manager or the personal shopper what the store does for loyal customers.

It doesn't matter if the item you get a discount on is priced at $1. You are practicing for $10,000 or $100,000 items in the future—it's the same process. I used to practice on practically every situation imaginable. My friends would make fun of me. They stopped making fun of me when they needed help and I did things they could not.

Great negotiators are made, not born. Excellence comes from focus and practice. I have taught people who were initially terrible at negotiation, but they soared in a single semester. In other words, creating a List is not enough. You have to implement it, over and over, and learn from your mistakes. It is not hard to learn.

Wei-Wei Wang, a slight woman in my negotiation class at the University of Southern California, was very timid at first. She avoided most negotiations and had a hard time meeting her goals.

So I suggested that she take a communication and presentation course first, to get her confidence up. "No, Professor Diamond," she said. "I really want to take this course. Throw the book at me."

"Okay," I said. So for the next twelve weeks of the course, I pitted her against the class bully every chance I could: a hard bargainer four times her size, with the sensibilities of a meat-ax. But she was very diligent and learned the course tools very well. During the last session, she had a negotiation with this guy in front of the class. And she handed him his head, to a standing ovation, including from this guy.

She didn't realize how good she was getting. Halfway through the course, she wrote me a note: "Professor Diamond, I'm very frustrated. I've done everything you said. I've learned the negotiation tools, I've practiced the negotiation tools. I prepare for negotiations, I go on negotiations. But before I get to use everything, they say yes. How do I practice more?"

If you have prepared and practiced, other people will sense it. And they will give you more. No matter where you start from.

Of course, you have to consciously *decide* to negotiate. Our surveys show that most people think they negotiate about fourteen hours a week. In reality, almost everyone negotiates more than forty hours a week. They're just not conscious of the rest. The more you consciously use negotiation tools, the more you will get more.

Learning these tools does not happen in a straight line. This is why I repeat certain ideas in this book in different contexts to give you a better understanding of what you have to do. I find that when I provide a new idea for my students, and later double back and repeat the same idea in a slightly different way, they learn more. In that sense, *Getting More* is delivered like a course. You deconstruct your behavior, you look at each part and improve it, and then you put it back together again.

It's like learning a sport. To get better, you identify every part of your game, focus on the weak spots, improve them, and then put your game back together again. It's similar to learning how to play the piano or drive a car.

Different strategies and tools work better in different situations. But using the three questions to organize a process is the same for any negotiation: whether you are asking for a discount at a deli or trying to work out a billion-dollar deal. This is why good negotiators can negotiate anything, and bad negotiators can't negotiate anything.

Even the smartest, most capable and respected people around make mistakes if they don't use the kinds of tools in this book. This is a new and evolving field. Good instincts are not enough.

So use the List. Take it with you from negotiation to negotiation. Figure out what you did right and wrong the last time. Modify your List. Do this often. Practice one strategy at a time. See what happens. Learn from it, then do it again.

EVERYONE BENEFITS FROM COACHING

Getting More is essentially a series of coaching sessions. It is designed to take anyone at any level and make them better at negotiating. *Everyone* needs coaching. In fact, the more expert you are in something, the more you need a coach to stay competitive.

Imagine Olympic swimming champion Michael Phelps, or seven-time Tour de France winner Lance Armstrong. When Armstrong wins a race, does he say, "Well, I've got this nailed; don't have to practice anymore"? Of course not! The same is true with anyone who is negotiating something, whether it's a million-dollar contract or a shirt with a missing button that has to be returned to the dry cleaner.

Ilan Rosenberg is a seasoned attorney in Philadelphia who took my course to improve his negotiation skills. After just one class, he went to Mexico to try to restart a long-stalled deal. Following what he learned in class, he didn't start by discussing the deal terms. Instead, he tried to get to know the other person—his hopes, dreams, fears. After initial surprise, the other guy opened up and told Ilan what was bothering him. The result? "We closed the deal," Ilan said. "It was worth $20 million."

As you learn these negotiation methods, you will soon be able to teach yourself by practicing and debriefing yourself. You will improve month by month, year by year.

But in order to meet your goals, you will also need to help other people get better.

This may sound counterintuitive. But unless the other party does well, they will not likely do a deal. Or they will try to modify it or wriggle out of it later. You can't get more unless the other side is reasonably satisfied.

And you will need to help others because most people don't know how to set their goals or meet them. They don't know how to listen or find the pictures in other people's heads. They are mostly confrontational and defensive and have the wrong attitude.

You'll need to help them define their goals, meet their needs, get more.

Most hard bargainers are unskilled negotiators; they don't know any other way. But until the other party shows you they are a lost cause, you should try to help them. That doesn't mean taking a lot of risk yourself. Take a small, incremental step and see what happens. Ask, "Would you like to make an agreement that is reasonable for both of us?" If they say yes, then define how the parties might go about it.

Bob Woolf, the retired sports-agent superstar, essentially said to others in a negotiation, "I have one thing that's not negotiable. I *demand* that we meet your interests." When the other person expressed surprise, he would say something like, "The reason we need to meet your interests is that if we don't meet your interests, you won't meet mine. And I'm a real selfish guy. I want my interests met."

PERSISTENCE

A negotiation is over when you say it is, not before. It doesn't matter how many times the other person says no, or disagrees with you, or gives you a hard time. Keep asking, stay focused on your goals (without making yourself the issue). Persistence, after all, is a focused effort, over time, to meet your goals.

If the other party bridles at your persistence, say something like, "Well, I'm just trying to meet my goals. Is there some way I could do this better?" Some people won't be interested in helping you. But more people than you think will help you, let you keep trying, and eventually give you what you need.

In the first class in my course, students tend to try to negotiate for something a couple of times and then give up. By the end of the course, there is no limit to how many times they will ask. Each time, they ask a little bit differently.

Diego Etcheto needed to rebook his ticket on a flight from Philadelphia to Miami. He missed the flight the day before because a storm prevented him from getting to the airport. He wanted Delta to remove the $150 change fee. He called thirteen times. Delta's answers: no, no, no, no, no, no, no, no, no, no, no, no, yes. It took ninety minutes, but he got the $150 fee waived. "Be polite, but firm," said Diego, who now works for his family's food business in Washington State. "When you hear no, ask 'Why not?' I was prepared to negotiate all day."

The Dr. Seuss classic *Green Eggs and Ham* is one of the best books on persistence ever written, in the eyes of Jack Callahan, one of my NYU Executive MBA students. I agree. After more than 100 lovely requests and denials, green eggs and ham are happily eaten. "I read it seven times tonight to my persistent one-year-old," Jack said.

With persistence comes self-confidence: the belief that you can do it. Students describe self-confidence as their number-one benefit from the course. Tim Essaye, by using the course tools in a company deal, secured a 25 percent bonus. The self-confidence the course gave him made a lifetime of difference.

Colleen Sorrentino got the confidence to tell her husband, Bob, without nagging, that he had promised to go food shopping so she could study. "I didn't argue and for once I didn't get emotional," she said. Colleen said that Bob has done all the food shopping for the more than ten years since that negotiation. "I always tended to feel guilty when I asked for something," said Colleen, now a managing director at her family's brokerage firm, Wall Street Access. "I now have a way of going about things that helps me be stronger."

YOU MUST CONSIDER THE DEEPER MOTIVATION

People do some of the most important things in life not for money, not for rational benefits, but for how it makes them feel. The emotional and psychic rewards they get, and the anguish, must be part of the negotiation process.

Sharon Walker's mother was dying of breast cancer. Although Sharon, a student in my Wharton course, was making plans for a family, she realized that her mother would likely be dead before her first grandchild was born. Sharon wanted her mother to read children's books on videotape so that her unborn grandchildren would know who their grandmother was.

"The memory of her making the animals talk in children's stories is an especially dear memory of my childhood," Sharon said. She wanted the same for her own children.

But Sharon didn't know how to approach her mother. The sickness caused great emotional distress for the entire family. Indeed, Sharon's father and sister would oppose Sharon's plan if her mother got any more upset. So, in class, we did a role reversal—a negotiation simulation—in which Sharon played her mother, to try to figure out what her mother was thinking and feeling. And other students played Sharon, so she could essentially watch herself negotiate. Sharon particularly did not want to appear selfish to her family, or to upset her mother further.

By doing the role reversal, Sharon realized that her mother would most likely want to have a role in the lives of her as-yet-unborn grandchildren, whom she would probably never see. She also realized that her mother, deep down, very much wanted to read children's books on videotape. But Sharon also understood that her mother was afraid, and already very sad. Her mother lived in California, 3,000 miles away, and couldn't go through it by herself.

Sharon also realized that if she went out to California and spent some time with her mother, then her mother would be able to go through it. She would remind her mother of the wonderful times they had shared with the children's stories when Sharon herself was young. She would talk about how the family all felt cheated by the cancer, but that her mother could provide a special legacy. "Whatever happens, don't you want to be able to read to your grandchildren?" Sharon would say. "Don't you want them to know the sound of your voice?"

Was Sharon trying to manipulate her mother, to take something from her mother? I tell this story to my classes, and some people think so. The right answer, though, is of course not. Was Sharon trying to *win* the negotiation? And would reading the books cause her mother to *lose* the negotiation? Not hardly. More broadly, should we even talk about this in terms of win-win or win-lose? In fact, these are irrelevant terms in this and other negotiations. They don't capture the fundamental dynamic of what really goes on when people interact. A lot has to do with emotional baggage, with things that have nothing to do with the negotiation at hand.

When you give a present to someone you love, who benefits more? When a store clerk gives you a discount because you are the first person all day who was nice to her, who benefits more? It is much more complicated than buzzwords, and requires one to look much more deeply into the people and the situation.

In Sharon's case, by the time she got back to California from school, her mother was too sick to read the books on videotape, even though Sharon was able to persuade her. Her voice was gone. Sharon's mom died without the task being completed. Today, Sharon, a Boston high-tech strategy consultant, said she wishes she had learned the negotiation tools earlier in life, so that she would have known how to do the negotiation before her mom was dying.

But she now teaches what she learned to her own children, two boys and a girl, ages five, seven, and nine. Especially about understanding and focusing on the feelings of others. And they are better for it, Sharon says.

It is also important to underscore that Sharon did not meet her goals in the negotiation just described, since her mother died before the tapes were done. These processes are not perfect, nor should you expect them to be. But if you keep trying to use them, they will make your life better in many unforeseen ways. So use these tools now. Don't wait.

CHANGING YOUR LIFE

I often hear from students that the negotiation course has changed their lives. There are many benefits to negotiating effectively: confidence, a detailed approach to solving problems, greater control over one's life, more money, more peace of mind.

"The benefits of this course are potentially immeasurable," said Evan Claar, a hedge fund manager in New York. "I see here the keys to unlock everything I want. Not just in my business life, but in my personal life and relationships."

The experience of Carol McDermott is typical. Using course tools, in one semester she: (1) was offered $45,000 more at work, (2) got $90 back from checks the bank bounced in error, (3) got $100 from Continental Airlines after they didn't have her chosen meal, (4) got $240 a year in discounts from her cable TV company, (5) negotiated an $8 "volume discount" on four flower purchases, (6) convinced a restaurant to serve her group after closing time, (7) persuaded two friends who had not spoken in three months to reopen relations, (8) convinced her boyfriend to attend Thanksgiving at her house, (9) learned not to become flustered during tense negotiations, and (10) did better at avoiding being dragged into arguing over unimportant issues at the expense of her goals.

These are just some things she happened to write down. There were dozens more. These results were just while she was a Wharton student. They increased exponentially after graduation. And her results are typical of what students report.

"The negotiations course divided my life into two parts—before the course and after the course," said Alexei Lougovtsov, now a trader for Merrill Lynch in London. "It allowed me to have a much happier and easier life, a more successful career, and better relationships."

Alexei mentioned two important negotiations, one professional and one personal. During the financial crisis of 2009, the investor community expected the Royal Bank of Scotland (the world's biggest bank by assets) and Lloyd's Bank (Britain's biggest mortgage lender) to suspend dividends. Alexei, using course tools, thought about the pictures in the heads of each party, including investors, and how items of unequal value would be traded.

He said he realized that the financial institutions would never suspend dividends to ordinary investors, who were the backbone of the economy. And he realized that the government depended on the investors for its political future and therefore would help the dividends get paid. So he recommended that his clients invest in the companies even with the threat of default. He was right. The dividends were paid, and the stock value increased by more than five times. His bank made tens of millions of dollars. "I had arrived at my conclusion not by analyzing legal documents and financial statements, but by thinking about the pictures in the heads of each party," Alexei said.

His second important negotiation was to convince his girlfriend, Qin, to come to a boxing camp with him for a week. His girlfriend works on Wall Street, and her friends were making fun of her for not standing up to her boyfriend and demanding, say, Barbados and beaches. "I painted a vision," Alexei said. "I asked how many people get to work out next to world-class boxers. It almost had résumé value." He took her to a boxing camp started by legendary promoter Don King in Florida. She worked out, sweaty, next to some of the greats. Her horizons were broadened. "She wants to know when we can go back," Alexei said.

As Cindy Greene, a Boston consultant, said, "I evaluate all interactions in a different way now. My awareness of others is incredibly acute. My life is fundamentally changed." It will be the same for you.

2

People Are (Almost) Everything

The Writers Guild in Hollywood in early 2008 had been on strike for three months. John Bowman, the Guild's chief negotiator and now its president, spoke with me on a phone call set up by a prominent Hollywood agent. "Listen to what this guy says," the agent, Ari Emanuel, told Bowman. "Take notes."

It was a Tuesday afternoon. Bowman had a breakfast scheduled for Thursday morning with representatives of the major Hollywood studios, to talk about the dispute. He had a number of substantive issues and wanted to know the order in which to bring them up—royalties, basic compensation, etc.

I told him to put aside these issues, at least for now. That's not the problem. The problem is that everyone is mad at everyone else and everyone is losing money. "Make small talk," I said. "Ask them, 'Are you happy?' " They will not be happy, and they will admit it, I said. They may start blaming the Writers Guild. That's okay, I told Bowman. "Commiserate with them," I said. "Ask them, 'If we had to start over again, what process would *you* like to see?' "

Bowman was skeptical. I told him a negotiation is about the people. I gave him some of the examples I include in this chapter—how it's almost always about the people, first. People like to give things to others who listen to them, who value them, who consult with them. I told him to get rid of the two confrontational New York garment-district negotiators who had been working for the Guild and whose very presence drove laid-back Hollywood studio executives crazy.

During the phone call, Bowman said he would give my advice a shot. At this point, what did he have to lose? The result: At the breakfast meeting, the parties agreed to restart negotiations after months of failure. The garment-district guys were replaced by Bowman. It took only a few days to get an agreement. Almost immediately, the strike ended. "This process solved the writers' strike," said Ari, the real-life model for HBO's *Entourage* and the brother of former White House chief of staff Rahm Emanuel.

One can also say two other things about this: first, it wasn't rocket science, and second, unless you already know how to do this, the skills are completely invisible.

From time immemorial, people have come to negotiations armed with their lists of topics to push from the start. Here are my issues. Here is my proposal.

Wrong! Unless you connect in some way with the people you are negotiating with, you won't get a deal. Or, if you do get a deal, it won't be a good one, or it won't stick. Even if you hate the other side, you need to connect with them.

Remember, you are the *least* important person in the negotiation. The most important person is *them.* And the second most important person is a third party important to the negotiators. If you don't accept this, you won't persuade many people of anything. This chapter will show you how to focus on the other parties and thereby meet your goals.

PICTURES IN THEIR HEADS

First, the characteristics and sensibilities of the people sitting across from you dominate every other part of the negotiation. It is not even worth thinking about race, religion, gender, culture, creed, or any other issues until you know *the pictures in their heads that day.* If you each bring three people to a negotiation on Monday, and you bring a fourth person on Tuesday, it's a completely different negotiation. Even with the same six people, someone may have had a bad commute that morning, someone else may not be feeling well, someone's kid might be sick, someone might be distracted by something else.

So the first thing you have to do is take the emotional and situational temperature of the people sitting across from you, even if you know them very well. Even if you are married to them.

This is a very different way of thinking about the process of negotiation. Traditionally, people thought mostly about the issues: "This is my proposal. Here's my agenda." Later, people thought about interests: "Why do you want this deal? Let's talk rationally about this." This was farther back from the issues, focusing on benefits, so it was better. But neither issues nor interests are good enough. To be really effective, one has to start all the way back at the beginning. What is the other person feeling? How do they perceive the situation? What are the pictures in their heads?

If you don't start there, how can you possibly know where to start? And each person is different—even the same person is different on different days and at different hours of the same day. You must focus on how they are feeling and thinking and viewing things at the moment of your discussion with them. Otherwise, you are just walking around in the dark.

Most people think that the negotiation is about substance: I'm a financial expert, I'm a medical doctor, I'm an environmental lawyer, I'm an energy expert, I'm a mechanic. But studies show that less than 10 percent of the reason why people reach agreement has anything to do with the substance. More than 50 percent has to do with the people—do they like each other, do they trust each other, will they hear what each other has to say? Just over a third has to do with the process they use. That is, do they decide to explore each other's needs (rational and emotional)? Do they agree on an agenda? Do they make genuine commitments to each other?

If you believe that negotiations are about the substantive issues, sadly, you will be right more than you are persuasive. That means that the truth,

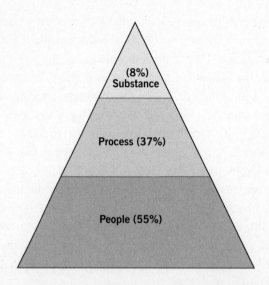

the facts, are only one argument in a negotiation. The people and the process are much more important. This is particularly hard for people who are focused on the substance—doctors, engineers, financial experts—to accept. But, based on research, it is true. You can't even use substantive issues to persuade effectively unless and until the other party is ready to hear about them.

Why was O. J. Simpson found not guilty by the criminal jury in Los Angeles for the murder of Nicole Brown Simpson and Ronald Goldman, despite a wheelbarrow full of DNA evidence, including his blood type at the site? Few attorneys I know who looked at the evidence could understand the verdict. There is a simple explanation, however, embodied in this question: how did the inner-city jury, mostly minorities, feel about the prosecution, and about its racist witness, Mark Fuhrman?

First, the jury didn't like the prosecutor. Moreover, the jury didn't trust the prosecutor. And if the other side doesn't like you, and they don't trust you, *they won't hear you.* Just because you're yakking at them, and they are going, "Uh-huh, uh-huh," doesn't mean they hear a word you say. And when people are angry, confused, or uncertain, they *physiologically* hear less. Even if they are taking notes furiously, they might be writing, "I hate this person." Watch an umpire and baseball coach screaming at each other, nose to nose. Do you think they hear very much of what the other is saying? In order to persuade them, you first have to get them to listen to you. It must be a separate, focused, conscious effort.

So, many of the arguments that the O. J. Simpson prosecution made, and the evidence the prosecution collected, literally fell on deaf ears. The prosecutors were smart, experienced lawyers, but they failed miserably. That's because when it came to understanding people—the *first* requirement in a negotiation—they were clueless!

The defense team talked to the jury as people. "If it doesn't fit, you must acquit," Johnnie Cochran told them about the glove O. J. Simpson tried on. It gave them a simple statement to apply to the case. You might not like it, but this is how the real world actually works.

Why did George W. Bush win the U.S. presidential election in 2004? I think it's because he said, "Even when we don't agree, at least you know what I believe and where I stand." A highly credible statement. And credibility is what matters most. This statement contrasted sharply with the perceived switching of positions by his Democratic opponent, John Kerry.

In 2008, why did Barack Obama win the U.S. presidential election? I think Obama won the election in the second presidential debate. Every time it looked like Republican candidate John McCain was going to slug him, Obama smiled and tried to be collaborative, calm, and, well, *presidential.* Indeed, a *New York Times*/CBS poll at the time said that McCain's angry tone and personal attacks had caused negative reactions in 60 percent of voters.

What does this mean in terms of a negotiation? It means that if you are having trouble with the other party in discussing the issues, *stop!* Go back to talking about the people, and then fix any problems there. Don't forge madly ahead. If you do, you won't get a deal, or if you do, the deal won't stick.

A woman was in a very sensitive job buyout negotiation in Los Angeles. Day one was fine, day two was not fine. So she stopped talking about the issues and said to the other person, "Mark, we had a good day yesterday, but today we're not. If it's something I said or did, I'm sorry. I want to get us back on track. What's going on?"

Mark apologized for being distracted. It turned out to be something else entirely. They rechecked their process and successfully finished the negotiation.

THE HUMAN CONNECTION

Focusing on the people will get you much more. Even in a transactional situation, people are five times as likely to help you if you treat them as individuals. The numbers are staggering: 90 percent versus about 15 percent willing to help.

Even if you don't know them, or you dislike them, making a human connection will usually get them to help you meet your goals. This is true with the bored bureaucrat at the government office, the curt service representative with the phone company, or the leader of a disagreeable nation.

What you don't want to do is blame such people for being ornery or hateful. Blaming them will just bring you further from your goals. Being nice to them will bring you closer to your goals.

Aliza Zaida had a center seat on a five-hour overnight flight on US Airways from San Francisco to Philadelphia. And all they had left were center seats. People were grumbling to the gate agent about this. When she got to the podium, Aliza noticed that the gate agent had been fielding all these complaints with a cough, and didn't appear to be feeling well.

Aliza had an extra bottle of water, which she offered to the gate agent along with cough drops and condolences. These were gratefully accepted. It wasn't a manipulative thing; Aliza, now a Pittsburgh consultant, is like that. "I would have done it anyway," she said.

Aliza asked respectfully if the gate agent might consider her for an aisle seat if one opened up. No pressure, no complaints. She left her ticket with the gate agent and sat down. In a few minutes the gate agent called her name. "She gave me an exit-row aisle seat, which had more room," Aliza said. "She also gave me a free meal. She didn't want me to sleep on an empty stomach. I thanked her again and she gave me headsets in case I wanted to watch the movie. Kindness counts."

You might say, if everyone did this, the negotiation tool would become ineffective. Or, it seems manipulative. Maybe, but everyone won't do this. Most people will just complain and think of themselves, not the other person. Besides, too many people being nice isn't a bad problem to have. I'd like to live in *that* world. Wouldn't you?

Focusing on the people also means that when you are negotiating with representatives of a group, you should be focusing on the *individuals* in the group. Not the company or the culture, not their gender, race, or religion. Each individual is different and unique. Talk to them as individuals.

There are lots of books and articles with titles like *How to Negotiate with the Russians*. What's wrong with this? These titles presume that all Russians, Japanese, Chinese, French, Americans, etc., are the same. My response to such titles goes like this: "What? You're going to negotiate with a hundred and thirty million Japanese?"

In fact, you are going to negotiate with one person, or a couple of people, who may be more or less the same as the cultural norm. And it's not the whole culture or group that will say yes or no; it's an individual, with his or her own perceptions and experiences. To be sure, there are differences among cultural *norms*, but norms are averages. They are not precise enough for you to know how to persuade the individual sitting across from you.

Indeed, you may have more in common with someone in Mongolia, who doesn't even speak your language, than with the person sitting next to you at your company.

"It is certainly not true that all Americans are individualistic and aggressive, and all Japanese are team players," said Wei-Wei Wang, our much-improved USC negotiator from Chapter 1.

I once sensed a client was unhappy. So I asked, "What's the problem?"

They replied, "We don't like lawyers." I'm a lawyer. I said, "Tell me more." So they mentioned a problem they once had with some lawyers in Cincinnati.

I told them, "I've got really good news for you. I don't know them. I'm not related to them. I'm not responsible for them . . . I'm just me."

Why should you be responsible for everything your company has done in the past ten years? Or what others in your profession or culture have done for 100 or 1,000 years? Would they take the rap for something someone in their country or company did ten, twenty, or fifty years ago? It's not fair, and what's more important, it's not relevant.

Focus on the people in front of you, and what you and the other party can do now. What is in your power to do? It is a very empowering way to think about a negotiation. You discard all the frustrating stuff over which you have no control, and deal with the things you can affect. It helps set priorities. It helps get things done. And if they say that company culture can affect the negotiation, you can respond: "Maybe, but don't you really want to know instead if I can make a decision that meets your needs, and then make a commitment that sticks?"

Even the most extreme of parties are not monolithic. Imagine you were a Jew in Poland in 1944. You thought all Nazis were evil. If you then met Oskar Schindler, you would have lost your life. That's because Schindler, although a Nazi, was willing to save your life. But you never asked him, because you thought all Nazis hated Jews.

What a source of competitive advantage it is to know who's really the same and who's really different, whether in business or personal life. And you can't tell just by considering external features or affiliations. As such, you will be able to make alliances and deals with people from other groups, where the less precise and less skilled negotiators will fail.

The president of Georgetown University, Jack DeGioia, was in one of our executive negotiation workshops at Wharton one year. As we were discussing this point, he said that he had done some research after the terrorist attacks of September 11, 2001, about the Arab American culture. He noted that appoximately 63 percent of all Arab Americans are Christian.

In other words, this research, and subsequently our own, found that more than half of all Arab Americans are not affiliated with the central religion of the Arab culture: Islam. Instead, they belong to the central religion of Western culture: Christianity.

So what happened after 9/11? It became open season on numerous Arab Americans by a variety of U.S. government officials, some very visible and senior, as well as by airlines, educational institutions, and many ordinary Americans. There are thousands of documented incidents, from murder to assault to illegal arrests and detentions, to being booted off aircraft. Some comments blamed all Arabs (presumably Christian ones, too) for attacking Christians. You might say it was a small percentage. But why is *any* percentage acceptable, especially in the United States?

More Americans might instead have worked with the many Arab Americans who love Western culture, gathering contacts, information, and assistance in the struggle against Arab extremists. This is an example of a missed opportunity due to a failure to treat people as individuals. This is not to criticize Muslim practitioners. The key point is the lack of differentiation, and the lack of effective and precise judgment about people.

As the years pass, uncomfortable incidents continue. After a Nigerian man tried to detonate a bomb on a U.S.-bound plane at the end of 2009, U.S. officials put Nigeria on the terrorist watch list. Nigeria responded by threatening to sell its oil elsewhere. Did not officials of both countries overreact? One Nigerian terrorist does not make Nigeria a terrorist country. And a few people who overreacted in the U.S. Transportation Security Administration do not make all American leaders prejudiced, either.

THIRD PARTIES

Anand Iyer worked for a company selling technology for currency exchange. One of his clients said his "company" believed Anand's fees were high. "I told him we negotiate with people and not with 'companies,'" said Anand, now a currency and equities trader in San Francisco. He told his client that he'd be glad to talk to the exact people who thought the fees were too high. It turned out that those people just wanted "progress" on some front in currency exchange. They worked out a trade involving public relations and some extra work. The fees stayed the same.

There are almost always at least three people in a negotiation—even if only two people are present. The third party, or parties, are those people, real and imagined, that the principals think they must defer to in some way. They may be ghosts and goblins of their past. They may be people whom a principal told about the negotiation—a spouse, colleagues, friends—in front of whom the principals need to save face. It may be a boss. The point is, you need to account for these people to achieve your goals and get more.

For example, the other person might agree with you personally, but he or she has an unreasonable boss. In such a case, you might ally with the other person to find arguments to persuade the other person's boss.

Scott Brodman, a sales manager for a major chemical company, wondered to himself why the purchasing rep of a new account kept asking for things even though the deal was already a very attractive one. He asked questions in order to find out about any third parties behind the scenes. "I found out that the other side's management was looking over his shoulder and second-guessing him," Scott said.

Scott helped his counterpart show his bosses industry standards, as well as how their needs were being met. "He told his management that he got the best deal he possibly could," Scott said. They agreed.

Very few people ignore the opinions of third parties who are important to them. When you need to influence someone, and you don't think you have enough influence by yourself, think about who else is important to the other person and whom you may have an easier time influencing.

Bernard Burton, a New York attorney, represented a contractor in a suit against the builder of a racetrack on Long Island in the 1970s. The track, Suffolk Meadows, got into financial trouble and the builder, Ronald Parr, stopped paying at least some creditors. Burton was worried Parr would not tell the truth on the stand about the debt, since Parr had not been forthright before.

So Burton subpoenaed Parr's secretary of thirty years. Not to testify, but just to sit in the courtroom. Burton figured that Parr would never lie in front of his secretary, a kindly, honest old lady. And as he hoped, Parr told the truth. Burton got the money for his clients. "Every penny," he said. That is the importance of third parties.

VALUING THE OTHER PARTY

A student went into Strawbridge & Clothier's, at that time a major department store in Philadelphia, to buy a suit for a job interview. He found a $500 suit reduced on sale to $350, and brought the suit to the counter. There, a harried salesclerk was fielding all sorts of demands and complaints by other customers.

The student waited until the other customers cleared out and the salesclerk had some time. He started a conversation with her by apologizing for everyone else's behavior. He said she must be tired after a full day of work. It wasn't fair for other people to take out their problems on her, he told her. The student was probably the first person all day who was nice to her.

The student noted the existing discount on the suit and asked if there was anything else that could be done—an additional discount for store credit card, payment in cash, and so forth. The salesclerk said none of those programs applied. Then the student said, "Can I suggest this? I am probably the first person in a while who is at least trying to understand how difficult your job is. Could I have a nice guy discount?" The salesclerk smiled and said, "How about $50?"

Now, granted, this is a little thing. But the student received a 14 percent discount just because he made himself a person to the clerk. He made a people connection. It's not a fancy technique, but it is invisible to most people. And there will be times when it will be a big deal in a negotiation. How would you feel about increasing your annual disposable income by, say, 10 percent?

A key to getting other people to give you what you want is to value the other party. The way most movies and books portray negotiation, you beat up the other party and you get more because they are ashamed or bested. But this is entirely wrong! Think of your own reactions. You want to give people more when they value you. In family situations, when people get upset, it is because they feel devalued. In job situations, people grumble because they feel devalued.

And you can adjust your approach immediately in a negotiation if you start out doing it wrong. I was once late for class at Wharton. A Pepsi truck was blocking one lane of a two-way street. Into the space of the other lane, a car and a taxi had inserted themselves in opposite directions. There were maybe five cars behind each one, honking, but neither car in the space would budge. I decided to help negotiate it. I got out of my car and walked up to the taxi, figuring that I could better negotiate with someone who was clearly a local.

"Do you have to be so macho?" I said. Wrong question! It insulted and devalued him. He dismissed me with his hand and said, "Bah!" I realized I'd made a mistake and tried a more empathetic approach.

"You could be a nice guy," I tried. Of course, he probably felt beaten up for being too nice a guy in the past. He considered this, though. "Well," he said. But he still didn't move.

So I thought about the pictures in his head. I thought about what he does every day. Finally it hit me how I could value him. "You know," I said conspiratorially, "between you and this other car, you are the only professional driver here."

He backed up.

Understanding the pictures in the head of the other party is a theme to which I will return over and over again. It is the single most important thing you can do in trying to persuade another person. If you try to understand the pictures in their heads, you have a starting point to changing their minds.

The next time a police officer stops you for a traffic infraction, apologize and thank the officer for doing his or her job. You are valuing their judgment in stopping you. You are valuing the time they have spent building a career. And when you value other people, they give you stuff. If you are worried about liability, tell them you are sorry "for what happened" or "for any part I might have had in this." I tend to say respectfully to the cop, "You're the boss."

I was stopped on Thirty-seventh Street in New York City a few years ago for not wearing my seat belt. It looked clearly like three cars on the side of the street were all getting tickets for the same thing; the police had just set up shop there. So I decided to value the police officer. I said, "Thank you so much, Officer, for stopping me and doing your job. You probably just saved my life." Did I get a ticket? Absolutely not.

Of course, you have to mean it. If you say things like this without genuine sincerity, you are going to get a ticket. If you hate all police officers, it will come across. You need to think about all daily encounters as negotiations, and practice to the point where you can focus on the other party quickly. In other words, they must genuinely feel that the negotiation is about them and their needs and perceptions, not yours. The police officer wants to feel that you have learned a lesson. The main question is what that lesson will cost you.

When I was a journalist, I used to have to gain people's trust in a few seconds. My first goal was to keep them in the conversation. I would try to insert myself, figuratively, into their brains. What are they thinking and feeling? What would cause them to keep talking to me? What would cause them to make a connection with me? You need to be open and curious enough to try to find out the pictures in their heads, or you are lost.

Denis Zaviyalov's five-year-old daughter, Regina, wanted to be a princess. "She watches princess cartoons. The walls in her room are adorned with princess posters," he said. There's only one problem: "Her room is a complete mess." So Denis thought about Regina the person, the pictures in her head, the world through her eyes. He asked her to show him how to make sunflowers out of paper plates. She did. "Thank you, Princess!" he said. Then he added, "But look at the mess we made." He looked around the room. "Does this look like a princess's room?"

Regina thought about this. "Princesses don't have messy rooms," she said. "So what should we do?" Denis asked. Regina said, "I could clean up the room, throw away all the dried Play-Doh, and make it look like a princess's room." Deal!

Everett Hutt had sixteen guys waiting for him early one morning for crew practice at one of the boathouses along the Schuylkill River in Philadelphia. A car was blocking his reserved spot. It was 6:00 A.M. After some effort, the night attendant called the owner, who told him where the key to the car, an Acura, was. The attendant brought down a Honda key and kept trying to force it into the Acura ignition, saying it had to be the correct key because he got it from the spot where the owner said to look in the key box.

Instead of muttering "You idiot, can't you see it's a Honda key?" Everett praised the attendant for his efforts. Then he told the attendant that "not everyone is as orderly as you are; maybe the key was put in a different spot by mistake." The attendant agreed to go back upstairs, where he found the right key.

Now, you say, "I will *never* do this." Well, Everett's actions got him to his practice on time. If you take actions that don't meet your goals, you're going to spend a lot of time arguing with parking lot attendants and everyone else.

Often, the rewards will be unexpected and profitable. When she was a student at Columbia Business School, Jennifer Prosek decided to strike up a conversation with Jimmy Lu, a quiet Chinese student whom hardly anyone talked to. Within five minutes, Jimmy, grateful, offered Jennifer public relations work in China. Curiosity about others will itself lead to business.

Jennifer has since become the founder and CEO of a PR firm in New York and London. "We look at business development as the outgrowth of one's natural curiosity," she said. Viewed in this context, she added, a simple conversation about anything can be part of the sales-negotiation process.

So how do you find out about other people? You make small talk. Not just because you read somewhere that it's smart to make small talk. You do it because you are interested in them. Because you want to try for a point of connection with other people. It's a way of approaching life.

It's also a way of approaching others. A new waitress at Champps Restaurant in Philadelphia was trying to handle a lot of tables. It was taking a long time for one of my students and her friends to get their dinner. So she called the waitress over and thanked her for her efforts, valuing her. The student said she realized the waitress was new and very busy. Could she bring an appetizer while they were waiting?

The waitress brought a free appetizer and then took the price of the entrées off the bill: everything but the drinks was free. "The waitress essentially paid me for being nice and understanding," my student said.

"Finding a common bond with other people pays huge dividends," said Ruben Munoz, an attorney in Philadelphia. Ruben got a translation rate for birth and marriage certificates halved by looking up the translator on the Internet before his meeting with her, and talking about their common interests in Spain and travel. You don't want to do this? Okay. But you won't profit, either.

The public often treats people in service positions like servants. They will be extremely grateful if you treat them with dignity.

Gaurav Tewari was about to be charged $100 to have boxes delivered to him that had been stored over the summer at a public storage place. He found the manager of the warehouse and chatted with him. The manager said he was hoping to get an MBA someday. Gaurav, who was getting an MBA, gave him advice on applying to business school. The result? There was no charge for delivery.

By their own accounts, my students have saved more than *$1 billion* in such small ways. That is not chicken feed.

Making a personal connection means you have to focus on other people, not just yourself, bringing them into a conversation with you. A student in one of my Wharton classes was driving around an expensive Philadelphia suburb one day, looking for a place to live after graduation for himself, his wife, and their infant son. The student wasn't paying attention and went through a stop sign. A police car parked on the side street pulled him over almost immediately.

The student apologized profusely and said what he did was unsafe. "The thing is," the student said, "I was so busy looking at these beautiful houses for a place to live after graduation for myself, my wife, and my infant son that I didn't see the stop sign.

"Whatever you decide to do to me here," the student continued, "could you advise me where I should look in this community for a place to live where the houses are a bit less expensive? I'd love to live in your community, but I was hoping to find something more affordable." Whereupon the police officer took out his wallet and showed the student the officer's own baby pictures. Not surprisingly, there was no ticket.

Does this happen all the time? Absolutely not. But again, what you are looking for is that one extra hit every nine games.

FINDING AND ACKNOWLEDGING THEIR POWER

By valuing others, you are also acknowledging their power. This includes not just the CEO. It also includes the maître d' at the fashionable restaurant, the administrative assistant who knows where the files are, the harried bureaucrat behind the window at the Department of Motor Vehicles, or the child or counterpart who can save or waste your time. Valuing what they do recognizes their position, capabilities, or perceptions. They will want to give you something in return. Even if they have little power, giving them power by acknowledging what they have control over will lead them to give you something back. This is the opposite of exerting your power over them; as a result, it has the opposite effect: people want to help you.

So the next time a hotel clerk or a customer service representative on the phone or a gas station attendant or other service provider makes a mistake or doesn't give you exactly what you want, don't chastise them or treat them poorly. Doing so won't help you meet your goals. Instead, value them by acknowledging that they have the power to do it differently. This is the opposite of the typical reaction, but it works—and works far more effectively.

Dawn MacLaren, a management consultant, was at a crowded restaurant with a friend. The waiter didn't bring drinks despite four requests. Dawn's friend screamed at him, demeaning him, and the waiter walked away. Dawn followed him across the restaurant, apologized for her friend, and for cranky customers in general. "If you could bring our drinks and a check, the next time you will have to come to our table is to pick up your tip," she said.

Drinks arrived less than two minutes later. "Instead of making him seem incompetent, I tried to see the situation from his viewpoint," Dawn said.

The key is not being reactive even if the other person is in a bad mood. Often, people will lash out at you just because they are frustrated from some other encounter. Don't assume it's about you. Tell them you're sorry they are having a bad day. You will reap all the benefits. It takes discipline, but the rewards are worth it.

You will face thousands of encounters like these in your life. How you choose to resolve them will have a significant effect on the quality of your life.

Finding and acknowledging the other person's power also means finding the *decision-maker.* Or the person with direct influence over the decision-maker. How many of you have wasted hours of your lives negotiating with the *wrong person?* Everyone. When you call someone up, you should know if the person can help. "Hello, do you have the power to do *x?*" Life is short.

A French company had negotiated with a Korean company for three years. Every time the French company thought they had a deal, the Korean company kicked it up to the next level. After three years and the expenditure of $500,000—for travel and other expenses, not even counting the opportunity costs—the French company gave up. The reason they failed is that they hadn't asked what they should have asked at week one. That is, what does this process look like? Who makes the decisions?

Closely related to that is, *who is the right negotiator?* It may not be the most skilled or senior person. Indeed, studies have shown that the more powerful people are, the less attention they pay to the other side's needs. That means the less successful they will be at expanding the pie. It's a real irony, then, that some of the most junior members of a team might end up being the best negotiators. So your question should be "Who on my team will be most likely to get the other party to meet my goals?"

An important way to empower them, too, rarely used, is to *give them the problem.* Use empathy or just ask them for help. When you involve people in your problems, they will feel empowered, they will take ownership, they will be more likely to help you. Ask them for help.

In all of my years as a negotiator, I did one advisory session for the CIA. Someone at the inspector general's office called me. It seemed the administration was being overwhelmed with employee grievances. Management couldn't handle them.

So I went down to Langley, Virginia. I told them that a good way to reduce the number of employee grievances was to give the problem away to the employees. Form an employee grievance committee. Put various employees on it. Have people rotate in and out, say, every six months. Offer a small bonus for it, or a positive letter in the employee file, that sort of thing. All grievances from employees would first go to the employee grievance committee for review. If the committee approved, the grievances would then be forwarded to management.

In such a situation the number of employee grievances goes way down. People feel embarrassed bringing frivolous or vindictive grievances to their peers. What is left are the legitimate complaints. Ask your colleagues, bosses, and employees for advice on how to solve your problems. Let them know you might not accept every answer. But you *will* get more.

TRUST

A colleague was a friend of mine for almost twenty years. One day he saw an opportunity and appropriated for himself a project we had worked on together for more than a decade. Spouses are married for years; suddenly one cheats and *poof!* The marriage is over.

Clearly, trust is a major people issue. The benefits of trust are huge: faster deals, more deals, bigger results. Not having it is costly. A French study showed that there is so little trust among people in France that employment is 8 percent lower and gross national product is 5 percent lower than they could be. The comparison country was Sweden. This is a multibillion-dollar difference. In general, Scandinavian countries and the United States had the most trust.

Part of the economic problem in many developing countries is that transaction costs are so high because there is very little trust. Part of the economic problem in the United States is that since 9/11, trust among people and institutions has dropped. So transactions, such as airport security or loans, are more time-consuming and costly. This takes away money that could be used for more productive enterprises. A 2009 Danish study found a direct correlation between societal trust and foreign investment, especially with the hated lower trust rates in post-Communist and developing countries.

Let's define trust. Trust is a feeling of security that the other person will protect you. With some trust, another person will help you until it's too risky for them or a better opportunity comes along. With a lot of trust, the other party will help you even if it harms them. It is *very* important to understand the trust dynamic.

The major component of trust is honesty—being straight with people. Trust does *not* mean that both sides agree with each other, or are always pleasant to each other. It does mean, however, that the parties believe each other. Your credibility, as I mentioned earlier, is the most important negotiation tool you have.

The opposite of trust is, of course, dishonesty, or lying. It includes any action that deceives other people. That includes telling the truth in such a way that you omit facts and create a false impression. It can be clever manipulation of emotions. It can be the distorting of information, bluffing (making threats or promises you don't intend to carry out), undermining the credibility of others through selectively chosen information. It's anything that doesn't pass the "smell test." Lying destroys trust and ultimately hurts successful negotiations.

You have to make sure there is a basis for trust. If someone you have just met in a business situation says to you, "Don't you trust me?" your answer invariably should be something like, "Why should I trust you? We just met each other. And if you trust me on that basis, you're crazy!" Trust is something that develops slowly, over time. It is an emotional commitment to one another based on mutual respect, ethics, and good feeling. It includes the notion that people care about others and will not try to grab everything for themselves.

If you are unsure of the relationship, *don't* trust the other person. Don't make yourself vulnerable to them. The right response to an untrustworthy person is *not* to be untrustworthy back. Why destroy your credibility just because they have destroyed theirs?

A colleague, Michel Marks, was chairman of the New York Mercantile Exchange (NYMEX) from 1974 to 1986. He invented energy futures, a trillion-dollar industry. I once asked him for the secret of his success. "I always leave money on the table," Michel said. "I never leave them with nothing." He added that people trusted him, so they brought him deals, and he did more deals. And he said he did each deal faster, so he did a lot more deals.

Michel was no patsy; he didn't expose his throat when he wasn't sure of the trust situation. But he made his credibility the major part of his own competitiveness. And his milieu, NYMEX, is a pretty transactional, short-term place, as popularized in the Eddie Murphy movie *Trading Places*.

Now, lawyers might say, "How is leaving money on the table consistent with my responsibility to zealously represent my client?" My answer would be, "Over what time frame? If you take everything today and they won't deal with you again, have you really gotten your client the most that was available to you over all relevant time frames?"

Some people may say that trust varies from culture to culture. That's true. But it is also true that the more the human connection in any culture, the more trust. And lack of trust still has a cost. Some years ago I conducted a negotiation workshop in Moscow for a number of the most successful businessmen in the former Soviet Union. After the first morning, three of the participants took me to lunch to set me straight.

"All this stuff about collaboration is very nice for your students in the West," one of them said. "But it is irrelevant to us. Whenever we want something, we just steal it." The three of them chuckled, but they meant it. I asked about bribery. Yes, they said, they bribe people, too.

I said to them, "This may work for you today inside Russia. But the international business community won't stand for it, and it will cost you in the long run." Of course, they didn't believe me.

In 1998, the Russian banking scandal erupted, and U.S. banks lost billions of dollars due to bank fraud in Russia. U.S. investment in Russia dropped from 28 percent of the world total to 2.9 percent. If you were to ask many international financiers about Russia, the first association that would come to mind is "cheating." Even if it's a minority of people involved, it's expensive. The French study cited earlier said that about 90 percent of the people in Russia have "no trust at all" in the justice system, compared to about 23 percent in the United States and about 12 percent in Norway, the two countries found to have the highest degrees of trust.

Lying and bluffing in negotiations feel risky. People can call your bluff. If it's an organization and different people tell different lies, someone on the other side will eventually detect it. Internally, lying or bluffing may cause dissension and distrust among those with higher ethical standards. Someone may detect the inconsistencies and use them against you.

That doesn't mean you have to tell the other person everything. As noted in Chapter 1, tell them you're not ready to disclose some things "at this point." If the relationship develops, you can disclose more.

It also helps to figure out what they are really asking. A woman moved away from her Manhattan neighborhood but came back to one of her former local stores a short time later to buy some music CDs. She wanted about $150 worth. At the checkout counter, the manager asked if she lived in the neighborhood; there was a discount for neighbors. Her question later to the class was, should she have lied? She did not and paid full price.

What was the manager's real question? Did he give a hoot where she lived? No. He wanted to know if she was a frequent customer. Why couldn't she have answered, "I used to live in the neighborhood, and recently moved away. But I come back just to shop at the stores that I love. This is one of them."

Isn't that more powerful than lying? It responds to what he was really asking. What if she lied and showed her driver's license with her old address and the manager knew someone else had moved in there? Stores do have databases. She'd be toast forever in that store.

To prove the point, the student went back to the store and told the manager what the class recommended she say. And she got the discount, after the purchase. It may take a little more thought about the other party and the situation, but the results involve less risk and more gain over time.

NEGOTIATING WITHOUT TRUST

As we know, the world is often an untrustworthy place. How do you negotiate in situations where there is a lack of trust? After all, untrustworthy people pay money, too.

The fact is, although trust is best, you *don't need it* for successful negotiations. This is a big point and most people miss it: trust is not the major requirement for a successful negotiation. Something much more fundamental is needed.

What is needed is a *commitment*. Trust is only one way to get a commitment. Contracts, third parties, and incentives are other ways to obtain commitments.

The important thing is, you need to get a commitment in the way *they* make commitments, not in the way you make commitments. Your word is your bond? Who cares? Is their word their bond? Don't just assume that because you make a commitment one way, they will make a commitment the same way. You should spend as much energy on getting commitments that you are sure really commit them as you spend in setting your goals.

U.S. companies doing business in China have whined that many traditional Chinese companies don't use contracts to make price commitments. They make commitments differently. First, the Chinese company gets the structure of the deal done in a contract—supply, delivery, length, and so forth. Then, they look at the market and propose pricing based on market conditions. Prices in contracts are viewed as advisory. Indeed, the *China Economic Review* said in April 2010 that Westerners who don't plan for such a second, post-contract negotiation should "plan on failing."

However, if an elder of the community in China, respected by the company, announces in the press that this contract, with its embedded pricing formula, is an excellent example of U.S.-China cooperation—now *that* would be much more of a commitment. That's because face-saving is important in both business and personal behavior in China.

A U.S. consulting firm was owed a substantial debt by one of the largest companies in China. This debt was 700 days old—almost two years. The U.S. company tried attorneys, and it didn't work. They tried diplomacy, and it opened the door a little: for a meeting.

I suggested to the U.S. company that its executives meet in person with the heads of this traditional Chinese company and say something like: "Your not paying this debt has dishonored us. It has dishonored us in front of our colleagues. It has dishonored us in front of our friends. It has dishonored us in front of our families. It has dishonored us in front of our employees, consultants, customers, government, neighborhoods, and communities."

Moreover, the Chinese company should be advised that the nonpayment has also dishonored *them* in front of their own government. That's because China was trying for international trade respect. Not paying legitimate business debts for work performed is against international standards. The Chinese company paid the debt in full within three weeks.

In many markets in the Middle East, a handshake is a binding commitment. One trader sticks out his hand, arm straight, and says, "How about this price? Give me your hand." The other trader snaps his arm behind his back: offer not accepted. The negotiation continues. If they reach a deal, they shake hands in front of witnesses. Binding commitment.

For several years, one of my companies exported bananas from the jungles of Bolivia to Argentina. In the particular markets we dealt with in Argentina, I found out that the following statements were *not* commitments: (a) "I swear." (b) "I swear on my mother's life." (c) "I promise." (d) "I signed the contract." (e) "I absolutely guarantee it."

But if we owed them money, they would keep the agreement, at least until we paid them. So we developed a structure in which they paid the up-front costs of ripening, delivery, sales, and so forth. We received the payment from the ultimate consumers—here, supermarkets. Then we paid our partner for their costs and profit split.

In the six years that we dealt with them, they never broke any term of the agreement. Did I trust them? I didn't even know them! So here is a key. In the absence of trust, you need a mechanical substitute to give them an incentive not to cheat. It can be a monetary structure as above. It can be money in escrow or potential negative opinions by third parties. It can be the net present value of future profits from the deal.

As the singer Tina Turner once said, "What's love got to do with it?" In a negotiation, trust is nice, but not necessary.

There are many other ways to protect yourself against lying or cheating by the other party. The first is being incremental. Give a little information or value that doesn't cost much if you get cheated. See if you get something back in kind. If so, go a little further. Be careful that you don't get into a sting situation where you have given a lot and they have given little that's of value to you. Make sure you get sufficient value in return each step of the way.

A Ukrainian businessman, Alex Dogot, said that when he meets someone in a business setting, for the first few months he always asks questions to which he already knows the answers. "If they lie, I don't deal with them again. If they tell the truth, I go to the next step," he said.

There are other ways to test them. Ask them to prove to a third party that their other offer is bona fide. Tell them that you will give them better prices and terms up to your limit, which only the third party will know. The third party would then review any other offers against yours. If your offer is better, the other party gets the money you have deposited with the third party. If they balk, you should become suspicious of their veracity.

I like former president Ronald Reagan's comment about the Soviet Union: "Trust, but verify." It's an old Russian proverb.

Here is a list of things for you to keep in mind:

- If they have a lot more information than you do, you are vulnerable. Be incremental and don't make commitments until you have more information or a lot of trust.
- Collect lots of information ("due diligence") on them. Ask them for details. See if all the information matches up. Check and test everything. Use trusted third parties to help.
- Do they evade your questions or change the subject? The more secretive they are, the more risk there is that they are hiding something.
- If it would be more profitable for them to cheat than be honest, change the incentives. For example, compensate them for performance (value) they provide over time.

- Don't provide your assets (inventions, time, buildings) without *explicit* protections.
- Make guarantees of truthfulness part of any agreement. Tell them: "It will give me comfort and cost you nothing if what you say is true." If they balk, watch out!
- Put in your agreement the consequences of breaking the agreement.
- Meet in person; it's harder to hide things. In some cultures, many parties will not negotiate except in person, where the parties can observe each other.
- If you feel uncomfortable that something has been left unsaid, ask them, "Is there anything else I should know?"

Trust your instincts. Is the other person nervous? Looking guilty? Trying too hard? Looking away (unless it's cultural)? Keeping long silences? Declining to make commitments? These are not conclusive evidence of dishonesty. But they should raise questions that cause you to go slower, ask more questions, be more incremental.

Getting more also means not getting less. Take the trouble to follow these guidelines. Don't be sorry later.

LOSING AND REGAINING TRUST

A thousand years from now, someone will look up newspaper articles for the twenty-first century and see an obituary of the widely respected style guru Martha Stewart. The article will start with something like, "Martha Stewart, who changed the way the world viewed style, and who was indicted and convicted for lying to a grand jury, died yesterday." Cheating, or even the perception of cheating, is forever.

Let's say you are at a law firm. You overbill a client once in your career by $1,000. You get found out. For the rest of your life, people will look at you as the attorney who overbills. The law firm will be looked at as the law firm that overbills. It just takes once.

The cost of cheating is loss of trust. The cost of loss of trust is actual dollars, reputation, credibility, and your effectiveness as a negotiator. Michael Phelps, who won a record eight gold medals for swimming in the 2008 Summer Olympics, lost millions of dollars in sponsorship contracts because he was found smoking marijuana, once. He still does sponsorships, but at a fraction of the opportunity he had before. And, of course, we all know what happened to the endorsement career of pro golfer Tiger Woods when he was discovered to be cheating on his wife.

In class negotiation sessions, there are opportunities for one party to cheat another. Once, a lawyer and a law student made an agreement with each other during a negotiation. The student's team broke the agreement and beat the lawyer's team soundly. The lawyer was outraged. He stood up in front of this large class and said to the student: "I have all the information I need about you for the rest of your life."

The student responded, "Hey, lighten up, it's just a game." To which the attorney said, "If this is what you'll do for points, just think what you'll do for money."

Even the *perception* of cheating can destroy negotiations and the relationships that go with them. One manager in my Columbia University Executive MBA course said he was working for an industrial equipment manufacturer that ten years before had a problem with its major customer over the contract for the annual purchase.

The client was buying $80 million a year in equipment. In the contract negotiation, the client specifically opposed a particular pricing formula. The vendor agreed to take it out. It didn't affect much of the purchase, and it was far down in the contract. But it had been heavily negotiated.

When the contract was finished, the vendor signed it and sent it to the customer. As the customer's purchasing people were going through the contract, the purchasing manager discovered that, lo and behold, the pricing formula was still in the contract! The customer was livid, saying it had been cheated. The vendor apologized profusely, but no matter. The customer didn't believe the vendor, since the formula had been so heavily negotiated.

For ten years after that, that customer bought nothing from that vendor. In all, with inflation, it cost the vendor $1 billion in sales. After ten years, there was no one left in the vendor's senior management who had been involved in that deal. At the customer's company, there was only one person left. It was the CEO, who happened to have been the purchasing manager ten years before.

One of the most dramatic, and applicable, examples of the effects of loss of trust concerns a customer of a big producer of chemicals.

The customer was a large printing plant in central New Jersey. The purchasing manager told me he was buying less than 10 percent of his chemical needs from the vendor, perhaps $100,000 a year. He said his company *could* be buying at least $500,000 a year, and perhaps much more. But, he said, instead of getting this business, the vendor had lost the printing plant as a client in 1990, eleven years earlier. In fact, 2001 was the first time the printing plant had bought anything from the vendor since 1990.

"What happened?" I asked.

"Well," the purchasing manager said, "in 1990, the company tried to force a new product on us, saying the old product was no longer available. The new product didn't perform and we lost production time." Then, he said, he found that the so-called new product was actually "test material." As a result, he said, "trust was lost." He said the vendor lost more than $1 million in business from his firm.

"So, why did you start again?" I asked.

"Well," he said, "the company's sales rep has been great. He's been coming around, giving us information, really nice guy. So we thought we'd give him a shot at the account again." This explained the relatively small order in 2001, the purchasing manager said.

"How long has the sales rep been coming around trying to win the account back?" I asked. "Every month for six years," the purchasing manager said.

It is possible to regain trust after you have lost it. It's not easy, of course, and it's not fail-safe. Your request can resonate if you frame it in terms of a "second chance." The process needs to be incremental. "You have to be polite, you have to apologize, you have to promise to do better," said Vera Nakova, a senior marketing manager for Sanofi-Aventis pharmaceuticals who gave a second chance to an underperforming market research vendor. "You have to be open to change. You need to discuss past miscommunications." She said a key to reestablishing trust is to demonstrate your ability to collaborate and solve the problems that have occurred.

CHANGING EVERYTHING

Having an understanding of people through the tools and strategies in this chapter can have extraordinary results. Here is one from Dr. Chris Shibutani, a former student of mine at Columbia Business School, about a twenty-seven-year-old autistic patient named Jean.

Chris, who is now a portfolio manager at UBS, was a pediatric anesthesiologist at Memorial Sloan-Kettering Cancer Center in Manhattan during the 1990s. Jean, the adult patient, was noncommunicative and uncooperative. He repeatedly became violent when approached with needles for tests.

"I thought about his needs and who he was as a person," Chris said.

"He simply needed more concrete reassurance and had more limited coping mechanisms."

Chris realized that Jean was afraid of pain and symbols of pain. So he made a display of putting away visible needles. Chris also realized that Jean hated being talked down to. So he sat next to him at eye level and had a nurse calmly lie down on a nearby stretcher. This acknowledged Jean's power and valued him.

Chris figured that Jean disliked surprises, so the doctor made very slow movements. Chris demonstrated the use of monitors on himself first, then on Jean's mother, while both smiled. Human connections.

Chris knew Jean was hungry before the tests, so he laced the anesthetic mask with sweet strawberry scent and let the smell waft over to Jean. Because Jean rocked and hummed sometimes, Chris did the same, humming, "Who's afraid of the big bad wolf?"

Reassured, calm, and cooperative, Jean went quietly off to sleep. You can move even the most difficult people a long distance by figuring out who they are, valuing them, and giving them even a little more control.

3

Perception and Communication

Take a look at the picture below. (Picture the circle as red and round.) In two words or less, write down what you see. Ignore the arrow; it's there as a guide.

What did you write down? The most common answer is a red dot, but only 33 percent of observers wrote that. Next is a red circle, 18 percent. The question has produced many different answers. Someone from the

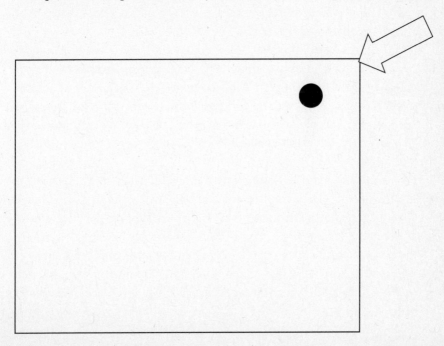

medical school wrote down "streptococcus." About 7 percent wrote "white space." More than 40 percent wrote something other than "red." Here is a partial list of answers:

Red Dot	Japanese flag	Rudolf
Upper Right	Goal	Eyeball
Streptococcus	Black Dot	Blood Drop
Target	Stoplight	White Space

How could people have so many different answers to the same simple question? Put another way, there is widespread disagreement over what people saw. Multiply this by 1,000, we have litigation; multiply it by a million, we have armed conflict. It's all on the same continuum.

In addition, almost everyone processed a small amount of the information inherent in the question. I pointed to the red dot, but said, "Write down what you see." Clearly, there is much more white space than red dot. And if you argue that the question focused you on the red dot, why do 7 percent of the people see white space?

Perhaps the biggest cause of negotiation failure, worldwide, is communication failure. And the single biggest cause of communication failure is misperception. Two people look at the same picture, but each sees a different part. And as is too often the case in the world, they will "kill" each other fighting over different parts of the same picture.

What causes different perceptions? First, we are all different people, so we are interested in different things. We have different values and emotional make-ups. Different people influence us. We experience and observe different information; often we ignore or dismiss information that doesn't fit. In arguments or negotiations, we selectively collect evidence that supports our views. We also selectively remember. Our memories color our perceptions.

These are the main reasons for virtually all human conflict since the beginning of time. Their importance cannot be overestimated.

There are two women in the well-known picture on page 59, an old woman and a young woman. The old woman is in profile, with her mouth as the horizontal line just above the fur coat, her large nose left above her mouth, and her eye just below her black hair. The young woman, seen from behind, is looking away; her necklace is the old woman's mouth; her chin is the old woman's nose; her ear is the old woman's eye.

In some of my classes, the students knew there were two women in this picture when we first displayed it. I passed out copies of each half of the picture—the old woman or the young woman—to different halves of the class.

Then I took the combined picture off the screen at the front of the room and asked people to stare at their half for five minutes. Next, I put the combined picture back onto the screen at the front. What do you think happened?

Almost no one could see the other half. If people have trouble seeing a picture they know is there after seeing a contrary image for five minutes, how much trouble does one culture have seeing another culture's point of view, after seeing the same picture for a thousand years?

THE PERCEPTION GAP

For many people, the other person's perception is not there at all on all kinds of subjects. Many people think that others who don't see their point of view are being thick, stubborn, or unreasonable. That's not necessarily so. The problem is usually much deeper than that. Often, the things you hold so firmly and dearly are *invisible* to the other party—they don't exist.

So to persuade people with different perceptions, you must start with the notion that your "facts"—your ideas, thoughts, and perceptions—are invisible to them. What you see so clearly the other party may not see at all.

What do you think happens when schoolchildren in the Middle East see a map of their region for all of their young lives without Israel in it? When someone finally tells them that Israel exists, they don't believe it.

Even using ordinary language can lead to dramatically different perceptions. A client worked in the marketing department of PolyGram Records in New York City. After he and other colleagues argued one day at work, they realized that each was using the term "marketing" differently. One of them thought it was closer to sales; the other thought it was closer to strategy. And yet they sat near each other in the same department for years. Their differing perceptions affected how they approached their jobs, spent resources, dealt with clients—indeed, spent their time.

Clever lawyers negotiating complex contracts know they need a section defining terms used in the agreement. They realize that even the most ordinary words are open to interpretation. If parties have different ideas of what the same words mean, the entire agreement can be in jeopardy because there is no meeting of the minds.

This is even more important in everyday language, when opportunities for misinterpretation are vast. But people rarely define the terms for their talks. Even more rarely do they question something that seems ambiguous.

Examples of misinterpretation abound. "The client said our $430,000 fee was too much" for the architectural service package being offered, said Anup Misra, a founder of a real estate development firm. "He wouldn't tell us what fee he had in mind." Finally, the client was asked to define "architectural service package." It turned out the client wanted fewer services than outlined in the initial fee. The final fee was $230,000 for half the scope of work. Dispute solved.

Bob Brown was dissatisfied with his son's high school grades. After closely questioning his son, Alex, Bob found out that Alex thought his grades were "good enough" to get into the college of his choice. Bob introduced his fourteen-year-old to a college admissions counselor who told Alex they were not. Rather than arguing with Alex over who was right, Bob helped to show him what the real standards to get into college were, by using a respected third party. "It worked perfectly," said Bob, a health science advisor at Merck. Alex got into the University of Wisconsin and maintained a 3.8 ("A") average as an electrical engineering student.

I taught a three-day negotiation workshop a few years ago for executives in Riyadh, Saudi Arabia. One executive who had lived in the United States said, "You know, when you are in a restaurant in the United States and you want some more coffee, you raise your cup and sort of rock it back and forth. The waiter comes over and refills your cup. But if you do that in Saudi Arabia, the waiter takes your cup away. And they think they understood you perfectly." Imagine a day full of different perceptions like this.

In millions of different ways, people get into personal conflicts because they haven't asked the question "Do they mean what I think they are saying?" In psychology, this mistake is called *fundamental attribution error*. You assume that everyone else reacts to things the way that you do.

When you say to someone else with some force, "It's hot in here!" and they reply, "I'm cold," the wrong answer is to say, "You're wrong!" People react to things in different ways. The more you are exquisitely conscious of this in all of your encounters, the less conflict you will have and the more problems you will solve. This means that their perceptions are more important than your proposals; that is, if you want to persuade them.

Not communicating effectively in companies is expensive: more expenses and frustration, lower efficiency and service, loss of customers, poor response time (including to competitive threats), inability to capitalize on the collective wisdom, lost opportunities, less time to build the organization. One major company calculated the loss as 3.5 hours per worker per week: millions of dollars per year for even a 500-worker company.

CLOSING THE PERCEPTION GAP

How do we solve these problems of miscommunication and perception? The first thing you must realize is that these problems occur all the time, everywhere. First, question the language being used to see if you both mean the same thing.

Jocelyn Donat, an executive director at JPMorgan Chase, told her two-year-old niece Annalisa at bedtime, "Now it is time for a story from Aunt Jocelyn." Immediately her niece said, "Two stories." After some back and forth, Jocelyn finally asked her niece why she wanted two stories. "Because I'm not tired" was the answer. They settled on one longer story. They each had a different perception of story length.

From now on, when you have a conflict with someone, ask yourself: (a) What am I perceiving? (b) What are they perceiving? (c) Is there a mismatch? (d) If so, why?

You may have done this in an ad hoc, unstructured way at times in your life. Now you should make such questions a specific, conscious part of your negotiations repertoire. This means that you need to understand both parties' biases, try to articulate their perceptions, and then explain yours.

Here are two statements with the same words. Statement number one: "I'm going to New York City. Where are you going?" Statement number two: "Where are you going? I'm going to New York City." Experience shows that sentence number two will be heard by the other person much more often than sentence number one. When you ask someone for their perceptions first, you value them, so they are then much more interested in listening to what you have to say.

Two sentences, same words, different order. There is a reason I said these tools are invisible to those who don't already know them.

And this is why it is generally senseless to interrupt someone. When someone is interrupted, the tapes are still playing in their head. Mostly, they don't hear you. Listening declines further if they get mad about the interruption. What you must do first in a negotiation is get them *ready* to listen to you.

Most people start with the facts. "My proposal is to offer you $200,000 for this house based on market conditions." But as we have seen, the facts comprise less than 10 percent of the reason why people reach agreements or not. Other people will begin a negotiation by explaining the rational "interests." "Housing prices are continuing to fall, so it's best to sell now."

But neither facts nor rationality speaks to most of the people in the world. Rather, we need to start at the beginning: is the other person even ready to listen to me? To know that, you have to understand the pictures in their heads: their perceptions and feelings, how they view you and the rest of the world. If you don't, you don't have a starting point. You're just walking around in the dark.

In the example above, try something like this: "Hi, this is such a nice house you have. How long have you lived here?"

Explaining *your* perceptions is the last thing you should do. First, learn *their* perceptions.

Tim McClurg, an account manager at a major life insurance company, was told by a broker that the company's prices were 15 percent too high. Tim questioned the broker more closely about his perceptions. What about the high prices didn't the broker like? "The broker didn't think that we would make him look good to his own customers," Tim realized. So they provided a package of additional services to the broker with a blended price.

One good way to find out the other person or party's perceptions is to ask questions. In a negotiation, questions are far more powerful than statements.

A statement commits you to whatever you said; it doesn't get you any information, and it gives the other side something to throw things at. You become the target. A question, on the other hand, doesn't commit you, usually gets you information, and gives you something to throw things at if you wish. Questions focus the other side on themselves.

Almost everything you say in a negotiation should be a question. It helps you find out if they really intended to communicate what you first think they mean.

Damian Olive, a senior investment officer at the International Finance Corporation (World Bank) in Washington, D.C., wasn't getting financial information or even return phone calls from a Mexican company in which the bank had invested.

Instead of threatening, Damian thought about what problems the Mexican company might be having. He sent a note asking if everything was okay. "We found out that the client didn't have the time, money, or people to collect the financial information immediately," he said. The firm was embarrassed. In the end, the company offered to provide a little information at a time. An unnecessary blow-up was avoided.

Try turning your statements into questions. Instead of saying, "This isn't fair!" try saying, "Do you think this is fair?" Instead of saying to your son, "Clean your room!" try saying, "Could you tell me why your room isn't clean?" Now, you might not like the answer. But remember, the negotiation isn't over with the answer to your question. It isn't over until you decide it is.

Questions also give the other party a better chance to participate in the conversation. You might learn something valuable. At the least, by asking them for their perceptions first, you have valued them.

Jack Douglass had tried unsuccessfully to convince a customer to use his company's new website to order products. With the existing system, the customer had to visit the store in person several times a day to pick up chemical products. With the new Internet system, the customer could order only once a week by computer.

"He got very angry," Jack said. "He said he would no longer buy from us if he had to use the Internet." So Jack tactfully asked him questions about his buying habits.

"I found out his real issue," Jack said. "It was a people issue. He liked the human contact. He wanted to protect the jobs of our local people." Jack explained that the new Internet system would not take the jobs of the people he liked. And he could still go see them for advice. It would, however, make the company's inventory allocation more efficient, and result in fewer invoices and less extra work for his buddies. The customer began ordering on the Internet.

Many people say they don't have the patience for this. Actually, conducting interpersonal relations this way saves a lot of time over the long term. The dialogue becomes less hostile, less emotional, and eventually more persuasive.

Jordan Robinson received an unexpected phone call from "an attractive woman" who lived nearby. She invited him to lunch. She showed up with two female friends, all of them showering him with compliments and questions. Flattered, he answered them. When he finally became skeptical and started asking questions back, he found out they were trying to sell him a seminar on life improvement for $450. When he declined, high-pressure sales tactics ensued. "I wasted two hours by not asking questions," he said.

You don't have to be obnoxious asking questions. Many people assume that questions can be seen as hostile. But there are all sorts of ways to ask questions. A favorite of mine is the tactic of the somewhat dated TV character Columbo: "Help me out here, I'm confused . . ." It's a powerful way to ask a question—asking for the other person's help.

Here's another powerful question stated in collaborative terms: "Please tell me where I'm wrong here." If they tell you where you're wrong, you get information that will help you in the next negotiation. Again, the negotiation isn't over until you say it is. If the other person can't tell you where you're wrong, you become more persuasive.

I am forever asking people to tell me where I'm wrong, from a colleague to the CEO. It's a small thing, but remember, negotiations are very sensitive to the exact words used.

It is the precision that matters. God, not the devil, is in the details. The more precise you are in communicating your thoughts, hopes, dreams, feelings, and information in general, the less chance there is of miscommunication and a failed negotiation.

THE COMMUNICATIONS GAP AND HOW TO FIX IT

At the beginning of a course I taught at Columbia Business School, I asked, "How do I get to Broadway from here?" Someone said, "Go down 118th Street until you reach Broadway."

I then asked: "How do I get to 118th Street?" They said: "Go north across the campus." I responded: "How do I get to the campus, and which way is north?" Them: "Well, go outside the building." Me: "How do I get out of the building, and by which exit?" Them: "Take the elevator to the first floor." Me: "Where's the elevator?" Them: "Leave the classroom." Me: "Through which of the two doors?"

Once we painfully went through this exercise, it became clear why we miscommunicate so often, leading to conflict and failed deals. We assume certain knowledge and pictures in the head of the other party. But that knowledge and those perceptions are often not there. You have to start at the beginning and go step-by-step—at their pace, not yours—if you want to persuade them.

Here are the basic components of effective communication: (1) always communicate, (2) listen and ask questions, (3) value, don't blame them, (4) summarize often, (5) do role reversal, (6) be dispassionate, (7) articulate goals, (8) be firm without damaging the relationship, (9) look for small signals, (10) discuss perceptual differences, (11) find out how they make commitments, (12) consult before deciding, (13) focus on what you can control, and (14) avoid debating who is right.

FIRST THINGS FIRST: YOU *MUST* COMMUNICATE

This goes against the conventional wisdom, but it is ignored to bad effect. Except in the most extreme cases (if they have harmed a loved one, for example), you should try to talk with the other person—even if you hate them.

That's because if you don't talk to them, it means you don't even value them enough to listen to what they have to say. This makes the principal alternatives no agreement, litigation, or war. If you talk to them, you can get information you can use, either to get a deal or to use extreme statements against them before third parties.

Whatever you might think about the other person, including your enemy, isn't it smarter to find out what they are thinking before making a decision about what to do? Even if it is to attack.

Talking is a sign of strength. Not talking is a sign of weakness. Yet that is exactly the opposite of conventional wisdom. I'm amazed at the number of labor-management negotiators, sports negotiators, attorneys, diplomats, and leaders of all sorts who, when things are not going well, walk out. That *guarantees* that things won't go well. How does that make any sense at all?

Yet people all over the world wreck negotiations by walking out, thinking they are doing the right thing. If you are afraid of being seen as weak, why not say, "Hi, I'm here to hear any concessions you might want to make." It depends on how things are framed.

In 2002, former Israeli prime minister Ariel Sharon said that he should have killed Yassir Arafat, then head of the Palestine Liberation Organization, twenty years before. That statement by itself did not make Sharon a bad negotiator. What made him a bad negotiator, at least in that instance, is what Sharon didn't say. Sharon should have said: "Arafat, I hate you, I should have killed you twenty years ago . . . *We have to talk!*"

If Sharon wanted to reach a deal to end violence, then he needed to talk with Arafat, no matter how the two felt about each other. This also means talking with all manner of characters as long as you can get information from them that *could* improve the situation. That includes people who might otherwise sympathize with terrorists. If you are worried that talking to them will legitimize them, take incremental steps about who negotiates and how it's framed.

The FBI, National Security Agency, and other federal agencies concerned with hostages and terrorists have sent people to our negotiation workshops at Wharton to learn these tools. Some of the military in Afghanistan is now using these communication tools to build coalitions against the Taliban. I will include more on this in Chapter 15, Public Issues.

Here is another counterintuitive communication tool: many negotiators demand concessions from the other party to start or restart negotiations. This looks good on television and portrays the negotiator as strong and tough to their constituents. But it is often ineffective. Worse, it creates hostility and sometimes retaliation.

Unless I have some form of a relationship with you, I am not going to willingly give you anything. You want a concession from me for the privilege of talking to you? My first response is, go jump in the lake! If we develop a relationship during our negotiation, then concessions might be in order, including something for an injury you suffered yesterday. But at the start of negotiations—when we have no trust or relationship—no way.

This notion of "Give me a concession and then we'll talk" puts the cart before the horse. Talk first, proposals later.

THEIR WORDS AND PERCEPTIONS ARE
MORE IMPORTANT THAN YOURS

This brings up the second point about the list on page 65: Listening to the other side and asking questions. Validating their perceptions. What *you* say is less important than what *they* say. What you think you said is less important than what they think they've heard. In order to persuade them, you need to listen to what they are saying, verbally and nonverbally. The more you try to blame them, the less they will listen. The more you value them, the more they will listen. This is true for virtually everyone, including children, government officials, sales reps, and customers.

An uncle of mine, a very successful insurance salesman, would go to see a potential client and ask a couple of questions. They'd talk for the better part of an hour. At the end of that time, the client would usually buy insurance. "Boy, are you a good conversationalist," they would say to my uncle.

Most people persuade themselves by talking. If the other party insults and threatens you, the correct response is, "Tell me more." The more you know about a person, the better you can see how they think, the better you will be able to visualize the pictures in their heads. And the better negotiator you will be.

Not doing this can have disastrous results. It is instructive to look around and see the number of visible and costly mistakes made because "experts" are wrong.

Much has been written about the errors that German authorities made during the taking of Israeli Olympic athletes in 1972. The authorities in Munich were antagonistic, divisive, and contemptuous. German sharpshooters opened fire on the terrorists with the hostages still at gunpoint. The terrorists killed eleven hostages. The Russians used the same tactics in negotiations with a Chechnyan warlord in 1995, resulting in the deaths of more than a hundred hostages.

Some years ago a hostage negotiator from a major Sun Belt city police force came to Wharton and told of an unsuccessful hostage negotiation that ended with a highly emotional man killing his girlfriend. She had just broken up with him and he was holding her at gunpoint.

The hostage negotiators used harsh tactics from their "by the book" training, such as gassing the apartment.

As noted above, such tactics tend to destabilize people, and make them more emotional, more unpredictable, and often more extreme.

Instead, why did the hostage negotiators not think hard about the man's perceptions? He was clearly distraught about his girlfriend leaving. He needed to be calmed down by being valued as a human being.

In a discussion after the negotiator's talk, I suggested that the hostage negotiators might have offered that his girlfriend still loved him and things could be worked out. If the girlfriend was astute, she might have been able to go along with this. The man was distraught; he very much wanted to hear comforting words. The situation might have been saved. The hostage negotiator turned ashen, realizing the outcome might have been different.

In recent years, many hostage negotiators have given up such extreme tactics. But now many negotiators in all kinds of situations use false niceness to cause others to give up things not in their interests. If people think they are being manipulated by false flattery, then emotion, instability, and danger result, just as if the old, hostile tactics were being used. This is different from the Sun Belt hostage suggestion above, since that strategy was designed to help the parties, not hurt them.

VALUE THEM, DON'T BLAME THEM

Studies done with both children and adults over the past fifty years show that blaming people reduces performance and motivation. Praising people, on the other hand, improves both. I mentioned valuing them in Chapter 2. Here is the communication part.

Following are the results of a study showing just how much negativity is a part of the repertoire of less skilled (and presumably less successful) negotiators.

NEGOTIATING BEHAVIOR	SKILLED NEGOTIATORS	AVERAGE NEGOTIATORS
Irritators per hour: self-praise, implied unfairness	2.3%	10.8%
Options per issue	5.1%	2.6%
Blaming	1.9%	6.3%
Sharing information	12.1%	7.8%
"Long-term" comments	8.5%	4.0%
"Common ground" comments	38.0%	11.0%

Compared to skilled negotiators, average negotiators cast blame three times as much, consider half the creative options, look for common ground less than a third of the time, share much less information, make half the number of comments about the long term, and make more than four times the number of gratuitous comments that irritate the other side.

More negativity, less negotiation success. Period.

SUMMARIZE WHAT YOU ARE HEARING

Sum up what you think you are hearing with some frequency, and play it back to the other side in your own words. It values them and makes sure you are both still on the same page. They can see that you are listening to them, making it more likely that they will listen to you. And if you don't have it quite right, they can correct a misunderstanding.

To emphasize, just because you think you are being crystal clear doesn't mean the other side understands it the same way, whether it's your customers, friends, competition, or spouse.

It also gives you a chance to package, or frame, information in ways that put things in perspective: "As I understand it, you like our products better than theirs but you are still buying theirs." Or "I got the highest rating in the department but I'm not getting a bonus, while others have. Is my understanding right?" Or "You're saying, son, that even though you got Bs and Cs on your report card, you still believe you can get into an Ivy League school? How so?"

Citibank was charging Lori Christopher, now a Los Angeles consultant, 17.9 percent annual interest on her credit card. Another bank offered her 11.6 percent. The Citibank customer service rep would not budge. "So," Lori said, "you're telling me that I should transfer my balance from your card with its 17.9 percent APR to the other bank offering me 11.6?" This made it crystal clear for the Citbank rep. Lori got an 8.9 percent rate. Framing paints them a picture.

ROLE REVERSAL

Role reversal means putting yourself in the shoes of the other party. It is one of the most important tools in this book. It will give you a better idea of the other person's perceptions, of the pressures they may be under, of their dreams and fears. In other words, to understand people, you have to try to feel their pain, their happiness and uncertainty, and address it in your negotiation strategy. And you have to let them know you are trying.

A student was offered a job at Citigroup along with about fifty other graduating MBAs among thousands of applicants. Like most of my MBA students, no matter how much money he was offered, he wanted more money. The student came to see me for assistance.

"What are your goals?" I asked. The student said that he wanted to differentiate himself among MBA graduates so he could rise faster in the company. He also said that he wanted the vice president who had hired him to be his mentor.

I said we should take the goals one at a time. "First, if your goal is to differentiate yourself and most MBAs ask for more money, how does asking for more money differentiate yourself?" I said.

"Good point," he said. It's always a good idea to see if your actions are meeting your goals. "Okay," I said, "let's take the second point. Who is this guy who you want as a mentor?"

The student said it was the vice president for whom the student had worked the previous summer. The vice president, he said, had just developed a new program to rotate the fifty new hires through various departments the following September. The vice president was nervous about the rollout.

So I said, "Put yourself in the shoes of the vice president. What are his hopes and fears? How can you help him?"

The student did a role reversal, putting himself mentally in the vice president's shoes, and realized what he needed to do. He called up the vice president and thanked him graciously for the job. Then the student said he was hoping that the vice president could be his mentor. In return, the student volunteered to do whatever he could to help in the intervening ten months. The student offered to interview people, conduct research, and do any other administrative tasks needed.

"Interesting," the vice president said. "Let me put you on hold for a minute or two. I'll get right back to you."

When the vice president came back on the line, he said, "I'm going to tell you two things. First, I'm issuing you an immediate $15,000 bonus. Second, I want you to come to the worldwide Citigroup board of directors meeting next month to meet the chairman and the CEO of Citigroup."

That student's career was made. Before even joining a company with thousands of employees and almost half a trillion dollars in assets, he was meeting the two people who ran the company. And it came from creating an opportunity from an ordinary incident, using the negotiation tools from this book. Role reversal will help you become exquisitely sensitive to the perceptions of the other side.

People frequently are unable to express their feelings. It's your job to find out what is really behind people's comments. How do you do this? By trying to find out more about them, by putting yourself in their shoes, by trying to see the pictures in their heads.

I once advised a clothing supplier, Comark, in Montreal. One of the buyers, Katherine Korakakis, was having delivery problems with her Chinese manufacturer. In class, she played the role of the factory owner based on their last meeting. Suddenly, she stopped.

"I just remembered," she said. "We walked down a row of shirts. He was giving a bunch of us a tour. He picked one shirt off the rack and displayed it. 'This is Kathy's shirt,' he said." Kathy at that moment realized that what this owner was doing was not making shirts for Comark, even though he made tens of thousands of them. He was making shirts for Kathy. She realized that the owner was not her problem. He was her solution.

She sent him a gift. She thanked him for making all these great shirts "for me." She called him up. He finally confided to her that the shirts were late because he was having problems with his own supplier of cloth. It turned out to be a common problem that Kathy and her vendor needed to fix together. Her whole approach to the negotiation changed.

Thinking from the other person's point of view often turns up surprising results. Barbara Troupin, a medical student getting an MBA, was staffing a clinic in a poor section of Philadelphia. She was visited one day by a battered-looking woman asking for a pregnancy test.

Upon further questioning, Barbara discovered that the woman (a) was a prostitute, (b) was a cocaine addict, (c) practiced unprotected sex, (d) was beaten up regularly by her pimp, (e) couldn't practice her trade if pregnant, (f) didn't know who the father was, (g) would be beaten up further by her pimp if pregnant, (h) wanted an abortion if pregnant, (i) was poor, (j) was undereducated, and (k) had never been to a clinic before.

The class was asked to analyze this situation. Only a few students thought to ask why this woman showed up at the clinic for a pregnancy test. Clearly there are home test kits for pregnancies. The mere fact that this woman showed up at all was a cry for help. She wasn't there for a pregnancy test. It is critical to recognize what people are actually saying, not just what they appear to be saying.

Barbara gave the woman a pregnancy test and talked to her about her options. They included a halfway house in another city away from her abusive pimp.

Even if you are wrong, others will appreciate the effort you make to try to understand them.

Practice being the other side. Have your colleagues play you. Go through a negotiation simulation. You don't need a lot of fancy theories. You just need knowledge of how to practice, the will to practice, and a little time. It will make you a stronger negotiator.

BE DISPASSIONATE

What is the correct response to the statement "You're an idiot"? You might think, "Go jump in the lake!" or "You're even more of an idiot!" or "Drop dead!" All are wrong. The right answer is, "Why do you think I'm an idiot?"

Why is it the right answer? First, you get information for that negotiation, or the next negotiation. The best negotiators are dispassionate, and continue to ask for information.

As mentioned in Chapter 1, if someone says to you, "I hate you," ask why. Ask what they like most about your competitors and least about you. If they threaten you, ask why they are so angry. Respond to what is behind what they are saying, not just to their often ineffective efforts to express their feelings. Even if they tell you only a little bit, you will get valuable information that you can use to persuade them.

David Horrocks, a health information executive, was working on a five-day project. "Halfway through day two, a team member angrily and publicly declared that I had purposely misled him," David said. David did not express anger. Instead, he asked specifically what he had done. "When I understood what he wanted, I showed him that I had no possible motive to purposely mislead him," David said. The other party's anger quickly subsided and the team functioned smoothly again.

How many blow-ups do you see at work or in your personal life that cause frayed tempers or lasting scars because they are not handled effectively?

STATE AND RESTATE YOUR GOALS

Goal-setting is not just something that is done at the beginning of a negotiation—you need to check on your goals frequently.

Are you all still on the same page? Have new events or information caused you to rethink your goals? Are your actions still consistent with your goals? When you drive a car to a destination, you make all sorts of adjustments with the steering wheel to get there, including detours if needed to avoid roadblocks. How you achieve your goals in a negotiation needs to be similarly adjusted.

TONE AND EMAILS

Negotiation is very sensitive to the exact words—and tone—used. If you have a hostile tone, if you insult someone, if you are ornery, the impact of what you are saying will be lost. You can be firm without putting people off, as in "I really need to have this, and here's why." Sarcasm may feel good at the moment, but is often ineffective in a negotiation. You may see successful negotiations in which sarcasm is used. These people are successful in spite of their sarcasm, not because of it.

Many people in the world live by email. Entire companies owe their existence to email. In 2009, 34 billion emails were sent *per day* worldwide, or two thousand times the 15 million per day in 1998. That's 10 trillion emails in 2009. If you include spam, the number is five times higher.

How good is email as a communication device? "Terrible," most people say. One reason is that email has no tone. It's sort of like tofu—it takes on the flavor of what the recipient is feeling at the moment. If the other person is feeling defensive, they may think you are attacking them. It is clearly better to meet in person if possible, or talk on the phone.

If you have to use email to communicate, what can you do to minimize problems? Here are some suggestions:

- Add tone back in. Start with "Please hear this email as . . ." And then insert words like "friendly," "constructively critical," "sad," "frustrated," etc. This increases the chance that the recipient will read the email in the tone that you intended. At the least, it will soften negative reactions.

- Never send an email based on your first reaction to one you've received. Most people know to avoid this, but too few people do it. You want to get it off your plate or save time. Actually, you will save more time by holding on to it and looking at it half an hour later than by sending it and spending hours or days correcting a misimpression.

- Before sending the email, reread it as the other person would read it in their foulest mood. Most emails come across as more aggressive than intended. You should think about the pictures in their heads in the worst case. It will reduce risk.

- Do role reversal. Mention something relevant to them first in the email—the equivalent of small talk. "Hope you've recovered from your cold." "Heard you had a lot of snow." It tends to make you more of a person, and will better approximate a face-to-face meeting where there is more human contact.

- Try never to send an email if you are upset or angry. You will say things you didn't mean to say. Write the email if you wish, store it as a draft, and reread it later.

- Try to keep your emails short. Emails are not the best place to make complex proposals that take a lot of time to review. If you need to send a report, enclose it as an attachment; note the time frame ("at your convenience" or "in the next few days") in which you would appreciate a read. This is sensitive to their time and avoids their putting their hand to their forehead and saying, "Oh geez, another long email!"

- If you are writing a particularly sensitive email, have a colleague or friend review it before you send it. A fresh pair of eyes usually helps.

- If you have to send the email and you are in a bad mood, take yourself out of the equation. Start the email by saying, "I'm in a really bad mood, so please forgive the tone," or whatever else needs forgiving.

- Humor is effective if they view humor the same way. Wry turns of phrase are like small talk.

Finally, think about the other person's communication style. Try to approximate it as closely as possible. You are not trying to mimic them; you are trying to translate for them.

If the other person is a busy executive, he or she may want just a few words. The point is to make sure that the other person is hearing what you intended them to hear. And the manner in which you communicate has a lot to do with that.

The invitation designer for Bill Coglianese's wedding was more than a week late on the samples and was available only by email. The designer's assistant told Bill to wait another week. Instead of dashing off an irritated response, Bill sent an email thanking the designer for taking on the job. The email then matter-of-factly explained the wedding stresses and said he and his fiancée really had to make a decision on the invitations. How could the designer help the couple stick with them on the project? Bill wanted to know.

He got the design by overnight courier the next day. "Even in an email, you don't have to be rude in pushing back," Bill said. He added that the email took out the emotion and made it easier for the designer to act quickly and positively.

PAY ATTENTION TO SIGNALS

Most people will give you the means to persuade them if you watch and listen carefully. Too often, we don't notice enough about others. Noticing signals of all sorts—verbal and nonverbal—provides much information that can be used for persuasion.

If the other person says, "I can't possibly do that for you at this time," you should ask, "When can you do it?" or "Who else can?" If they say, "This is our standard contract," you should ask, "Have you ever made an exception?" If they say, "We never negotiate on price," you should ask, "Well, what *do* you negotiate on?" Look at every word, inflection, action.

Melissa Grouzard asked that the rent be lowered for her apartment. The landlord declined. She asked if he recently charged less. "Two years ago, but not today," the landlord said. Melissa, now an attorney in Chicago, picked up the signal about "not today" and responded: "Well, if not today, how about tomorrow?" The landlord reduced the rent.

Fabio Vassel wanted the investment bank UBS to hold his job offer if he could not get a visa in time. The human resources manager said, "There is nothing I can do." So Fabio said, "Well, who *can* do something?" He found the right person and got the job offer held. Fabio, now an investment banker at Nomura International in London, had listened carefully and heard the signal: the HR manager was speaking only about her own ability to do something.

Japanese companies often bring a lot of people to meetings to carefully watch and listen to the other side: subtle turns of phrase, hand or eye movements, when they take notes, when they look down, and so forth. This provides a great deal of information. After the meeting, the Japanese team gets together and compares notes.

What does this mean for you? It means that when you go to a meeting of any significance, bring someone with you. When your colleague is talking, listen and watch carefully. You will pick up signals invisible to those not paying close attention.

A few years ago a not-for-profit health care club at Wharton was holding a conference for 500 people and needed to buy binders. Staples, the office supply store, wanted to charge $1,300. The student group could not afford this much. So they called up the manufacturer in California and tried to get the binders cheaper by buying direct.

The manufacturer's sales rep said she was unable to sell directly to ultimate customers. "I just can't sell these binders to you," she said.

There were three major signals—three words—in that sentence that were relevant to the students' goals. What were they? "I," "sell," and "you." The "I" word: if the sales rep herself could not sell the binders to the students, could some other department at the company sell them to the student group? The "you" word: if the student group could not buy them from the sales rep, perhaps some other department of the university could buy them and provide them to the student group?

Finally, and this is the question the students asked: if you can't "sell" them to me, can you *give* them to me? The answer? Yes! By offering the company some advertising at the health care conference, the company would provide, for free, off-spec binders in inventory from last year—no problem!

In thousands of different ways, small and large, if you listen and watch other people carefully, they will give you the means to persuade them.

In 1998, the U.S. government accused Microsoft of illegally steering its software customers toward its own Internet browser. It was a major antitrust suit. In this case, the U.S. government missed a settlement signal from Microsoft big enough to drive a truck through.

In court-ordered settlement talks of 1999 and 2000, the government demanded that Microsoft put on its Windows products the codes to access competing browsers such as Netscape. Microsoft refused. "Bill Gates said no one was going to tell him how to design his products," said Steven Holley, a partner at the law firm of Sullivan & Cromwell, who represented Microsoft in the negotiations. So the two sides went back to court and fought for nineteen more months, which cost a lot of time, money, and effort.

When Microsoft said it would not put the codes on its products, what *should* the U.S. government have asked? How about "Where will you put it?" or "What *will* you put on your products?" Microsoft sent a big signal to the government by saying that it wouldn't put the codes on its products. But the company didn't say anything about Microsoft's website or advertisements, or about what else Microsoft might place on Windows.

And that is very close to the settlement Microsoft and the government came to in 2001: Microsoft would put on its Windows menu a link to Netscape if someone besides Microsoft—the consumer or the computer manufacturer, for example—put the Netscape codes on the computer. Holley said it might have been possible to come to that conclusion nineteen months earlier. But, he said, the government really didn't want to settle in the earlier mediation, and people weren't focused on what became the eventual settlement.

It shows, again, that even if you are terrific at what you do, the often-subtle negotiation tools are a separate skill.

FIND OUT HOW THEY MAKE COMMITMENTS

This was discussed in Chapter 2, as effective commitments involve both the pictures in their heads and how those pictures are communicated. The subject is noted again among the major communication tools listed on page 65 for easy reference. Of course, there is some overlap. For the communication part, suffice it to say that you need to have an *explicit* conversation about how they make and keep commitments. Otherwise, you may face what happened to a big Swiss company.

After getting what it thought was a "binding agreement" signed by its Middle East counterpart, the Swiss company asked for performance under the contract. The Middle Eastern company refused. When the Swiss company pointed to the Middle Eastern firm's signature, the firm said it was not bound by the contract and signed it only not to be "impolite." The Middle Eastern firm's representative said he would feel bound only if they and the Swiss firm's representative met in person and "reached an oral agreement with a handshake."

For the Swiss, the written contract was a binding commitment; for the Middle Eastern company, only the handshake was binding.

CONSULT BEFORE DECIDING

Let's say you are making a decision that affects other people. It may be a decision to go to the movies or a restaurant, build a new store or factory.

You don't consult everyone that it affects; you make the decision on your own. What happens?

The first thing that most likely happens is that people will oppose you just because you have devalued them. You didn't think enough of their opinions to ask them, even though the decision affected them. It doesn't matter whether they have anything worthwhile to say, or whether you already know what they are going to say. By failing to consult them, you are alienating people. Instead of saving time, it will cost you time. They will go out of their way to think of roadblocks. This is because you sent a nonverbal signal that their opinions were not worth hearing.

The second thing that most likely happens is that you won't get what are often good ideas that you might not have considered.

If you are pressed for time, send out a note that says: "I need to make a decision on this by x time tomorrow. If I don't hear from you by then, I'll assume it's okay to proceed as outlined." That way, people feel consulted, and many won't feel compelled to contact you. If they contact you after the deadline, you can talk reasonably about the need for deadlines. If they don't like the deadlines, you can all work out a better process for the next time.

You don't have to use their opinions. You can explain why you made the decision you did. If you get pushback, you will at least have consulted them. And they will be less emotional, because you have valued them.

An international bank sent increased costs for banking services to its customers. A bank manager said, "Customers got really annoyed." It wasn't the fees; it was that customers were not consulted about timing and method. They refused to pay the increase until the bank's people talked to them about it. Relationships had to be repaired.

Greg Gewirtz wanted to visit Israel. His family was concerned that Israel was too dangerous. He consulted each and every person in his family who expressed concern. He got each and every one of their reasons for concern. He addressed each and every concern. "I would not visit areas with the most conflict," he said. "I let my family know I was consulting with them before I committed to the tour. I let them fully air each of their concerns."

The result was that his mother "calmed down" and his father became "satisfied that it is safe."

Not consulting others before making a decision can have extraordinarily bad consequences on the world stage, too. Before a speech to the

United Nations on September 12, 2002, President George W. Bush declined to consult other countries on a subject of key importance to the world: whether to invade Iraq, a sovereign nation. Instead, then and in the weeks that followed, he outlined the new policy of unilateral U.S. military action anywhere in the world, if the United States felt threatened.

As such, President Bush devalued the opinions of the leaders of 200 countries and territories in the U.N. He angered much of the rest of the world in the process. Many nations did not send troops to Iraq to help the United States. Others sent fewer troops, or pulled them out sooner. He got much less support.

President Bush could have given the same kind of speech, providing the United States the same degrees of freedom, without causing such an adverse reaction. All he had to do was use better persuasion skills: consulting before deciding, and valuing the other countries. He might have said:

"I know this is a difficult time for many of you. Some of you represent Arab nations who feel conflicted. Others represent developing countries that have their own beef with the United States. But I respectfully suggest that we have a common enemy, and that is international terrorism.

"At the end of day, each individual sovereign nation here, the United States included, will need to make its own decision about what to do—whether to use diplomacy, military action, or something in between. But before we make our decision, we are going to try to consult as many countries as we can."

Same speech, allowing the United States the same degrees of freedom. Takes just about one minute to say. But it sounds different, doesn't it? And it would likely have enlisted more countries and more troops, perhaps producing a better outcome than the multiyear loss of life.

YESTERDAY IS GONE

We have no control over what happened yesterday. As much as we'd like to change yesterday, we can't. Fighting over what happened yesterday will never get you anywhere in a negotiation.

Fighting over yesterday has three main outcomes: (a) war, (b) litigation, or (c) no deal. It is expensive, time-consuming, and painful, and often will not end the conflict. And it leads people to lose sight of their goals.

There will never be peace in the Middle East unless the Arabs and Israelis stop fighting over yesterday. No matter how many treaties and envoys they have, there will always be someone who is trying to take revenge on someone else for yesterday.

That doesn't mean that we can't account for yesterday in the context of an agreement. But first we need to talk to each other as people, and use the kind of negotiation tools discussed in this book. We must find a way forward. Then, it is possible to do something about yesterday. But it is always touchy. If you can't do a deal with someone unless they account for yesterday, the deal is almost never worth doing.

The orientation of the parties—either toward yesterday or tomorrow—is one of the major differences between negotiation and litigation. Litigation focuses people on yesterday and blame. Negotiation focuses people on value and tomorrow, or, indeed, today.

Mark Hood, an oil industry supply-chain manager, was trying to address a supplier wanting "payback" for yesterday's problems. The supplier was angry at its treatment by Mark's predecessors, and started becoming difficult on terms and payment of a completely unrelated project. "It was a trust issue," Mark said. "First, we had to have a series of lunches and dinners and talk to each other." They heard the supplier out, apologized for the behavior of others, and made a commitment to do better.

Not fighting over yesterday is liberating in a negotiation. You encourage the other parties to talk only about those things over which they have control. It helps separate what's relevant from what is not. It empowers both parties. You can say, "Why blame me for yesterday; I wasn't involved, and I don't speak for those who were."

WHO'S RIGHT IS POINTLESS IN NEGOTIATION

Assigning blame and punishment is a natural human reaction. Yet it is very difficult, psychologically, for the other person to agree to be punished. And it's hard to admit you are wrong; it makes you appear less valuable, to yourself and others. Blame almost always requires a third party: a judge, a jury, a referee. If you want to argue over who is right, you will find it much harder to get them to meet your goals. Instead, you will have to pursue the more expensive alternatives—litigation, third-party arbitration, or war.

It is better to ask negotiation questions: What do we do now and how do we prevent this from happening again?

In 1993, Malden Mills, the maker of Polartec, a popular synthetic fleece, had a $400 million fire that destroyed its factory outside Boston, Massachusetts. The CEO of the company, Aaron Feuerstein, kept the union workers on duty at full salary for two years as the plant was being rebuilt.

It was a time of significant unemployment, and Feuerstein became a national hero. He was on the cover of *Time* magazine.

But Malden Mills was worried about possible federal violations from the fire. The federal investigators were planning to interview two local fire departments: the Malden Mills plant fire brigade and the Malden Mills city fire department.

The plant fire brigade arrived immediately after the fire started, but was unable to put it out. The city fire department arrived twenty minutes later, after the fire was out of control. The city ultimately put out the fire but the plant was destroyed.

The plant brigade was "infuriated" and wanted to blame the city fire department, said Jeff Bowman, then the company's crisis coordinator and marketing director. I was a consultant to the company during that time, assisting Bowman. The two of us urged Feuerstein in strong terms not to let his firemen criticize the city firemen. Blaming the city, we said, would not meet the company's goal of getting a clean bill of health from the federal government.

Being right was not the company's goal. Not having a big regulatory fine was the company's goal. Preserving the company's great reputation was the company's goal. Feuerstein was particularly concerned about his own reputation being tarnished. Blaming the city would only alienate its fire department.

"Don't lie," I said. "But your firefighters can certainly say that while the city fire department got there twenty minutes after the plant fire brigade, the city people live farther away. Perhaps in the future they might live closer. Also, they trained the plant firefighters, and they ultimately put out the fire."

Even though this was reasonable framing, you can imagine how difficult it was to get the plant fire brigade to do this. They wanted to be right, in public. Eventually, however, the CEO prevailed upon them. The plant firefighters offered a tactful response, in public. The city fire department then supported the plant.

The plant got a clean bill of health from the feds in significant part because of the local fire department's support. "The company would not have survived without them," said Bowman, who has since retired and is the chief operating officer of Massif, a military apparel maker in Ashland, Oregon. Malden Mills survived because they focused on their goals, not on who was right.

Each tool in this chapter is subtle. Each requires only small changes in what you say in a negotiation. You don't have to use all these tools at once. Try one or two of them. Practice them. Build some confidence, and get results. Then try something else.

But remember the watchword of this chapter, immortalized by Professor Godbole in David Lean's film *A Passage to India*:

> *One cannot tell anyone anything*
> *unless they are ready to hear it.*

4

Hard Bargainers and Standards

One of my students went to McDonald's to get some French fries at five minutes to 11:00 one night. The fries were soggy. He asked the counter clerk for fresh fries. The clerk snapped at him in reply, "We're closing in five minutes!" So the student calmly walked to the end of the counter, picked up a printed copy of McDonald's freshness guarantee, and walked back to the clerk.

"I'm here at McDonald's, right?" the student said. The clerk grunted affirmatively. "Well," the student said, "this freshness guarantee says your food is absolutely fresh during all business hours." He pointed to the French fries part of the guarantee, which promised "the perfect texture" that customers have come to expect.

"Isn't this store open until eleven P.M.?" the student added. "It doesn't say here that this freshness guarantee expires five minutes before closing time, does it?"

Did the student get fresh French fries? He did.

Many people would have accepted the soggy French fries, or stormed out, or argued angrily, or otherwise gotten upset. This student decided to calmly use the standards that McDonald's set for itself. It's a small thing, for sure, but in thousands of negotiations, large and small, from restaurants to your job to geopolitics, using other people's standards is a highly persuasive way to achieve your goals.

Using the other person's standards is one of the great negotiation tools that most people don't know about. Standards are especially effective with hard bargainers. Few people know about them, fewer people use them, and almost no one understands the psychological levers that enable them to work in all kinds of situations. I'm not talking about "objective" standards, or criteria that you think are fair. Standards are criteria that the other party thinks are fair.

When invoked, they usually work like magic. And you can use this negotiation tool every single day, in some cases more than any other.

Using their standards is important because the world is an unfair place; people and companies violate their own standards all the time. They make service promises and break them. You order something from the store and it is not delivered as promised. They promise great service and treat you terribly. You rely on what they said and then, often unapologetically, they go back on their word. It drives many people crazy. Now, you can calmly use their standards to get what you want.

The late Tim Russert, host of NBC's *Meet the Press,* was often praised for his brilliant reporting. One of the things he would do while interviewing national politicians was play back to them, on national TV, previous statements they had made that seemed to contradict their current behavior. The politicians would squirm and then be forced to justify themselves. This was using their standards.

I discovered the power of using other people's standards as a journalist more than thirty years ago, and refined my use of it as an attorney and businessman. It has been an essential part of our tool kit in my class.

How does it work? It is a fundamental tenet of human psychology that people hate to contradict themselves. So if you give people a choice between being consistent with their standards—with what they have said and promised previously—and contradicting their standards, people will usually strive to be consistent with their standards. Of course, no tool works all the time. But you will get much *more* from using these tools. People will violate their own standards less often, and you will get what you want more often.

THE POWER OF STANDARDS

A standard is a practice, policy, or reference point that gives a decision legitimacy. It can be a previous statement, promise, or guarantee. Or it can be a practice agreed upon by the other party for a negotiation.

Company policy is a standard. Essentially, it says, "These are our rules." Another standard, equally powerful, that can be invoked is "Has your company in its history ever made an exception to company policy?" The next time an airline ticket agent tells you it's $100 to change your ticket, ask whether the company, in its history, has ever made an exception to this policy. If it has, try to fit into one of the exceptions.

Start by trying this negotiation tool with service providers, since they are in the business of serving others and almost always have guarantees or standards of service: cable TV companies, phone companies, airlines, credit card companies, banks, hotels, etc. If you have an issue to bring up, find out what the company says about customer service on its website or in print or TV ads.

If a service representative is unhelpful or rude to you, say to them: "Your ads talk about how customer service reps always try to be helpful to customers. I'm curious—how does that compare to this situation?"

People will not hang up, walk away, or punch you out. In fact, they will usually do what you want them to do.

Some years ago a Wharton student, Jason Klein, tried for three years running to get into Penn Law School. He wasn't admitted the first year; the second year he was on the waiting list and not admitted. The third year he was on the waiting list in late April and needed an answer immediately in order to pursue a joint degree program with Wharton, where he had already completed the first year of a two-year program.

The law school did not usually make waiting-list decisions until the summer—too late for him, given the requirements of course registration and summer plans. So he wanted to be admitted *and* get an exception, that is, fast consideration. Anyone who knows the application process to a top school understands that his chances seemed to be about zero. Jason was a student in my negotiation class at Wharton, so he asked me what he might do.

I suggested that he go through the Penn Law admissions catalogue and research the school's standards. Then he should write a letter to the dean of admissions and simply say, "Here's your standard, here's how I meet it; here's your standard, here's how I meet it; here's your standard, here's how I meet it." At the end of the letter, I suggested he say, "Please tell me where I'm wrong here," or something similar. All of which he did.

He gave the letters to the admissions office on April 28; he was accepted on May 2. Jason was sure this was not a coincidence, especially since he had been told by the law school that the earliest he would be considered would be June.

Once you recognize the power of using other people's standards, you see it everywhere. Until then, these tools are invisible. "This process provided a powerful lesson," said Jason, who is now the vice president and chief investment officer for Memorial Sloan-Kettering Cancer Center in New York. "It is one thing to talk about these tools and concepts. It is entirely another to actually see them work for me when I use them."

In situations where there are no previous standards you can use, look for ways to define standards they will agree to use in the negotiation. A young executive went to Hermès, the expensive French store in New York City, to buy a scarf. It was a $500 scarf, reduced on sale to $250. The young executive asked the salesclerk to gift wrap the scarf, since it was a present for his wife's birthday. The salesclerk responded, "We don't gift wrap sale items."

What an outrageous thing to say for a store of that quality. But instead of getting angry, as most people would do (and getting nothing), the executive asked, "So if I paid full price, $500, for this scarf, you would gift wrap it?" "Certainly," said the salesclerk. The executive responded, "So Hermès these days is charging $250 for gift wrapping?"

Did the executive get the scarf gift wrapped? You bet!

There are two basic reasons people will almost always follow their own standards. The first is that their own internal moral compass tells them it's the right thing to do; they don't want to admit to themselves they are not honest. The second is that they are concerned that violating the standards they are supposed to follow will annoy or anger a third party important to them: their boss, for example, who upholds the organization's standards. The person violating the standards would appear unreasonable and, in the worst case, could be fired.

Let's say you're asking for something that is perfectly reasonable and the customer service rep on the other end of the phone is being unreasonable. He or she is in fact violating the standards of the company. You can bring the third party into the equation, by asking, "If the CEO of the company himself were on this phone call, would he approve?"

What you have done is brought the vision of an 800-pound gorilla into the conversation. The other party now knows that he or she faces a bigger risk in violating the standards of the company.

In doing due diligence on a small cargo airline I bought with a partner in the Caribbean several years ago, I visited various islands to check out the facilities. It was just a company pilot and me, flying in a single-engine plane. It was a lovely, clear afternoon. When we landed in Tortola, in the British Virgin Islands, there was no one in the arrivals lounge but an immigration officer.

The officer gave the pilot a hard time in filling out various forms, even though she knew the pilot and had seen him often over the previous ten years, and the pilot and I both had airport passes. All I wanted to do was to make sure the company's small office was in order. It was located fifty yards from the arrivals lounge; we could see the building from where we were standing.

I looked around the lounge for a standard. And there on the wall was a plaque that one sometimes sees at tourist destinations. It was a statement from the prime minister of the British Virgin Islands, and it read something like, "Welcome to the British Virgin Islands. Our customs and immigration officers and other service providers value our tourists and other guests and will treat you with courtesy, dignity, and respect."

So I walked over to the immigration officer and said, "Excuse me?" "Yes," she said, looking up, annoyed. I pointed to the plaque and said, "Are those really the words of the prime minister?" She said, "Yes," a little more tentatively. I said, "So how do the words of the prime minister compare to this situation?"

We were out of there in five minutes. According to the government, the plaque has since been removed.

USING STANDARDS

Here is a possible response to the dry cleaner upon getting a damaged shirt back: "Is it your policy to send shirts back to the customer with fewer buttons than they arrived with?" Certainly it uses standards. But this might feel too aggressive for you. That's okay. Use the words you are comfortable with. The principle, however, is clear: isn't it the dry cleaner's job not to lose buttons?

Or you might say to your spouse or significant other, "Dear, we went to the last seven movies that you wanted to go to. Isn't it my turn to pick a movie?" Again, you might want to use other words. But what you are doing here is asking the other party if they believe the choice of movies should be distributed fairly between the two of you.

One of the great things about standards is that it is a transparent process. It is NOT manipulative. You can tell the other party exactly what you are doing. If they say, "Are you using standards on me?" you can reply, "Of course! What's wrong with using your own well-considered criteria as a basis for decision?" Here you've made it a standards issue to discuss their standards. "I'm simply asking your company to do what it said it would, right?"

Some psychologists label standards as "consistency traps," and lump them in with manipulation techniques. This gives the wrong idea about standards. You are not trying to trap anyone into anything. You are just trying to get other people to keep their promises, and to do what is reasonable. What's wrong with insisting on honesty and fairness?

What do you do if the other person decides to violate their standards and be dishonest? Well, they become more extreme, which has its own risks, as I will explain shortly.

The next point to keep in mind is that you can hurt people with these tools. There is no doubt that they work; your decision will be how far to go with them.

Here's an example of how using standards can hurt people. It involved the brainwashing of U.S. prisoners of war in the Korean War in the early 1950s. The Chinese military, which supported the North Koreans, would ask American POWs, "Is the United States perfect?" The U.S. soldiers, of course, would respond, "Nobody's perfect." So the Chinese military would ask, "Would you mind writing this down? That is, if you believe it. We'll give you a couple of cartons of cigarettes for your effort."

So, many POWs then wrote down, "U.S. not perfect."

A couple of weeks later, the Chinese interrogator would ask the POWs, "What are some ways that the United States is not perfect?" The Chinese would essentially ask the Americans to back up their statements. Many of the POWs would write down some ways that the United States was not perfect, and get another carton of cigarettes for their efforts.

This would go on for several months, in increasing levels of detail. The Chinese military would then publish these long diatribes against the United States by U.S. soldiers, written in the soldiers' own handwriting. Very few of the American POWs would go back on what they had said, since the comments were in their own handwriting. In fact, they vigorously defended what they had written. The U.S. soldiers, by definition, had been brainwashed. It was a significant psychological blow to U.S. efforts to keep up morale.

Here is an example closer to home: A Penn Law student, Neil Sethi, now the general counsel of a big real estate firm, went out with some friends to Don Shula's sports bar, a franchise started by the former Miami Dolphins football coach, for drinks and dinner. He ordered a beer, which did not arrive until half an hour after dinner was served. "In the spirit of the class, and almost without thinking," he said, "I asked if drinks are supposed to come before dinner."

The waitress apologized profusely, Neil said; she added that there had been a mix-up with another table. He asked if any of this was his fault. She said no. Neil then told her to take back the beer. The waitress said she could not do that, since she had already opened the beer and put the charge into the computer.

"I asked if it was the restaurant's policy to penalize customers for its mistakes," Neil said. "Of course not," she said. Neil then asked if a drink charge, or any charge for that matter, had ever been taken off a bill after the charge had been put into the restaurant's computer. The waitress answered yes. So Neil wanted to know, if this was the restaurant's mistake, and charges had been taken off the bill before, why wasn't the charge being taken off the bill now? The waitress took the charge off the bill.

After the waitress walked away, a friend of Neil's expressed astonishment that the waitress had taken the charge off the bill. "I know this restaurant chain," Neil's friend said. "That money is coming out of that waitress's meager salary." Rather than appear like a fool, the waitress had essentially agreed to deprive her family, maybe of a food purchase.

"The news that the cost of my beer was going to come out of her check stunned me," Neil wrote. "I began to genuinely realize the power of these tools. I realized that with this power I have learned came a responsibility to use it wisely." He paid for the beer and thanked her for the lesson in human relations. He said this lesson would greatly influence his career.

Knowing this, you have to decide what is comfortable for you in negotiating with others. I might try for some things that you would never attempt, thinking it unseemly. Though I might ultimately get more than you, you may decide it would not have been worth it for you to feel bad.

One woman in my class was sure that using the other party's standards could not possibly work. So I told her to pick any situation and try it out. She had bought a lot of clothes from Eddie Bauer, a well-known clothing retailer. Eddie Bauer had a written lifetime money-back guarantee for its clothes.

So this woman went back to her apartment, took all the clothes from her closet that she had bought from Eddie Bauer over the previous five years, went to the local Eddie Bauer store, slapped the clothes on the counter, and said, "I don't like these clothes anymore. I want my money back."

Store personnel gave her all her money back, in full, in cash, on the spot.

"I was never so embarrassed in my whole life," the student reported the following week.

This was going too far for the student; she found out what her limits were. I advised her to avoid situations that made her uncomfortable. "But don't tell me these tools don't work," I said.

Let's look more deeply into the mechanisms that cause this strategy to be so effective. A few years ago I was in Taiwan for a week on business. At the end of the week, the hotel where I stayed charged me $150 in access fees for 150 credit card phone calls—$1 per call. I was prepared to pay the tolls. But there was no notice in the room about access charges. So I found the manager, the decision-maker, and started to negotiate with her.

"Is it your policy to charge customers for things you have not first notified them about?" I said.

By asking that question, I gave her the choice that I always give people when I use standards. That is, "Be extreme or come to me." What was she going to say, "Sure, we break the law, no problem"? Not likely. By law, you must give notice before charging people for anything.

So she said, "Of course not."

"Well," I said, asking a second question, "there was no notice in the room about access fees for credit card calls, was there?" "Well, no," she said, "but other hotels charge you."

"Of course they do," I said, "but they notify in advance, don't they?" She thought for a moment. "You have a point, Mr. Diamond," she said. "I'll tell you what I'll do. Why don't we split the difference, and you pay $75."

To which I responded: "Please help me out here, I'm confused. If I'm right about this, I don't owe you anything. If I'm wrong about this I owe you $150. Where does $75 come from?"

Compromise is often a lazy, ineffective way to negotiate. At the very end, after every other tool is used and there is only a short distance to bridge, it might be okay. But standards are much more effective. "You're right," the manager said. "We'll take the charge off your bill."

You might find this a bit harsh. Clearly, using the right tone in such a negotiation is important. You should say all this in a calm, very sweet, and reasonable tone. The key is to give them the choice as to whether to be extreme or meet your goals. Over the years, my students have gotten millions of dollars back using such methods. The real question is whether the money should be in your pocket or theirs—particularly when they have been unfair.

What if the other person doesn't want to answer your standards question? Ask them if there is something wrong with the question. That makes answering questions a standards issue.

One caution: you will frequently fail if you ask for exceptions with a lot of people around. Why? Because that makes it a bigger decision for the other party. If others overhear, then they will also ask for exceptions.

BEING INCREMENTAL

Underpinning the use of standards, and indeed all of *Getting More*'s advice, is the notion of being incremental. Break up a negotiation into multiple steps. Most people who are less experienced at negotiation ask others to take too big a step at once. They ask other people to make a big jump from where they are to where you want them to go. For example, "My computer is broken, give me a new one."

Asking the other person to make this big a jump makes it easy for the other person to say no. Big steps seem more risky, too different from the current status.

So you should divide the negotiation into smaller steps. You get anchoring and buy-in at each step. The distance traveled between each anchor is small. You can bring people great distances through incremental steps. You lead them from the familiar to the unfamiliar, one step at a time.

Essentially, you are building the foundation in each case to persuade people to go to the next step. If the other person asks where you are headed, tell them that you are trying to determine their standards, to find out what is possible in this situation. If they ask you more questions, you disclose the information that brings you closer to your goals. "What is possible here?" is thus better than "I want you to give me twenty percent off," a much bigger increment.

You need to start far back enough that they can't say no to a point you've raised without their feeling foolish. Start with the pictures in their heads. That's what a standard is—a picture in their heads. Most people don't go back far enough in a negotiation. You need to start with what is familiar to them, and to proceed incrementally from there.

What do I mean by going far back enough? Ask, for example, "Do you want to reach an agreement?" "Do you want to make a profit?" "Do you want to make your customers happy?" It provides an anchor for the negotiation. If they say at the beginning that they want to reach an agreement, but later start making outrageous demands, you can ask the other party how this dovetails with their indication that they wanted to reach an agreement.

In a negotiation you should lead people from the familiar to the unfamiliar, step-by-step. The more difficult the situation, the smaller the steps you have to take, and the more steps you'll need.

The pictures in their heads should be simple, something to which they can't say no and that you can accept.

Here is an example of being incremental, starting from what is familiar. A student of mine, Rocky Motwani, went to pay a traffic ticket at the Department of Motor Vehicles in West Philadelphia. There, in huge type, he saw a sign that said ABSOLUTELY NO PERSONAL CHECKS ACCEPTED. Rocky only had a personal check, so he decided to see if he could negotiate this.

He searched around for a standard. On the back of his ticket was an address to which one could mail a personal check. There was something familiar about the address.

Rocky approached the window. "It says on the back of my ticket that I can mail a personal check to the address listed here. Is that right?" Rocky said to the clerk. "Yes," the clerk replied.

"Where exactly is this address?" Rocky asked. "It's this building," said the clerk.

Rocky paused for a moment. "And where exactly in this building do the checks come to that are mailed in?" Rocky asked. "Why, that desk over there," said the clerk, gesturing to a desk about six feet away.

"Really," said Rocky contemplatively. "Could I ask you a question? Is there something special about that six feet? Six feet away, a personal check is okay. Six feet closer, a personal check is not okay . . . What if I take my check and put it in an envelope and waft it over you and it lands on the desk over there? Can I pay by check then? I'll even put a stamp on it."

Did Rocky pay by check that day? He did. And 3,000 people before him did not. And probably 3,000 people after him did not. Now, you may not prefer the bit of sarcasm Rocky displayed. You might instead have asked if there were ever any exceptions to the rule of no personal checks. The point is, Rocky pointed out the apparent inconsistencies in the DMV's rules, and in doing so met his goals. If he had tried to negotiate all at once ("Why can't I pay in person by personal check if I can mail one in?"), it would have likely been too big a jump for the clerk to make. The clerk needed to see every step of the thought process.

Rocky has since become a managing director at JPMorgan Chase Bank, running a $200 million business. Today, he says, "I use the negotiation tools actively, and daily." Particularly being incremental.

Here is an example from a business situation. Murray Helmsley, a manager for BASF, was told by a large customer that BASF needed to put bar codes on all of its packages. The customer said it would withhold $450 per package if BASF did not do this to defray the customer's manual sorting costs. But BASF's home office told Murray they would not do this for just one customer. What was Murray to do?

"I ignored the threat, and looked at more incremental options," Murray said. He persuaded BASF to do a one-month trial using customer-provided labels. BASF's logistics and marketing people agreed to meet and coordinate with the customer. The test worked.

Attorneys find that being incremental is similar to cross-examination. You lead people step-by-step to where you want them to go. The steps lead toward a goal. The difference in negotiating is that the process is not intended to trap people but to have them understand precisely where the other party is coming from.

One of the most famous uses of being incremental in a hard-bargainer situation is a scene in the 1970 movie *Five Easy Pieces*. The Jack Nicholson character asks for a side order of toast in a diner. The waitress says they don't serve toast. So he orders a chicken salad sandwich on toast. Then he tells the waitress successively to hold the mayonnaise, the butter, the lettuce, and the chicken. His tone is hostile and he gets very angry, but he doesn't have to. He shows the diner's standard to be unreasonable and that they could meet his goals. (In this case, though, he causes a scene and doesn't get the toast.)

Those in my class learn from the mistakes of others. Kris Davenport, one of my Columbia Business School students, ordered a Virgin Mary (Bloody Mary without vodka) at a restaurant. She was told this could not be done. "Do you have tomato juice?" she calmly asked. "Yes," the waitress said. This continued with Worcestershire sauce, Tabasco sauce, and ice. She got the drink.

I know, some of you may think they will spoil your food. Not if your tone is nice. Not if you ask if anyone is going to do that. I once said that to a restaurant and they were absolutely shocked I would think of that. You might also say that a nice tip is coming if they meet your needs.

Even if they won't give you much at first, take what you can get and come back another day. Remember, "Every ceiling is a new floor." Take the 1 percent cut in your credit card interest this month; renegotiate next month; $50 here and $75 there is a lot of cash at year's end.

FRAMING

The key to standards—indeed, to all successful negotiation—is framing. I've referred to it earlier in the book. But nowhere is it more important than with standards. Framing means packaging information or presenting it using specific words and phrases that will be persuasive to the other party.

Negotiation is very sensitive to the exact words used. The idea is to give people a vision of what the key issues are. Barack Obama used "Change." The late Johnnie Cochran, in the O. J. Simpson murder trial, said to the jury about the glove, "If it doesn't fit, you must acquit." Coca-Cola made billions of dollars on "the pause that refreshes."

Here are a few other examples of how you might frame an issue: If a restaurant is late with your reservation, ask, "Does this restaurant stand by its word?" Or, to any service provider, "Is it your goal to make customers happy?"

Figuring out how to frame things comes from asking yourself the question, "What is really going on here?" Great negotiators have a firm grasp of the obvious.

A Wharton law student, Lina Chou, received an invitation for an American Express card. The bonus for signing up was 5,000 free miles on a participating airline, worth up to about $250 or so. She called American Express and was told that she didn't qualify for the offer because she already had an Amex card. The offer was valid only for new members, she was told.

Lina thought about this. Then she called back, asked for a supervisor, and told her the issue. She then said, "Could you tell me who I should talk to about American Express's decision to change its worldwide advertising and positioning for the entire company?" "What do you mean?" the supervisor said.

"Well," Lina said, "it used to be that American Express had this slogan, 'Membership has its privileges.' But now I find that nonmembers have more privileges than members. So you must have changed your slogan to 'American Express: Nonmembership has its privileges.' Who do I talk to about that?"

The supervisor gave the miles on the spot to Lina, now a finance analyst in New York. Can you imagine this situation getting out to blogs?

Framing the issue, and using standards in the presence of third parties (or implied third parties), are very effective. Here, Lina's framing showed that Amex was implying that new customers were more valuable than existing customers. Put in these terms, Amex preferred to provide the miles.

Studies have shown that one person will be much more persuasive than another with the exact same facts because of framing. The more success-ful negotiator packages the information in a way that creates a different picture in the other person's head. One study often cited has to do with survival rates for surgery. Some patients are told that an elective surgery has a 90 percent survival rate. Others are told that the surgery carries a 10 percent risk of dying. Even though the information is exactly the same, many more people elected the surgery when the choice was presented as a 90 percent survival rate.

A student bought a computer from CompUSA. After a month, the computer broke. He called the salesman, who told the student to send the computer back to the manufacturer because it was still under warranty. The student didn't want to do that—it would take time and he needed a computer for school.

So the student called the store back and asked for the manager. The student said to the manager, "Is it your policy to stand behind your local customers? Or do you send them away to someone else at the first sign of problems?"

"Of course we stand behind our products!" said the manager.

"So why are you sending me to the manufacturer when I need a com-puter for school today?" the student asked. "That doesn't sound like you are standing behind your products, does it?"

The student got a loaner computer. In other cases, other students got new, replacement computers. Most people would have just complained that "the computer is broken," or asked, "Why should I have to go to all this trouble to get it fixed?" And the store manager wouldn't have been swayed. Instead the student framed it in terms of the store's own customer service standards, and achieved his goals.

You may say, "This isn't rational." Most important negotiations are not about rationality. They are about people's feelings and perceptions. And that is why framing, the way information is presented, is so impor-tant. We can use framing to make the world more fair.

PNC Bank in Philadelphia made a mistake on the account of Shehnaz Gill, but the student was charged a fee for the overdraft anyway. He asked the bank manager, "Should PNC customers pay for the bank's mistakes?"

The manager clearly didn't have a good answer to that and didn't know what to do. It was hard for him to make such an admission.

So Shehnaz, now a strategy manager at Coca-Cola, applied a second PNC Bank standard: the bank's widely advertised commitment "to create solutions" for customers. How could the bank manager create a solution here? he asked. Shehnaz got the refund.

Standards can be used not only with hard bargainers, but also in all sorts of relationships. The key is to do it in such a way that you preserve the relationship. Remember, you are on the other person's side; you are just helping them to see the issue in a different way.

Tahir Qazi had a two-and-a-half-year-old daughter, Nadia, who was very unhappy being placed in her high chair for dinner. She wanted to sit at the table with the rest of the family. But instead of telling Nadia what to do or making something up, her father went around the dinner table, chair by chair, and asked Nadia: "Who sits in this chair?" This was a fun game for Nadia, one that gave her power to decide where everyone would sit. She played enthusiastically. Soon all the chairs were taken.

Tahir, now a Comcast vice president, didn't then say to Nadia that there was no place at the table for her. Instead he asked her what to do. Nadia realized that if she sat in one of the chairs, someone would have to be left out who usually sat at the table. And she realized that she was the only one who could fit in the high chair.

Now clearly, an older child might say, "Get another chair." Or be more difficult. For Nadia, *in this situation*, this was the perfect set of tools. It gave her power, decision-making authority, and an incremental process that helped her see she was the only one who could fit in the high chair.

You don't have to accept the other person's standards and framing. A big part of framing is "reframing." You start with how they phrase something, and you find a different way to interpret it, so that they get insight—and hopefully will meet your goals.

Framing will often change the balance of power in a negotiation, no matter how big or powerful the other party. As noted earlier, it should be used carefully and in a positive way. A woman in my MBA class at Wharton was offered a job at McKinsey, one of the world's leading consulting firms. She thought she deserved an extra $30,000 signing bonus because of her years of experience in the sector for which she was hired—media and entertainment. Her boss-to-be thought she deserved the bonus, too. But he told her he could not offer it because McKinsey's firm-wide policy was to treat all incoming MBA graduates the same.

So the student thought about how to reframe McKinsey's standards to meet her goal: get an extra $30,000 soon. She asked her future boss when the soonest was that McKinsey could pay a bonus to a new hire. "Three months," the boss replied. "So why don't you just pay me the $30,000 three months after I start?" she asked. "Sure," the boss said.

That negotiation took less time than it has taken you to read this account of it.

It is much more persuasive to let others make the decision, instead of telling them what the decision should be. You want to lead them to where you want them to go, through framing and by being incremental. For parents, as I will show later in the book, these tools work particularly well with children.

John Roche's wife, Rosemarie, wanted to get rid of their dog, a large Dalmatian. "She hates the dog," John said. For one thing, the dog, Houdini, kept going through the family's invisible fence, setting off the alarm, and running all over the neighborhood. Neighbors complained.

"I gave her the opportunity to vent," said John, CFO of a real estate investment trust in New York. "Then I asked if the dog provides security and companionship to our kids." "Yes," she said, now a little more willing to think about the benefits of the dog. Then he said, "If we get rid of the dog, what do we tell the kids? That we got rid of the dog because he was an inconvenience, that we couldn't be bothered?"

There is an old proverb: Don't use a sledgehammer to kill a mosquito. The dog problem wasn't actually a big problem. In fact, it wasn't even a dog problem—it was a fence problem. The solution: adjust the fencing system to keep the dog from setting off the alarm and running all over the neighborhood. Drill down and find the smallest solution necessary to fix the real problem.

You can use framing and being incremental to meet your goals in work relationships, as well. Peter Tauckus, a debt instrument trader on Wall Street, returned from vacation to find his seat taken. "Location is important on the trading floor," he said. His boss had given Peter's seat to a trader who was hired back. One of the conditions of acceptance was that the trader sit at the trading desk, where Peter's seat was empty. Most people would have given up at that point. But Peter decided to negotiate it.

"I asked my boss if Tom was going to trade par debt or distressed debt," Peter said. "Distressed debt," his boss replied. "So why isn't he sitting with the other distressed-debt traders?" Peter asked. Peter then asked if all the traders should sit at the trading desk. His boss answered yes. Then Peter asked if there were any salesmen sitting at the trading desk. There were. So Peter asked if the *salesmen* had to sit at the trading desk.

Peter summed all of this up, and then added that it had taken him a long time to get his seat. Bottom line—he got his seat back.

Framing and being incremental are two of the hardest things for people to learn. Most people want to rush ahead, and find it hard to break things up into smaller steps. Also, it takes time to get just the right framing; many people don't have the patience. But great framing can immediately conclude a negotiation in your favor.

Kevin Sherlock, a managing director at Deutsche Bank, framed the situation for a customer demanding a lot of extra work without paying for it: "Should we work for free?" Said with a collaborative tone, this is very good reality-testing for a customer.

SETTING STANDARDS

You should always try to set the standards before the negotiation starts. People see the value of a general rule at the start of the process. If you don't do that and try to set standards later when it clearly benefits you, others will think you are being manipulative and taking advantage of the situation.

A good standard to set at the start of a business meeting might be: any item we can't solve in fifteen minutes, we go on to the next item. So at three o'clock in the morning, instead of being on item 4, we are on item 30, with four to go. Then we go back and solve the hard ones. This is called a "process" standard, or a standard to govern the process that people will use to negotiate.

An agenda is a process standard. Most people don't think agendas are a big deal, so they don't set one. They have an idea of where they want to go, and that's good enough. I disagree—it's not good enough.

I can't imagine having a meeting without an agenda. Even if you know what you want to talk about, an agenda sets a standard for proceeding. If you get lost, it helps you get back on track. You need to make sure that everyone *agrees* on the agenda. That way, if someone interrupts and tries to go off on a tangent, you can note that everyone agreed to the agenda. You can write the new subject on the board for all to see, under "other business."

Even for a simple meeting, you need an agenda. If you have set an agenda before the meeting, check it again at the start of the meeting in case things have changed. We all know how easy it is for meetings to go off track. Not having an agreed-upon agenda at the start is like getting in the car without directions to your destination.

In negotiating, start with the easy things. It gives both parties a sense of accomplishment. An easy thing is "When is the next meeting?" Even if the first five items are merely logistical, they are not trivial. Accomplishing anything makes the parties feel much better about the meeting and become much more collaborative.

At the final negotiation for a $300 million merger between two high-technology companies, progress was glacially slow, with lots of bickering. I realized that the committee was too large to reach an agreement anytime soon, and I caught the eye of someone on the other side, Rick Seifert.

"Hey Rick, want to have a cup of coffee in the next room?" I said. Maybe Rick and I could start to work something out.

The reaction of Rick's colleagues was swift. "I don't know about that!" said the CEO of Rick's company. They were thinking I was going to divide and conquer, that Rick would give something away or that I would somehow take advantage of Rick. This was, of course, ridiculous.

So I said, "Oh! I see! You think I'm going to brainwash Rick in fifteen minutes. Is that right, Rick? Am I going to be able to brainwash you in fifteen minutes?"

Well, his colleagues felt foolish. They realized that they had shown no confidence in Rick, a seasoned negotiator, and that their fears were unfounded. I thought of the pictures in their heads and I realized they were probably wondering why I wanted to meet with Rick privately.

So I added, "I'll tell you what. Rick and I are going to have coffee, I'll bet we both need some. Why don't you guys give Rick and me something to work on while we're having coffee? We'll try to come back with a solution."

This seemed reasonable to everyone. So they gave us a problem to work on. Rick and I went into the next room, commiserated on how slow this was going, worked on our task, found a solution, and then came back to the negotiation. Our collaborative answer changed the whole tenor of the negotiation, and the merger negotiation was successful.

What if you don't know what the other party's standards are? What should you do? *Ask.* In your job, ask for the criteria they use to decide raises and bonuses. If they won't tell you, mention, nicely, that you can't meet their needs unless you know exactly what they want from you. Get them to be as specific as possible—both about their needs and the amount of the bonus. Then, when you meet the standards, it will be much easier for you to make the case for a raise. Find out the consumer price index and see if you are being paid more or less in real dollars this year versus last year. If less, ask if you aren't at least as valuable this year as last. Or find some measurement of the company's success to use.

There are situations where this won't work. As I said, no tool is perfect. But it works more often than if you don't try. And even a small increase in your success rate will have a major positive impact on your life.

Asking the other party for their standards often values them, particularly if you do it respectfully. I was late on paying a big bill to American Express. Amex refused to give me the attached airline miles as a result. I was about to get angry at the Amex customer service rep, since I was a longtime Amex customer. Then I stopped myself and thought about her day.

"I'll bet people scream at you all day long," I said to her on the phone. "They do," she said.

"I'll bet a lot of people threaten to cancel their card when they don't get their miles," I said. "Absolutely," she said.

"What do you do in such a case?" I said. "Well," she said, "I just transfer them to the card cancellation department. I don't have to take that garbage."

"Do you ever restore people's miles when they have been late paying their bill?" I asked. "Sure," she said. "When?" I asked.

She said, "When they apologize, when they thank me, when they promise never to do it again, and when they are nice to me."

I said, "You know, I really apologize for being late on my account. I'd really thank you if you could restore the miles for me. I promise never to do it again. And I think you are a really nice person." She laughed and said, "The miles are already back in your account."

It's something you will get better at with practice.

Control the criteria by which decisions are made. It used to be that female executives and managers bridled when their male counterparts asked that the women take the chalk and write the meeting points on the blackboard. My advice is, you should always take the chalk. That way you control the process.

I once had a negotiation in Atlanta with CEO Buddy Wray and CFO Wayne Britt of Tyson Foods, the world's largest producer of chicken, beef, and pork. I was representing a Croatian client that owed Tyson more than $75 million for chickens that my client had distributed in Russia. I was trying to reduce the size of the debt and negotiate a plan that would enable the client to remain in business.

I was much younger than they were, and knew how to type. So I offered to take the meeting minutes. The Tyson CEO sort of waved me off with some condescension and said fine, I should take the minutes.

So I wrote down the meeting notes exactly as I wanted, organized the main points exactly as I wanted, typed up the meeting memo exactly as I wanted, typed up the agenda for the next meeting exactly as I wanted, and sent it off to the Tyson executives.

At the next meeting we had, this silver-haired Tyson CEO walked in, holding a laptop computer awkwardly as if he never held one before. He gestured pointedly at me and exclaimed, "I'll take the minutes!" No fool he.

No matter what your level in an organization, just by asking some well-placed questions, you can soon control the meeting. "What are our goals here?" you might say in a nonthreatening way. "What's the problem?" you might say tactfully. You might offer to write these up on the board, asking permission to do so. Soon you will control the meeting.

NAMING BAD BEHAVIOR

It is just one step from naming their standards to naming bad behavior. A person who behaves badly implicitly violates his or her own standards by acting counter to the practices of the society, company, group, or other organization to which they belong.

"Society" in this case includes third parties to whom the other party appears beholden. And third parties are key, whether present or absent. A person who appears unreasonable before important third parties would lose credibility and could be criticized or even fired.

Often, when people behave badly to you, you can get a "chit," or an I.O.U., in return for their bad behavior. An apology is a chit. If your car gets delivered back late from the shop, you might get a free oil change if you note the bad behavior. Some of the examples above involve implied third parties, as in the case of the immigration official in Tortola (what if the prime minister found out she violated his pledge?).

Naming bad behavior is particularly useful for women executives in male-dominated corporate suites. There are a lot of different ways to do it—directly, with humor, etc. Almost all are effective. One female vice president was a particularly collaborative person. This was ordinarily wonderful, but she was in a shark's den.

One day she was talking to the CEO of the company with another vice president, a man. The other vice president repeatedly interrupted her. Then, in the middle of a sentence as she was talking, the other VP walked away, embarrassing her. She thought that this was the time to make a stand. After she finished talking to the CEO, she caught up to the male vice president.

"Let me ask you a question," she said. "Yes?" he said.

"What were you thinking about when you walked away in the middle of a sentence when I was talking to the CEO, embarrassing me?" she said. "What were your goals? What kind of relationship did you want to have with me? Would you have done it if I were a man?"

She said that he apologized to her for two days.

Great negotiators have a firm grasp of the obvious, and they say it. So you need to be direct about naming bad behavior. "Is it necessary for you to be shouting at me?" you might ask. Or "I promise to try hard to never interrupt you. May I have the same consideration?" Remember, these are tools you can use often with hard bargainers who don't seem to get the concept of relationships and are trying to undermine you.

In the movie *Get Shorty,* the John Travolta character is giving negotiation advice to the character played by Gene Hackman. Travolta tells Hackman that when he negotiates, he should open the blinds to make sure that the other party sits with the sun in his eyes and therefore gets distracted. Now, if that happened to you, wouldn't you want to call the other party on it? "Why am I sitting here with the sun in my eyes?" Or you might say, "This sun is distracting. Why don't we close the blinds so I can focus more on our conversation and on what you are saying."

You need *tools* to deal with hard bargainers. Not all negotiators are nice. Some people advise you to be nice in a negotiation, that it contains a lot of power. Well, that depends on the situation. If you are in the water with sharks, you need shark repellent. I'd rather be nice, but I am not going to leave myself—or you—unprotected if the situation does not call for niceness.

Here is the key to naming bad behavior—and this is one of the most powerful tools of all: in naming bad behavior, you must NEVER make yourself the issue. If you do, you lose the chit, because then you are also unreasonable. Attorneys make this mistake often. They may say, "How dare you call me a jerk, you jerk!" In fact, the meaner and more difficult they become, the calmer and quieter you must become. This is one of the few tools against which there is no defense. For example, say in a very sweet voice, "Why are you swearing at me? I would never curse at you. Why, we respect you."

You want to put all the focus on them. They will drive themselves off a cliff, appearing increasingly unreasonable.

The best modern practitioner of this tool was Mahatma Gandhi. He took the jewel in the crown—India—from the British Empire without ever raising his voice or ever raising a weapon. The more vicious the British became, the more passive he became. Finally, Britain became so extreme they could not withstand the onslaught of world opinion, and they gave up India.

The Reverend Martin Luther King Jr., with his strategy of nonviolence, produced the same reaction. White supremacists finally became so extreme that they lost the support of the political system and most of the rest of the nation.

Naming bad behavior without making yourself the issue is so powerful because it turns the other party's entire being against them—all the focus is on them. In the second debate of the 2008 U.S. presidential election, every time John McCain insulted Barack Obama, Obama was respectful. When McCain refused to shake Obama's hand after the debate, Obama was gracious. All the negative focus was on McCain. As noted, McCain probably lost the election then and there.

In corporate or relationship settings, you have to be careful about the way you name bad behavior. Tact is often required. One example is someone trying to take credit for your idea. You bring up a great idea in a meeting, only to have someone paraphrase it as their own later in the meeting. This is a perfect occasion to name bad behavior—without making yourself the issue.

First, compliment them. "That's excellent!" you should say, without sarcasm. "When I brought this idea up a few minutes ago, I was hoping someone else would endorse it. Glad to see we agree!" Or, if you want to be even tougher (without making yourself the issue), you might say something like, "Terrific! When I brought up the idea a few minutes ago, I didn't know anyone else was working on it." Then review what your group has done with the idea and ask sweetly, "So what have you all been doing with the idea?"

They may waffle their way out of it that time. But they will never do it again.

Clearly, practice makes all of this better. Practice framing questions in which standards are embedded. You will get better and better at it. Ask, for example, "What's fair here?" "How do we decide?" "Should I pay for your mistakes?" "Is it your company's goal to make customers happy?"

Not getting upset when the other person violates their own standards is key. It takes a change in attitude to get it right. For example, every time someone tries to cheat me, I tell my team not to get upset. "Look at it this way," I say. "We just made money!" We name the bad behavior and get a chit. I am happy when others try to cheat. Now, I have them pegged as cheaters. And I can use it forever.

When people don't return phone calls or emails, try not to get upset. Just keep a list of the dates and times of your calls. When you get enough of a record, email them, saying, "Gee, we called you fourteen times in the past two weeks; we were hoping to reach you. Is there something else we can do?" Now you've got a record you can use with third parties. But you probably won't use it often; they almost always call back.

Moira McCullough got to her beach house one rainy summer weekend only to find the landlord there with some of his friends. "The landlord had assumed that we wouldn't be out for the weekend," she said.

Many people would be angry at the landlord. This would have gotten her nowhere. The landlord would have become defensive and Moira would have had to sue the landlord to enforce the lease. Instead, she was cool as a cucumber. "I asked him if we had paid for use of the house for the entire summer, seven days a week, for sixteen weeks," she said.

He admitted he had acted improperly. Still matter-of-fact, Moira asked him for concessions. She got two more weeks in September at no charge. "People too often lose focus on their goals," said Moira, later a telecommunications manager in London and New York and now a stay-at-home mom for her kids, ages seven, ten, and eleven.

Train yourself to do this. You will get *more* this way. You will meet your goals more often.

Ben Young went to an electronics store in Manhattan to buy an extended-life battery for his camcorder. "$200," the salesman quoted him as a price. It was four times the normal price. Ben was ecstatic. "So why is the price four times normal?" Ben said sweetly. "$100," the salesman said. "Why did you just drop the price so much?" Ben said. "You must really be trying to gouge me."

The price then went to $80, to $65, and then to $55, "the best price I can offer," the salesman said. At this point, Ben, now head of a real estate hedge fund, asked for the manager. "Is it your usual policy to quote four times the price of a product to a customer?" Ben said. The manager said no, criticized the salesman, sold the product for $50, and threw in a free carrying case, "for my hassles." What a rush! Hard bargainers are fun!

Ka-ming Lim couldn't get repairs done in his apartment by the maintenance staff. But the staff did respond to angry complaints to the manager's office. So he said to the manager, "Do you think it's fair for residents who make the least noise to receive attention last?" Ka-ming, now director of a Singapore bank, essentially named bad behavior with good framing. The maintenance people showed up within four hours.

When *you* do something wrong, do others try to exact too big a penalty from you? You can use framing here, too. Essentially, they have behaved badly in "overcharging" you for your bad behavior. In such situations, you can ask, "So how much do you want to hurt me for this?" It gives people a sense of perspective.

Terry Jones bought the wrong ticket for his New Jersey Transit commuter train. The ticket collector started to berate him and demanded that Terry buy an expensive one-way ticket to New York and pay a surcharge. "So you want to give me the death penalty?" Terry said jokingly. "The conductor smiled and said he would come back. He never came back."

James Ciarletta's fiancée received an unqualified coupon from Cohen's Optical for a new pair of glasses for $34. But the store's salesclerk told her they were only for a limited number of (cheap) frames. Most people would just give up, not wanting to make a scene. But James decided he would calmly use standards and hold the store to its promise.

James's fiancée picked out a pair of frames for $174.54. James introduced himself to the owner, who confirmed it was a franchise and she had complete authority for items in the store. She also confirmed that customer satisfaction was very important at Cohen's, as its ads say.

"I asked if it was Cohen's policy to honor its published coupons," James said. "She said it was." Then she declined to honor the coupon. James asked again if Cohen stood behind its published advertising.

"She began blaming the advertising agency for making a mistake," James said. "She started to get very heated about it. I kept my cool. I kept bringing her back to the same standards issues: her authority, customer satisfaction, honoring its policies. I asked if money is more important than customer satisfaction and honoring its policies."

Finally she started screaming at James and his fiancée, "Okay, that's right, making money is most important to me!" James took a step back and waited. Suddenly people in the crowded store stopped and looked at the owner, surprised looks on their faces. A few seconds, seeming like an eternity, passed. James was already thinking about the letter he would write to corporate headquarters about this franchisee. He knew she knew that.

"I calmly started to restate her words to the rest of the now-quiet store," James said. "The owner stopped me, apologized, and said I was right. She said customers are in fact more important and the store would stand behind its advertising." He asked his fiancée to give the owner the chosen frames and the coupon. "They gave us the completed glasses in thirty minutes," he said.

This goes farther than a lot of people would go to achieve fairness. James did report that he felt his lip quivering during this exchange—something I said would disappear with practice. But James stayed calm throughout; it was the owner who got upset. Would some people think the store shouldn't be penalized for the mistake of its ad agency? Maybe.

But I included this story to show you, again, how to go about doing this. Notice that James was incremental in his approach, and never got rattled. You can apply it to things large and small in life. You only have to decide that you will hold people to their promises.

Now let's look at some significant business negotiations and see how these tools apply. Some years ago, Hewlett-Packard was involved in a major project to upgrade the computer facilities for Telecom Egypt in Cairo. Another contractor was rude, sexist, racist, and confrontational, according to HP; the American staffers there were up in arms.

HP sent a couple of people to my office in Philadelphia for a few hours to talk with me about what to do using negotiation tools. For various business reasons, HP did not want to approach Telecom Egypt directly with the anecdotal evidence they had.

I asked the people from HP if there was any U.S. aid in the deal. There was, a small amount of money from the U.S. Agency for International Development (USAID). A company is not allowed to participate in a project where U.S. laws are violated. The actions by the contractor clearly violated U.S. laws. And the most interested party in protecting U.S. laws would be the U.S. government, I suggested.

So I advised the HP people to issue each of their employees notepads and pens. I suggested that for the next month, the HP employees should simply write down in their notebooks everything this guy said and did—not to argue with him, protest, get angry, etc.

At the end of the month, I said, HP should collect the notebooks, put a rubber band around them, write a short summary, send them off to USAID in Washington, and ask, "What do you think?"

Within a short time, the contractor was gone. No muss, no fuss, no problem. This is a great example of using standards to deal with bad behavior.

One of the most difficult hard-bargainer situations I've been in occurred a few years ago during a major financing for a company in Ukraine. It was a $107.5 million Eurobond issue for Ukraine's largest company, Yuzhny Machine-Building Plant, or Yuzhmash. Yuzhmash built most of the former Soviet Union's land-based intercontinental ballistic missiles (ICBMs) for nuclear warheads. After the fall of the Soviet Union and Ukraine's independence, Yuzhmash sent its nuclear warheads to Moscow as part of a disarmament effort brokered by the Clinton administration, to limit the number of countries with nuclear weapons.

This good will by Ukraine got some Western business. One was the production of rockets by Yuzhmash for a commercial joint venture with Boeing to launch communications satellites.

Yuzhmash needed working capital to build the rockets. The bond would be the largest foreign-sourced commercial financing in the history of Ukraine. I was Yuzhmash's counsel, charged with putting the deal together. Eventually, I persuaded JPMorgan in London to raise the money.

The project began in 1998, when we received from the Ukraine Ministry of Finance an unconditional, irrevocable Ukraine government guarantee that I wrote for the $107.5 million to be borrowed by Yuzhmash. The guarantee was very tough; I thought financiers would need such a guarantee because Yuzhmash had no history of Western borrowing and would be considered a big credit risk. In fact, the World Bank's European arm, the European Bank for Reconstruction and Development (EBRD), turned down the loan twice as too risky.

The Ukraine finance minister, however, was happy to provide the guarantee. It was an excellent political gesture, since the immediate past president of Yuzhmash was Leonid Kuchma, then the president of Ukraine. Also, it didn't cost the Ministry of Finance anything, since the guarantee wasn't worth the paper it was printed on: Ukraine had no investment-grade international debt rating.

I held on to this guarantee for five years, until March 2003, when, lo and behold, Ukraine got an international investment-grade debt rating. We went back to the Ministry of Finance and said, essentially, "Hi! Here we are again! Ready to do the deal!" Both JPMorgan in London and its law firm, Linklaters, wanted the guarantee reendorsed because five years had passed.

The Minister of Finance essentially told us to get lost. President Kuchma was on his way out, the ministry was borrowing billions of dollars from other governments, and the terms of our guarantee were too draconian. The minister was in the driver's seat, believing he had all the power. Since they were bringing in all this government money from abroad, they thought they had enough power to challenge President Kuchma's wishes. Remember what I said earlier about the misuse of power.

We tried being collaborative: This was great for Ukraine; it would establish a foreign-sourced commercial lending market and open the way for all sorts of private economic growth in Ukraine. To no avail. Finally, we had to use standards.

The Yuzhmash officials and I sat with the Minister of Finance and various deputy ministers. We made copies of the guarantee the ministry had signed five years before. I asked the minister, "Does this guarantee say, 'Irrevocable'?" It did, of course. I then asked, "What does 'irrevocable' mean? That you can revoke it later when you feel like it?" Clearly, that wasn't what irrevocable meant. Everyone got a bit uncomfortable. We were using their own standards against them.

I then said, "Does this guarantee say 'unconditional'?" Of course it did. "What does 'unconditional' mean?" I asked. "That you can set conditions later when you want to?" They grunted. Of course, it didn't mean that, either.

Then I turned to the last page of the guarantee and asked them to do so, too. "Is this the seal and signature of the Ministry of Finance of Ukraine on this irrevocable, unconditional government guarantee?" I asked. Clearly, it was.

Finally, I said: "So the standard that the Ukraine Ministry of Finance is setting for all those international lenders from whom your government wants to borrow billions of dollars is that the Ukraine Ministry of Finance will break its commitments to foreign lenders when the ministry finds it convenient to do so." I suggested that this would not likely bring in many lenders.

This was not a happy meeting. One deputy minister got so upset that he pointed out that we, Americans, were in the middle of Ukraine. I asked if he was physically threatening us. His extreme statement just undermined his credibility. The ministry reendorsed the guarantee and we did the deal.

I didn't just want to leave the relationship with the ministry in shambles—which is where it was at the end of the meeting. So afterward I talked to Yuzhmash, and we decided that the company would invite the minister to come on the road show with us. We were going at least to London, Vienna, and Frankfurt to meet lenders. Yuzhmash told the minister that he could meet new investors to whom he could pitch his own deals, after he verified to them that he had reendorsed the Yuzhmash deal. This was clearly a benefit to him. So the ministry sent another deputy minister with us.

Finally, on the road, I had a couple of meals with the deputy—not alone, but with others. By the end of the week he said hello to me when he passed me in the hallway. It had been very much a hard-bargaining situation. But we met our goals and in the end, I think, did what was best for all parties.

Of course, it is very important in all of this to make sure the other party is actually behaving badly. That means you still first have to go through the process of collecting information. You have to find out what's really going on.

Bryan Holmes was the brand manager for a major nonprescription medicine. He got a call from his factory manager saying that the quality-control people "had rejected another batch" from Puerto Rico. Bryan said he wanted to see all the facts before making a decision. What are the rejection standards?

Bryan found out that the standard rejection rate for nonprescription drugs was 3 percent. But the Puerto Rico factory was being held to a much stricter, 1 percent rejection rate used for prescription medicines. "This was a mistake," Bryan said. "One percent is almost impossible to meet" for a nonprescription drug. When the 3 percent rejection rate was restored, the factory did just fine. The wrong standard had been used. It seems obvious when broken down into its elements. But how many people do this?

Shawn Rodriguez was told that "federal regulation" required his lower-interest loans to be paid off first. This turned out to be incorrect. But Shawn's conversation with the loan rep did not have to be hostile. All Shawn needed to do was to get her name and ask for whatever backup she had. Once he checked it out and found out the claim wasn't true, he was able to get something for it.

"I didn't assume a war," said Shawn, now an associate in the law firm of Gibson, Dunn & Crutcher. "To be contentious would have been counterproductive. I just fixed the problem, got the credit, and met my goals."

WRAP-UP: YOUR COMPETITIVE ATTITUDE

Think about when you played competitive sports: baseball, football, hockey, swimming, etc. When you were in the thick of competition, what were you thinking about? By far the number-one answer in my courses is winning—at least 95 percent of the answers. But it's the wrong answer. If you think of winning, you'll lose.

Here is a better question. What were you focused on? The answer should be *the ball, the puck, your stroke, your breathing.* The minutest details of your craft. If you are a gymnast and don't do that, you'll break your arm on the parallel bars.

Competitive negotiation is exactly the same. Don't get distracted by, well, distractions: winning, losing, what happened yesterday, unfair play, a referee's call, what might happen tomorrow, the next period, a penalty, the emotion of the moment.

Instead, execute and focus: what are my goals, what standards should I use, what are their needs, can I invoke any common enemies, can I form a vision of a relationship, who is their decision-maker, etc.

Before you negotiate, to be sure, you will strategize and prepare. Then you will focus and execute your strategy, dispassionately. If you see a problem, you'll take a break, reexamine your strategy, make any needed changes. Then you will go back into the negotiation and execute again. This is a powerful process. It works for the best sports teams and the best negotiators.

It's also important to consider this method with hard bargainers, because the world is a place where many people cheat. People who cheat are hard bargainers—they make it hard to get fair processes and results. So your attitude in approaching hard bargainers is important. Don't let them get to you so you become emotional and make a mistake; focus on your goals. By going through the dispassionate process just described, you are much better able to deal with hard bargainers.

In competitive life, there are two kinds of people: those who are qualified, and those who try to steal from those who are qualified. What this really means is that many, if not most, hard bargainers act the way they do because they lack the skill to meet their goals fair and square. So they have to lie, cheat, and steal.

The key is to not get upset or take it personally. Less skilled people have to eat, too. Indeed, in tough economic times, studies show, the number of people who cheat goes up.

So just figure out your goals, use negotiation tools, meet your goals, and move on. They are who they are. Lower your expectations of other parties' trustworthiness. That way, you will never be disappointed. And you will often be pleasantly surprised.

Again, these tools don't work all the time with all people. John Layton asked a manager at Neiman Marcus some years ago for a discount on a damaged humidor. The manager said no. "Is it the position of Neiman Marcus to offer damaged merchandise at the same price as undamaged merchandise?" asked John, managing director of an asset management fund.

The manager refused to lower the price and walked away. This happens sometimes. The world has all sorts of people, though it's unlikely this would happen in today's economic climate. John could have reported her to Neiman Marcus executives. Others did and got all kinds of goodies. Or he could have posted this on a blog.

Your ability to use standards is often limited only by your creativity. Helene Rutledge, now an innovation director at GlaxoSmithKline, shared the course notes with her husband, Jon. She rightly figured that if two people understand these tools, the way they negotiate with each other will be even better.

One day he said to her, "You don't love me." Helene was startled. She wanted to know why he thought that. He told her that she had a really bad cough and refused to go to the doctor. "He told me that since I'm not taking care of myself, I am not living up to the bargain of a long and healthy life together." He said, "If you die early, you will leave me alone; thus, you don't love me."

Overdramatic, perhaps, but a lovely way to make a point as an alternative to nagging. Helene went to the doctor.

5

Trading Items of Unequal Value

A few years ago, a paper industry executive told me about a multimillion-dollar deal that he just couldn't close.

"We thought and thought about the deal and the customer, and tried to figure out what they wanted," said the executive, Larry Stillman, who is now an entrepreneur in Utah. "We finally figured out what it was. It was four basketball tickets." Tickets to the finals of the National Basketball Association, but tickets nonetheless.

To the customer, this was just the kind of validation it wanted: that its vendor would do almost anything to make its customers happy. As a result, Larry's company got a paper supply contract worth millions of dollars.

Larry discovered something that day that few people practice and even fewer understand enough to use consciously, consistently, and successfully. It is the notion of trading items of unequal value. All parties value things differently, and often unequally. Once you find out what they are, you can trade them. In the process, you will get what you consider valuable things for yourself. In exchange, you can give up things that have relatively little value to you.

Trading items of unequal value will cause the overall number or value of items in the negotiation to rise, making more available for all. The other party will become less price-sensitive, the relationship will get better, trust will be higher, and your own value to the other party will increase—whether in business or personal life.

Some people call this "expanding the pie." Others label it "win-win." Still others call it "interest-based negotiation." Others describe it as "collaboration." But none of these catchphrases really captures the mechanism you need to understand in order to use this powerful tool with confidence and consistency. None of these phrases tells you how to do it.

"Trading items of unequal value" tells you what you have to do. First you have to find the pictures in their heads. Then you have to find the pictures in yours. You find out which ones don't cost one side much but are valuable to the other side. Then you trade them.

The pictures in their heads don't have to be in the deal itself. They can be from anywhere. In fact, the more you look at the whole world as your potential resource base, the easier it will be to find something the other side wants.

The CEO of a major company in Philadelphia once said that the most important thing he ever did for his most important business client in a twenty-year business relationship was to pick up the client CEO's mother-in-law at the Philadelphia airport one Saturday night. His action had nothing to do with any deal. But it affected every deal forever after.

As with many of the tools in this book, trading items of unequal value may seem counterintuitive. But the more you practice with it, the more you will see how effective it is.

HOW IT WORKS

In 2000, I taught a two-day negotiation workshop in London for the forty senior mergers and acquisitions (M&A) executives for Tyco International. At that time, Tyco was the world's most acquisitive company. It was buying an average of a company a day.

One of the executives, Matt Rogers, who was Tyco's head of M&A, took to heart the concept of trading items of unequal value. The next week he persuaded a British company that wanted to sell Tyco a subsidiary for 3 million pounds (about $6 million U.S.) to instead *pay* Tyco to take the company off its hands.

Here's how it happened. The British company's major condition was that it had to unload the subsidiary within three weeks. By asking questions of the company and others associated with it, Matthew found out that the subsidiary, a closed-circuit TV installation and maintenance business, was losing a lot of money. In fact, its parent company would violate its bank agreements on debt if the subsidiary wasn't divested in three weeks. "The entire enterprise, worth at least thirty million pounds," was in jeopardy, Matt said.

So Tyco offered to take the subsidiary off the British company's hands within three weeks if Tyco got the subsidiary for nothing. Tyco would save 3 million pounds (cost of company), and the British company would save at least 27 million pounds (savings from not losing its bank credit and going under). Matthew promised that Tyco would drop everything if need be to do the deal.

At the last moment, the British company agreed to pay Tyco 60,000 pounds for Tyco's "administrative costs," including, of course, dinners at fancy restaurants. That is how Tyco was paid to take a subsidiary off another company's hands. In essence, Tyco offered to trade the ability to fast-track the sale for a reduction in the sale price from three million pounds down to zero. The British company gave up 3 million pounds instead of its whole company worth 30 million pounds (net savings, 27 million pounds).

"Trading items like this has been part of my negotiation tool kit ever since," said Matthew, now M&A head of H Control, a cable TV and Internet company based in Miami.

This was terrific; the trade doesn't need to involve a very big thing. We are all familiar with the positive effect of buying a single flower for a loved one, or bringing back something unusual and inexpensive from a trip. It's not the monetary value of the gift you are providing that matters much of the time. You are providing respect, friendship, love, and the value of your time. You are valuing the other person. In return, they love you more. And this, as they say, is priceless.

Throughout the book there are examples of ordinary people trading items of unequal value: You do the wash on Monday and I'll do the shopping on Tuesday. You take the kids on Wednesday and I'll take them on Thursday. This chapter is designed to give you a structure around which you can do this in a more conscious, effective, and profitable way.

Even in business, the thing you trade can be very small, in return for a big benefit (say, getting their account). I often ask executives questions like this: On Monday, you deliver a truck filled with your products to a customer, and they pay a price for it. On Tuesday, you deliver a truck of exactly the same products to the same customer, and they pay the same price for it. In addition, however, on Tuesday you give the customer's purchasing manager the name—the name only—of a good, inexpensive hotel in the Caribbean for a second honeymoon for him and his spouse. Have you delivered the same product on Tuesday as Monday?

Of course not! You will have increased the value of your customer's life on Tuesday relative to Monday. Marginally, for sure. But marginally is often all that is needed to succeed in a highly competitive world.

Think of your counterparts as the repository of a billion synapses. Some are in the deal, many not in the deal. The more of those synapses you light up, the less price-sensitive they will be, the better the relationship, the more value in the deal. Some of my clients like the fact that I teach at a university. I provide them and their kids advice on how to improve college entrance applications.

This process is very different from the "interest-based negotiation" that has been a staple of business in recent years. The "interests" usually refer to the proximate reasons why people want things they are asking for: if the bank gives me a lower interest rate on my purchase of a house, I will transfer my accounts there. Or, if you let me watch football with you on your new HDTV, I'll bring the snacks.

This is good, and you should find as many such trades as you can. But *Getting More* is much broader. The "interests" or "needs" to be traded can be anything, including respect or help with one's home computer system: in the deal, outside the deal, rational, irrational, explicit, implicit, long-term, short-term, verbal, nonverbal, big, small.

If I get you some consulting business or let you use my box seats at the sports stadium, you will let me borrow your fancy car. If the bank gives me lower interest to buy a house, I will be the cook at the bank's annual picnic, using my culinary skills. If I can watch football on your HDTV, I will mow your lawn all summer with my tractor, saving you landscaping costs.

The entire world is at your disposal to get an agreement. You are not constrained by the negotiation subject itself. The chance of *Getting More* is greater. People want a lot of things in life. The more you find out what they need, the more of it you can use to trade.

Some of my course participants have sought refunds, lower interest, or lower fees from credit card companies because of customer loyalty. When the credit card rep was not able to do that, the participants asked what else could be done that didn't involve money. The reps then offered double, triple, or quadruple the value of the requested monetary item, by providing frequent flier miles or other benefits almost as usable as cash.

A company may be able to offer its clients travel discounts or office supply discounts through the company's superior contacts or buying system. This can enable a company to hold the line on pricing during a discounting cycle: the clients essentially got the "discount" by saving money on travel or supplies.

When you focus on the other party's needs, you can move a long way from seeing money as the most important part of the deal. The intangibles will substitute for high money requests. Prashant Desai was trying to hire a live-in nanny for his family. A single father had offered the nanny twice the salary that Prashant could afford to pay. So Prashant, a Pittsburgh computer networking expert, invited the nanny over to chat.

He found out she was a single mother and was trying to find local medical care for her son, who had recovered from blood cancer. It was her first job. "I showed genuine care," Prashant said. "I informed her that my wife is a physician and my father owns a pathology lab. I communicated our philosophy of the nanny being an extension of our family."

He noted the family's informal lifestyle and support structure. He also showed her comparable nanny salaries demonstrating she would not be underpaid. The nanny took the job with Prashant's family at half of the competing offer.

"Getting past the salary and knowing her was key," Prashant said. "In the past, I would not have pursued this deal." Course tools helped him succeed, he said.

INTANGIBLES

A key driver behind trading items of unequal value is "intangibles." That is, things besides money that have a value to others. In business deals, for example, the parties often wind up with pretty similar monetary valuations. What usually seals the deal for one party are the things offered other than money—the intangibles—that make the overall package more valuable to the other party. It is often something of small value to one party, but which exactly fits the dream (or fear) of the other party.

Janice Brue of GATX, the big aircraft leasing company in San Francisco, needed to get back a bunch of airline seats it was owed by Air Canada. But it was getting hung up by bureaucracy. Finally, Janice found the right item to trade: a round of golf at Pebble Beach. It was easy for her to arrange, and the executives at Air Canada appreciated the offer.

As you will see later in this book, trading things of unequal value works wonderfully with children. Children trade intangibles all the time: my baseball card for your marble; my doll for your stuffed animal. While the underlying item is tangible, the intangible component is the special attachment that someone has to a specific item. Sometimes the attachment is quantifiable, but often it is not.

For example, a specific item to be sold might be a cookie. If it's an ordinary cookie, you might pay $3 for it. But if it's an oatmeal cookie that prompts fond memories of your grandmother's cookies and the smell of cinnamon, you might pay $5 for essentially the same cookie. The intangible value is $2 to you.

The human economic system started by trading items of unequal value: you have too much meat, I have too much bread, we trade. Money was aimed at standardizing things. But it can never replace the very specific intangible that you might provide them, something perhaps they alone value.

Debbie Simoncini-Rosenfeld, vice president of an insurance company, was trying to deal with her eight-year-old daughter, Jessica, "screaming and yelling" to stay up later than her 8:30 bedtime. Her daughter wanted to read later at night. So Debbie traded her daughter a 9:30 P.M. bedtime in exchange for no bare-belly shirts at school and no riding her bike in the street. Debbie valued her daughter's decorum and safety more than a later bedtime; her daughter valued a later bedtime more than decorum and safety. "Children like to be involved in making the rules," Debbie said. "If they get something, they will give up something."

Nobuko Aoki, one of my former students and now at a leading U.S. computer company, was managing a joint venture with a Japanese company. At first, both companies insisted on owning 51 percent. But by closer questioning, Nobuko, now a finance manager, found out that the Japanese company would accept 49 percent if the U.S. company kept the Japanese employees.

Trading items of unequal value has more universal application in business than one might think at first. The legal system's business judgment rule, which governs most mergers and acquisitions worldwide, says that if you are a company director, you do not have to take the highest stock price offered by a buyer for that company. You can take a lower stock price offer if, in your reasonable business judgment, the lower-priced offer, plus the value of intangibles, makes long-term shareholder value higher.

It used to be that the courts made the directors, particularly of public companies, take the highest price per share offered for the company. The theory was that the directors must get the highest price they could. Even in nonpublic companies, shareholders often sued to force the directors to take the highest price.

In recent years, however, the courts have come to realize that intangibles such as the company brand, the skill of employees, and company reputation may be very valuable. Buyers who offered to protect these intangible assets in some way were sometimes allowed to buy the company, instead of buyers with higher, all-cash offers.

There has been an effort to quantify intangibles. Some years ago it was estimated that the value of United Airlines' brand was worth 3 cents per seat-mile, or $90 per passenger on a 3,000-mile trip. This is a vast amount of extra value. Coca-Cola's brand has been valued at $84 billion; two-thirds of Kellogg's stock value has been attributed to its brand. If you save a counterpart in a negotiation an hour, a week, or freedom from care, or worry about risk—what could that be worth? If you start thinking like that, a whole set of new options will open up to you.

Don't expect the other parties to think up these things. Often, you will need to do the work for them. They won't know how to add the value.

Clearly, there are some situations where it is unethical to provide certain kinds of intangibles to people: gifts to doctors by pharmaceutical companies; bribes or favors for government employees. Trading items of unequal value is not intended to encourage illegal or unethical behavior. You need to find an intangible that is legal. And since there are so many intangibles, this is not difficult. A computer expert at one major company got a new client by helping a prospect's daughter with her computer on a Saturday.

The network acquisitions manager at a large technology company saved hundreds of millions of dollars for his company by getting a more than 90 percent reduction on cable prices. The vendor needed to finance another deal. The big technology company helped them with the financing in return for their extra inventory at low prices.

Eric Schwartz, vice president for law at Johnson & Johnson, was able to persuade his company to develop an artificial pancreas for diabetics not on the basis of the economics, which were uncertain. A partnership with the Juvenile Diabetes Research Foundation improved the rapport with the U.S. Food & Drug Administration, and the positive publicity and the consistency with the company's credo were intangibles that more than carried the day.

Now, you might think, "He's asking us to think outside the box." I'm not. I'm saying, "There is no box." There is only your ability to be creative, to think broadly about goals, needs, and the pictures in the heads of the other parties. In fact, the more broadly you think about needs that are not part of the deal, the more you can add value to the deal by making the entire pie larger.

NEEDS

Many negotiators like to talk about "interests." People often have a hard time figuring out what it means. How does it differ from goals? Well, "goals" refers to what you want at the end of the process. In most negotiations I have one goal, and I have various needs that the goal would satisfy—that is, various reasons why I want this goal.

Let's say you want a salary increase but the company can't give you one. Your real goal should be to afford a better life. So maybe the company instead can cosign a loan that will get you a better house for a lower monthly payment. Or the company can give you more vacation time so you can do some outside consulting. Or it can provide you with a cheaper way to take that dream vacation. The more that the company knows about your underlying needs, the more of those needs it can fulfill.

Another issue is that "interests" has generally presumed a certain rationality. Most people assume that the parties can have a rational discussion about the benefits they want. Truth is, the world is full of irrational people. The world cannot be made rational, despite efforts by many well-meaning people to make it so. People get angry, adoring, fearful. I'd like to make them rational and calm, but I live in the real world, as do you.

So, to meet people's intangible needs and make the pie larger, you need to know the emotional and irrational needs of others, too. These may include fears like being alone, having an office on a high floor, or bugs of any kind. They may include dreams like baseball camp with the pros or a seminar on fishing. We ask people in our courses for their dreams and fears. We get dreams like travel, sailing, owning a restaurant, running a marathon, and running a company. We get fears like snakes, crowds, public speaking, flying, and heights.

If you know that the other party likes travel, you can use it in a conversation to break the ice or offer them something you know about the subject. If you know a prospective employee fears heights, you can offer an office on the ground floor. And the employee will trade something for it.

The point is, the more you find out about the other party, the more persuasive you will become in the negotiation. You expand the pie, meet your goals, find options, trade items of unequal value.

Take the case of family-owned businesses. More than 90 percent of all businesses in the world are owned by families. At least two-thirds of the gross national product of developed countries comes from family-owned businesses, as well as two-thirds of employment. The numbers are higher in developing countries. The world of *The Wall Street Journal,* that of widely held public companies, is not where most people spend their time.

In the world where most people spend their time, intangibles are much more important than most people think. In many family-owned-business deals, the founder and builder of the company often asks an outrageous price to sell his company. But, probing deeper, you might find that what he really often wants are intangibles. He wants respect; he wants to keep the brand name; he wants to have his picture prominently displayed in the lobby of the building; he wants to get a summer job for his niece, or be appointed emeritus on the board. In other words, he will accept a lower price plus intangibles.

Missing these cues makes you less likely to make a deal. In much of business, money is not the most important item of importance to *either* side, regardless of what they say. The price has to be reasonable, but so much more is required.

Intangibles can bridge the gap between seemingly inflexible positions. Geoffrey Dubus's wife wanted him to kill the two mice that sometimes ran around their apartment. "They transmit diseases," she said. Geoff, a venture capitalist in Paris, didn't mind the mice. He thought of them as "inoffensive living animals."

Whatever you think about their positions, the real need of Geoffrey's wife was not to kill the mice. It was to not have them in her apartment. So Geoff found the holes where the mice entered their apartment and plastered them up. Everyone was happy: Geoffrey, wife, and the mice.

Rosemary Ford, then a Penn Law student, had given her five-year-old daughter a department store fashion catalogue that Rosemary was finished reading. By and by Rosemary decided she wanted the catalogue back to copy a design from the cover for a craft project. So she asked her daughter, Cordelia, to give her back the catalogue, but Cordelia refused. She hid the catalogue. "It's my magazine, Mommy, you gave it to me."

Instead of getting angry or annoyed, Rosemary tried to find out her daughter's intangible needs in wanting the magazine. "Why do you want the magazine?" Rosemary asked. "To look at all the pretty pictures inside," Cordelia responded.

So Rosemary, now an attorney in Philadelphia, said, "Well, Mommy wants to copy a design from the cover. Why don't you get the magazine, give Mommy the cover, and keep all the pretty pictures inside?"

Cordelia got the catalogue, carefully tore off the cover, gave the cover to her mother, and kept the rest of the catalogue. Whereupon Rosemary explained to her daughter the *principle* of trading items of unequal value.

Rosemary's five-year-old daughter thought this was so cool that she spent the next week telling everyone she could think of about this: friends, family, neighbors. And finding items of unequal value herself to trade. This is an example of how a mother made her daughter a better negotiator and improved their relationship. If you want to have better negotiations, don't hide the process from your counterparts. Tell them about it.

GETTING THE INFORMATION

What if the other side won't tell you what they want? Not everyone is as forthcoming as you would like. Some people are scared, some are reticent, and some just don't know. What you do is *guess.* If you guess right, you will usually get the information you need. You will likely improve the relationship and the chance of a deal. If you guess wrong, they will often tell you so and give you information about their needs. Either way, you get more.

Again, nothing is perfect. The point is, if you do all of this, you will be more successful—you will get more.

For every important meeting you attend, find out as much about the individuals at the meeting as you can. This goes for a job interview, a meeting at work, a conference call. Do research before the meeting. Ask people.

I tell my students to find out before an interview exactly who is interviewing them. Research the interviewer. What has he or she written? What are their likes and dislikes? What about the firm? What have been its biggest successes and biggest concerns? By the time a company has decided to interview you, it probably thinks you can do the job. The rest is intangibles: fit, motivation, loyalty, interest in the company. They are already mentally putting you in the company and thinking, how would this person react as an employee?

One student was in his final interview at an investment bank. He researched the managing director, but when he arrived at the investment bank, the bank had changed interviewers because of scheduling issues. He was escorted into the office of another managing director, about whom the student knew nothing.

As the student was being introduced, he looked around the office casually to establish some point of connection. He saw a small picture in a frame on a stand behind the managing director's desk. It looked like a picture of the director and two of his kids standing in front of a sailboat.

So the student asked the director if that was a picture of him and his children. It was, the director replied. Whereupon the two started talking about sailing. The student didn't know much about sailing, but he didn't need to. He asked, "Do you sail a lot? Where do you sail? Do you race, or do you just sail recreationally? How would someone learn about sailing?" And so forth.

The two then spent forty minutes talking about all sorts of subjects—sailing, other sports, travel, food. Not once did any business subject come up. At the end of the forty minutes, the managing director offered the student a job. Did they have a business discussion?

Of course they did! What business information did the director learn about the applicant in the course of having a forty-minute discussion about nonbusiness subjects? Well, the director learned that the student was a great listener. Curious. Perceptive. Interested and interesting. Would probably be great with clients. Can think on his feet. Someone the director wouldn't mind working all night with. Terrific people person, good for sales.

By the time you have a final interview at an employer, they are already sure you can do the job. It is not your hard skills they are looking for, but your soft skills. The intangibles.

Getting the information on what they value had particular significance for Mike Leskinen, a mutual fund principal in New York. He said his mother lived on some land the family owned in Pennsylvania and received $500 a month from a company that had built a cell phone tower there. Eventually the company needed to get a permanent easement and offered his mom $80,000. He and his mother thought they'd be thrilled with $120,000 as negotiations began.

Mike consulted course tools. "I tried to figure out what this was worth to them, not just to me," he said. "I did research on the Internet. I thought about the pictures in their head," including moving the tower. After doing all that, he called the company. They paid his family $750,000. But he wasn't greedy; the value was up to $1.2 million, he said.

EXPANDING THE PIE

The information you collect from others gives you the ability to better meet your goals and fulfill your needs. Remember, it is not about gaining power at the expense of others. Your having more power doesn't mean less power for the other person. The pie is expanded. It is like the development of new technology. While certain kinds of jobs are lost, overall both employment and prosperity almost always increase.

If you know the other person's needs or interests (broadly), you can also deal more effectively with hard bargainers. Let's say you have figured out how to expand the pie: include more in the deal than originally thought. They, on the other hand, keep insisting you take a lower price if you're the seller, or pay more if you're the buyer. They don't want to talk about anything collaborative.

So you say, "You don't want to talk about the much greater value in this deal? The greater profit for you? Our paying you more money? If you don't want to talk about this, is there someone else in your organization—a business development person perhaps—who will talk to me about the larger profit available here that you are not asking about?"

They wouldn't dare turn down a discussion on that subject. They could get fired if a higher decision-maker in their company found out about it. You own this negotiation. So whether the other party is a hard bargainer or soft bargainer, there are tools for both. With collaborators, expand the pie together. With hard bargainers, offer to show third parties how the pie can be expanded.

Counterparts in negotiations have said to me things like, "I want $100,000!" To which I have replied, "Why not $200,000? Why not $300,000?" And they've responded, "What?!" And I've said, "Well, we don't even know what's in the deal yet. How do you know I won't pay you more? I need to know first, what's in the deal? When I know all of your interests, all of your needs, I can make a proposal."

For example, there may be cross-selling opportunities, there may be potential operational synergies (from back offices to travel). So let's address needs and intangibles first, and make proposals later. When they say, "What's your proposal?" you should say, "I don't know, what's in the deal?"

Others are not going to know how to do this. You're going to have to help them at first. The more they understand the process of expanding the pie by trading items of unequal value, the easier the negotiations you will have with them. Clever clients have even brought their own customers to my workshops. The result was much better deals among all parties.

One of the more remarkable business success stories of expanding the pie involves Brad Oberwager, the founder and CEO of Sundia Corporation of Oakland, California, producer of high-quality fruit cups. Brad, who took my course about fifteen years ago, has raised trading items of unequal value to a high art.

Several years ago he approached ten of the twenty largest watermelon growers in North America. He offered them part of his planned fruit cup business if they would simply let him put "Sundia" stickers on the watermelons they sold in stores. It cost the growers nothing. For two years store owners saw the stickers. Then, one day, Brad, with the growers' support, started making sales calls to the stores. He offered a fruit cup with higher value added than the brand they had come to know. "Overnight we represented thirty-two percent of the market," he said.

He said he has reduced overall his business strategy to one question he learned in class: "What costs you nothing that gives me what I want, and what costs me nothing that gives you what you want?" He added that he discloses a lot of information, is transparent about his plans, and over-prepares. "Being smart is not what makes you a good negotiator," he said. "You are a good negotiator because you can see the future. And that comes from preparation."

LINKAGES

A key memory aid to think about in all of this is *linkages.* You link things together that are not necessarily related: they may be inside the deal or outside the deal. You can link them by issues, time, or other parameters: if you do this for me now, I'll do something for you later.

Why do families fight over where they are going to go on vacation this year? Unless you are all going to die this year, there is next year. There is also, for this year, not just where you go but what you do when you get there, how you get there, what you eat, how much you spend—all sorts of things to trade. And there are things outside the deal that you can trade, too.

If you think more broadly about the things you can trade off, you will make your relationships better. Things that seemed completely inflexible and difficult suddenly will become easier. That means if you really have to have the Corvette, then your wife should get something for her hobby, too. If he helps with the gardening, she doesn't complain when he watches football. She decorates the living room, he decorates the garage. He plays cards with his buddies; she has a "girls' night out."

We do negotiation clinics at school. A student with a negotiation problem sits in front of the class and has to negotiate each side, successively, with me and other students, as we all offer ideas on how the negotiation can be improved. At one point, we had two people in the class who were engaged to each other, and of course this raised all sorts of interesting negotiation issues.

For one thing, the male student had a job offer in New York City, while his fiancée had a job offer in Los Angeles. They had argued for months about where they were going to live and which one of them was going to give up a hard-won job. So we put them together to negotiate with each other in front of the class. She hated New York and he hated Los Angeles, where he was born. Her job in Los Angeles was much better than his in New York. The economy had just turned sour; there were many fewer investment banking jobs in Los Angeles for him than in New York.

The class gave various pieces of advice to the students, using course tools. Finally, the male student said, "I'll be glad to move to Los Angeles, without a job, and look for a job, as long as I can (a) set up and make every decision regarding the wedding, (b) pick the honeymoon location, and (c) pick where we are going to go on vacation for the next ten years."

The underlying question he was raising, of course, was, "What are you willing to trade for me to be jobless?"

His fiancée thought about this for less than a minute. Then, she said, "I'll stay in New York if I don't have to work."

Suddenly, the whole negotiation had changed. It was clear that she had an intangible need that they had *never* discussed in all their months of haggling. Her future husband had thought there was *nothing* he could do to get his wife to stay in New York City. But working wasn't as important to her as it was to him, or as he had thought it was.

We didn't need to finish the negotiation for them in class. We had reestablished a meaningful negotiation for them. They would be able to reach an agreement in private.

Even in the most hostile situation, you can try to expand the pie. And you will be able to do it at least some of the time. In other words, you'll *get more*. If the other person says, "I'm going to wreck your business," your next comment should be, "Okay, but can we make more money in some other way?" Such a response seems counterintuitive, but it works.

I co-own and head a small cargo airline in the Caribbean, which operates from various properties—warehouses, hangars, offices.

A company named IvyPort had been leaving its ground handling equipment—belt loaders, tugs, trucks—on one of our properties for months. Our people had called the company repeatedly to move the equipment, but had gotten no response.

After eight months, I told my people to start using the equipment. Within hours, I received an angry call from the owner, Alfonso Fernandez Jr., now associated with Ivy Investments, telling me that I had stolen his property and he was going to call the police.

"You don't know the laws in Puerto Rico!" he fumed on the phone. "I'm an attorney! You can't do this!"

"Oh," I said calmly. "You're an attorney. That's great. I am, too. Where did you go to law school?"

"Columbia," he said. So I responded, "Congratulations! Columbia is a great school. I went to Harvard Law School, just up the road, so we're practically neighbors."

"I also have an MBA, so I know about business," he said. "And what you did wasn't businesslike." I responded, "That's great. Where did you get your MBA?"

"Wharton," he said. "Me, too," I said.

"And," he said, "I've taught business." "Me, too," I said.

By not being reactive, and continuing to find out about the other party, we both got more. A lot more. He could keep his equipment on our property at no charge, and we could use his equipment at no charge. And, over the next couple of months, he gave us $100,000 in cargo warehousing business from his clients that we could accommodate at lower prices. We became friends.

You might say we were lucky. This doesn't apply all the time. Again, of course it doesn't! What is important is the *process*—trying to get more from every deal. I would venture to say that too few people put themselves in a position to get more in this fashion. They are too busy being defensive, accusatory, or argumentative. Remember, you just want to get that one extra hit every nine games.

Managers I know say to their counterparts: "Why fight each other when we can profit together?"

A CHANGE IN ATTITUDE

What all this involves is an attitude change. It means thinking more about the upside than the downside. It has a lot to do with the way people look at problems.

Here is the thought process: You are going to get hit with a certain number of problems in your life. You will have to spend time dealing with them. The attitude adjustment you should want to make is, as long as you have to deal with these problems, what kind of opportunity can you make out of them? You only have so much time in your life. Why not use it more wisely?

It doesn't take a lot of time to figure out opportunities hiding inside problems. You just have to look for the opportunities. Instead of thinking that a problem is a drag to deal with, think of a problem as an opportunity waiting to be recognized and developed.

Every time you have a problem with another party, think: How can you make money from this problem? Is there a way to trade intangibles? How can the pie be expanded? And slowly but surely, you will start to get more.

This process does involve going out of your way to try to make the other person happy. That means you have to all but give up the idea of getting "leverage," advantage or power, over others, unless it's a hard-bargaining situation. Pushing other people just causes others to try to protect themselves—or hurt you—instead of expansively finding opportunities.

It reminds me of a joke. A guy goes into a store and buys a lamp. He goes home, rubs the lamp, and a genie comes out. The genie says, "I'll give you anything you want, but your neighbor has to get twice as much."

The guy says to himself, "I want a house—*but my neighbor will get two houses!* I want a million dollars—*but my neighbor will get two million.*" Finally, the guy gets an idea. "I know what I want," he says to the genie. "Put out one of my eyes."

Yes, this is sick. But isn't this how many, if not most, people negotiate? "This will hurt you more than it hurts me." "You'll lose more than I will." Rather than figure out who can hurt the most—the seeming basis for all Cold War and many legal negotiations—why not talk about the *opportunity* for everyone involved? When people threaten to walk out of a meeting, I usually try to get everyone to agree in advance that anyone can walk out of a meeting and be fine. "Having said that," I say, "is there a better deal we can do in the room?"

As with standards and other negotiation tools, framing is a big part of being persuasive in trading items of unequal value. Try to frame their needs in a way that meets your goals. Dawn MacLaren, the management consultant mentioned in Chapter 2, had a sixty-six-year-old father who was hard of hearing. For more than two years he refused to get a hearing aid—he was a stubborn man.

Finally, Dawn went to see him one afternoon. She said to him (in a loud voice), "Dad, don't you want to hear the sound of your children's voices?" He got a hearing aid *that day*. She achieved her goals: her father got a hearing aid. And he satisfied his needs: to hear his children's voices.

If you want to work on a particular project that you think is promising, a good way to approach your boss is to say, "Boss, I have an idea on how to increase the department's profits this year." I can guarantee you that your boss wants to increase profits (needs). And you want to work on a particular project that increases profits (goals).

One of the more interesting assumptions about negotiations is that the more things that are on the table at a negotiation, the more difficult and complex that negotiation is. Actually, the more items on the table at a negotiation, the easier the negotiation is. That's because you have more items of potentially unequal value to trade. I like to get as many issues and items on the table as possible.

Many people assume it's hard to get others to disclose their needs. People often play their hand close to the vest, to use a poker analogy. I have found the opposite. When you start trying to figure out the needs of the other party, and let them know you are trying to meet their needs, the problem is not getting them to talk. The problem is getting them to shut up.

A Wharton Executive MBA Program student once asked me to help resolve a business dispute that had been going on for six years. The owners of a software products company were a husband and wife in the midst of a divorce. He owned 60 percent, she owned 40 percent.

The company had no money. However, a public company was interested in merging with them. The public company had a great stock price but no product. Separately, neither could make it. Together, they were worth more than $300 million.

But the merger couldn't occur because the wife refused to vote her 40 percent stock, effectively blocking the merger. Both companies were on the verge of litigation. Her company was about to go bankrupt without the merger.

I went to see the wife. She had no money, her savings were almost depleted, and her husband was late on payments he promised to send to her. I asked her what she wanted. She said she needed some money to live on. She said she wanted sole custody of the children. And she said she didn't want her husband to get more than she did—she wanted her husband to feel more pain than she did.

I told her that she could never bring back the better times of the past, and she would never be able to hurt her husband in the way she'd like to in the future. I asked her why sole custody was so important to her when her children would be leaving home for college shortly, and why was it so important to fight each other and lose several more years of her life? And I asked her, in particular, why was it so important for him to feel pain, since she'd have to feel pain, as well? That was because without the merger, everyone would be broke.

Finally, she saw that her actions were not helping her to accomplish her real goals and needs. She agreed to get the divorce and do the merger. I told her I had to talk to her husband, too. After all, both parties had to agree; that's how it works. She was understandably nervous about this. But she finally agreed to let me talk with him.

So I went through the same drill with the husband. He had his own set of issues, which we walked through. He finally came to realize that he would never meet his goals in life, never meet his needs, unless he left his wife with enough for her to live on comfortably for the rest of her life. And it wasn't reasonable for a mother not to be able to see her children (he wanted sole custody, too). He agreed to the divorce terms.

Both of them then wanted me to represent them in the merger with the public company. I did, going through the same process that I did with the husband and wife. I talked to each side about their needs, their goals, their perceptions, what was bothering them, and so forth. The merger went through.

What was most interesting about this is that none of it is rocket science. It just involves asking people about their needs and goals, finding out the intangibles that matter to them, and focusing on the upside, not the downside. What is it that will make them happy? What's also interesting here is that until you see how to do this, it is invisible.

The following story ending this chapter is near and dear to my heart, literally and figuratively. It shows how helpful these tools can be, even in life-and-death situations.

In January 2001, I had two heart attacks. I was being stabilized at a hospital in Philadelphia in preparation for open-heart bypass surgery. But the hospital kept giving me medicines that produced bad reactions, so I wanted to get the surgery elsewhere.

I checked around for the best heart surgeon I could find. I came across the name of Dr. Wayne O. Isom, one of the world's best heart bypass surgeons. He did the bypass surgeries on David Letterman, Larry King, and Walter Cronkite.

Of course, I couldn't get near Dr. Isom. His schedule was full for months. He didn't know me, I didn't have any connections to him. Moreover, the only access I had to him was by email. And as we know, email is imperfect at best as a persuasion tool.

How could I establish a connection with him through email that might be meaningful enough for him to operate on me? So I started doing research on Dr. Isom from my hospital bed in Philadelphia. I searched for who he was, what his interests were, how he spent his time, what kind of person he was: I was looking for a point of connection.

One of Dr. Isom's main research topics at the time was small artery cholesterol build-up. I have small arteries. So I did research on his research, and wrote him an email. I told him who I was (a professor and former journalist), gave him some of my heart history, and asked him if he could operate on me. I acknowledged that he might be too busy to do the operation. I understood that he had a long waiting list.

Even if he could not operate on me, I mentioned, we did have a point of connection, which I described. Could he do a consultation with me? I asked a couple of specific questions from my research. I wanted to convey to him that I hadn't just dashed off a letter to him, but that I had really studied some of his life's work and taken the time and trouble to understand it.

My family and I also contacted every person we knew in New York who had had heart surgery and asked if they knew a doctor who practiced at the same hospital as Dr. Isom. We found one, a cardiologist, Dr. Michael Wolk, who called Dr. Isom's office.

To make a long story short, Dr. Isom cut short a vacation by one day and came back to New York City to operate on me. The results were fantastic.

I asked Dr. Isom why he cut his vacation short to operate on me. Certainly someone of his stature didn't have to do this. I asked him again in a lovely meeting we had in his office as I was writing this book. He said it certainly helped that Dr. Wolk, a highly respected cardiologist I had found through third parties, called his office. But he said it was more than that: I was one of the few patients who had ever asked him about his research. I had made a "personal connection" with him.

Imagine that! The negotiation tools discussed in this chapter worked: Understand who the other person is, understand his concerns and perceptions, his needs and intangibles. Trade items of unequal value. In effect, I was negotiating for my life.

I later read a news story that said former president Bill Clinton wanted Dr. Isom, too, but Clinton's staff would not even tell the surgeon who the "VIP" patient was. Dr. Isom suggested that someone else do the operation. It might have been different if a personal connection had been made, Dr. Isom said.

Dr. Isom said that even as he has gotten more skilled at medicine, he has found that personal connections are at least as important. He said he has operated on the indigent, whether or not they could afford it, because of their efforts to make a personal connection with him. After her operation, an indigent woman from Brooklyn gave him a $50 contribution for his research, something that was a bigger percentage of her income than some of the $5 million contributions that come in, he said.

What this means for negotiation is that no product or service is ever just a "commodity" as long as you make sure that you key on the personal connection. It is your synapses, your experiences, your time, your efforts, your interest in others that you have to trade. And that differentiate your offering from everyone else's. Those are the intangibles that enrich the lives of others and cause better deals to happen. It causes everyone to get more.

But why end there? The use of the negotiation tools I've described in this chapter found other uses in the hospital, too. Even in great hospitals like New York Presbyterian, I realized, nursing care varies. I needed to stay in the hospital for a few days before the operation for tests and to be stabilized again since I had moved from Philadelphia.

So I let every nurse, nurse's aide, and nurse practitioner who happened to come into my room know that I taught negotiation—and that I was available for free, 24/7 consultation on how to get a better job at the hospital, how to get a raise at the hospital, and in fact any subject on which they wished negotiation advice.

I had a steady stream of nurses, nurse's aides, and nurse practitioners coming into my room, both before and after the operation. And I received great care. The staff could not ask me enough about what I needed. ("Want more morphine? No problem!" "We'll get the doctor right away!") I was also moved from the hall side of a two-bed room to a VIP room with three big windows facing the East River.

Trade items of unequal value. It works.

6

Emotion

A woman in my class at Columbia Business School, Lisa Stephens, had a five-year-old daughter who fell in the kitchen one Saturday morning, gashing her forehead on the sharp corner of the kitchen table. The child, Aubree, was hysterical. The child's grandfather, Lisa's father, was hysterical.

Aubree clearly had to go to the hospital to get stitches. But she refused to go, clinging to the table for dear life. No one could pry her little fingers off the kitchen table.

Lisa was about to become hysterical, too, when she suddenly stopped. She said to herself, "Wait a minute. I'm taking a negotiation course. I'm going to negotiate this."

So Lisa walked over to her daughter and touched her gently on the arm. "Does Mommy love you?" Lisa asked. "Yes," her daughter sniffled, calming down.

"Would Mommy do anything to hurt you?" her mother asked. "No," her daughter said.

"When we get to be big people, do we have to do things sometimes that we don't like to do?" her mother asked. "Yes," Aubree said.

"Mommy has stitches," Lisa said. She showed her scar. "Granddaddy has stitches," she said. Lisa's father showed Aubree his scar. And within five minutes, her daughter let go of the table and walked to the car by herself.

Here are some things that we know for sure about this event. First, Aubree's refusal to go to the hospital was entirely irrational. It was in Aubree's interests to go to the hospital, and get there quickly. But, as in millions of negotiations every day, she wasn't being rational.

The second thing this story shows is that we must start a negotiation thinking about the pictures in the heads of the other party. Lisa's goal was to get Aubree to the hospital without traumatizing her further. The mother realized that the picture in Aubree's head was "I'm hurting and alone, I need love."

So, having considered What are my goals? and Who are *they*? the mother thinks, what will it take to persuade Aubree? So Lisa asks, "Does Mommy love you?" The question shows her daughter that her mother understands that her daughter needs love. Lisa draws her daughter out as Aubree answers the question.

Lisa then realizes her daughter is probably thinking, "Okay, Mommy loves me, but I'm in pain." So her mother asks, "Would Mommy do anything to hurt you?" And Aubree realizes that her mother is thinking about her daughter's pain, too.

This whole process is incremental, starting from the mother thinking about the pictures in the child's head to achieving the mother's goals. It doesn't take very long—it happens step-by-step. And in the end, and within five minutes, Aubree walks to the car of her own free will, rather than being dragged kicking and screaming—a more common and more traumatic way to do it.

In sum, what Lisa gave Aubree was a series of *emotional payments*. They directly addressed Aubree's fears and showed her that her mother understood. In other situations, the emotional payment could be an apology, words of empathy, or a concession. It could just be hearing out someone who is upset.

Emotional payments have the effect of calming people down. They get people to listen and be ready to think more about their own welfare. They start from irrationality and move people, little by little, toward a better result, if not a rational one.

EMOTION AND NEGOTIATION

Emotion is the enemy of effective negotiations and of effective negotiators. People who are emotional stop listening. They often become unpredictable and rarely are able to focus on their goals. Because of that, they often hurt themselves and don't meet their goals. Movies often show scenes of impassioned speeches, suggesting these are highly effective. Whether that is realistic depends on whether the speaker is so emotional that he or she is not thinking clearly.

Emotion, used here, is when one is so overcome with one's own feelings that he or she stops listening and is often self-destructive. The person can no longer focus on his or her goals and needs. Empathy, by contrast, is when one is focused on the feelings of the other person. It means being compassionate and sympathetic. In other words, emotion is about you, empathy is about the other party. Empathy is highly effective. Emotion is not.

Genuine displays of emotion—love, sadness, joy—are of course part of life. But it's important to recognize that these emotions, while real, reduce listening, and therefore are not useful in negotiations where processing information is critical. People feeling such emotions are almost always absorbed in the moment, for solace or gratification. The goal is not necessarily reaching the best outcome. The long term, and the broader world, often recede. The feelings can be needed and important, but not effective to reach well-considered results. Indeed, emotions have often been used to push people to do things they later regret, including testing physical limits, which can be dangerous, since emotional people are less immune to self-harm.

In contrast to the above, the emotion strategies in *Getting More* are designed to enhance relationships both personally and in business. The premise of this chapter is that it is possible to be dispassionate and compassionate at the same time.

"By reducing the emotional content, I learned that negotiations are not tests of sentiment, but rather an opportunity to systematically define the path to success," said Umber Ahmad, a former Goldman Sachs vice president profiled in a documentary about up-and-coming women in Wall Street finance. She added that the tools of *Getting More* are particularly important in showing many women how to be more dispassionate.

Here are some of the things that cause emotions in a negotiation. When the other party:

- Misrepresents: lies about themselves or the facts, makes false accusations.
- Breaks commitments/agreements or won't make them.
- Devalues the other party by insulting, threatening, being hostile, causing loss of face, going over their head, questioning their authority or credibility, blaming them.
- Is greedy or self-centered: makes excessively high demands, oversteps

their authority, doesn't reciprocate goodwill (doesn't thank you for a gift).
- Is undisciplined: doesn't adequately prepare, is inconsistent, loses control, personally or professionally.
- Dashes the other person's expectations: fails to show up for a meeting, treats others unfairly.

When people get emotional, here is what happens. Instead of focusing on goals, interests, and needs and effectively communicating, emotional people focus on punishment, revenge, and retaliation. Deals fail, goals are unmet, judgment is clouded, and people don't meet their needs. Emotion destroys negotiations and limits creativity. Focus is lost. Decision-making is poor. Retaliation often occurs.

Emotion in negotiation has received increasing attention since 1990. Researchers, teachers, and practitioners began to realize one had to address the emotional side of people, not just the rational side. The results of this attention have generally been mixed and not always helpful.

For example, there has been a trend suggesting that it is okay to feign emotions, such as anger and approval, to get others to do what you want. This is, of course, dishonest, and usually manipulative. The tactic aims to get other people emotional so they are scared or flattered into doing something they would not otherwise do, and which too often is not in their best interests.

The tactics are called things like "strategic emotion," "false-positive feedback," "a display of fury to extract a concession," "on-demand emotional expression," "tactical emotions," "impression management," "strategically angry," and "emotion manipulation." These are variations of "good cop, bad cop"; they destabilize situations and make them unpredictable; they often aim to get the other party to make a mistake, such as disclosing information that can be used against them.

That's why people hurl insults or wave obnoxious banners at sports figures during games. The object is to get the players angry and emotional so they get distracted and lose focus on their goals: that is, to execute effectively to win the game.

Most of the advice on using emotion to manipulate a negotiation doesn't consider the long-term effects on the relationship, which usually ends when the manipulator is found out. Credibility and trust take a big hit. If you find the other party displaying false emotions just to get you to act in a certain way, I suggest that you *never* deal with them again if you can help it.

View anyone who feigns emotion to get something out of you as a cheat. In the most extreme case, terrorist leaders convince some of their followers to blow themselves up to satisfy an emotional need for revenge or a heavenly reward. In whose interest is this? Not bystanders who become victims, and not the person blowing up himself or herself. The beneficiaries are terrorist leaders, who get political aggrandizement without physical harm. They get additional funding from others who are equally emotional.

Some people point out times when they have used emotions as negotiation tools and they have worked. The problem is that they are risky and unpredictable in terms of the results, and cynical and untrustworthy in terms of attitude. They destroy relationships. Demands to "take it or leave it" increase rejection rates, studies show. People perceive them as unfair and will sometimes reject good deals out of spite. Only half as many offers are accepted when negative emotion is used.

One can see this in business. A customer of Richard Holland threatened to switch vendors because of a price increase. Yet even after the increase, Richard's prices were less than those of other vendors. "When the other person is mad at you, they may do things just for spite," said Richard, an industrial account manager.

So Richard decided he would be much more empathetic to customers about their rising costs. He asked customers how his company could add more value in exchange for a price increase. It worked. Empathy and consultation were emotional payments.

Let's look more specifically at what the introduction of emotions often does to a negotiation. First, they destabilize the situation. You are much less sure of how the other person is going to react. The outcome is less predictable when the parties are emotional.

Emotion reduces people's information-processing ability. That means they don't take the time to explore creative options. They don't look at all the facts and circumstances. They don't look for ways to expand the pie. As a result, they don't get more. In fact, emotional people, studies show, care less about getting a deal that meets their needs than about hurting the other party.

It is true that positive emotions have been shown to increase creativity and the likelihood of reaching an agreement. But such negotiations are often conducted at a pitch and with a fervor that are risky. You've seen an ebullient group suddenly turn on someone or something that had previously been the object of their affections. That kind of instability should worry you. Try to conduct negotiations that are calm and stable. Warm feelings, perhaps, but laced with solid judgment. The emotional temperature needs to come down if you want to meet your goals and solve thorny problems.

What about the strategy of good cop, bad cop? This is a favorite tool that participants in negotiation courses say they use. The police use this tactic to try to destabilize a suspect by causing emotion. They hope the suspect will make a mistake and make an admission (against their goals and interests). So, yes, anger and emotion work in a situation where you want to try to harm the other party and get them to make a mistake. Unless that's your goal, you probably don't want to use anger as a negotiation tool.

Another problem with using emotion on purpose is that the more you use it, the less effective it becomes. If you raise your voice or shout once a year, it can be very effective. If you do it once a month, you become known as "the screamer," and you lose credibility. This applies to walking out of negotiations as well.

A tone change is fine once in a while. If you are normally quiet, every once in a while you might raise your voice. If you are normally a pretty loud person, once in a while you might be especially quiet or soft-spoken. But such tactics must be well-thought-out and measured.

Negotiations are more effective when they are stable and predictable.

EMOTION-PRODUCING TACTICS

To listen to many negotiations, one would think that threats are the method of choice. But threats are one of the *least effective* negotiation strategies. Threats cause people to get emotional, making them less able to see things clearly enough to do what you want them to do. Since emotion makes people less resistant to self-harm, your target will likely not care as much about your threats as you would like them to.

Studies show that people who threaten are only half as likely to reach an agreement as those who don't, and with the very same facts. So why do people threaten? Lack of negotiating experience or skill. When people try to force you to do things, you lose face. In some cultures, loss of face has driven people to acts of violence, including murder and suicide. Losing face, in turn, is tied to self-esteem and self-worth. So threats cause loss of face: the result is resistance.

Related to threats is another common but ineffective negotiation tactic, "take it or leave it." It causes people to get upset and fewer agreements result.

Here is a study on the "take it or leave it" approach. Researchers told a subject that he or she would be given $10 to divide with another person—but the other person had to agree to the split. If the other person rejected the offer, both parties would get nothing.

When the other person was offered $1—meaning the offerer would get $9—75 percent of the other people *rejected* the offer. Now, this makes no rational sense. It is better to go home with $1 than with nothing. But the unfairness of someone else getting most of the amount available caused them to act emotionally, against their goals and interests.

On the other hand, 95 percent of the other people agreed to the split when it was done 50/50. But when $3 was offered, two-thirds of the other people rejected that.

As such, you must take irrationality into account when deciding how to approach others. If the other person is likely to act irrationally, you need to offer emotional payments. You need to make adjustments.

One example of adjustment is "collaborative threats." In a normal threat, you tell the other person: "If you don't lower your price, I'm going to someone else!" Often the other person will become emotional and respond with something like, "Go jump in the lake!" Although it would be better for them to lower their prices and keep you as a customer, you made them react emotionally by flexing your power with them.

Another way to frame this is to say, "I really like you guys, I've been buying from you for some time. But now some of your competitors are offering us more value. We'd like to stay with you. What should we do?" The same threat to leave is inherent, but you are asking for their help. How do we stay in business together? It is framed in the context of a relationship. And it opens the way for more creative solutions.

By reframing and, essentially, *giving* them the problem, you have reduced the emotion and improved the result. You've made the situation a common problem to solve together. You have valued them more.

CONTROLLING EMOTION

So how do you control emotion in a negotiation? There are two kinds of people to think about. You and others. I've talked a bit about the other person's emotion already; we'll pick that up again shortly. But let's address your own emotions.

If you are emotional, you are no good to anyone in a negotiation. If you start to get emotional, stop! Take a break; calm yourself down. If you can't, perhaps you are not the right negotiator, at least not at that time. Take a longer break until you can calm down, or enlist the help of someone else. If you try to negotiate when you are upset, angry, or otherwise emotional, you will lose sight of your goals and needs. And you will make yourself the issue.

You can try to take the issue away by saying, "I'm feeling emotional now, so I might not mean everything I say." This works best if they then empathize. Exquisite preparation is a defense against losing sight of your goals. If you start to get upset, reviewing the materials you have prepared may calm you down.

Lower your expectations. If you come into a negotiation thinking that the other side will be difficult, unfair, rude, or trying to cheat you, you won't be likely to have dashed expectations—and you won't be as emotional. When you lower your expectations of what will take place in a negotiation, you will be rarely disappointed—and you might be pleasantly surprised. Getting yourself psychologically prepared is important.

You might feel, "Hey, I shouldn't have to do things like that." Okay, maybe not. But we live in the real world, not in the "should" world. If you follow these tools, you will gradually make your negotiations better. Other people will behave better. The results will be better. Slowly, the world will become better. The human race has lived a certain way for thousands of years. Don't expect it to change overnight.

Remember that great expression "Revenge is a dish best served cold." When everyone else around you is angry, it doesn't help to join them. Don't let your emotions match theirs. A colleague once said, "Just because you're in an insane asylum doesn't mean you want crazy doctors."

Say to yourself, "They're trying to get me to take the focus off my goals." Don't let others manipulate you into getting less, or getting nothing at all. Getting mad at someone destroys your goals. It's like saying, "I'm mad at you, I think I'll kill myself." Don't let the other side cause you to hurt yourself.

I once saw two attorneys with their clients outside a courthouse. One attorney was screaming at the other attorney and his client in an endless tirade. The attorney on the receiving end just stood there with his client, silently listening.

Finally, the attorney who bore the brunt of this looked at the other attorney and said in a light voice, "Good try!" It completely destroyed the effectiveness of the outburst.

So you *can* control your own emotions. Dealing with the emotions of others can be trickier.

DEALING WITH EMOTIONAL SITUATIONS AND EMOTIONAL PEOPLE

- Recognize when others are acting against their goals/needs.
- Try to understand the other party's emotions and perceptions.
- Find the cause of their emotion and their needs and goals.
- Consider whether your negotiating style is contributing to the situation.
- Make emotional payments: concessions, apologies, empathy.
- Try to create trust.
- Avoid extreme statements—they just produce more emotion.
- Use third parties and their constituents to help you.
- Apply their standards.
- Correct erroneous facts.

The first step toward dealing effectively with the emotions of others is to recognize when they are being emotional. It is not always obvious. Brits and Swedes, for example, are culturally less emotive than Brazilians and Italians, but that doesn't mean any individual in those cultures is less or more emotional. Some people are calm outside and seething inside, and vice versa.

The key is whether the other person is acting against his or her own interests, needs, and goals. You have probably watched people do exactly the opposite of what benefits them. You ask yourself, "What's wrong with them? Can't they see this won't help them?"

They can't. They have lost focus on their goals and needs. They are being emotional. They aren't listening clearly.

To persuade them, you have to begin by increasing their ability to listen. That means you have to calm them down. You have to become their emotional confidante. Try to understand their emotions. What gave rise to them? What can you do to calm them down?

You've had heated discussions with your friends, partner, or spouse. The more you tell them to calm down, the madder they get. That's because telling them to calm down devalues the legitimacy of their emotions. And when people feel devalued, they become *more* emotional.

So empathize with them. Try to understand the cause of their emotion. It doesn't work to simply tell them, "Be rational" or "Be logical." If they wanted to be logical or rational, they would be. They want to be emotional. So commiserate with them. This will usually calm them down enough to have a conversation together. The more you listen to them, the calmer they will be.

You have to figure out what kind of emotional payment they need. It's an oft-repeated request from women to men: "I don't want you to solve my problems; I just want you to listen to them." For many women, being listened to is the emotional payment. Anything that values their emotions through some demonstration by you is an emotional payment. It could be a compliment. It could be a touch on the arm. It could be just listening. It's different for every person. So first you have to try to understand the pictures in their heads.

I first discovered the impact of emotional payments about twenty years ago when I was involved with the Harvard Negotiation Project. Both there and elsewhere in the negotiation industry, people were talking about negotiation strategies for "reasonable people," "rational actors," and "wise negotiators." All around me, however, I saw evidence of irrationality driving decisions: from children to businesses to governments.

Students, professionals, and others kept asking how to deal with irrational and emotional people. I then realized that almost all the studies were dealing only with the world as it should be, not as it was. So I started developing tools and strategies to deal with emotions.

Shortly after that, I mediated a high-society divorce in New York. The husband had hired male lawyers to whom he was paying a lot of money. The wife had hired female lawyers, who were working pro bono. The assets, which had been large initially, had been whittled down through legal fees and losses in the stock market.

When I was asked to assist, the couple still had about $400,000 left in assets. The husband was basically ready to just give his wife all the money as the divorce settlement. The divorce was a continuous drain on his business. But she refused to take it. She was so angry at him that she wanted to rake him over the coals in court, embarrassing him and leaving everyone with nothing.

She was clearly emotional. She was acting against her own interests. So I thought about what I could give her that she would recognize as an emotional payment so she would take the money.

One day, as I sat with her, I said, "You know, if you take this settlement offer, it will be all the money he has." She thought about this for a moment and said, "Do you mean to say, if I take this settlement offer, it will be all the money that son of a bitch has?" I said, "Yes." She said, "I'll take it." She wanted, in her own mind, for him to feel pain—and this was an emotional payment for her.

To find out what the other party might consider to be an emotional payment, you need to focus hard on the pictures in their heads. How do they view the world? What are their needs and perceptions? How would they like to hear things framed? Do they need concessions? If so, what kind? A simple apology? An elaborate apology? No apology, but flowers? In other words, emotional payments are very specific to the person and the situation.

Spencer Romney, a Penn Law student, was on the phone with his wife, Lisa, a dentist. She was trying to tell him about her stressful day. "I was with friends, and distracted," he said. "She got mad, hung up, and refused to answer my calls." When he got home, he immediately started to give her a foot massage, without saying anything. Then he asked her about her day. Crisis solved.

Only when you get the other person to start listening can you do things that will begin to bring them back. What standards have they used before—standards they might now accept? Using standards first would be too much for them to handle in their emotional state. First, they have to be ready to handle possible contradictions. And you must *avoid* extreme statements, including threats. They are emotion-producers.

One idea is to get them talking about themselves, so they can vent or express their feelings. Try guessing at things that may be bothering them. They will often tell you that you are right or wrong. Ask questions. The mere act of considering a question takes energy from their emotional fit, as with the child at the start of this chapter. Articulating what you think is the other party's pain, even if you are wrong, will have a calming effect even as they look inward to see if you are right.

Jim O'Toole and his wife, Anne, were having an argument about how little time he was spending with her and their two children. He had a full-time job and was pursuing an advanced degree. "For once I decided to take the time and just let her tell me her side of things completely," he said. As she talked, she became calmer. So did he.

Clearly, they all wanted to spend more time together. "Then I reviewed my current obligations and how it would provide a long-term benefit to all of us," said Jim, now president of a paper distribution company in Chicago. "She was much more understanding than in the past." With their argument over, they had begun a new communication process for the future.

Doctors are beginning to see that apologizing to patients for mistakes, or for less-than-perfect care, goes a long way toward avoiding lawsuits. Traditionally, attorneys and insurers have seen any apology as an admission of liability. This is not necessarily true. Things can happen that only with hindsight seem wrong. And even if there is liability, you can be sure that if medical professionals empathize, the patient or the patient's kin will be less out for blood.

In Riyadh, Saudi Arabia, Ziyad Al Saleh was in the process of buying a food industry company. The owner was reluctant to sell, even though he knew the offer was a good one. "He was fearful of losing control, and thus emotional," Ziyad said. The solution was to first talk with the owner about his fears. They also offered him a key position in the firm, with some job security. Third, they gave him a vision of global expansion. Finally, they pledged extra compensation if he could help turn the vision into reality.

The owner saw that with additional people, he would be able to accomplish something he had been unable to accomplish on his own, due to his lack of size and resources. So he agreed to the deal.

Mark Robinson, a student at the University of Southern California Business School, drove to a jewelry store with his wife to pick up her engagement ring, which had been repaired. The store was in a fairly tough area of Los Angeles. It was hard to find a parking space relatively close to the store. Mark saw someone walking toward a parked car. So Mark pulled ahead of the car, patiently waiting for the parked car to leave.

After what seemed like an eternity, the parked car left, pulling around Mark waiting to back in. As he started to back in, another car came up from behind and pulled into the space. Inside were two tough-looking guys. Mark decided to negotiate the situation. His wife was horrified. "My wife wanted me to drop the matter," Mark said. "I, on the other hand, focused on the other driver. Maybe he didn't see me. Maybe this was negotiable."

Calmly, Mark got out of the car and walked over to the two tough guys. He went to the driver's-side window, smiled, and waved. "Hi!" he said. After a few seconds, the driver rolled down the window. "Yeah?" he said.

"I spoke to him like we were acquaintances," Mark said. "I said, 'You probably didn't see me patiently waiting for the space. But I've been here for a long time. Would you allow me to have the space?'" He gestured to his wife. "I was hoping not to look bad in front of my wife," he said. "It's up to you. But I appreciate anything you might do."

The two guys looked at each other and then at this guy. Clearly, he wasn't a threat. He accused them of nothing. Moreover, he gave them a chance to be magnanimous.

"Okay man, we're cool with that," one said. Mark shook the driver's hand. The driver then started his car and pulled away. Surprised? Well, Mark had given them a big emotional payment. One that the guys could tell their friends about—how they helped some guy not look bad in front of his wife. "My wife was in shock for some time about the power of this process," Mark told me afterward.

If this feels uncomfortable or dangerous to you, then don't do it. But the student presented his argument in a way that carried very little risk. He tapped into the other guys' psyches. So if you feel this tool won't work in a given situation, ask yourself if you are using the right tools.

A student at Wharton was held up at gunpoint in West Philadelphia. He gave the robber his wallet, saying, "I'm probably not even worth wasting your gun on, it will make too much noise. You're the boss." In the end, the robber gave the student back his driver's license and student I.D. card. They were not usable to the robber, and the student said, "We all know those SOBs in the bureaucracy give everyone a hard time over this stuff." (Common enemies.) Why did he do that? When do you think the last time was that the robber heard anyone say to him, "You're the boss"?

One use of emotion in a negotiation is to bond people together. People who have been through an emotional ordeal tend to bond together. This is true if the experience is a negative one, such as a war, an accident, or danger, or a positive one, such as winning a big sporting event. While it can be a basis for team-building, used wrongly, it can leave lasting scars. It is like playing with fire.

What about when you have tried to get through to the other person and are unable to? Think about third parties. Who might the other person or party trust enough to listen to, if not you? Do they have friends, colleagues, or constituencies who might be able to calm them down? Are there third parties you can blame, in an attempt to unite the other person around common enemies?

If all else fails, are there more rational people on the other side you can appeal to? For example, if you are dealing with a company or a team, rather than an individual, it may be easier to find more cooperative people. Going over the head of the emotional person carries with it the risk that he or she will retaliate, and that you will destroy the relationship. In personal situations, this is not advisable. In business situations, it sometimes is necessary.

If you have an emotional, extreme person on the other side in a business negotiation, ask every other member of the other team if they agree with each and every word, in tone and substance, that was just said. Make your tone one of trying to understand the situation. It is not accusatory. If there is any hesitation by the other side, ask for a break. (*Telling* the other side to take a break is too aggressive.) During the break, hopefully members of the other side will calm down the emotional person, or exclude them from the negotiation.

You also need to recognize when someone is using emotion to manipulate a negotiation, and do something about it. I tend to mistrust general praise. "You're a great teacher," in my view, is just a throwaway line. "In what way?" I want to know. "What specifically did you learn that's valuable?" I want to see if they are just jockeying for position (or a good grade). Are they trying to manipulate me, or sincerely expressing appreciation?

If you see the other side playing good cop, bad cop on you, ask them directly, "Are you playing good cop, bad cop with me?" Call out the bad behavior. Or you might want to say, "I see that your approaches to me are very different. One is nice, the other is not. Do you want to take a break and get your approaches straight?" This also shows why manipulation is risky. Good negotiators will call it out and the manipulator will lose credibility.

Deadlines and time limits are often used to hurt the other party emotionally. With deadlines looming, people are less able to process information, less interested in expanding the pie, and less creative. If someone imposes a deadline on you, ask if they would like such negative things to occur. Better yet, find out any deadlines in the beginning, so you can manage your time and not settle for a lesser deal. Having enough time to be creative is essentially having enough time to *get more.*

Some negotiators suggest that you start with an extreme demand, to leave room for concessions. When you make an extreme demand, the other party will almost always say no. The thinking is that you can then make a more modest demand, which seems more reasonable and acceptable.

This is just another manipulative tactic. If someone tries that on you, say something like, "So how come you changed your first offer so much?" Put them in the hot seat for trying to manipulate you. The net result of such tactics, though, is that trust and the chance of a deal both go down. Be careful of being too aggressive in naming bad behavior, as noted earlier.

Then there are food and gifts—cookies, trinkets, or more. Lunch at a fancy restaurant. This is supposed to soften up the other side and make them indebted to you. To break the ice in a negotiation, it's fine. In trading items, it's fine. But you have to evaluate the source. If the other side is being genuine, okay. But make sure they don't later try to exact a concession in return.

Ask yourself if their actions seem genuine. If you think they are feigning an emotion, ask yourself what kind of relationship you're going to have if they are acting this way.

Such manipulative tactics are often used by hard bargainers.

I went to Springdale, Arkansas, for negotiations with Tyson Foods, the giant food company, on behalf of a Russian client who owed Tyson millions of dollars. They did not try to kill me with kindness. Quite the contrary; under the guise of showing me around, they gave me a tour of the chicken-processing plant.

I heard one of the executives whisper to another before the tour, "Should we show him the kill room?" The other said, "Absolutely."

I'll spare you the details of the tour of this slaughterhouse. Afterward, they took me into a conference room in the slaughterhouse where they had a lunch of—you guessed it—Southern fried chicken. I made sure that I had steeled myself and expressed delight at the offering. I also made sure I ate more Southern fried chicken than anyone else in the room.

These kinds of manipulative tactics are meant to take advantage of unskilled negotiators. They don't work on skilled negotiators. Displays of rudeness, fake emotion, anger, and other bad behavior such as violence *can* be gotten away with if the negotiator has a vast amount of power over the other party. Remember, not all negotiations are solvable.

To deal with such emotional violence, first try to use the tools in this book: find their needs, use standards, try for a relationship, use third parties that could influence them, make emotional payments, understand their perceptions, and so forth. They may not be conscious of their behavior and may be willing to listen to you. Or they may be Machiavellian and not care.

If none of these work, try to remove yourself from the situation. Don't be a punching bag. They are trying to hurt you and don't care about you. Manipulative tactics run the risk of creating instability. When the person being manipulated comes to their senses—and I say *when,* not if—they will know they've been manipulated. These kinds of short-term strategies eventually backfire.

Even if the other side is being extreme, your remaining calm will give you more options. With a little humor, sometimes, and questions, you can turn an entire crowd around.

Stuart Meloy, a former student, sent me this anecdote. "A couple of years ago," he said, "one of my wife's horses ran away and came to rest on the property of the most disagreeable redneck in our county, in the middle of his birthday party. When I showed up, he came out into the yard, drunk, demanding payment for damage that the horse had allegedly caused to his truck.

"Very quickly we were surrounded by his family and friends, most of whom had been drinking. Frankly, I was concerned for my safety. But then I thought of your teaching and calmly asked him to show me the damage. He pointed to a dent on the driver's side. The man is a logger and his truck was covered with dings and dents.

"So I just started asking questions without any judgment or emotion," Stuart recalled. "Are you sure it was this dent, and not that one? What about these other dents? If the horse caused this dent, how did it get rusty so fast? By the time I was done the crowd was roaring with laughter and he retreated. We got the horse back without further incident." He added, "I use these tools constantly."

PERSONAL STYLE

A pleasing style can be helpful in opening communication and, essentially, not making emotion the issue. We generally like to give things to people we find pleasing. It is very useful to think about the impact and use of one's personal style in negotiations.

The importance of style is in how it affects the other party's willingness to meet your goals. One could imagine a situation where a nice person on your side might resonate with a sweet person on the other side. Or vice versa. The weakest member of your corporate team might be the best negotiator. Their style could give the other side a sense of comfort and confidence. So the real question to ask is, "Which person on my team is the most likely to get the other party to meet my goals?"

Studies have shown that the more powerful people are in a negotiation, the less attention they pay to the other side's needs. And that means the less successful they will be at expanding the pie. It's ironic. Most companies pick the most senior person to negotiate, when some of the most junior members might be better.

I cofounded a medical services company in Florida. We raised millions of dollars, mostly from investors from the Deep South. I knew more about negotiation than anyone else in the company. But I did no negotiation with the investors. All of us knew that no matter what I said, the potential investors would think of me as that aggressive guy from New York.

I don't like this kind of stereotyping, but I have to realize that it exists. And this book is about reality, not pipe dreams. So others in my company, also from the Deep South, did the actual negotiation. They consulted with me offline for tools and strategies, but I was not present at the negotiations.

Of course I would have loved the chance to change the investors' perceptions of me and New Yorkers. But the negotiation was not about me. Our goal was to raise the money (and we did).

One way of improving as a negotiator is to find out how you come across to others. All sorts of diagnostic tools are available to assess one's style. The more I have used them, the less helpful I think they are. How do you reduce a person's entire personality to a score or a number? People have different styles, and act differently with different people and in different situations.

Moreover, people can change their style based on the needs of the situation. However assertive you might be otherwise, you might be a sweetheart when confronted by a man with a gun.

But we can still draw some conclusions about personal style. I ask students to assess themselves and others qualitatively in various situations. This gives us enough information to make recommendations on what to do differently.

Some people are better in a crisis than others. Some people love pressure; others hate it, or freeze in the face of it. Some people's first reaction is to accommodate others. Some people run from conflict; some run toward it.

I try not to make such personal differences more than they are, since it's only one part of a negotiation. But it can be helpful. And I've seen people change as they learned better negotiation skills: for example, screaming less and becoming less emotional. This doesn't make them different people; they are just able to make better use of their skills.

One executive's self-assessment showed he was noncollaborative and confrontational. When he saw this result, he stood up in front of the class and started screaming at me. "What are you talking about! I'm a collaborative guy!" Everyone laughed. His behavior undercut his beliefs. I wish he'd taken it as constructive criticism.

A personal assessment is not meant to make you feel bad. It is meant to give you more information about yourself to enable you to become a better negotiator. The more information you have about yourself, the more conscious you will be of the process, and the more you will be able to make effective changes to meet your goals.

I once used a style-assessment tool for about 160 people at the headquarters of Johnson & Johnson, one of the world's largest pharmaceutical firms. One person stood out as highly confrontational. We released the assessments to everyone, by name. This particular person happened to be a highly placed counsel of the company. He called me up and started sharply criticizing me, saying that I ruined his reputation at the company, and that the results comprised confidential information.

So I checked back with my sponsors at the company. They had given me permission to release everyone's name and results so the participants could compare notes and help one another improve. When I mentioned what happened with this attorney, they chuckled. "We knew he'd be like that," one of them said. "Now he's outed. It will be good for him to see this." The sponsors actually wanted the attorney to see that he was too aggressive with others in the company.

An American woman won custody of her two young children in a divorce. Her husband, a Brazilian, promptly kidnapped the children and took them to Brazil. She didn't have the funds or skills to navigate the Brazilian legal system. She wanted to call him and work it out. I asked her to assess her negotiation style, and his. She thought she was very accommodating and he was very aggressive.

I advised her not to deal directly with him; he would eat her for lunch. I suggested that she deal with his family, whom she knew well, to get her children back. The standards should be: (a) a young child should be with its mother, (b) laws should be respected, and (c) kidnapping is bad. His family agreed, and prevailed upon him as a group to send the children back to the United States. So knowing the *relative* styles of individuals can be a key tool in deciding how to conduct a difficult negotiation.

It's important to understand corporate style (to the extent that there is one) as well as individual style. In 1997, I did a negotiation workshop for second- and third-tier management at the Seoul, South Korea, headquarters of Daewoo. Daewoo was then one of the world's premier companies, a $60-billion-plus conglomerate that made everything from cars to ships to appliances.

The Daewoo managers I taught, almost to a person, were extraordinarily accommodating and routinely gave away the store. I mentioned to Daewoo's chairman, Kim Woo Choong, that the fire in the belly that he and others had in founding and growing the company did not seem to have been transferred to those he expected to follow him in leading the company. And, indeed, the managers I taught were saying that the Vietnamese and Brazilians were eating them for breakfast, competitively.

Chairman Kim was alarmed at this. He started a strategic program to increase his management's negotiation skills, training them to be more assertive and better at meeting goals. But it was too late. Daewoo essentially went bankrupt. Companies are run by people, and if its people aren't skilled in negotiation, the company is in trouble.

Even with cultural norms, in a negotiation, one needs to address individuals. The norms are a good starting point, as in "Are these attorneys as aggressive as the reputation of their firm or profession?" But that is a question, not an answer. You still have to focus on the individual. For Daewoo, as it so happened, there was very little difference among the individuals—an unusual situation.

I have found, by the way, only small differences in the style of men and women in corporate America. We have statistics on this, despite the popular books that emphasize major gender differences. Corporate women tend to be a little more collaborative and corporate men tend to be a little more avoiding.

I have also found from both studies and experience that people who are highly confrontational reach fewer deals, unless their counterparts are highly accommodating (in which case the one who gives in will often be resentful sooner or later).

Companies can effectively choose a strong negotiating team based on the styles of the people on the team. Aggressive, goal-directed people are good closers. They will make sure the deal gets done. Accommodating people, who are often much better listeners, are good openers. They help connect with the other party. Compromisers are good in an emergency: they can make decisions quickly. Collaborators make good facilitators: they consider the needs of all parties. As you look at the descriptions below, think of yours and others as either low, medium, or high.

What are the common negotiation styles?

Assertive

The more aggressive you are, the more you try to meet your own goals at the expense of others'—and you will get *less* in a negotiation. That's because other people sense that you don't care about them. "Tough" people fall into this category. If you fight every battle, you fit this profile. Back off a bit: the key is to meet your goals while still considering and fulfilling the needs of the other party. Listen to the other party. Acknowledge their value.

Collaborative

Highly collaborative people tend to be more creative, look for joint gains, and find ways to expand the pie. They look for items of unequal value to trade. They solve problems. Every problem is seen as a potential opportunity. But they need to be incremental with people whose trustworthiness is uncertain.

Compromising

Compromisers get less. They settle. They tend to pursue speed instead of quality. They "split the difference." Busy people are often compromisers. They take the first reasonable option and move on. But they sacrifice their ability to get more.

This is not to say that one should never compromise. After you have used every negotiation tool in this book, bridged every gap you can, used every intangible available, and are still a little apart, you can split the difference and feel you've done the best you can do. But it is a last resort for good negotiators.

Avoiding

High avoiders generally meet no one's goals. They don't engage, they avoid conflict, and as a result, they not only don't get more: they often get nothing. There are extreme situations in which one actively *wants* to avoid—like not talking back to a crazy guy with a gun. But in everyday life, you mostly want to engage others. It will get you more. Try starting to engage by being incremental. Ask for something more modest. Instead of asking for a discount, for example, ask if the store ever has any sales.

Accommodating

Accommodators tend to be great listeners. But they can go overboard in trying to reach a deal at the expense of their own goals. Focus on standards of fairness, getting commitments, and using third parties. By contrast, if you don't accommodate much, you probably don't listen well. You need to collect more of the basic information necessary to be effective in negotiations. If you don't collect enough information about the other person and the situation, you will have a much harder time meeting your goals. Ask more questions before making statements. Try not to interrupt the other person. It is not hard to fix this.

The more you learn and practice the tools of *Getting More,* the less extreme you will be in terms of any of these traits. As always the key questions are paramount: What are my goals? Who is the other person? What will it take to persuade them? You can be as nice as pie while being very persuasive. Don't let your negotiation style get in the way.

ETHICS

Ethics—or, I should say, the perception of a lack of ethics—is an emotional topic. Like so much of negotiation, ethics is usually situational. There are some absolutes, but far fewer than you might think.

Let's define ethics: it's a system of behavior in which people are supposed to treat one another fairly. "Fair" includes judgment, but clearly it includes not hurting people on purpose, except as part of a socially agreed process of justice. It also includes acting in a way that people think is fair.

"Ethics" varies depending on culture and perception. While the law is a guide, most ethical issues don't reach the level of legal intervention. The problem with ethics is that when people think others are unfair, they become emotional. Their ability to process information declines. So they don't often see that the situation is more complicated and nuanced than they originally thought. In such cases, perfectly good deals often fail. What I am proposing in *Getting More* is that you ask more questions before simply assuming that something is unethical.

The Israeli economic consul in Kazakhstan was complaining about the lack of ethics in Kazakhstan. As an example, he said the Israeli government canceled a $50 million investment in a factory in the early 1990s because a dozen local inspectors wanted bribes. "We don't pay bribes," he said emphatically.

Fifty million dollars was a huge amount for a newly independent, developing country such as Kazakhstan, on the eastern end of the former Soviet

Union. "Tell me about the inspectors," I said. "Were they decision-makers? Were they in the government ministry in charge of approving the plant?"

He said the inspectors were not in the government ministry approving the plant. But, he said, they were in a sister ministry with influence over the deciding ministry.

They were asking for "$600" in bribes over a six-month period. This was one ten-thousandth of one percent of the project. The consul said it was the principle.

I then asked him how much each inspector earned monthly. "$12," he said. So the twelve inspectors each wanted another $8 a month for six months: a hefty two-thirds increase in their salary. Finally, I asked the consul to describe the lifestyle of these inspectors: well-off, middle-class, poor, etc. He said the inspectors and their families barely had enough to eat.

I reminded him that in New York and other cities, government employees are sometimes hired part-time by private enterprise to serve as "expeditors" to help a company navigate the bureaucracy in getting a project approved. It is all disclosed, legal, and especially popular in countries trying to attract foreign investment.

"So," I said to him, "do you know why the inspectors asked for bribes? Because they didn't know how to ask for a job."

The Israeli economic consul was embarrassed. He said that he and his government had made a mistake. It is an easy mistake to make. It's back to that term "fundamental attribution error." We all think that everyone else has the same thought processes, set of experiences, and perceptual framework that we do.

So here it didn't have to be an ethical issue. And everyone would have been helped by the reduction in reflex emotion.

A bribe is typically defined as payment to someone, usually a government employee, to do something they are already being paid to do by the government. (Extortion, its sister behavior, is threatening to harm someone unless they pay you.) You might say a bribe is a bribe, no matter how small. But that isn't really true, is it? If you take someone out to lunch, or give them a small trinket, that's not considered a bribe. Sometimes the key is in thinking more creatively—that is, finding better options for all parties.

How about one closer to home. A job interviewer asks if you have other offers and you don't. Fearful of not getting an offer, many people want to lie. Don't think of it that way. First, the other person is essentially trying to find out how the market has valued you. If other offers are possible, you might say, "I have other opportunities that I am actively pursuing." It is true, and it doesn't force you to lie.

Let's say the question is more specific. "Did you get a job offer at your internship with Morgan Stanley last summer?" If you did not, then you needed to prepare for that question long before the interview with another firm. What is the other person likely to perceive? That if you didn't get the job offer, there may be something wrong with you since Morgan Stanley is perceived to have good judgment.

Given those possible perceptions, you need to think in terms of framing. Was the reason you didn't get an offer at Morgan Stanley that you weren't good enough? Was there some other reason? For example, perhaps the fit wasn't right. Then you should talk about how the new firm's fit is better. In other words, talk about it in a way that is true and ethical. Or suggest that the present firm should use its own judgment, not that of another firm.

What we are trying to do is improve your negotiating situation. We are trying incrementally to move people in a direction where the cost is less, the risk is less, and the ethical insult is minimal. We are not going to change thousands of years of human nature or cultural norms overnight. In the real world—where you and I live—any improvement is a plus.

DOES MOMMY LOVE YOU? A REPRISE

Today, more than a dozen years later, Lisa Stephens and Aubree still talk about the extraordinary experience they had in the kitchen that day, profiled at the beginning of this chapter. "We see the small scar on Aubree's forehead and remember the twelve stitches and how we handled it together," said Lisa, now a senior manager for a major accounting firm in Washington, D.C. "Not a day goes by that we don't use the negotiation tools to improve our lives."

Lest you still think the anecdotes in this chapter are exceptions: I had an executive in one of my programs at Wharton, Craig Silverman, a financial advisor on Long Island. Craig went to a local medical laboratory one day for a routine blood test. In the next room was a young girl, about five years old, screaming at the top of her lungs "as if she was being tortured," Craig said. She was supposed to get a blood test, too, but she wouldn't let the nurse stick her arm with the needle. Her mother, soon joined by

Craig's nurse, was holding the girl down, while a second nurse was trying to stick the needle into the girl's arm. It was a nightmare of a scene.

Craig, remembering the story of Lisa and Aubree, decided to be of assistance. He went to the girl's room and asked her mother's permission to talk with her, which he received. "Look at me," he empathetically said to the girl. The others wondered what was up. The girl looked at him. "Do you think your mommy loves you?" Craig asked, kindly. "Yes," the girl said. "Do you think your mommy would do anything to hurt you?" Craig asked. "No," the girl said.

Craig went through the entire litany, with some variations, of what I described at the beginning of this chapter, including "Don't you want to get better?" and then, when the girl had calmed down a bit, "The doctor and Mommy can't make you better unless they do this test." Within two minutes, he said, the young girl calmed down and was ready for the needle.

"Her mother and the nurses looked at me like I was some sort of magician," Craig said. "Where did you learn *that*?" they asked. I'm happy to say he referred them to this book.

7

Putting It All Together:
THE PROBLEM-SOLVING MODEL

Eric Holck, an attorney at Google headquarters in Mountain View, California, said the sales and legal teams were not seeing eye-to-eye. "There was disagreement over what we should offer, how much risk to take, whether to concede points, how the negotiation should be conducted," he said.

It's a common problem in many organizations. The legal department protects against risk. The sales department brings in the money. So the lawyers put in tough clauses to protect intellectual property and other company assets. The sales department wants the deal done fast for payment: work out the fine legal points later. Arguments ensue. Things take longer. Sometimes customers complain.

But Google, the world's foremost brand, is about solutions, so the participants in my workshops there embraced the idea of a problem-solving model. In one of the workshops I taught, Eric decided to play the role of a sales rep during a role reversal exercise. He used the process that will be described in this chapter. Eric found that the basic issues between legal and sales were: not enough trust; not enough communication; disagreement over standards; not as much joint preparation.

"I was shocked how quickly my allegiances changed," Eric said. Before the exercise, he could easily argue the lawyers' side. But quickly he found himself disputing the lawyers who were role-playing him. He said his ability to deal with sales—and appreciate their perspective—increased considerably after that. He and the other attorneys he's talked to now attempt to explain more to sales up front about why certain things might be needed. And the lawyers make greater efforts to loop sales in throughout the negotiation process, including collaborating on client calls.

"It doesn't mean you have to give in more," Eric said. "But the outcomes are generally better now."

The best negotiators are problem-solvers. They find new, creative, and better ways to solve both their problems and other people's problems. They turn problems into opportunities more often than most people do. And that is the key to negotiation success. Because you can't meet your goals unless you can identify and solve the specific problems standing in the way.

Over a twenty-year period, I have developed a comprehensive problem-solving model. Thousands of my students and clients have used it all over the world. It helps structure negotiations, and provides a checklist of tools. I have included it in this chapter and in a wallet card downloadable from my website, www.gettingmore.com. It organizes the twelve strategies and supporting tools, and puts everything together in one place to help you better meet your goals throughout your life.

The *Getting More* Model (I call it the Four Quadrant Model in my negotiation class) is essential to getting more. It provides an organizing principle in preparing effectively for negotiations. You can use it by yourself, or you can use it with a team of people.

"The Four Quadrant Model is the most powerful tool I have seen in negotiations," said Kenneth Odogwu, an executive who took one of my courses. "It is useful in all kinds of situations."

Kenneth said that he used it, for example, to solve a negotiation among Swiss, Israeli, and Nigerian firms over production and distribution of cosmetics in Africa. "It greatly assisted us in setting the stage for the negotiation, and providing a watertight solution that was acceptable to all."

First, here it is:

THE *GETTING MORE* MODEL
(aka the Four Quadrant Negotiation Model)

Quadrant I—Problems & Goals

1. **Goals:** short/long term.
2. **Problem(s):** in reaching your goals.
3. **Parties:** List. Decision-maker. Counterpart. Third parties.
4. **What if no deal?** Worst case?
5. **Preparation:** Time, relative preparation. Who has more information?

Quadrant II—Situation Analysis

6. **Needs/interests:** of both parties: rational, emotional, shared, conflicting, unequally valued.
7. **Perceptions:** Pictures in the head of each party? Role reversal, culture, conflicts, trust.
8. **Communication:** style, relationship?
9. **Standards:** theirs, norms.
10. **Reexamine goals:** Why say yes, why say no? For both parties.

Quadrant III—Options/Risk Reduction

11. **Brainstorm:** options to meet goals, needs. What to trade or link?
12. **Incremental:** steps to reduce risk.
13. **Third parties:** common enemies, influencers.
14. **Framing:** to create a vision, develop questions to ask.
15. **Alternatives:** to improve/effect deal if necessary.

Quadrant IV—Actions

16. **Best options/priorities.** Dealbreakers. Giveaways.
17. **Who presents:** How and to whom?
18. **Process:** Agenda, deadlines, time management.
19. **Commitments/incentives:** Especially for them.
20. **Next steps:** Who does what?

The Twelve Strategies on Which the Model Is Based:

Goals Are Paramount	Use Their Standards
It's About Them	Be Transparent/Ethical
Emotional Payments	Communicate & Frame
Each Situation Is Different	Find the Real Problem
Be Incremental	Embrace Differences
Trade Unequally Valued Items	Make a List

The twelve strategies are the building blocks for the *Getting More* Model. You will not need to use all the strategies and the entire Model in every negotiation. You'll look at the principles and figure out which items to use, based on your goals and the other party in that situation. For a big negotiation, you might go through each step laboriously.

It's best to outline each step. An oft-quoted maxim in Hollywood is: "If you can't write your idea on the back of my business card, you don't have a clear idea of what you want to say."

Let's go through the *Getting More* Model, step-by-step.

Steps 1 and 2 comprise about half of what is important: figuring out your goal(s) and figuring out the real problem in meeting your goal(s). The goal is what you want at the end of the negotiation that you don't have now. The problem is what is preventing you from getting to your goal.

Your first attempt at a goal might be, "I want to go to Chicago for a job interview." Your problem, or roadblock, might be, "Flights have been canceled due to snow." However, when you finish going through the Model, you might well realize that your *real*, underlying goal is not that you want to go to Chicago for a job interview. It is, "I want a job at X firm." And the real problem is, "They need more information on me to make a decision."

This will open up all sorts of other options that should enable you to find creative ways to deal with the fact that flights have been canceled. Maybe a phone interview would do, or a more detailed résumé, or other information you might prepare for them today. Are there other things that would show them you are a creative problem-solver?

A long time ago I was accepted to Columbia Journalism School, the best journalism school in the country and my longtime goal. The next day I was offered a job at *Newsday,* one of the best newspapers in the country. I called the dean of admissions at Columbia and asked what I should do. He said, "You idiot! You go to Columbia *to* get a job at *Newsday.*" I went to *Newsday.* As far as the dean was concerned, I had the wrong goal.

You can start your analysis with your goal. Or, if you don't know what your goal is, you can start with what you think the problem is. But you need to get to the root problem in each case. You do that by continuing to ask yourself "why" until you run out of answers.

For example, "My car is broken" is not, in and of itself, a problem if you've got two cars. So a better problem statement would be, "I have no way to get to work today." Or "I'm going to be late getting to work today because my only car is broken."

The reason to clearly state the root problem is that your goal in this specific instance is not to "fix my car." It is to get to work. Stating the problem in this way opens up other options: taking the bus, calling a taxi, calling a friend, taking the day off, and so forth. A clear statement of the problem will help you to come up with clear options of how to fix it.

Step 3 is to identify the key parties in the negotiation. You *must* identify the decision-maker, as well as the people with direct influence over the decision-maker. If you leave any required parties out, they may become upset because you didn't consult them. Are there hidden third parties who might become involved?

Step 4 helps you figure out what happens if you can't make a deal. Some people like to use the acronym BATNA, or Best Alternative To a Negotiated Agreement. But this term too often leads people to be too willing to walk away without achieving their goals, because they focus on the *best* option. If you want to review walkaway options, use WATNA, or *Worst* Alternative To a Negotiated Agreement. It shows the risks of not achieving an agreement. Better yet is to think about *all* the other alternatives, from best to worst, and the likelihood of achieving each. You want to be *realistic*.

Another less useful term is "bargaining range," described as the range between the most the buyer will pay and the least the seller will accept. Good negotiators can change the bargaining range—for example, by trading items of unequal value. They can focus on intangibles, come up with creative framing, and use some of the other creative tools from this book to change the situation. Most people assume the bargaining range is fixed and centers on money. That isn't true; it's only a starting point.

Say a buyer will pay up to $325,000 for a house and the seller won't accept less than $300,000, the *initial* bargaining range is $300,000 to $325,000. That will change if the seller agrees to a deferred payment on part of the price, offers to help finance the loan, or throws in the furniture.

Step 5, preparation, cannot be stressed enough. If you are not prepared, you are like an amateur race-car driver in the Indianapolis 500: you will encounter more crashes. If the other side is unprepared, they may be overly emotional, less focused on their goals, less creative, etc. You may have to help them get prepared. You may need to help them calm down.

This may seem counterintuitive. But *Getting More* is intended to be a transparent process, not a manipulative one. You can even give a copy of the *Getting More* Model to the other party. If both parties know about the concept of trading items of unequal value, they will both get more. It may take more time to get them prepared, and you may have to revise your time frame. But it is often the difference between reaching a deal and not reaching one.

This does *not* mean you should give away the store. But you must leave them with something they will be satisfied with, today and tomorrow. If not, they will retaliate in some way. If they are an employee, they won't work as hard or as well. Other companies or individuals may try to change the deal, get out of their commitment, or both.

If the other party is a hard bargainer, and they don't have your needs at heart, you don't have to help them. In that case, knowing how prepared they are will help you decide how to out-prepare and outmaneuver them. A lot of this centers on how much time and effort you are willing to take to collect information about them and the situation.

Here is a simple example: You want a discount on a flight. You call an airline agent and they swat you aside. You should realize that they do this kind of negotiation all day long. So if you are going to negotiate with someone like that, you need more than a wing and a prayer. You have to prepare more.

Quadrant I sets the stage on which you will negotiate. It helps you develop basic information. A significant part of *Getting More*, however, concerns Quadrant II—analyzing the situation—that is, the pictures in the head of each party.

Step 6 comprises needs and interests, broadly: rational and irrational (or emotional) needs, long-term and short-term needs, shared and conflicting needs, and so forth. Your "goals" are what you want at the end of the negotiation. Your "needs" are why you want it. For example: You want to spend the holidays with your family. Your problem is you have to work. Your needs are to make your children happy, give them presents, spend quality time with your family, make a special dinner with your spouse. If you know that your family wants to spend time with you when you are not hassled, and they care more about spending quality time with you, then various other options open up, including postponing the celebration a few days. The more you know about yourself and the other party, the more needs you can identify, and the more you have to trade.

Steps 7 and 8 are related. "Perceptions" refers to how the other person views the world. Use role reversal. What are they thinking and feeling? What are the pictures in their heads? Step 8 refers to how this manifests itself in your conversation or communication with them. What is their style? Are the other person's perceptions affecting your ability to communicate effectively?

Step 9 is about standards. What are their stated standards? What other standards would they accept?

After completing Quadrant II, stop and take stock. Reexamine your goals (Step 10). Why do you think the other person will now say yes or no to your goals? You may have to adjust your goals if your analysis shows them to be unrealistic.

By the time you have finished going through Quadrant II, you will have a list of issues to address. You need to develop options to solve them, and then prioritize everything. This brings us to Quadrant III, options and reducing risks. Step 11 consists of brainstorming options, either alone or with your colleagues. Don't let people cavalierly shoot down options they don't like. It will stifle the creative process.

Studies show that some of the best, most innovative ideas follow some of the silliest suggestions. Even an ill-formed idea can spark a great idea in someone else. So don't criticize anyone else's idea until everyone runs out of ideas. Write them all down on a piece of paper, whiteboard, or blackboard. Look them over—smart, stupid, contradictory or not. As Nobel laureate Linus Pauling said, "The best way to have a good idea is to have a lot of ideas." Start with items you can link to other deals or relationships. The more you can do this, the stronger an option will be.

A British study in 2006, "Why Bad Ideas Are a Good Idea," found empirical evidence that bad ideas prompt creative processes that produce good ideas. "Bad is the new good," it suggested, especially in technology. This is exactly opposite to what many people seem to think. Ideas that are different, or suboptimal, are often criticized, when they can be the grist for better solutions.

The next three steps (12, 13, 14) will help you improve your decision-making process in choosing the best options and prioritizing your approaches. Can you reduce the other party's perceived risk by making your proposal more incremental—that is, suggest a series of smaller steps? Which third parties are important, both to support the deal or to avoid?

Can you frame or package the information in ways that are more persuasive to the other person? Something that gives them a vision? For example, "6 and 6 program," that is, 6 percentage point profit rise in 6 months. Or, "party for smarty," the child gets more party time for good grades.

Step 15, the last item in Quadrant III, has to do with improving your alternatives to reaching an agreement, or changing the power balance. A powerful third party, for example, can change the balance of power if they join or support you.

As noted throughout this book, the use of power in a negotiation is fraught with risk. Seeing a negotiation in terms of gaining power over the other side sets up a conflict situation. If they perceive you as trying to grab power over them, they may well have an emotional response—as in "I don't care if I undermine the negotiation, I'm going to get even with you." Once you play the power card, the relationship is usually over.

I can't say it enough: While the tools in this book will give you power, they should be used selectively and constructively so that extreme reactions are not provoked. You should be sensitive to the needs of everyone along the way.

The last steps in Quadrant IV, actions, help you pick your best option(s) and turn them into commitments for all parties.

Step 16 is picking the best options. These are the ones that the other party will most likely accept, that appear the least risky, that move you toward your goals, that would be supported by third parties, and that create a vision of the future.

It is important to decide how to present your proposal, which is Step 17. This depends a lot on your audience. Some people need only two or three lines in an email. Others want a binder. Some want to talk it out face-to-face in a meeting. Others want a Word file. If someone has to go through your proposal in a format unfamiliar to them, it will take energy away from their focus on the proposal. They will become less interested sooner. They may dismiss it for reasons that have nothing to do with the proposed ideas themselves.

I once wrote a *109-page* memo on environmental liability in property transfers and submitted it to a partner at the law firm where I worked as a summer associate. The partner's assessment was that the memo was too short, because it did not include enough case references.

Later that summer I worked for an investment bank. I submitted a *two-page* strategy memo on an $800 million merger between two utility companies. The managing director said the two-pager was too long: CEOs would not read more than a page. You have to know your audience. Presentation is a more important part of persuasion than most people realize.

Next, you need to figure out the process that will be used to consider your proposals. This is Step 18. If criteria need to be set by which success will be measured, make sure you are involved in setting that criteria. Using the wrong criteria can hurt in achieving your goals.

Step 19 focuses on commitments. It is imperative that you get a commitment from the other person or party in the way that *they* make commitments, as noted earlier. Otherwise, you will have just wasted your time. Spend the necessary time on this. Are you sure that everyone is fully committed? How do you know? What incentives and penalties are provided for?

Many perfectly good negotiations fail to produce the desired results because of poor follow-up. That is the purpose of Step 20. What's the next step? What's the deadline? Who is going to do what? Without these things, people shuffle off and many of the options are forgotten.

The more you put yourself, psychologically and strategically, in the negotiation before it begins, the better off you will be during the negotiation, and afterward. In fact, that is what this entire Model is about: learning as much as possible about the negotiation before you get there. I will address conducting the negotiation itself in Chapter 16.

Clients and students have found the *Getting More* Model to be deceptively powerful. When you use it, at least three things will probably happen. First, you'll discover the problem you start with is usually not the real problem. There often will be some underlying problem lurking behind the obvious. When the real problem emerges, you will be better able to find the solution.

For example, Rhonda Cook at SEI Investments, a major financial management firm, thought the problem was that a client kept asking the company to do work not included in the contract. But after going through the Model, she discovered the real problem: "SEI contracts are too vague." This is what caused perceptions to differ between SEI and some of its clients. The fix was to write clearer contracts.

The second thing that will very likely happen is that you will find more options for solutions than you thought you had. Even experts in a field, when they use this Model, find new ways of thinking about goals, problems, and solutions.

A technical program manager at a major technology company did not want to pay higher prices to a major supplier. But the company was cutting its volume with that supplier. Using the Model and doing role reversal, the manager found out that the supplier would not raise prices if the supplier could be introduced to some of the company's other divisions.

"It's very hard for suppliers to penetrate major technology companies," the manager said. "By offering introductions elsewhere, we broadened the deal." The supplier essentially traded actual cash in holding prices the same today, in return for introductions, an intangible: the possibility of broader future business with the technology giant.

The third thing that will happen is that you will have a much better idea of the pictures in the heads of all concerned, how they differ, and what you should do about it.

A woman in one of my executive programs could not get her daughter to call in when she was out late. Her daughter wouldn't even discuss it. The mother thought the daughter was irresponsible. Then we went through the Model and the mother played the daughter. The mother realized that her daughter thought the only problem was the unreasonableness of her mother. Now the mother knew how to start a discussion with her daughter: "So tell me how you think I'm unreasonable."

You will get many other new ideas, too, including how to frame things better, how to get commitments, and how to be incremental. Overall, the breadth of new insights that come from this Model can be profound.

One of the first ways I used this Model in an important setting overseas was with the Lithuanian science sector in 1993, soon after the country's independence from the former Soviet Union. Some colleagues and I were assisting the science sector in commercializing former Soviet science in the West. We had a room full of people: the minister of industry, the head of the science sector, and dozens of scientists and officials.

We were scheduled to meet for the day. The purpose of the meeting was for the various groups involved to try to find effective solutions. We had already assigned the problems, and I had just finished going over Problems and Goals at about 10:00 A.M. Suddenly, the country's chief scientist stood up and wagged his finger at me. "We're not in school!" he scolded in English, with a thick Russian accent. "We don't do *this*!" Much of the rest of the room chimed in, *"Da, da"* (Yes, yes).

Now *that* was a problem. I had a mutiny against our process by a hundred Lithuanian leaders in front of a minister. There were long-term implications for all of our work in the country (which was sponsored by the U.N.). At the least, I needed to persuade them to stay in the room and work through our model, even if the day was shorter. There were benefits to be gained for the country.

But the most credible guy in the room was insulted. He felt he was being treated like a schoolboy. He needed an emotional payment. "All right," I said, "that's fair." I could hear a sigh of relief from one of my U.N. colleagues behind me.

Then I needed to keep them involved in the process long enough to get them to see the power of the Model. So I slowed things down; I became very incremental. I said, "It's time for a coffee break. Why don't you have coffee and pastries with your assigned groups, and just start on the beginning of Situation Analysis, Quadrant II? When the coffee break ends, if you don't like the process we've laid out, you can leave and never come back."

Having coffee and pastries was a small step, so people were willing to go along with it. How could the chief scientist oppose a coffee break? And what I asked them to do was such a small step that it would be impolite not to do it.

At six o'clock that evening, almost eight hours later, we could not get them out of the room. Finally, the cleaning staff kicked us all out. The group generated so many ideas during that one day that it took the country three years to implement them.

Working through the Model, however, during a negotiation uses only half its potential. The other huge advantage comes from doing a simulated negotiation with it beforehand.

The idea is to try to replicate what the negotiation is going to look like when you later actually sit down with the other party. It is highly unlikely that the other party is going to say before the negotiation, "I know you're preparing to negotiate with me. So why don't I come over and help you prepare?"

Using the *Getting More* Model is the next best thing. Run through the negotiation with another person or team as it might occur. It will provide you with insight as to what might happen. You'll be amazed at just how much information you will come away with. The person who "owns" the problem plays the role of the other side to get further insight into how to persuade them.

The point of the negotiation simulation is not necessarily to obtain a result—although results and additional options are useful. The point is to see what the *process* will look like. What do good and bad openings look like? What should be said, and in what way? What shouldn't be said?

For example, we once had a negotiation simulation in which someone made a suggestion, whereupon someone on the other side reflexively said, "Drop dead." Everybody realized that if that suggestion were made during the real negotiation, the deal would probably fall apart. So we made sure that suggestion was *not* made in the real negotiation.

Jennifer Morrill, a San Francisco attorney, said that when she was at Yahoo! she was having trouble with an advertising client. "They wanted more control over the look and feel of their content posted on the Yahoo! site than we were prepared to give them," she said. So she played the role of the client in a simulated negotiation. She found that the real problem had nothing to do with the content on the web page. "It was lack of trust dating from the beginning of the relationship," she said.

The client was afraid Yahoo! would steal its customers. So when the actual negotiation occurred, Jennifer was able to articulate the client's fears. The client thought she was a mind reader. She was able to allay the client's fears enough to have a discussion and solve the problem.

In conducting a negotiation simulation, you need at least two people negotiating each side of the problem; otherwise, it's harder to brainstorm. (You can have as many as four people on each side, or eight people total. After that, it gets a bit unwieldy.)

Remember, this is a two-party negotiation. So you have to have a specific person on each side to negotiate with. Also, while each side has one spokesperson, everyone should be able to speak up. In a real negotiation, that is not optimal. But in a brainstorming session like this, the point is to get as many ideas out as possible.

You can do a simulation with more than two parties. Don't attempt that until you've really got the Model down. Otherwise there are too many variables. Two parties is optimal, or a series of two-party negotiations.

In the simulation, the owner of the problem must play the *other* side. That is, in the simulation, the problem owner must make the best case possible against himself or herself. This kind of role reversal makes the problem owner stand in the shoes of the other party and really try to understand their perceptions.

In other words, the problem owner prepares as the other side would prepare. The problem owner, assisted by at least one other person, negotiates as the other side would negotiate. At the same time, others prepare and play the role of the problem owner. The problem owner essentially gets to see himself or herself negotiate. This is what Sharon Walker, whose mother was dying of cancer, did, as described in Chapter 1.

Often, you'll discover great insight about the effect of the problem owner's arguments on the other side, and what arguments might better be used.

Make sure everyone has the same facts; give a brief background for everyone beforehand. Then the sides separate physically (out of earshot of each other) and go through the *Getting More* Model, answering each item *from the point of view of the role they are playing*. It should take forty-five to ninety minutes to go through the checklist properly, and answer all the questions.

This will be hard for some problem owners. But as the Tom Hanks character said to the Geena Davis character in the baseball movie *A League of Their Own* after she wanted to quit: "It's supposed to be hard! It's the hard that makes it great!"

After preparing, both sides should come back together again and negotiate the roles they just prepared. Don't be a fly on the wall. Don't lapse into philosophy. Stay in character and make the best case you can for your side. This will give you a sense of the dynamic that is likely to occur when you are in the real negotiation. Do it for at least forty-five minutes, although you can do this for hours if you wish.

After the negotiation is over, reflect on what happened. Talk to the other party about what happened. Show each other your preparation notes. Ask what worked and what didn't. What insights did you glean that can be used in the real negotiation?

Finally, you need to turn this into a plan on how to conduct the real negotiation. Write up all the notes in one consolidated *Getting More* Model for the owner of the problem. Now, instead of thinking for a few minutes about the other person's perceptions, you will have the ideas of several people who have spent ninety minutes on it, thinking deeply about both parties' needs, about the standards to use, the options available, and so forth. The result will be a much richer preparation.

Remember, the problem owner doesn't need people who are experts; he or she just needs a fresh pair of eyes. This is because most of negotiation is about the people and process, not expertise.

I once prepared a six-person corporate negotiating team for a $300 million negotiation. We enlisted thirty other people who were not involved in the negotiation. We divided the group into six teams of six people each. We put one member of the actual negotiating team on each of the six teams.

Then we ran six simultaneous negotiations with the same set of facts. We spent the whole day on it. The results were terrific. The negotiating team got a lot more perspective and ideas. They discovered a lot of issues that had not previously surfaced. They were much more prepared.

You can take as little or as long as you wish on this: fifteen minutes, or all week. Each moment you spend makes you more prepared. In 1993, just after the fall of the Soviet Union, I assisted the prime minister and twenty-eight ministers of the newly independent Latvia in organizing their first popularly elected government since the Russian Revolution of 1918.

The government officials had asked for a three-day session at a retreat outside Riga, the capital city. As I approached the main meeting lodge at about 9:00 A.M. on a Friday, I could already hear people screaming at each other.

One big area of dispute involved government subsidies. The agriculture minister thought that much of the available money should be used to grow wheat. Wheat is made into bread, which feeds the populace and, as an export, brings in foreign exchange.

But the defense minister thought much of the subsidy should be used to buy arms. Latvia was a bit unstable after the fall of the Soviet Union. Without a strong defense, the government could be overthrown, the defense minister argued.

I told the group that this dispute was a *very* good topic for discussion. Everybody got a big emotional payment and calmed down. I then said that I had a really good way to deal with this. However, I needed a specific commitment from everyone, including the defense and agriculture ministers, to my being in charge of the process.

They were not totally clear on where I was going with this. But since I was respected enough that they had hired me for a weekend, they made the commitment.

"Okay," I said, "we're going to have a debate in front of the group between the agriculture minister and the defense minister." There were cheers. "The subject is subsidies. And also anything else you want to debate over."

The agriculture minister and the defense minister each strode to the front of the room. They were flushed with the anticipation of battle.

"There's only one process rule," I said. "Each of you has to debate the other side's position."

Pandemonium broke loose. "No! You can't do this! I won't!" the two ministers said, one by one. Half of the other ministers laughed with delight. The other half took sides.

"Didn't you say I was in charge of the process?" I said. "Didn't everyone in this room make a solemn commitment?" (Standards and commitments!)

"But, but . . ." the defense minister said. "I can't do it!"

"Of course you can," I said. "You know each other's positions cold. What you don't have is that you don't feel each other's perceptions. You have to feel it. You have to perceive it deeply to find an agreement."

I promised that it would be worthwhile. I reminded them that they hired me for my process expertise. I told them we didn't have to do it for more than an hour, maybe even less. Grudgingly, they agreed.

I asked each of them to prepare separately, helped by whichever other ministers wanted to help them, and gave them a simpler version of the

Model. We started with five-minute opening statements. Then we had a negotiation. I wrote up the various points they were making on flip charts. Various other ministers called out points for the two debaters to make.

After about an hour, we ended the debate. I went over the points they had made, which I had written down. After a break, I said the two sides needed to meet and figure out what their proposals were, based on what had come out during the debate.

Then the two ministers met again in front of the group, this time in their own roles. I told them to figure out a reasonable agreement, based on what they had just been through. As one could imagine, they developed stepped goals and provided subsidies to meet each incremental goal. They agreed to check frequently against the targets. Priorities were set.

The two ministers told me and the group it was the best experience they had solving problems in all their years as government officials. But, as I've said throughout *Getting More,* it was not rocket science.

Thousands of problems, professional and personal, have been solved in and after my courses using this Model. One woman at Columbia Business School insisted that her learning team use it to solve a dispute with her husband over birth control methods. And it was resolved.

A potential client of Heidi Vanhamme, an investment banker, refused to accept the fee schedule in the bank's engagement letter. By putting herself in the client's shoes, Heidi realized it was not about fees but about performance. The client wanted to make sure they got value for their money.

"We put in a performance-based, incremental fee schedule," she said. This reduced the client's perceived risk. As value to the client increased, the consulting firm's percentage rose. "We were able to understand their real reasons," she said. All this was just from the role reversal exercise before the negotiation.

The Model also reveals the weaknesses in one's own position. "We found out that we were not taking as much risk as I had thought," Heidi said. "The client wanted us to take more risk." She added: "We found the holes in our story."

With such information, you can start the negotiation by asking more specifically about the other party's perceptions, what is likely bothering them, and subjects they might consider more important to discuss.

The Model is especially good for identifying the overall process that led to the problem. If you fix your problem, but you don't fix the process that led to the problem, you will have another problem next month with the same bad process.

If one of the radios breaks on an airplane that is part of my airline, I know the maintenance department will fix it. That's not my concern. I want to know *why* a radio broke in flight. I want to see if there is some generic process I need to fix. If I don't do that, I'm likely to have a flat tire next month, a propeller problem the month after, and a cylinder problem the month after that. I need to find the process that led to the problem.

The Model will also help you figure out who is the right counterpart. For example, both Stryker and Synthes, producers of high-quality hip and other joint replacements, are favored by many doctors for the quality of their products. But hospital purchasing departments, which want to buy more cheaply, have cut into their margins by turning to lower-quality competitors.

Using the Model, the companies discovered they should be getting doctors to negotiate for them with their own purchasing departments. The doctors should be talking about product performance and longevity, not the price of a hip component.

"We are going to use this process all the time now," said Ben Pitcher, director of the health care division at Stryker.

Years after John Marotta took my course, he wrote to me, saying his wallet had been stolen. He asked me to rush to him another laminated Model checklist card, claiming it was the most valuable thing in his wallet. "I use it religiously," said John, the CEO of a medical device company in Denver. "It's more important than my credit cards."

8

Dealing with Cultural Differences

In San Francisco, an eight-year-old Chinese boy came to school, bleeding from his arms. He was taken to the school nurse, who said it was a case of child abuse. She notified the authorities and said the child should be taken away from his parents.

It turned out that the boy and his parents had just come from a remote region in China. There, one of the cures for the common cold was to scrape the arms to let out the evil spirits.

Was this a case of child abuse? Not in the classic sense. Should the child be taken from his parents? Of course not. Well, who should talk to the parents? And what message should be conveyed? The answer is, someone who is respected by the Chinese community and knows both cultures: perhaps a Chinese doctor who has lived in the United States for some time. He should not say to the parents, "Your way is awful." He should say, "Your way was fine where you were. But I have other suggestions that are better and more effective. Your child will cry less."

This example shows what can go wrong in dealing with people from other cultures, and how to fix it.

Dealing with people from other cultures—people who are different—is one of the key success factors for this century. As everyone knows, the world is getting smaller and people who are raised differently are running up against each other more and more.

And yet, many people are clueless about what "differences" really mean, and even more clueless about what to do about them. As a result, perfectly good deals fail, wars are begun, and conflict, both interpersonal and international, seems to occur daily.

Indeed, our collective inability to deal effectively with our differences is the root cause of almost all human conflict since the beginning of time. But to make headway, we first need to understand what "difference," "diversity," and "culture" actually mean.

WHAT IS DIVERSITY?

Who is more different, (a) a black manager and a white manager who work together in your company, or (b) two white Southern boys in rival motorcycle gangs in Nashville? The two white boys may kill each other on sight. In that sense, they are likely much more different from each other than the black manager and the white manager. In other words, "differences" may not be as much about race as many people think.

Who is more different, (a) a Jewish middle-class family in Tel Aviv and an Arab middle-class family in Cairo, or (b) a Jewish middle-class family in Tel Aviv and Jewish extremists nearby, who killed an Israeli prime minister? Clearly, the Jewish and Arab families are likely much closer in sensibilities than the two Jewish groups. So maybe "differences" aren't as much about religion as people think.

"Diversity" is not as much about the externalities of race, religion, language, food, dress, music, gender, national origin, age, and profession as it is about where people think they get their identity from—that is, the pictures in their heads. People may get their identity from externalities, but more and more often, they don't.

Volumes have been written about diversity, too much of it wrong. That is, the ideas expressed are not supported by the way people think and live. In trying to persuade other people in a negotiation, people's perceived psychological affiliation is much more important than the way they look or the house of worship they attend.

By culture, then, I am referring to the affiliations from which individuals think they get their identity. The production department and the marketing department in the same company may have two completely different cultures. The same may be true for New Yorkers and Los Angelenos, oil and solar advocates, accountants and mechanics, club members and nonmembers. This will affect their perceptions of one another and how they treat one another in all manner of interactions.

So you need to understand first what culture they *believe* they belong to. If you don't know that, you won't even know where to start persuading them. The bourgeoisie in Europe between World Wars I and II, who all spoke different languages—French, German, Italian, Spanish, English— probably had more in common than two people living on the same block in New York City do today.

A major U.S. newspaper once had the headline "U.S. Hispanic Lobby Still Weak." This is a symptom of the problem. First, it purports to treat the tens of million of people of Hispanic descent in the United States as part of the same culture. This just isn't true. Hispanics are doctors, lawyers, accountants, mechanics, Spanish speakers, French speakers, Democrats, Republicans; they originate from Spain, Haiti, Cuba, Mexico, the Dominican Republic, and many other countries. The newspaper account treated them as a monolithic group where none exists. It is this kind of behavior that leads to prejudice and discrimination.

Second, something called a Hispanic lobby could not possibly represent such a very, very diverse group of people. It is likely that their interests coincide only on certain issues on certain days.

Thinking that all "Muslims" are from the same culture is just as inaccurate. There are different Muslim sects, and different nationalities, and they are sometimes at war with one another, as is frequently the case with the Shi'ite and Sunni sects in Iraq. Some people in some of those sects love the United States; others don't.

Dealing with superficial, often physical differences in an attempt to identify and solve differences is like throwing darts at a dartboard, blindfolded. Sometimes you hit the mark. But it is an imprecise and ultimately ineffective way of addressing the true differences among people.

I define cross-cultural differences as those differences stemming from dramatically different perceptions in the heads of the people I am negotiating with. Their differences may or may not have much to do with race or religion or gender. But they have everything to do with the other person's beliefs—the influences on them, their worldview, their hopes and dreams and fears, and so forth. Until we know the pictures in their heads, or try to know them, we cannot determine whether the people we are negotiating with are truly different from us or not.

At a workshop for various Russian managers in Moscow, problems they faced were submitted in Russian and then translated into English. A lot of the participants did not speak English. One participant, a consultant named Tatiana Polievktova, wrote that she was having a hard time convincing her son to do his homework.

"We found incentives and rewards for the child doing his homework right," she said. "Both sides were proud: parents and happy son. I found out what he wanted. I split big steps into smaller pieces."

Tatiana spoke a universal language here: the issues involved in raising kids. She handled the problem exactly the way many parents would have handled it in the United States, Iran, Argentina, China, or Japan. Just because she has a Russian passport doesn't mean she experiences these concerns differently. Perhaps the strongest cultural bond she feels in her life right now is with "parents with young children" everywhere. In negotiating with her, the fact that she is Russian may not even be among her top three ways of thinking about or identifying herself. These are the kinds of questions you should be asking.

Those who learn to deal effectively with differences among people have a tremendous competitive advantage in negotiating. They will reach more agreements. They will form better relationships. They will gain a truer and quicker understanding of others. They will ask better questions. They will be more successful in many dimensions.

On the other hand, some may call another person "brother" or "sister" or "man of the tribe" without knowing them or asking anything about them. This suggests common ground, but there may not be any. You can't depend on externalities; you actually have to do the work to find out if there really is a connection. Otherwise you risk its being just another manipulative tactic, as in "We are the same, so please do something for me."

Broadening your definition of "culture" will make you more successful in dealing with the diverse world we live in. One of Sebastian Rubens y Rojo's neighbors, for example, complained twice to the landlord when Sebastian had parties. The parties weren't particularly loud, according to Sebastian. So he went to see the neighbor to talk about it directly.

"I told him we were from two different cultures," said Sebastian, who is from Argentina. "He was from the workaholism culture, which I told him I very much respected. But I was from the student culture, along with many others in the building." Students, he noted, often have parties on the weekend, as the neighbor must have done when he was younger.

Sebastian, who now works for the education ministry in Abu Dhabi, told both the neighbor and the landlord that the students could adapt, but that flexibility was needed on all sides. The result was a constructive set of ground rules that worked for everyone. "He was very interested in the international students," Sebastian said. "He even let us dance the tango in my apartment."

Some people around the world profess to hate Americans. All 300 million of them? We can't *all* be the same. In fact, some people who live in the United States may identify themselves not as Americans first, but as vegetarians.

Not understanding genuine cultural differences has caused many historical problems. One of the most celebrated moments in diplomatic history occurred in 1960 when Soviet premier Nikita Khrushchev banged his shoe on the table at the United Nations, threatening the West. While there are conflicting accounts of this, a number of research papers claim that when Khrushchev was banging his shoe on the table at the United Nations, he was wearing two shoes at the same time.

Was this the emotional rambling of an out of control leader who might actually cause a nuclear war? Or was this the calm, cool negotiation strategy of someone who knew exactly how to push the West's buttons? Certainly, greater knowledge of the Russians' negotiation style would have been helpful to the West in 1960, early in the Cold War—whether Khrushchev had two shoes or three.

It is easy to turn gender, race, and similar issues into full-blown workplace blow-ups where everyone loses. And there are legions of lawyers, journalists, and government officials who know exactly how to help people do that. But it is much better to use negotiation tools to identify your goals, find the real cause of the problem, and put things back together again.

Often it's a cultural misunderstanding: the parties have different perceptions and ways of communicating. Frequently, a cultural interface manager, a kind of cultural mediator, is necessary to help the parties translate, like the Chinese doctor at the start of this chapter. Sometimes each party needs its own interface manager, someone they trust, to explain the other side.

Cultural averages are interesting starting points, but they do not provide answers about what to do in any particular negotiation with individuals. You still have to get inside the head or mind of the people you are negotiating with. And you can't assume a cultural trait has validity in your case without first finding out the pictures in the other person's head—unless, of course, you want to be wrong a lot (or worse).

Following are the results of one of the politically incorrect surveys I take from time to time. This particular survey was done among seventeen executives at Wharton in a program soon after 9/11.

IS THERE ANY VALIDITY TO THESE STATEMENTS?	Yes	No
Some races are better at sports than other races.	9	8
Certain races have a certain smell.	5	12
Certain cultures dance better.	4	13
Certain cultures produce better lovers.	4	13
Certain cultures are less trustworthy than others.	7	10
Orthodox Jews bathe less than other people.	1	16
Most Muslims support "evening the score" with the U.S.	2	15

As you can see, we had disagreement on every question. Clearly, the executives had lots of preconceptions and stereotypes.

I then asked each participant who said "Yes" to a stereotype to stand up. Then I asked that person to *prove* to the class how they knew that particular stereotype was valid. I started with "Certain cultures produce better lovers." I asked them: "What? You've slept with twelve million people from your favorite amorous culture?"

I want people to *prove* that their stereotypes are valid. "Now," I say, "my laboratory says there are no intelligence- or performance-based genetic differences among the races. What's your laboratory say?" I continually ask for evidence. And of course, often there isn't any.

I once had a conversation with some white racists. I asked if there were real cultural differences between whites and blacks that they didn't like. "Or," I said, "is this just a skin pigmentation thing?" It was a standards question: be extreme or come to me. If they said, "Nah, we're just skin pigmentation guys," that's like saying, "Gee, I'm a jerk."

"Oh, no," they said, "there are real cultural differences."

So I said, "Tell me, do you like jazz?" "We love jazz," they said, nodding in unison.

"Well," I said, "jazz comes from the black culture." I leaned forward. "So are you part black?" "What!?" they retorted, aggressively.

"I'm sorry," I said. "Is this just a skin pigmentation thing, then?" They stopped in their tracks, mumbling that that was only one example.

"Okay," I said. "Tell me, do you like grits?" A little more uncomfortably, they said, "Sure, we love grits."

"Well," I said, "grits was the traditional food of the slaves." I paused. "Does that make you mostly black?" I paused. "Or is this just a skin pigmentation thing?" I added, "As far as I can see, you guys have a lot in common with the black culture, don't you?"

THE ROOTS OF STEREOTYPES

Where do such cultural stereotypes come from? Perhaps from ignorance. Perhaps from fear. Certainly, stereotyping is as old as the human race, when survival and protection depended on one's family and tribe. People who were the same were safe. Strangers were risky. They were assumed to be "enemies," often based on little more than the fact that they looked, spoke, or acted differently.

But they might not have been different in their psyche, where it counts. Those with the same blood, on the other hand, might be very different. In the Bible, Cain killed Abel, his brother. So we need to ask more questions to find out who is really the same and who is really different.

So where do people get their ideas about stereotypes? Ignorance, a single bad experience, the influence of others? In a negotiation, you need to find that out. Often the key to removing stereotypes is simply providing information to others about the humanity of individuals. Start with this principle: *There is no Them.* There are just people with individual perceptions. You are trying to meet your goals in a sea of different perspectives and views.

Overcoming stereotypes can be as simple as asking people to live a week, a day, or even an hour in the other person's shoes. In the business world, people in marketing and production should trade jobs for a few days—or at least do role reversal. Managers and employees should trade jobs for a few days. A few of the smartest companies do this. It decreases mistrust and communication problems, and increases teamwork and productivity. Often, the main problem is that people from one culture haven't ever been exposed to those of another culture.

DEALING WITH DIFFERENCES

Sadly, understanding different cultures is not a strong suit for many in the United States. Part of this is because of the structure of our legal system.

The United States has a legal system that usually works. It is generally fair, accessible, less corrupt, and less expensive than the legal systems of other countries as a percentage of income. Legal services cost only half of

1 percent of the gross national product, and that cost has been slowly trending downward in percentage terms. In India, the cost of legal delays alone is estimated at 2 percent of the gross national product.

The problem with the U.S. legal system is that you don't have to form a relationship with the other person. You just sign a contract and you can sue them if they break it. Plenty of attorneys will represent you for a small or contingency fee. This produces a system that is highly transactional; it minimizes focus on relationships.

Most of the rest of the world doesn't have this luxury. Their legal systems are often inaccessible, unfair, corrupt, and very expensive. That means that for most of the world, all that people have is each other. And it dramatically changes the way people interact with one another.

If you get hosed by your business partner in Bolivia, or Yemen, or Mongolia, the legal system is not likely to help you. There is no unemployment insurance, food stamps, or welfare system. You and your family may literally starve to death. Corruption is viewed simply as a business expense in many developing countries. "The courts of many developing nations are often used not to eradicate corruption, but to punish and eliminate any perceived threats to the government," according to the University of Iowa Center for International Finance and Development.

As such, in the United States, relationships are a very nice subject. People write books about it; they go on television and talk about it.

For most of the rest of the world, however, relationships are not just a nice subject. Often they are a matter of life and death. So the focus on the other party is intense.

Let's say an American and a Peruvian executive go out to lunch in Lima. It is supposed to be a one-hour business lunch. For fifty-five minutes of the hour, the Peruvian executive asks the U.S. executive about friends, family, and hobbies. The U.S. executive is thinking, "What's wrong with this person? I came here for a business lunch."

Does the Peruvian executive think they are having a business lunch? Of course. The question the Peruvian executive is asking himself or herself is, "Do I trust this person? Before I put my life, and my family's life, in their hands, without recourse, who are they?"

This is the question that is asked by most of the rest of the world. It is not a question that appears to be asked by most people in the United States. The United States focuses more on punishment and contracts than on relationships. And this hampers the United States and its citizens in their negotiations with the rest of the world. There are studies to this effect. "Let's get down to brass tacks!" is an oft-repeated American business expression. But for meeting one's goals in a world where cultures increasingly run up against each other, it is ineffective, and often insulting.

Even in societies where lying is considered common, there are certain people to whom one just does not lie without thinking long and hard about it. Who? Those with whom you have relationships. Your family. Your close friends. Business associates that you have dealt with or will deal with for a long time.

Mike Finch of Marathon Oil was having trouble with a foreign supplier. "They delayed responses, shifted levels of authority, did not honor established points of contact," he said. "They continually provided less than adequate information."

We did a role reversal exercise, in which Mike played the role of the other side. The real problem became quickly evident to Mike. "Marathon is focused on the substance and the supplier is focused on the relationship," he said. "Marathon needs to reevaluate how it works with this supplier."

Essentially, the supplier didn't trust Marathon enough to give it the information needed to improve various oil processes. Cost-savings could not be realized as a result. Clearly, not focusing enough on the relationship with the other party was costing money.

Marathon saw similar problems in Mexico and in Asia. Marathon wanted to talk about the details of transactions. Their counterparts wanted to talk about the relationship. In more than one instance, U.S. Marathon people talked about their foreign counterparts as just "waiting." Marathon managers asked how they could "create a sense of urgency" among their foreign counterparts.

The Marathon people thought at first that the Asians and Mexicans were waiting for lower prices. Finally, it became clear that they were waiting for long-term commitments: people commitments as well as business commitments.

MetLife found out the same thing with its own Korean subsidiary. The Koreans simply refused to accept a new company-wide platform for various business processes. John Rao, a Met manager in the United States, found out that the Koreans were less focused on money saved or business efficiency.

"It was about trust," he said. "The Koreans wanted some say in the matter. They wanted some control." And the Koreans wanted the technical support to be in Korean, not English.

Even between developed countries there can be vast cultural issues. Mike Gallagher, a U.S.-based manager of BASF, got into a big argument because a company factory in Germany was late by four days delivering yellow pigment. The customer walked, and the German factory wouldn't take the pigment back.

"We didn't understand their culture," Mike said. And this was in his own company. It turned out that the American arm simply ordered the German factory to make what the Germans called a "nonforecasted order." It disrupted their carefully planned schedule. To them, it was the Americans shooting from the hip again.

As far as the Germans were concerned, they stopped on a dime and did the order. It was four days late, but it was the best they could do. And then the Americans criticized them. For the Germans, the response was, well, the heck with you! Germans versus Americans—the perception was a culture of order versus a culture of chaos. "It wasn't just a problem we had to fix," Mike said. "It was the whole process. It was all the communication."

"Given that the world is getting smaller very fast, almost every negotiation is a cross-cultural negotiation," said Igor Ojereliev, who was a student in my NYU negotiation class and is now an emerging-markets hedge fund manager in London. "It is important to remember that different cultures have different standards of what is fair and relevant." He said he found that in negotiating in China, most (not all!) street vendors need to haggle, so he doesn't usually start with a value discussion. At the airports in Egypt, he said, most taxi drivers (not all!) will take less if they think you are not in a hurry. "It's the pictures in their heads that count."

STEPS TO IMPROVEMENT

The first step to improvement is communicating effectively with others: understanding the signals they put out, especially when they are from another culture. If the other side starts making "relationship signals," they are interested in seeing whether or not they can trust you. Relationship signals include talking about nonbusiness subjects such as recreation, sports, food, and music. They are trying to get to know you as a person.

Too many people pay lip service to this—they ask a couple of questions without listening to the answer, and quickly move on to business. But others can sense when you are not really interested in them. *So you have to mean it.*

Christine Farner, a manager for Warner-Lambert, a pharmaceutical company, went to County Cork, Ireland, to discuss building a $275 million factory there. The local planning board was initially cool. Then Christine remembered the cultural learnings of the course, which she took at Columbia Business School. "So we took them out to dinner to learn about each other." By the end of dinner, everyone was on the same team, she said, with the same agenda and a planning process.

Next, you need to *acknowledge differences openly*. If you're different, or at least perceived as different, the extent to which you are honest about this will gain you trust and credibility. Even if the other party tells you that you should have learned more, you can apologize and say you'd like to start now. People look for honesty first.

After that, start somewhere. Agree to anything, no matter how trivial: where people will sit, what you will order for drinks. Acknowledge something you like about the other person and his or her culture. Talk about something you might have observed or read about the culture and ask if it is true. If not, what is? Be curious.

Donna Farrell, a consultant formerly with Arthur Andersen, found that clients kept looking at her as a young woman. They had misgivings about her abilities and sometimes asked for someone older and more experienced. Maybe, she thought, they wanted to work with a man. They couldn't say it legally, but to her it felt like the 800-pound gorilla in the room.

So she took the subject head-on. "I addressed their perceptions about age and gender directly, even if I didn't like their perceptions," she said. "I used humor. I found out their fears and addressed them. All of this established rapport."

This brings me to my next point. It is as counterintuitive as it is essential for dealing with differences.

- Do other people expect you to be like them?
- When in Rome, should you do as the Romans do?

The correct answers to the above questions are no and no. Other people who are different from you do NOT expect you to be like them. They know that you are not. They DO expect you to value and respect them. It is a subtle but important difference.

When I go to China, I don't eat monkey brains. What's more, I have special dietary needs. I don't wait until I have arrived to tell my hosts that, after they have spent a lot of money on a ceremonial feast. I call ahead and tell them my dietary needs. And they are pleased to cook for me what I need to eat. After all, the point in cooking the meal is to make me happy.

It should be of interest that *cultural fatigue* is not just a sociological term. It's a medical term. Cultural fatigue occurs when you have made the dozens of accommodations every day to try to be just like those around you in another culture. At the end of six months, you are physically exhausted. Cultural fatigue is the biggest cause of the failure of foreign executives and their families in adjusting to a new culture. The key is NOT to adjust. The key is to be yourself. You can learn some of the language, you can pursue some of the customs that you like.

But you do NOT want to be like them. And this is one of the major points of this book: there is value in being different. *Being different adds value.*

The single biggest cause of the growth of the U.S. gross national product since the end of World War II has been new technology. New technology has been largely developed by innovators, and innovators are *different.* They represent change. They represent a level of discomfort as new things are tried and instituted.

Many people hate change. Many people hate differences. Companies claim they love diversity and differences. But try to advocate change, and in many companies, it's a one-way ticket out. Yet it is difference that adds value. In differences there is strength.

So, if someone says to me, with some frustration, "We're different from each other," I'm going to slap the table and say, "Great! We're going to make money!" Homogeneity is not as profitable. Differences are more profitable. I like to say, "We have to get some people in here who disagree with us so we can make some money around here!"

It is the messy process of trying new things, the intensity of disagreement, the synthesis of the best ideas, that lead to value. Often, mistakes are made. Feelings sometimes get hurt. But the result is *more.*

So you *want* people with different perceptions and solutions. You do want to pay attention to the *process* of discussion. How you set your goals, what commitments you make to each other, your interest in discovering one another's value. When this occurs, people get more.

Research has proven these conclusions. One study looked at diversity in U.S. cities. The three most successful cities economically—New York, Los Angeles, and San Francisco—were the three most diverse. Each 10 percent increase in diversity resulted in a rise in net income of 15 percent in the original U.S.-born population. Diversity of opinion—tolerance of differences—is particularly important in the high-tech sector. It is not an accident that Silicon Valley developed just outside San Francisco, which studies show tolerates the most diversity of any area of its size in the United States.

To underscore this point: for this to work, the environment must support differences. In Rwanda, diversity led to ethnic genocide because differences were not tolerated. The more that differences are tolerated—indeed, embraced—the more economic benefit develops. Even in countries where the choice is not total tolerance or total intolerance, the failure to capitalize on differences has economic costs. Studies show that a company's failure to capitalize on the clash of ideas and perceptions results in higher turnover, less productivity, and lower profits.

The cost of extra turnover alone in a 2,000-person company in which differences are not embraced is $5 million per year right off the bottom line, studies show. This does not count the opportunity costs of losing the better ideas. It's a huge economic penalty.

Studies show that more creativity results from the clash of differing perceptions and experiences. The most creative people are those with widely varying experiences and skills from which to draw. In fact, diverse groups produce *three times* the high-quality solutions to problems than nondiverse groups.

But you need to be careful of just paying lip service to this. Someone who is different is someone with whom you will often disagree. Too many groups I have seen pick someone whose physical attributes might be different, and then pride themselves at having "diversity." But unless their *perceptions* are different, then they are really the same, and such benefits don't flow.

Here is an example of strength through differences. It ranks as one of the most rewarding experiences in my life. In the mid to late 1990s, my colleagues and I convinced 3,000 farmers in the jungles of Bolivia to stop growing coca for cocaine and to start growing bananas. These bananas were exported successfully to Argentina for several years until the value of the Argentine peso dropped and the venture was no longer profitable with us in it. The growers continued on their own.

The project started with a request from Donna Hrinak, then the U.S. ambassador to Bolivia, to assist in the antidrug campaign. She wanted to wean the farmers in the jungle region of Chapare off cocaine. I had met her through work I had done there on economic development.

After studying various agricultural markets, we decided there was an undersupply of high-quality bananas. And the prices that the bananas could fetch were actually more than the farmers got for their coca crop. In the drug trade, the processors and distributors made the real money, not the farmers. The government, meanwhile, kept firebombing coca fields, so it was a risky business for the farmers.

We started with 100 growers. The first time we talked, it was a sweltering January night (summer in the Southern Hemisphere). We met in a little clearing in the jungle. It was very dark except for the glow from my battery-operated computer and the shapes of people and animals. There were jungle sounds. No one spoke English except for me and an interpreter. The growers spoke Qetchua, an Indian dialect. The interpreter translated between English and Qetchua.

The growers—men, women, and children—wore little more than rags. Many looked malnourished. Barefoot children dressed in tatters were hanging out of two-story wooden shacks with big openings in place of windows. The skin of many was blackened with dirt.

I purposely wore a three-piece suit, a tie, and suspenders.

"Look at me," I began, talking to the group through the interpreter. "I couldn't be more different from you. I dress differently. I talk differently. I look different." I added, "My plane ticket down here probably cost more than many of you make in a year.

"But," I said, "I think we have some things in common. We both want a better life for ourselves and our children. And if we work together, we just might be able to do something together."

I noted that the growers had land, cheap labor, and diseased, nonproducing banana trees. We had capital, technology, and markets.

We talked about the life they led, how they made money, their complaints against the government, their interest in better medical care. Few could read and write, yet they were interested in education, especially for their children. I told them that I would need a commitment from each and every one of them that they wanted to attempt this banana-growing venture.

For several hours that night, we negotiated a lengthy contract. I typed it in English, and then the translator typed it in Spanish. Almost all of the growers were illiterate, but they weren't stupid. They asked very good questions and wanted all the terms one might expect in such a contract. It was subject to the laws of New York State. We negotiated each and every point, respectfully and thoughtfully. I would invest money in equipment, trucking, marketing, technology, and chemicals for the bananas. The growers would be guaranteed a certain price. They would commit to achieving certain production numbers. They promised to learn world-class banana production methods; and we promised to bring in the people to teach them.

They might make less money in some weeks than they would with coca, I told them. But we would form a brand that would have value, and over the long term they would get more. I noted to them that under Bolivian law, it was easier to get out of contracts for various technicalities. But under New York law, I said, if there is a meeting of the minds, there is an agreement. "So," I said, "when you put your names on the contract, or an *X* next to your name, it's for keeps. It's a commitment. You have to mean it."

We finished about dawn. There was nowhere to print out the contract since there wasn't any electricity. So the two growers who could read and write, and who spoke Spanish, drove the 350 kilometers (about 200 miles) with us back to Santa Cruz, Bolivia's commercial hub, where we printed out the contract and signed it.

In the years to follow, the contract with the Bolivians withstood the test of time and distance. This is because we had openly discussed our differences and how we could work together. We came from two dramatically different cultures, but we had similar goals. Our agreement was forged with human feelings.

This was a good start, but I didn't think it was enough to form the kind of long-term bond I sought. So we went back frequently, and took tours through the jungle. I wanted to understand their customs and how they lived. Then we hit on an idea.

The U.S. and Bolivian governments, which supported the project, wanted the growers to open a bank account to hold their money. A cash economy, they figured, is a drug economy. So the agency involved set the growers up with a bank account at the Bank of Santa Cruz, a regional bank located in the city.

But I wanted to value the growers more.

The best bank in the country was the Citibank in Santa Cruz. The best department at that bank was the corporate department. Companies like Mercedes banked there. The setting was elegant and quiet, with thick blue carpets. You could hear the soft whoosh of air conditioning. There were strict financial and corporate requirements. The growers hardly had two pesos to rub together.

Nonetheless, we asked the Citibank corporate department to make an exception for the growers. "Absolutely not," the head of the corporate department said, insulted that we even asked the question. So we used all of our various contacts, including political ones, to prevail upon Citibank to accept the growers as depositors. This was a highly visible project and Citibank, a major U.S. bank, was being asked to do something for Bolivia. They agreed.

Imagine this scene: a ragtag group of growers walking through the luxuriously appointed corporate banking department, where everyone else was dressed to the teeth in business suits and dresses. Imagine these growers getting their own Citibank card, their very first banking card and checkbook. And imagine the growers coming back to their shacks in the jungle, holding up their Citibank card and saying to each other, "We're as good as Mercedes."

A couple of years after we signed the contract, there was a big transportation strike. The road through Chapare (the jungle) was one of the country's principal transportation corridors. Only one truck was let through—our banana truck.

We took leaders of the growers to one of the best restaurants in Santa Cruz: white tablecloths and the like. They came in by bus from the jungle. We had them take back delicacies for their families. Others in the restaurant looked askance at them. But they were with us, and the restaurant could hardly afford to make a scene.

The number of growers in our project grew quickly and steadily. After six months, we had 3,000 growers from all over the jungle. The project became known in Bolivia. Protests by some coca growers were overwhelmed by the people turning to bananas.

But the biggest change occurred with the bananas themselves. The reason the project had never moved forward was because the banana trees in that part of the jungle were diseased. They had a fungus called black sigatoga, which causes the leaves of the banana trees to droop. Exposed daily to the sun, the bananas ripen on the tree, turning black, which makes them unusable.

The trees needed to be sprayed several times a day in part of their yearly growing cycle with a fungicide to kill the fungus. But it was too expensive to fly aircraft the 350 kilometers back and forth from Santa Cruz every day to spray the trees several times. As a result, the banana business had never gotten off the ground.

However, there was a small military airport in the middle of Chapare. If the small crop-spraying planes parked at that airport and used it as a base, the chemicals and fuel could be trucked in from Santa Cruz.

The airport was owned by the National Aeronautical Association, a joint effort by the U.S. and the Bolivian military. For twenty years they had refused requests from the growers to open the airport to agricultural projects to grow something other than coca. So we decided to use the negotiation tools outlined in this book to make our case: standards, framing, third parties, goals.

I wrote a letter to the U.S. Departments of State, Justice, and the Treasury, the three departments that dealt with the illegal drug trade. This letter essentially asked them if their actions were consistent with their goals. And it used their standards.

The letter said that if the airport remained closed, it showed that the U.S. government supported the illegal drug trade. But if the airport was opened to the growers, it would show that the government opposed illegal drugs, not just in word but in deed. Again, we got assistance from both the Bolivian and U.S. governments to help get our request to the right people.

At the same time, Alexa Sundberg, a U.S. marketing consultant, and Andres Judah, a Bolivian economist, worked for me on the ground and put pressure on politicians, got stories in the media, and organized the pilots' associations to join in the pressure.

The airport was opened. U.S. and Bolivian agencies appropriated $100,000 to build a new commercial airstrip next to the military landing field, in the heart of the banana plantations. We brought in technology from Ecuador to grow better bananas. We brought in new refrigeration and washing equipment. We found markets in Argentina. Our food label, Andean Gold, became a fixture in some of the Argentine supermarkets. The high prices the bananas fetched in Argentina showed that the Indians of Chapare were competing with the world's best banana producers.

Some months after the project started, banana prices dropped for a brief period. I was sure we would go into the red that month. But when I got the accounting reports, we were still in the black; the project was still making money. I didn't understand this. So I called down to the people who were handling our finances in Bolivia, and asked them why we were not in the red that month.

"Oh," one of them said. "The growers saw the market prices drop and they didn't want you to lose money. So they decided to drop their prices to you until the market recovers."

These are people that one would think I had nothing in common with. I didn't speak their language. I didn't understand their customs. But we made a connection, across time and space and culture, that endures to this day.

Does this happen 100 percent of the time? Of course not. But it happens a surprisingly high percentage of the time if you go through the process.

COMMUNICATION, PERCEPTION, AND CULTURE

Clearly, the way in which we communicate with people from other cultures is key. The way we interpret their actions. The questions we ask about their perceptions. When we think everyone else perceives the world just like we do, it causes all kinds of conflict.

One of the most interesting studies about this had to do with the misinterpretation of a smile. It was conducted on a college campus. Two Americans passed each other on a walkway and smiled at each other. Both felt good about this. Then, an American passed a Korean student. The American smiled; the Korean student did not. The Korean student thought, "These Americans are so superficial. All they do is smile, even at strangers. It means nothing to them." The American student thought, "These Koreans are so unfriendly."

An Arab student walked along a path in traditional garb, wearing a white flowing robe. People smiled at him in approval. But he felt only ridicule—because that's what smiling means in some Arab cultures in such a context. He quickly ran into the bathroom to check how he looked.

But the most interesting part of this research concerned an American woman and a Southeast Asian man. The female student was waiting for the off-campus bus to take her to her apartment after class early one evening. A man from Southeast Asia was tending to his two small children.

The young American woman was touched, and smiled at the man. The man, suddenly bewildered, looked back at her and said, "Oh. Do you want to meet later? How much do you cost?" He thought she was selling her services.

If just a smile can be the basis for such misunderstanding, think of the pitfalls in the blizzard of sentences in a complex or emotional negotiation.

The process to solve cross-cultural issues is the same as for other negotiation problems, although the perceptual differences are larger so it usually takes more time. The key, of course, is to start with the pictures in their heads, no matter how alien these pictures seem.

And you need to move incrementally. Across cultures, you often have to cross vast distances. Divide the negotiation into small steps. Take the steps one at a time. If they balk, shorten the steps.

When you are trying to bring someone a large distance, it's hard to do it without being very visual. They actually have to see it, both in their mind and with their eyes. Without the actual experience, it's very hard to change their perceptions. That's why this book is big on role reversal. For most people, you actually have to put them in the setting.

If they think they hate someone, you need to get them to spend time with that person. If they hate a culture, you need to find a way to have a positive experience with that culture. It makes no sense to give them data, to argue with them, to increase benefits that might not matter as much (salary, for example). Give them a picture, spark their imagination. Strike a chord they can feel.

STANDARDS AND CULTURE

Overcoming cultural norms is often incredibly difficult. But it can be done through the use of third parties, the reframing of standards, and an understanding of their perceptions. Carter Mayfield was invited to stay at his girlfriend Sheila's house, which was full of guests. Sheila's father, Justin Ali, who was Persian, prepared to sleep on the couch and give all the beds to his guests. This was a cultural norm; to do otherwise would be to lose face.

After consulting with Sheila, Carter looked through the TV guide and found a program he really wanted to see. He asked Sheila to tell her father that Carter really wanted to see the TV program, it could only be seen from the couch, and it would be rude not to let him see it. Another standard was found. Mr. Ali slept in his own bed, Carter said. Such a small thing, yet such a big thing. Carter, now a family business executive in Texas, married Sheila.

In Chapter 1, I mentioned that various women from India had gotten out of their own arranged marriages using course tools. Here's the story of one of them; let's call her Dena. Her parents wanted her to marry someone from her own sect. It's a tradition that began in the fourth century; even today, 90 percent of marriages in India are arranged.

But Dena loved someone else, from another sect. Her father seemed persuadable, but her mother was absolutely outraged at the thought during a talk one winter break. "We would have to walk with our heads down," her mother said. Indeed, one of Dena's cousins refused to marry her chosen spouse some years before and was disowned by the family: no one even spoke to her for years.

So, during the course, Dena did a role reversal exercise with some other

negotiation students to try to figure out what to do. "The first thing I realized is that I had to validate my mother's feelings and not argue with her,"
Dena said. "She wanted what was best for her children." Such an emotional
payment could get a conversation started.

Next, Dena would talk to her father, who was a lot more accommodating as long as the family's religion and traditions were followed. She would
also talk to a family friend who had married a non-Indian and had a happy
marriage. The endorsement of these third parties would further calm
Dena's mother down and enable a reasonable conversation with Dena—in
very incremental steps, over a period of time.

Dena would next introduce her beau to her parents—not in any formal
setting, but just for them to see him. Her parents would feel consulted.
Dena decided not to tell her beau of the significance of the first meeting; she wanted him to be natural. The man she loved was a professional;
Dena had good judgment in that regard. Dena also realized that if she got
emotional at all, all was lost, since the situation was so incendiary to begin
with. Dena's team in class practiced and prepared, and then did it again
and again.

When Dena went back to see her mother, she executed her strategy over
a period of weeks, sometimes talking to her mother alone and sometimes
with her father, always calm and empathetic. The result: "My parents paid
for the wedding and were proud parents," Dena said.

"The most important thing we learned was the power of using the negotiation tools in a structured way," Dena said. "It's one thing to hear about
the theory; it's quite another to practice putting oneself in the other's
shoes. Preparation is critical. Keeping out the emotional is essential." She
said the whole exercise fundamentally changed her relationship with her
mother for the better, based on mutual respect and value.

Dena is now living happily with the man she loves in California. She
bridged big differences in culture. Worldwide, 60 percent of all marriages
are arranged. Dena did what millions of women likely want to do but cannot because they lack the skill. She successfully negotiated for her life's
happiness.

Let's take a harder example—a young woman who is Israeli and who
wants to marry a young man who is Iraqi. Let's say it's the 1970s or 1980s.
What if they want to live in Baghdad? I don't think so. What if they want
to live in Jerusalem? Again, I don't think so. If they want to live in New
York City, maybe. New York is more diverse and, as such, more tolerant.

Let's think about what happens. The young woman talks to her mother.

What does her mother say? "Over my dead body!" Being calm, the young woman asks, "But why?" And, of course, we all know the refrain, "It'll never work!"

Now, that is *exactly* what we want to hear. Why? Well, what has the young woman's mother given her? *A big fat standard!* So if you are the young woman, you should be asking yourself, has it ever worked? And the answer is yes! My brother-in-law's sister, to name one. She's from a religious Jewish family that survived the Holocaust. Her husband is an Iraqi who worked for the World Bank. They lived in New York City for years, two kids and five dogs. Blissfully happy. And they aren't the only ones. In fact, there are at least several hundred mixed marriages of Arabs and Jews in Israel alone.

So you use standards, calmly, in this relationship situation, to make some headway here. But let's say your mother is clever. She says, "But the chances are almost impossible that it will work. I'll bet only one out of a thousand works, if that." What has your mother given you again? *A big fat standard!* If you are the young woman, you say, "But Mom, don't you always say that your kids are the best? So if anyone could succeed at this, wouldn't it be your kids?"

Of course, this is an emotional situation, and in and of itself, this will not be enough. Her mother needs to meet the guy. And you'll need to bring up the fact that there have been mixed marriages in the Old Testament; in other words, marrying non-Jews is not, in and of itself, against tradition. Indeed, in the Bible, Moses, Sarah, Ishmael, and Solomon all married non-Jews, and Abraham had a child with a non-Jew. Now *that's* a precedent.

What this example shows is that you can begin to bridge what seem to be big cultural differences by finding and addressing the pictures in the other person's head.

CULTURE AND BUSINESS

Let's look at an example that involves a business situation, one that has occurred several times with my students. It demonstrates the kind of incremental steps and role reversal necessary to bridge cultural gaps.

You are a smart female graduate of a business school. You have accepted a job as an associate in the Tokyo office of a major international consulting firm based in the United States. It's a two-year assignment. You've been to

Japan on various trips and speak Japanese pretty well from your studies and visits.

You are assigned to be the main contact with a traditional Japanese manufacturing company. Management and the board of directors are all male and very conservative. They will have nothing to do with you as a consultant. They go around you constantly to your boss, a man. Or they treat you like a secretary. A 2010 report by the World Economic Forum said women occupy just 24 percent of company jobs in Japan, second lowest only to India with 23 percent, among the twenty-seven major countries studied. And very, very few women are permitted into the corporate suite. Many women in the Japanese workforce do clerical tasks like serving tea: they are called O.L.'s, or "Office Ladies."

Your choices are either to mark time in the office for two years, returning to the United States with your career having advanced very little, or to do something about it, and shine. If you use the right negotiation tools, it will take about six months for you to become a full-fledged consultant, respected by the Japanese company.

Let's first consider how a traditional, all-male Japanese management views a young, bright foreign woman in their midst, inserted as an advisor and essentially as an equal. The word that comes to mind is *threat*. Let's spell this out. A threat to the established order. A threat to a thousand years of history. A threat to the cohesion of society. A threat to tradition. To them, it could easily suggest a break-up of the family ("What if all women behaved this way?").

So getting inside their heads is critically important. You may not like how this kind of inquiry makes some Japanese males recoil. But we're here to deal with the real world.

Of course, their perceptions and their feelings are just where we start our process of changing their perceptions to move toward our goals. As I've mentioned, problems are the start of the analysis, not the end.

Two key negotiation tools you need to look at here are their interests (needs) and third parties that could influence them.

Let's first make a partial list of their needs (interests): to profit and attract the best people, and to be seen as innovative, socially conscious, international, competitive, focused on the long term, and collaborative.

And third parties: shareholders, employees, customers, government, U.S. partner, public, competitors, board of directors, media, and colleagues.

Having done this, we can see how to reframe the situation. Far from being a threat, the young woman represents profit, the future, competitiveness: she is among the brightest of the new generation of young businesspeople. As an American, she can address the need to be international. There are likely an increasing number of role models of women executives in Japan who have increased their company's positive public image, and, as such, sales.

As you can see, we simply used the things important to the company's management: business needs and people. And we showed that their actions in excluding the American woman consultant did not meet the company's stated needs. If the company says that its needs also include keeping tradition, it could be pointed out that many traditional Japanese companies are moving in this direction as well. Tradition is not stagnant. The samurai were replaced by modern soldiers. Horses have been replaced by cars.

Now, the American woman is not the right person to make this argument on her own behalf to the traditional Japanese management. An American male counterpart in the consulting firm that already works with the Japanese company would make a better advocate. And the woman would have to prove herself professionally. But, little by little, she would be able to gain the trust of the Japanese company's management. They would view her as having changed from a young foreign woman to a smart business advisor.

The role played by the American male consulting firm manager is key in this situation. He is in the role of cross-cultural interface manager: someone who knows both cultures and is trusted by both. When the distance between people of two different cultures cannot be bridged by the parties, the cross-cultural interface manager can close the gap, and more quickly.

It is not the job of the interface manager to solve things. It is only the job of the interface manager to help in communications. The process is intended to get the parties to understand one another's perceptions, to send signals, to enhance understanding.

Remember, the differences here involve more than just language issues. In fact, if you have learned the other language fluently, it might work *against* you, because people in the other culture often incorrectly assume that you are "fluent" in all other cultural matters. In other words, they are actually less tolerant of mistakes.

I was working on a deal for the United Nations involving trade with

Cuba, and had a meeting scheduled with the executive vice president of a major pharmaceutical firm in Japan. I knew neither the Japanese culture nor the pharmaceutical industry culture very well at the time. I didn't need a translator between Japanese and English. The EVP of the pharma firm spoke perfect English. Rather, I needed help with the cultural issues, which were even more important.

I found a Japanese pharmaceutical consultant who had spent time in the United States and attended a program at Wharton. I retained him as my interface manager to help me handle the meeting.

We arrived at the company and were shown to a conference room. The executive vice president was not there yet. I immediately sat in the chair next to the door. In the United States, the chair across from where I was sitting, facing the door, was the chair of respect. I wanted to leave that chair vacant for my host.

No sooner had I sat down than my consultant gently pulled me up, led me around the table to the other side, and sat me down squarely in the chair facing the door. "In the U.S.," he said, "the host sits in the chair of respect. But in Japan, the chair of respect is given to the guest."

When our host came in, he immediately saw three things. One, I was sitting in the right chair. Two, I had taken the trouble to find out which chair it was. Three, I brought with me a cultural translator to make sure we started and continued with a minimum of miscommunication.

I was *not* trying to be like my host, speak his language or immerse myself in his customs. I was trying to send a small signal that I understood there were cultural differences and wanted to find a way to talk effectively. The meeting went very well.

This kind of strategy works in all kinds of situations, in many different cultural contexts. The first time I was planning to go to Ukraine, I was told that the standard for negotiations there was one bottle of vodka per person per negotiating session. This was not the kind of vodka that one buys in the store in the United States. This was the kind of vodka that one might use as lighter fluid. I don't drink, I don't drink vodka, and I certainly don't drink lighter fluid substitutes. But I needed to do the negotiation.

So I brought with me—please forgive the stereotype, but alas, this is true—a 350-pound Irish investment banker who told me that no one would drink him under the table. I introduced him to our Ukrainian counterpart as my "designated drinker." They were cool with that. I never saw so much vodka consumed in my entire life by two people. And we did the deal. We had found a way to bridge cultural differences.

THEIR REAL CULTURE

Often people have a wrong idea about what constitutes another culture. Just because someone is Chinese doesn't mean they belong to the Chinese culture. They may have been raised in America and would be insulted if you assumed they follow Chinese customs and traditions.

I once wrote an article about a professor at the State University of New York at Stony Brook. This professor, Hanan Selvan, had retinitis pigmentosa, a degenerative eye disease that gradually narrows one's field of vision until one becomes blind. Dr. Selvan, a brilliant independent thinker, was in the advanced stages of the disease. But he led an active life, traveling on trains by himself, armed only with his telescoping cane. He was an active member in a lot of academic societies, as well as Mensa, the society for those with a genius I.Q.

I asked him whether he belonged to societies for patients with retinitis pigmentosa. He responded indignantly. "They aren't scholars for the most part," he said. "All I have in common with them is a common affliction." Those words stuck with me. Here, the attribute that most onlookers would think was the most visible and defining part of his being was not even on his radar screen. One really needs to probe deeply to find out the culture to which the other party feels they belong.

Following is a list that captures what one should think about in dealing effectively with those who are different. It puts a lot of the tools from this book in a structure that can help anyone in getting more value from situations where people, at least at first, appear different from one another.

ACHIEVING AGREEMENTS WITH THOSE WHO ARE DIFFERENT
1. Develop goals. Find common goals. Invoke common enemies.
2. Paint a picture of the logical extreme: the risk in continuing the present course.
3. Do role reversal. Who are they? Question your assumptions. Find their dreams/fears.
4. Listen for signals: verbal, nonverbal.
5. Identify the "noise" that masks similarities (physical, language, style).
6. Articulate and value real differences.
7. Find standards: theirs and reasonable norms.
8. Name bad behavior and identify your own weaknesses.
9. Insist on evidence to support all views.

10. Be incremental in any suggestion. Focus only on what is controllable.

11. Consult before deciding: bring them into the process; ask their advice.

12. Find models where the suggestions have worked.

13. Insist on finding creative options. "Is this the ONLY way?"

14. Look for hidden agendas; develop incentives to change them.

15. Find their constituencies; appeal to their values.

16. Create a vision of the future. Discuss it with them.

17. Create a new "culture" of those who want to make the change.

The first thing, of course, is to identify your goals. Do the actions you plan meet your goals? Can you meet your goals given the people you are dealing with?

The picture of the logical extreme is a key one. It paints a vision for the parties as to what will happen if you continue on this path. Bankruptcy? Years in court? Nuclear war? I was once in a room with Israeli and Jordanian businessmen. I said, "How about this as the answer for the Middle East? The party that wins is the party that kills everyone on the other side: men, women, children, dogs, cats, goats, chickens, snakes, fish, worms, butterflies . . . ?"

They thought that was ridiculous. I said, "But that's what you have to do, right? You have to kill *everyone*. Because if one thing is left standing, you still have a war. Someone is still going to try to kill someone on the other side over what happened yesterday." They could see that this was indeed the picture of the logical extreme, and it was not going to accomplish anyone's goals. I wanted them to consider better options.

And I want to be incremental in the proposals; a little progress at a time. Are there some small examples where solutions have worked? Find them and apply them.

Start building a coalition of people. Start with those who want to join a new way of doing things. Bring more and more people into the process. Ask people's advice. Develop incentives to change things that are harder to change.

In May 2007, I conducted a two-day workshop for executives, educators, and government officials in Riyadh, Saudi Arabia. Riyadh is a very conservative city. We focused on the common bond that we had: improving processes and results through negotiation. In that sense we were all part of the same culture—educated people trying to do better. We had a great workshop in which we taught about forty-five people, many dressed in traditional Arab robes, the tools in this book.

At the end of the third day, I felt the freedom to say, "Not every Israeli is your enemy, and not every Saudi is your friend. Some Israelis will make you rich, and some Saudis will steal you blind."

They got it; there were lots of nods in the classroom at Prince Sultan University, whose namesake and benefactor is an heir to the country's throne. The group included the head of the city's Chamber of Commerce, the presidents of some of the largest companies in Saudi Arabia, and the head of Prince Sultan University.

It is possible to deal with vast differences between two groups, or individuals, calmly, effectively, and in a way that creates lasting value. You just have to try.

9

Getting More at Work

An honors graduate of Harvard Business School was hired by a major company in California. Within three years of her hiring, the three people who hired her—CEO, president, and executive vice president—were gone: retired, fired, or just left. The new management team intended to fire her along with the rest of the old team.

But it turned out that her job was inviolate. That's because when she was hired, she realized that she might be in trouble down the road. The three people who hired her were each twenty-five years older than she. She knew they would be gone long before her career hit its stride.

So for three years she did favors for a variety of company departments that had nothing to do with her job description. She did this after hours, on weekends, at lunch breaks, and sometimes when she could work it in as part of her job. She collected friends throughout the company. So when the new management team came in, there was a hue and cry throughout the company: "This woman is indispensable! You cannot get rid of her!" Her job was saved.

This manager was essentially involved in a three-year negotiation with the rest of the company. And they didn't even know they were involved in a negotiation. You think this is Machiavellian and manipulative? Well, whom did it hurt? No one. In fact, the company got free work for three years out of her. And the company saved a valued employee from being lost to corporate politics.

Relations between employers and employees are getting more difficult. The traditional trade-off was that employees would contribute their loyalty, skill, and time in return for job stability and a living wage. Unions sought to codify that. In recent years, however, the balance of power has clearly shifted toward employers in most areas.

In such an environment, savvy negotiation skills are critical. I tell my students who are having a hard time with prospective employers on job interviews: "This is the nicest they will ever be to you." So if there's a problem now, watch out!

The market is crowded with job advice: say this, wear that, ask this, prepare for that. The problem with much of this advice is that it is intended to be applied to every situation. But as noted throughout *Getting More*, one size does not fit all. Effective negotiation is situational. So the most important thing to do regarding jobs is to understand the other party. And to understand the people who influence the other party. Only then can you develop a negotiation strategy for a given situation.

That means you may have different negotiation strategies for different people in the same firm. It takes more work, but it is much more precise and effective. The goal is to make yourself more valuable in the company organization. The higher your perceived value, the further you'll advance in your career, and the harder it will be to get rid of you in an economic downturn.

Let's start with the woman from Harvard Business School profiled at the beginning of this chapter. First, she thought about her goals—a long-term career at the company. Next, she thought of any problems she might encounter in meeting those goals: her mentors leaving before she did. Then she identified the third parties who could help her: other departments. She thought about their needs—including event planning, advertising, and marketing advice. She prepared. She was incremental. She paid a lot of attention to relationships.

Expanding relationships is essential in virtually all job situations. Companies, even small ones, can be very political places. The more you identify and ally with the people who can help you, the better position you are in. Other people can serve as an early-warning system when things start to go awry. They will give you information to help you pursue company opportunities. They will come to your aid if things get rough. They will give your projects higher priority. They will help you out in a pinch.

Below are some of the key types of people who can help you after you get the job. Some can help you get the job in the first place. Reach out to them. Have coffee or lunch with them.

- People Who've Been There Forever. Look for someone who has been around for a long time, has been put out to pasture, and is often ignored by others. They know where everything is buried. Talk to them, value them. Every company has one or more people like this. They know all the pitfalls and politics. They will give you information that will be critical in meeting your goals and protecting yourself.
- People Who Have Left. Many of these people have seen the company at its worst. They know what the company can't do for people. You may need to take some of what they say with a grain of salt. They may have bad feelings or a hidden agenda. But you will usually get the unvarnished story. If you are looking for a job and they left on good terms, they may make calls for you.
- Information Technology (IT) People. Many people seem to hate the IT department. Learn to love the IT department, or at least one or two people in it. Most people could not do their jobs effectively without IT. When the IT supporting your work has a problem, you want someone to fix it immediately, even if it's the weekend.
- Librarians. Not all companies have them. But these people are better at research than almost anyone in the company. They will make your work—and you—better.
- Cleaning Staff. Most managers consider them invisible, but they know a lot. They hear a lot. They see a lot.
- Security Guards. When you've forgotten your pass, when you need a client to be quickly let in, when you want to get into a locked office where you've left some documents, a security guard you've made a relationship with will help you. Say "Hi" to someone daily. Give a holiday tip. Strike up a sports conversation.
- Administrative Staff. Also called the permanent staff. Executives and managers come and go; a lot of the administrative staff stays for a career. They can create ugly gossip—or positive buzz. Make them part of your team. Bring them cookies at holidays.
- Other Staff. Copy and fax room, cafeteria workers, travel department, maintenance people—all of these people will help you in a deadline when you have to have something to do your job, or you need information.
- Human Resources. The HR people are generally the captains of "No." Their main job is to protect the company. But they are not

monolithic. Make friends, starting with more junior people. Show an interest in what they do. They will be happy to explain their job to you. HR often has a fair amount of say on personnel (and personal) issues.

- People on Whom You and Your Department Depend. Are there outside vendors, restaurants, or printers that your department depends on? The more these people know and like you, the more you will be able to get favors for your department. Do you have their cell-phone numbers? Are there any tips you got from your travel department, for example, that you provide to outside vendors?

What I am talking about here is building your own *coalition*. It takes time, it takes effort and thought. But it takes less time and work than finding another job, or not getting the promotions and raises you might otherwise get.

Be incremental about this. Ask people about their job. Find out their dreams and fears. Give them information when you can. Offer them advice or a set of helpful hands. Start with a single person or two. What you are doing is collecting as much information as you can about the place where you work or want to work.

Is the organization nervous about something? Do they need help in a foreign language? A reliable intermediary with another culture? Staff in some region or on a holiday? Can you supply that information it is hard for them to procure except at great cost?

Ellen Walsh was new to a public relations company, working with two other people. No one knew her capabilities. Then she found out that a well-regarded employee was leaving. "No one wanted his job," she said. "His job was to hire interns." Ellen realized that volunteering for the job would make the company grateful. It would also allow her to meet a lot more people, some of whom would eventually work for the company, and help build her own base of support.

SPECIFIC SUCCESSES

Earlier in the book I referred to a student who, using course tools, was able to get twelve consecutive final-round interviews after being rejected eighteen times the previous semester. How did he do it? First the student, Mehul Trivedi, found out more specifically the needs of each firm and department to which he was applying. He used the negotiation preparation model outlined in Chapter 7 to prepare thoroughly for each interview. He identified the key decision-makers and collected specific information about each person who would interview him. Through the Wharton alumni network he found people who had recently left the firm, or knew the firm. He phoned associates with whom he had been friendly, and Wharton grads who worked at the firm. He asked about unfilled needs.

He realized that he had written a general résumé that would work only partially for all the firms to which he applied. But each of these firms had different specific needs: different skill sets, experience, locations, working hours, and conditions. Within each firm, different departments had different needs.

After he did that research, he rewrote his résumé, matching it to each firm and department. He sent it to the specific people who had the biggest perceived need: department heads, team leaders, human resources. He went through a role-reversal exercise with his wife, who videotaped him; they both studied the tape and made style changes. Mehul was able to anticipate at least two-thirds of the questions he was later asked. He showed in each case how he met or exceeded the firm's (or department's) standards, and he worked to make human connections in all cases.

"The results were astounding," he said. In many cases he was invited back for final-round interviews even before the first-round interview was concluded.

He said he had initially been skeptical of the course's model, noting that the people were at least half the reason why a firm reached agreements, and that the "substance" was, at most, 10 percent. But his experience proved the model's validity, he said. His chosen job was as a stock analyst, and he picked his firm before all the interviews were complete. Still, he said, the tools he learned can be applied to any situation. And he has applied them in the thirteen years since.

Mehul's approach was tailored specifically to each situation. That is how one gets good jobs. I look at hundreds of résumés per year. Yet *almost no one* writes a résumé reflecting *any* meaningful research about our enterprise. Mehul's experience has been replicated time and again by my students.

When Gaurav Tewari applied to work for a major technology firm in Silicon Valley, he knew *exactly* which two departments he could benefit most, and why. He asked people he knew to email reference letters to relevant interviewers. He had the firm's hiring standards down cold, including quotes from its mission statement. And sure enough, he got the job. He is now a principal at Highland Capital Partners in Boston.

Even in tough economic times, there are lots of ways to get in the door. Yi Zhang could not get a job at a venture capital firm in Silicon Valley because he didn't have start-up experience. But he learned the company was very interested in Internet phone technology, in which Yi had expertise.

"So I offered free consulting," Yi said. Once inside the firm, you are in the information flow; you learn about opportunities. Volunteers often become employees. The firm used Yi's work on technology and market analysis in an investment they were considering. He perfectly positioned himself for when the firm decided to invest. At the least, Yi built his résumé.

After a few months, the firm started to pay him. He turned it into a similar job in his native Shanghai. "Even after the door is closed, try a second and third time," he said. "Provide them with a specific solution. It takes time, but it works."

Some people cannot afford to give up their time without pay. Perhaps you can do this in lieu of a second job. Or on weekends. The key is to be persistent and to continue to find creative ways to get in the door.

Mark Sorial was rejected by the International Finance Corporation (IFC), the investment banking arm of the World Bank, for a job in Cairo. After the rejection, he asked the IFC why he was turned down. He was told that a senior IFC official didn't think he had the required technical skills. So he wrote a letter to his contact there, reframing his work at Wharton as two years of training in private equity and emerging markets.

"I realize that your team has made its decision regarding my candidacy, but I am hoping you will give me a chance should this position or another become available," Mark wrote, in a tactful and humble way. But Mark went further, and this is a key step: he offered to take a test of the IFC's choosing to demonstrate his technical skills. In other words, he was persistent, but not pushy.

Within a couple of months, a problem developed with the other candidate. The IFC took Mark up on his offer of a test. His results were great and exceeded the expectations of the skeptical senior IFC executive. Mark was hired for his dream job, as an associate investment officer in Cairo. "The negotiation tools I learned changed the way I view the negotiation process," he said. "I had a framework to prepare. It enabled me to be firm without damaging the relationship."

There are many situations at work in which the issue is thorny and can jeopardize the relationship if one is not careful. Many people just don't attempt the negotiation and get less. But with the use of the strategies in

Getting More, you can do the negotiation with far less risk. Besides identifying common interests, you can find common enemies. If you can find something both parties are against, it can strengthen the bond and reframe the entire situation.

Aleksandr Hromcenco, a director of clinical information in the pharmaceutical industry, wanted to change his annual performance review from "met" to "exceeded." He had just received the company's annual Clinical Innovation Award, a big emblem of his value. But it was announced after his review, so it had not been counted.

It's hard to get people to change a decision they have made. In this case, Alex thought his boss would simply say, "Well, we'll include it next year." So Alex reframed the situation: he asked his manager why annual reviews had to be submitted before all the data were in. That didn't seem fair to anyone, including managers, he said. Only two people in his department had ever received the Clinical Innovation Award. Surely if his manager had known about this, Alex said, his evaluation would have been higher. Alex showed his boss how they were both disadvantaged by the system. His boss redid the review. Result: a $13,500 increase in annual salary.

Another strategy to gain more at work is to reduce their perceived risk. A U.S. Air Force energy manager did not want to proceed with a $14 million solar energy project proposed by Honeywell for Luke Air Force Base in Arizona. The Air Force manager told Ranjit Bhopal of Honeywell that she had bad experiences with energy service companies. Ranjit immediately said, "If I were in your shoes, I would feel the same way." This validated the manager's perceptions, provided an emotional payment, and made her more interested in listening.

Ranjit then differentiated his project from her past experiences, using references and evidence. He proposed an incremental start: only $200,000 for the renewable-energy part of the $14 million project. This reduced perceived risk further. And Ranjit said a senior Honeywell official would show up for the dedication, valuing her efforts. She agreed. The test was successful, and now the whole project is being done. It took careful planning, multiple tools, and much sensitivity to the other party.

Simply by asking people about their fears, you can often get the information you need to persuade them. Ben Hughes lived far from a bar review course location. He wanted to do the self-study option at home. It was more expensive, and his law firm opposed self-study courses. Ben was told that some new associates who previously took the self-study course failed the bar exam.

But Ben decided to mitigate the firm's perceived risk, unfounded or not. So he noted to the firm's managers that he had worked at the firm for two summers already. "You know me pretty well," he said. "Don't you think I would study well on my own?" He also noted the firm's policy of being flexible with employees (standards). The firm agreed to the self-study and the extra $600 cost.

By now it should be clear that a key negotiation skill is asking questions: finding the perceptions and pictures in the other person's head, and finding out about the situation.

Dack LaMarque thought he was worth more to his new employer than the $85,000 he had been offered, even in a bad economy.

This is the kind of conversation that needs to be in person. So Dack went to Portland, Oregon, to talk face-to-face with the head of the company. "I started the conversation not about salary," Dack said. "I started with his vision for the company. I asked him how he saw me fitting into that vision."

As the CEO answered and saw more clearly the match with Dack, Dack's perceived value began to rise for the CEO. When the CEO finally asked Dack for his salary range, "I asked him what standard he was thinking about," Dack said. The CEO said he was willing to pay the money that Dack and his wife needed to maintain their lifestyle.

This was a great standard. Dack told him that figure was $120,000. The CEO said yes.

Dack then asked if equity was possible if he made "a significant difference to the organization." CEOs like to hear people talk like this. They settled on 3 to 5 percent to start, adjusted upward in two to three years if performance indicated it. So Dack received a 41 percent increase in salary, and equity, by asking for more information and using it to increase his value in the eyes of the CEO. Although he has since left the company for a private equity firm, Dack has maintained his relationship with the CEO and retained stock in the company.

Another student, an attorney from Brazil, wanted a promotion to senior attorney when he went back to his law firm after a year of study in the United States. But salaries and positions were frozen due to Brazil's economic crisis. The attorney met with the senior partner of the firm over lunch. First, he asked the partner about his kids, and the prospects for the firm. "The partner talked a lot about the firm and his expectations," the attorney said. Every time the partner mentioned an expectation, the attorney nodded his head and said he was committed to doing that. By the end of the lunch, the attorney had been made a senior attorney.

Christopher Damm, a physician, was trying to position himself as a marketing consultant for a medical products company. "The project leader did not know me or my skill set," Christopher said. "He saw me as a physician rather than a marketing consultant."

Instead of trying to sell the project leader, Chris asked questions. He asked the project leader about his goals, and the skills that were needed. He asked the project leader to describe his problems, vision, and standards. "Only late in the conversation did I match my qualifications to his comments," Chris reported. His engagement increased from four hours to six days, with the possibility of much more. He was now a physician *and* a marketing consultant.

He did it by (a) finding out the other side's needs, (b) discovering how they evaluated things, and (c) matching his skills explicitly to the other party's needs.

With compensation, it is especially important to know what the other party is thinking before asking for something specific. Otherwise you may end up negotiating against yourself. Paul Kavanaugh, a banker in New York City, was having a conversation with his boss at salary review time. "What are your expectations?" the boss asked. Paul said this was an "interesting" question, but could not specifically answer it without first knowing the standards against which salary and bonus were set. His boss described them.

"Where on this scale, roughly, do you think my performance fits?" Paul asked. To his astonishment, his boss "came up with a number that was almost twice what I had in mind." To make sure his boss felt he answered the question, Paul then asked for somewhat more than the boss offered. The boss then felt good about standing firm on his offer. I tend to look at this as an emotional payment, not manipulation. Paul was not trying to be extreme, but only trying to make the boss feel better. Most interesting about this is that Paul had not sufficiently prepared for the meeting, he said. By asking questions, he was able to gain time and information that helped him exceed his goals.

Small talk is almost always big talk, even in job situations. Will Chen wanted to transfer to a different group at the investment bank where he worked. He asked three times, and each time he was told no. So he scheduled an informational interview with the human resources manager in New York City. He wanted to make a personal connection with her. In the meeting, he asked what her favorite food was. Vietnamese. Will knew all the best Vietnamese restaurants, websites, recipes, and chefs. He found a connection. And he got the transfer.

INTERVIEWS

Entire books are written about job interviews, so I don't want to duplicate what's out there. But I do want to make suggestions through the lens of *Getting More.*

First, when someone asks you a question, answer it immediately and succinctly. Or let them know what information you need to answer it. People hate it when others don't answer their questions. Don't you? It's a bad politician's tactic: obfuscating, being evasive. The signal you're giving off is "I've got something to hide." Second, with some cultural exceptions (mostly outside the United States), direct eye contact is good. But don't stare! Smiling and other social niceties convey social skill. Stay focused on the other person. People want to work around others whom they like and trust. They read extra meaning into small things. If you're early, you come across as motivated. If you're late, well, will you be late for work if you get the job? Will you be late on work assignments?

Asking a job candidate to give an example of their reliability is more telling than asking them the best or worst experience they ever had. "Best" and "worst" are too often lazy questions. When was their character tested? If you're an employer, you want to find out what someone else is made of. When did they have to do something really difficult to support someone else?

If you're a job applicant, you want to ask how the company retains, trains, and promotes people in their careers. What is the company's philosophy of work? You should have a set of thoughtful questions gleaned from the research you've done on the company. When you've spent considerable time researching the company, it shows how motivated you are. It makes you appear as a self-starter. You don't need fifty questions, just three to five. You should have pitched your résumé to the company's specific needs. So you should talk about those needs, and your skills in meeting them.

STANDARDS

Standards are the law of an organization. People can try to use politics to go around the standards, just as people break the law in society. But the standards are always there. So one should always be conscious of them.

The organization's standards are a big protection—legal and organizational—against being treated unfairly. Read all the relevant personnel manuals. Document every instance of unfairness in light of the organization's stated policies. Be dispassionate when you point this out: don't make yourself the issue.

One student was hired by a major consulting firm, which offered him a $35,000 tuition reimbursement for the second year of his MBA program. His actual costs turned out to be $51,380. The firm would not renegotiate. The student did some research and found out that the firm had capped its tuition reimbursement at the cost of another, less expensive business school.

The student then researched his own firm's standards: it had offered to "reimburse second-year fees." It didn't say "second-year fees based on the cheaper school." Also, other firms in the consulting industry pegged tuition reimbursement to each student's chosen school.

The result: the student got the extra $16,380. "Framing the problem as one of fairness rather than one of compensation helped greatly," the student said. This is a great use of reframing standards in the work context.

Reframing standards is key in the job market. You often have to lead the other party, step-by-step, to where you want them to go. Don Cordeiro wanted to land a job with a large private-equity firm in Brazil. But he had no experience in the field. A large number of experienced candidates were applying.

However, Don understood that the real issue for firms is not experience but skills. Experience is only an indicator of skills. The best indicator is, of course, the skills themselves. So Don asked the hiring partner about the kinds of talent that the firm was lacking. "People-related issues," the partner said. "Team formation, entrepreneurial abilities, fit."

This was all Don needed. He pointed out the skills he had developed over the years in his various nonfinancial entrepreneurial ventures: developing teams, dealing with an entrepreneurial environment, finding ways to overcome differences in an organization. "I then mentioned that I had no experience in finance or private equity," Don said. "I let him establish the relevance of my background to the industry." Although Don took a management consulting job in São Paulo before the process was finished, the private-equity firm moved him up from nowhere to being a leading contender.

Himanshu Bahuguna was denied relocation expenses to Asia for a job after graduation from business school. But the firm did provide such expenses for new hires in the United States. He asked why the firm provided $10,000 in expenses for a new hire moving ninety minutes from Philadelphia to New York, but provided $0 to a new hire moving halfway around the world. He got the expenses. He added that instead of negotiating with human resources, he asked his own group, which valued him more, to go to bat for him inside the firm.

Roswell Osborne spent two hours on industry research and found that Microsoft offered $25,000 more to someone of his experience than eBay was offering him. When he brought that to eBay's attention, he was able to secure an additional $10,000 signing bonus. "That's $5,000 an hour for my efforts," he said. But after a month, his department was dissolved. He noted that he had given eBay a one-year commitment at their request, turned down other jobs, and that the company must have known about the restructuring before he came on board.

Roswell got a $70,000 severance package, gained from using standards and preparation. He decided to use all this extra money to start his own e-commerce business in San Antonio. "You keep preparing and practicing," he said. "And then, when you need it, it's there."

Here is one more, a bit thornier. A manager at a major company was denied a promotion due to the recession and a limited budget. Then the manager saw the employer's guidelines, which indicated that he should have been two levels higher. Politely, he showed the guidelines to his boss, and added that the higher title would prompt more credibility from customers. He got the promotion and a salary increase, using standards, third parties, and interests.

If the boss gets irritated, politely ask why. You are just asking the company to follow its own standards. Doesn't the company want persistent employees?

I teach my students not to accept ambiguous answers. Shervin Limbert, a consultant for a Lebanese gas-oil company, was told that he would get a "discretionary bonus." In Shervin's world, however, the phrase meant little or nothing.

So Shervin asked his employer how his value to the company would be calculated. Were there any standards? He then enumerated the value he had brought to the company so far. This included significant contacts in Kuwait for favorable terms on a contract he had brought in. As a result, he received a promise of a $30,000 bonus.

Once you become comfortable with using standards, they can serve you continually in doing a better job. John Moreno saved his company, Teton, $12,000 by persuading Fluor Enterprises to let Teton use Fluor's high-speed computer line.

Fluor technology people at first said security concerns barred Teton, a Georgia industrial construction company, from sharing Fluor's high-speed computer line. So John contacted someone else he knew at Fluor and asked if Fluor was sharing its high-speed line with anyone else. The answer was yes! How was security protected in that arrangement? The other company bought a router and firewall. John went back with this information to the Fluor IT people and offered to do the same. He also pointed out that Fluor and Teton had just completed a strategic agreement.

"Once confronted with the fact that Fluor had set the standard by allowing another contractor to share the connection," John said, "the Fluor IT people could no longer say, 'Corporate just won't allow it.' " John was very pleasant about it. But he was firm. And he met his goals. He's since been promoted to head of his division.

As noted throughout *Getting More*, a key part of framing is reframing. You take a company's framing and ask them to look at it a different way. This often makes it easier for them to meet your goals.

Judy Sher accepted a job at Fidelity Investments on December 4, thirteen days after the company's deadline for bonus checks that year. Getting a bonus check before year's end would save Judy more than $10,000 in taxes. She called up the decision-maker in human resources and blamed the bad economy (common enemy): her decision to join Fidelity had been delayed by the fact that her partner had a tough time finding a job. Judy then added that it was less than two weeks since the deadline, *which was very close to the deadline*. Couldn't they make an exception (standards)?

Judy got the check that year. She first established a human connection with the person at HR. Then she gave the HR person framing to enable them to sell it to their own constituency.

Adam Kane used reframing to get his company, Erickson Retirement Communities, to accept a $50 million project. Erickson develops and operates mostly upscale retirement communities; there are 30,000 residents in nineteen states. Adam, a senior vice president, wanted to go into the low-income market. The company was initially uninterested in this new market. So Adam contacted an executive who had just been appointed head of a new division: new products.

"They were thinking a new product meant, say, health care products,"

Adam said. But he reframed "low-income residences" as a "new product." The new product director, looking for something substantial, got behind the idea and the company approved it.

If you are good enough at using negotiating tools, you can find negotiation room in situations that appear watertight to others. Some years ago a former student wanted to transfer offices at McKinsey without having to go through a time-consuming, stressful review process similar to when the employee was hired. McKinsey said it was standard policy. So the employee used another McKinsey standard: its "One firm" policy; that is, the same standards throughout the firm worldwide.

If McKinsey is one firm, the employee asked, why do employees have to go through a formal review when transferring offices? Aren't the original hiring standards the same everywhere? McKinsey could have dug in its heels. But smart firms know that by violating their own standards, they will soon start to lose the best recruits. The employee got the transfer. This shows that you can meet your goals using their standards even when they are a big, powerful, worldwide firm.

Josh Furchtman's new firm said they would not move him twice, once to his parents for the summer and once to the city where he was working. He wanted to know: What if the total moving costs were less than the firm's usual cost for one move? Wasn't it really a budget problem? Josh found cheaper movers, and the firm paid for both moves. This was reframing the standard from "only one move" to "adhering to the budget limit."

Anders Bjork was rejoining a firm that offered him a salary similar to those junior to him. He asked his new manager if he had more experience and responsibilities than those junior. "Yes," he was told. "So should I receive the same pay?" he asked. Result: 15 percent salary increase. Anders, now a private equity director in New York, used framing, standards, and asking questions. Tone is also important; it was a relationship situation. He was very respectful in asking.

I could go on and on. A search of our database shows many hundreds of examples. They will work for you, too. Let's try just one more. Allan Castro was told his signing bonus was being cut due to a poor economy. Allan got a company brochure saying they "pay competitive rates." Allan brought this with him to a meeting with a human resources manager, along with industry standards showing that the compensation offered to him was low even in a poor economy. He received $5,000 more.

In using standards, it is important to ask for precedents. "Have you ever done this before?" and "Have you ever made an exception?" should be part of your everyday vocabulary.

TRADING ITEMS OF UNEQUAL VALUE

We've discussed the notion of intangibles. Here's how to meet your goals on the job by finding things to trade that don't cost you very much—but that the other side values.

Christopher Kelly could only pay a new hire the same salary as his old firm. This was unacceptable to the candidate. "I tried hard to understand his long-term goals," Chris said. "I wanted to find out the reasons for his unhappiness in his current job."

Chris found out that the candidate wanted to get an MBA eventually. Chris told him the company could pay for it. Chris asked what else the candidate was interested in. "He indicated that adding the word 'manager' to his job title would be very valuable to him," said Chris, who heads a weather services company. "Not a problem for us." The candidate accepted the job at the offered salary.

Once you see it in action, it seems simple. But you actually have to systematically and precisely go through the process.

Vikas Bansal, a manager at a major financial services company in New York, was trying to get one of his direct reports to work harder. Threats generally wreck motivation. Vikas realized that employee morale was already low due to decreases in salary and layoffs in a difficult economic environment. So instead he asked the employee, John, to explain his concerns and future career hopes. "I patiently listened," Vikas said. "I tried to understand his needs. Then I summarized them to make sure I got it right."

Vikas found out that John's wife was expecting a child that summer. Work schedule flexibility would be greatly appreciated. So Vikas listed his five top work priorities he wanted from John. In return, he offered John flexibility in working over the summer, including working from home. "He got excited," Vikas said. John left the meeting on fire, and his work greatly improved. It remains improved to this day, Vikas added.

Creative options to attract and keep employees are limited only by the imagination of either side. Similar to Chris Kelly, John Moreno was trying to hire an employee whom the company could not pay more in salary than his old job did. John, the Teton Industrial Construction manager mentioned a few pages ago, knew the candidate lived in a small apartment with his wife and three children. "His wife wanted a home of their own," John said. They owned a piece of land but couldn't afford the house. "We offered to install the foundation," John said. The result? The candidate accepted the job.

Ask for a list of intangibles that don't cost the company much, whether you are a candidate, employee, or manager. There are discounts on health club memberships or travel, moving expenses, lower-interest loans using the company's credit rating, flex time. All are good ways to bridge gaps in compensation and other negotiation terms.

Aravind Immaneni needed another staff member. And the compliance director at his company had an unused staff slot. But the compliance director was new and didn't want to give up the slot, Aravind said. "He thought giving up the slot could lower his status in the company," Aravind realized after doing role reversal.

So Aravind reviewed possible items to trade. They included sharing an administrative assistant and giving the new compliance director a corner office. Aravind also discovered that the compliance director hated doing audits. Aravind met with the director in the director's office (so he felt more important) and reviewed the various intangibles. The director picked getting help with the audit. Aravind did the audit and the director turned over the staff slot. "Role reversal made the negotiation easy," Aravind said.

Aravind, a senior vice president of a major financial services firm, was senior to the director. Thus, Aravind could have gone over the director's head and forced him to turn over the staff position. But Aravind found that trading things of unequal value preserved the relationship. "Looking at things from his viewpoint gave me a better way to do the negotiation," Aravind said.

To make such a trade, one has to be constructive. Tom Greer wanted to move an employee, Brian, from an engagement with one client to the team for another client. Brian had specific skills the second team could use. Brian's colleague complained that his staff was being unfairly taken.

Tom, a media and entertainment partner for a major accounting firm, did not respond in kind. "I offered to make a more experienced senior associate available as a substitute for Brian," Tom said. It met everyone's goals.

Work life is filled with millions of these daily negotiations. They will make work a hassle if not handled successfully. The tools outlined here are antidotes to hassle.

Susan Pirollo said her boss resented the "special treatment" she got by being allowed to attend an executive MBA program. He called her time off to attend school "excessive," even though the company had committed to it. But this wasn't about being right, Susan realized. She thought about what her boss was really feeling—overworked.

So instead of lashing back, Susan suggested that perhaps she could do more to help her boss. She asked which of his duties she could take over. She offered to use personal time to do it. By staying calm and pleasant, she reduced her boss's resentment. "It's so important in any negotiation to just *stop*, put yourself in their shoes, and think of the world from their perspective," said Susan, now a senior manager at a pharmaceutical firm near Philadelphia.

THIRD PARTIES

Allying with third parties is especially important at work. Organizations respect strength in numbers, since they are creatures of numbers. An organization represents an alliance by its members. Third parties also help if you don't have enough (a) authority, (b) persuasiveness on your own, (c) credibility, (d) connection to the decision-maker, or (e) emotional distance from the situation. Essentially, this is the skill of building coalitions.

Eric Lammers wanted to meet with the CFO of Reliance Resources to pitch a deal. He had never spoken to the CFO. And the CFO didn't generally meet with people he didn't know. Sending him a letter out of the blue seemed useless.

But Eric did know the company's treasurer, who in turn knew the CFO. Eric met the treasurer personally to show his motivation and present a stronger case. Eric also came up with framing for the treasurer to describe the proposal in one phrase: "liquidity options," a big need of the company. This was so persuasive that the CFO invited Eric, the treasurer, and the company's vice president of finance to the meeting.

Ram Vittal used third parties to collect information for him. Ram expected to get his green card upon joining a banking firm; it would reduce the risk to him in the event of a change in U.S. visa policy. But the human resources director told him the company's "standard policy" was a one-year probation. "They were intransigent," Ram said. So Ram went to the person in the company who would be most sympathetic.

He asked the vice president of the group that hired him. The vice president knew of other cases where green card processing had started as of the hiring date. The vice president got the process started right away. "I used to think that these stories about negotiation successes had fairy-tale endings," said Ram, who later joined Goldman Sachs, where he is now a vice president. "But I found that if you consciously use these tools and think the process through, in fact they are practical." Most important, he said, is making sure all parties get something from the process.

As such, the first choice, not available to Ram in the visa case, is to give something to the other side to further a relationship, instead of going around them. Shaping your proposal based on the pictures in their heads is one way to do it. Elisa Eiger wanted to be an internal consultant in her Alabama publishing company, but HR's policy was not to create new positions.

Elisa met with the HR director and asked what skills the company still needed. She "made a big effort to keep quiet" as the director outlined the skills. Elisa then summarized the apparent shared interests based on what she had heard, and explained how a position could be fashioned to meet those needs. Elisa had tailored the position to the director's comments. "The director offered to assist me in writing my job proposal and paved the way for me to get the job," Elisa said.

Ofotsu Tetteh Kujorjie, one of my students from Ghana, wanted to discuss the terms of a job offer with the company's CEO. The CEO didn't have time: take the job or leave it, now, Ofotsu was told. So Ofotsu phoned the CEO's executive assistant, whom he had met, and asked if there were any projects the CEO needed done. There were.

Ofotsu wrote to the CEO, saying he wanted to join the firm but had some questions about the terms. In return for having a discussion in person when Ofotsu returned to Ghana over Christmas break, Ofotsu offered to work on some of the CEO's projects, which Ofotsu named. This prompted a phone call from the CEO to say the delay was fine. Ofotsu did projects for the CEO, then went back to school and got an advanced degree in law at Georgetown. "The door is open; he still calls when he comes to town," Ofotsu said. He had used interests and third parties, and was also very straight with the CEO.

BEING INCREMENTAL

Most of the negotiations in this chapter, and in this book, are incremental: not asking for everything at once. This is one of the hardest things for people to learn. Other parties usually don't want to risk a big change. In every negotiation, think of ways to divide the process into steps. It doesn't necessarily take longer, because the alternative is often no deal at all.

Camilla Cho worked a summer at Warner Home Video and was offered a full-time job upon graduation. In the meantime she realized that she would rather pursue a finance/strategy career in Warner's media and entertainment division. But she knew she could not move inside the firm without the approval of her boss, Jeff.

However, merely asking Jeff about moving could make her appear ungrateful. Jeff had given her a great opportunity amid hundreds of applicants. It could damage their relationship and her career.

"After putting myself in Jeff's shoes," Camilla said, "I realized that my goal of an immediate transfer was unrealistic. So I focused instead on small steps: contacts and cross-company exposure first."

Camilla asked Jeff if she could do finance and strategy work some of the time, as this was a long-term interest. Jeff said that as long as Camilla did her current job, he had no problem with her long-term interests. Acquiring additional skills in key areas was always beneficial to the company.

"You can't always get what you want immediately," said Camilla, who is now vice president of Outside.in, an electronic news Internet company. "But you should be able to plot a course that will get you there eventually." Camilla got closer to her goals and met her boss's current needs. Success depends to a large degree on how you frame the issue.

Being incremental also means asking others questions about situations instead of taking on the whole problem yourself. When she was a student at the University of Pennsylvania Law School, Sarah Lewis was hired to work twenty hours per week for a premier New York City law firm. But she was assigned much more than that by two of the firm's partners.

Sarah wisely decided to frame this as not her problem. She contacted both partners and gave them the details of the amount and kind of work she had been assigned by each. She asked them to decide what she should do, since she could work only twenty hours per week.

"The partners talked with each other and reallocated my time," said Sarah, now a company counsel in New York. She started the negotiation with little control or power. But she was able to regain control over her job and life by giving away the problem in a first, small step. She didn't say she was overwhelmed. She didn't say it was a problem. She just presented the issue in a matter-of-fact way.

TERMINATION

If you are terminated from your job, this is also a negotiation opportunity. Many people get angry or otherwise emotional and don't think clearly. They often panic or threaten. Most regions, however, favor the employer, which usually has the resources to fight. If you calmly negotiate, employers are usually willing to give you more. They can give you many things that don't cost them much.

First, ask if you can resign. Find a reason that's true and well-crafted. Second, ask for a nondisclosure agreement limiting their comments when later asked for references. For example: "She resigned on March 23 for business reasons. Our privacy policy prevents us from disclosing other information." If you don't do that, your former employer may tell a potential employer that you are "not eligible for rehire."

Third, some firms may let you be an unpaid consultant for a period. Others may even let you maintain an office, keep a phone line, or have your phone line forwarded. Ask for the use of company outplacement services; some firms will pay a recruiter to help you. Others will give you a letter of reference. Extended health insurance is often available. Sometimes you can get your laptop or other equipment for free or cheap.

Most firms and industries have standard severance packages: for example, one week's pay per every year of service. Sometimes more is provided—find out when, such as elimination of your department through no fault of your own. Read the employee handbook for ideas. Browse the Internet. Don't sign anything immediately unless the package is clearly substantial. Tell them you want a day or two to collect your thoughts. If they try to fire you for cause, ask for chapter and verse—dispute it strongly. A high threshold of proof is usually required. And if you documented your good deeds, as suggested earlier, the employer will have a hard time proving cause.

If you fit into a special category, invoke it. You will get more, even without having a lawyer: women over forty, protected class of race or gender, and so forth. Don't be belligerent; just bring it up and ask what they can provide, saying you will sign a no-suit agreement. Again, be calm but firm: you will get more.

Unless the company is gracious and giving, I always advise fired employees to consult an employment lawyer. Even after that, you should still try to do the negotiation yourself, to preserve good feelings. But especially if they are difficult, you may want to cite specific rights that you have. Look for third parties in the company (or outside) who know the management and can put in a good word for you. It can make a significant difference in the employer's generosity. Only the most insensitive employers have the stomach for a messy process.

Finally, the more outrageous they are, the happier you should be. If they do something illegal or improper, you could be owed more money. Just take notes and find a third party to consult about it. Keep your head; it's not the end of the world. Eventually, you will get more.

All this advice goes as well for employers. The more you treat employees with dignity and fairness, even as you are firing them, the less likely they are to retaliate and cause you more grief than necessary.

THEIR SENSIBILITIES

It is important to focus on the signals a prospective employer sends. For example, a company scheduled Laura Beech for an interview in New York at the same time that she had been assigned a school presentation. Instead of suffering a bad grade, Laura presented the problem to the employer. The first scheduling person refused to help her. But Laura's interview contact at the firm agreed.

The first person was essentially saying that the firm felt it was okay to hurt Laura academically and force her to break commitments for its own convenience. Clearly, it wasn't the position of the entire company, but you should ask questions before accepting a job at that kind of firm. Laura is now a credit card company executive in New York.

Even if you are very junior in a company, without much power or influence, you can use these tools to enhance your career. Eric Delbridge was at a meeting with some senior people in his company. Instead of stating his opinion, he pointed out facts and standards, and asked what others thought of them. They began to see contradictions and support his private viewpoint. "Even though you are the most junior person in the room," said Eric, who is now a Chicago hedge fund analyst, "good negotiation skills can help you reach your goals in an almost invisible manner."

My students use the tools to learn from mistakes and eventually meet their goals. Dr. Stephan Petranker, who took my course at NYU, applied for the director of anesthesiology post at a hospital. He met the hospital's CEO without doing much research on the CEO's goals.

Stephan said he would improve patient care and focus on excellence.

But it turned out that the CEO was more interested in cost-cutting and logistics. "I thought the common ground was excellence in patient care," Stephan said. "The CEO wanted financial decisions that cut staff." He didn't get the job.

On his next job interview, ten members of a search committee interviewed him for thirty minutes each, back to back. "I asked each interviewer what I could expect from the next interviewer," Stephan said. "I consciously tried to put myself in the interviewer's seat and determine what would convince them I was the right man for the job. I asked each how I could present myself to make myself stand out from the other qualified candidates—and they told me." And he got the job.

If you use these processes, you will increase your chances of getting a job, keeping a job, doing better at a job—or finding better employees. The best thing about it is that it's not hard to do. And it will give you the most important thing you need in producing a better workplace: a structured process to *get more* with reliability and confidence.

10

Getting More in the Marketplace

One of my MBA students went to Bloomingdale's to buy a pair of shoes. There were two pairs of shoes near each other in the shoe department. They looked very similar. One cost about $130. The other cost about $250. It was clear that the more expensive pair was much better made.

"These two shoes look very similar to one another, although the more expensive one is much better made," the student said to the shoe department salesman. "You're right about that," the salesman said.

"I'll bet you don't move as many of these more expensive shoes. Most people probably buy the cheaper ones," the student said. "You're right about that, too," the salesman said.

The student asked if the more expensive pair was going to be discontinued soon since it wasn't moving very well. It was taking up space that could be used for a faster-selling product. The salesman saw where this was going. "We hardly ever discount merchandise," he said.

The student heard the words "hardly ever" and realized it was a signal that sometimes things *were* discounted. "I can't afford the more expensive shoes," the student said. "But I was wondering if I could buy them for a price that still left you a profit and helped you move them." "Move them" was a signal that the student understood the salesman's frame of reference.

The student then said she understood the mark-up was usually 100 percent on goods at department stores (she had done her research). She wondered if she could pay about $150 or so. She ended up buying the shoes for $160: a discount of $90, or 36 percent.

From the telephone company to a billion-dollar deal, people the world over continue to have trouble buying and selling things. It appears that the world is getting tougher: there are more hard bargainers, hidden decision-makers, broken promises, and inflexible policies.

Using the strategies and tools of *Getting More*, thousands of people have gotten extraordinary results in the marketplace: discounts at stores that otherwise never give discounts; millions of free cell-phone minutes; buying or selling a product, service, or company for terms that seemed impossible. The purpose of this chapter is to make the seemingly impossible become possible for you, too.

The first out-of-class assignment I give students is to go out and get a discount. I don't care if the discount is off a slice of pizza or a Tiffany necklace; I want my students to make an attempt to *get more*. They find that all sorts of things are negotiable with the right approach, even in the snazziest places. In most cases, all you need is a minimum of preparation, and the fortitude to ask.

When people first hear this, their most common question is, "Isn't this manipulative?" Here you are, taking people's hard-earned money. My response, as before in *Getting More*, is "not necessarily." If you get a discount from a store, who benefits more? You will like the store more and will likely come back, giving the store more business. If you get a discount for being nice to the sales clerk, the clerk may get a huge psychological lift, as so many shoppers are mean. It may make them more motivated.

In the Bloomingdale's example above, who benefited more? It's not clear, is it? Items of unequal value were traded. Bloomingdale's made a profit, and recouped its investment. It helped clear the shelves for faster-moving merchandise. Manipulation is really that which hurts other people. You don't have to be hurting others to meet your goals.

Much of the advice on negotiating in the marketplace is one-size-fits-all advice. How to sell a house, buy a car, sell a company. By now you know, however, that negotiation is very situational; it depends on the people and process in any given situation. While some tools are used more than others in the marketplace, you still have to focus on the specific situation, the people involved, and your goals.

As such, there is no one way, or even ten ways, to buy or sell a car, or purchase accounting services, or obtain an airplane ticket. There are a million ways, depending on your goals for the situation, who the other person is, and what process you have chosen.

STANDARDS AND FRAMING

Let's start with standards. This is the most common tool used in buying and selling things. The reason is that much (not all) of negotiation in the marketplace has traditionally been about prices and policies. Standards is not the only thing you will need. But you must master this tool to do well. This includes being able to frame the situation to fit into an acceptable standard for the other person.

We'll address easy consumer issues first. Most people know to ask for discounts, and sometimes they get them. These are not the situations we are dealing with here. I want to show you people who succeeded after the other party says no, often repeatedly. My students don't get frustrated or lose their composure. They just keep using the *Getting More* negotiation tools until they meet their goals.

Kenneth Reyes called Verizon Wireless many times to get his billing address changed. It wasn't changed, his bills got mailed to the wrong address, and he was charged late fees. Instead of getting aggravated, he got Nicole, a customer service rep, on the phone.

"Does Verizon have high customer-service standards?" asked Kenneth, an assistant at a Los Angeles talent agency. "Of course," Nicole answered. "Is calling four times to update a customer address in line with Verizon's standards?" Ken asked. "No," Nicole answered. Nicole fixed the address, then and there, and removed the late fees. "I'm a longtime customer," Kenneth said. "Could I get something for all my trouble?" By asking, he got two months of free cell-phone service, a $120 value. It adds up quickly.

One key thing about this negotiation, as I mentioned in the standards chapter, is that you must *never* make yourself the issue. Just because the other side is a jerk doesn't mean you should be a jerk. Also, the problem wasn't Nicole's fault. Why blame her for it? And note that Ken raised his points by asking questions.

So, you say, no big deal, Ken got $120 once. But try doing this once a day, or once a week.

Applying standards in a negotiation also means asking for exceptions to standards. Mark Perry had a Treo 750 phone that broke after thirteen months, one month after the warranty expired. He asked the salesperson in the store whether AT&T ever made an exception to the warranty. She took him aside and whispered, "Yes." Mark, now a Singapore commodities trader, got a new version of the phone for half price. Savings: $100.

Why did the salesperson take Mark aside? She didn't want the entire world to know. As such, whenever you ask for an exception, don't ask in front of a lot of people. It just drives up the cost for the other side, and makes it harder for them to say yes. (This is the opposite of what you would do if you want them to *meet* their standards. In such an instance, you want as many people around as possible, to expose their unfairness and inconsistency.)

A big part of standards is framing: asking the other person a question in which a standard is embedded. Andrew Dougherty wanted a bigger discount on a new bedroom set. Restoration Hardware offered 15 percent. He asked the store manager, Pam, if she worked on commission. She did not. He then asked her if she got any kind of bonus for anything she sold. Yes—for "exceptional sales." Is an expensive bedroom set an exceptional sale? he asked. Result: 40 percent off. Savings to Andrew, now a banking manager in New York: $1,800.

Charles Chen was renewing his phone plan with T-Mobile. There were five users on his family plan. He was told that T-Mobile limits family renewals to three free phones. Charles researched T-Mobile's standards. He found that each *new* customer gets a free phone.

So he asked the sales rep, "Does T-Mobile treat new customers better than existing customers? Haven't we, as existing customers, spent a lot more money with T-Mobile?" Of course T-Mobile's goal was not to treat existing customers worse than new customers. So Charles, who works for a cross-border consulting firm in Taiwan, got five free phones, in return for an additional year on his contract.

This is a big issue: companies often offer new customers better terms than existing customers. As a customer, you should key on the relationship. T-Mobile responded in kind, asking Charles to prove his relationship value by making another one-year commitment. Nothing wrong with that.

HBO was offering a great six-month, $6-a-month rate to new customers. Chris Hibbard, already an HBO customer, asked the service representative if HBO could give him the same rate. He pointed out that the selling costs to HBO are $0 for him, whereas they are more expensive for new customers. The sales rep did him one better. She gave him a *free* six-month trial.

Why did she do that for him? Because Chris, a supply chain manager in New Jersey, was friendly, mentioned his loyalty, and wasn't greedy. Many consumers, frustrated by something or someone else in the company, blame the rep who happens to answer the phone at that moment. And the rep hears this all day long. Being nice in a potentially hostile situation—even while using standards—is key.

Igor Cerc went to a store to have a clock engraved. It was a gift he was taking to a wedding the day he was picking it up. But when he arrived at the store, he found that the technician had broken the glass of the clock during the engraving process. They offered to replace the entire clock, after they got money from their insurance company.

But Igor needed the clock now. He realized it would not serve his goals to get upset. He calmly said he needed to go to a wedding in thirty minutes; the clock was his wedding gift. He noted there was similar glass in other clocks in the store. Couldn't the store take apart another clock to fix his? He was calm and polite throughout. "The clerk thanked me for not yelling at her as other customers do," said Igor, now a customer analytics expert for a Seattle financial services firm. "I realized that she would do everything she could for me as long as I remained polite." The clerk took apart another clock and quickly replaced the glass, and Igor went on his way.

By not making yourself the issue, you can ask companies hard questions about their service standards. But remember, *ask:* questions are more powerful than statements.

Comcast installed the wrong cable TV and Internet equipment at Alexandre Costabile's apartment. He called up and asked the service rep if these were Comcast's standards. No, they weren't, he was told. "How can Comcast restore my confidence in the company?" Alexandre asked. The result? The price of his service dropped from $127 per month to $67 per month for the first year, and he got a $45 discount on the equipment. Savings: $765. This is the sort of thing you should do routinely.

Alexandre, a consultant in Philadelphia, did something else that was key. He found the right person to negotiate with. Alexandre was looking for a friendly voice. When dealing with large companies, their size can work in your favor. If a customer rep treats you badly, call back until you find a friendly one.

Are you manipulating the situation? How? You're one person trying to navigate a major corporation over the phone. Why shouldn't you look for someone to be your advocate? Besides, you end up happier with the company and are more likely to come back.

Kenneth Ziegler saved $100,000 a year for his computer company using the other party's standards. He researched the slogan of a vendor that his company did business with: "Enriching life by enabling reliable and affordable communication anytime, anywhere." He showed the vendor the prices of their competitors and mentioned that for his company, the current prices were not "affordable," a key word in the company's slogan.

Then, he gave the problem back to the company. He said, "Find a way to make your prices affordable, meeting our needs at the same time." The company restructured its services. It found a way to provide similar services to Ken's company for $100,000 per year less. "I use standards whenever I can," said Ken, who is now chief operating officer of the company.

The ability to frame (or reframe) things creatively is a huge advantage in most successful negotiations. Learning this doesn't happen overnight. It comes with practice and preparation. Miranda Salomon Pearson and her husband, Larry, were charged $124 a month each as the "standard rate" at the New York Health & Racquet Club. That's $248 a month, or around $3,000 a year.

Miranda did some research and found out that health clubs often have a corporate rate that is half the individual rate. So she mentioned to the sales rep at the New York club that although she and her husband are not corporations, they work for corporations. This was reframing. Corporate memberships are intended to pull in a lot of people from the same companies. Miranda, a lawyer in New York, framed the couple's membership as accomplishing the same thing, through referrals. The result for Miranda: a savings of $1,500 a year.

Devin Griffin's fiancée, Sarah, asked him to buy gifts for the bridesmaids in the couple's upcoming wedding. A store wanted $975 for several bridesmaid's gifts. "I asked the retailer if they ever give discounts for customers with high-dollar orders," he said. Answer: yes. So Devin pointed out that there is no difference between buying ten items that total $975 or one item that totals $975. A sale's a sale, right? Point taken. Devin, who works in the digital media division of the Chicago White Sox, got a 20 percent discount.

A major professional sports team declined to sell sponsorship rights to Jeff Bedard's company because, they said, the offer was too low. Jeff said the team was exactly right—if all rights were being sold. "We only wanted to buy some rights," he said: national rights, not local rights. "Our offer was better than industry standards for that." He supplied sources to confirm it. Jeff was able to buy the rights. That is the value of reframing.

Josh Porter couldn't get a promotional discount rate from Comcast cable TV because he had already gotten one. So he asked the Comcast service rep if he could tell him the names of other discounts. This was after he expressed get-well wishes to the rep, who clearly had the flu. The rep told him to ask for the "retention rate." John, now a director at a private equity fund in Tokyo, did so—and got the discount. If you make friends with the other party, they will look for ways to help you meet your goals.

Consumers usually know a lot less than the seller does about the goods or services being offered. Don't be afraid to ask the other party what they have done for others in the past. They will tell you enough of the time that you will profit greatly.

Jared Weiner asked Sprint what it did when loyal customers had trouble with their reception. As a result, he got a year's worth of free text messaging (6,000 of them), worth about $200. "I then asked for and got the same deal for my mother and sister," said Jared, now a money manager near Philadelphia. "All family members should be treated the same." (Framing.)

Yan Li asked a Philadelphia jewelry store salesperson if she was empowered to give discounts other than those listed. The salesperson said yes. The result: Yan was given an instant 15 percent discount. Most people don't ask. Asking such questions will put a lot more money in your pocket by the end of the year.

Many people know to ask for discounts: coupons, seasonal sales, frequent buyer or flier, age (young and old). But this just scratches the surface: the list is long and intriguing. There are discounts for geographic residence, disabilities, smokers and nonsmokers, stranded travelers, professional groups, and even"friends and family" for people that store personnel like.

Airlines give discounts for funerals (bereavement), weddings, students, teachers, active and veteran military personnel and families, meetings, and conventions, among others. Anyone who buys almost anything without asking about discounts will waste money. Even billionaires say they ask for discounts. You should too. Be creative on the Internet.

As with other negotiations, the more you walk people through the details of their proposal, the more you will get.

Jason Weidman hired a San Francisco Conservatory group to play for an hour at his upcoming wedding. Their agent, Marcia, wanted to charge double the quoted price—two hours—because of travel time. The wedding was to be held in Tiburon, on the other side of the Golden Gate Bridge.

"I asked if the performers normally are paid for travel time if the performance is in San Francisco," said Jason, the marketing vice president of Medtronic, the medical device company. Marcia said no, but added that the wedding was in a difficult location. So Jason spelled out for Marcia how easy the commute was: "The group takes the ferry, the wedding party picks them up at the ferry stop. How is that difficult?" Indeed, although outside San Francisco, Tiburon was closer to the Conservatory than some parts of the city. Result: the agent dropped the travel charge.

Keep asking questions until you find the real decision-maker: the person who can meet your goals. Max Prilutsky needed to change his conference tickets from Friday to Saturday. But Ticketmaster cited its "no refunds/no exchanges" policy. Max, a researcher in Philadelphia, thought: Who's the real decision-maker here? It's not Ticketmaster, which is only an agent. The real decision-makers are the organizers of the conference that Max wanted to attend. So he called an organizer and walked him through the details, step-by-step. The agent said, "No problem."

Documentation is key to using standards in negotiation—either in writing or in descriptive detail. Ask for copies of things they claim; provide copies demonstrating proof of your request.

Laura Prosperetti bought a lot of merchandise at Douglas Cosmetics in Philadelphia. But she never seemed to get the free samples her friends got. Perhaps the clerks didn't realize she was a loyal customer? She thought it unlikely that the small shop would have the computer records to make her case. So she brought in her charge card bills for the previous year.

"I got a big gift," said Laura, now an attorney at Clearly Gottlieb Steen & Hamilton in her native Rome. She said that several years later, she still has the "big, shiny green purse" once filled with the full-sized samples. The key, she said, was combining a relationship with evidence collaboratively presented, and, of course, deciding to negotiate.

PERSONAL CONNECTIONS

In conjunction with standards, make as many personal connections as you can. Buyers will pay you more; sellers will take less. The personal connection is a kind of psychic payment that substitutes for money in a world in which aggravation seems rampant.

Ruben Munoz wanted a car rental discount from Hertz. Giovanna, the counter agent, said no promotions or discounts were available. Ruben, who had his two-year-old daughter with him, noticed that Giovanna was pregnant. He asked her if she had any other children. She said she had two boys and was hoping to have a girl. They chatted for a bit more, and Ruben told her about bringing up girls.

"Are you a member of any professional group?" she asked him, looking up. "Yes," Ruben said. "The American Bar Association. But I don't have my card with me." Too bad, Giovanna said. She couldn't give an ABA discount without proof. They chatted a bit more, and Ruben asked if the computer would allow a discount without proof. "She didn't respond, but typed something in the computer." Moments later, Ruben had a 30 percent discount for his two-day rental. She had overridden corporate policy.

Carlos Vazquez simply gave Jane, a store manager, his business card and said he was an Xbox fan. He wanted a 10 percent discount. He got a 40 percent discount. "It's the personal connection," said Carlos, a Goldman Sachs vice president.

Pick a few places where you like to shop, eat, and otherwise frequent. Then get to know as many people there as you can. It doesn't take much time to strike up conversations. In my experience, store personnel will be glad to go the extra distance for you if they know you.

Joaquin Garcia was a regular customer at Applebee's. So when he was organizing a birthday party, he called the maître d' to arrange for the party there. And he asked for a discount. He was told that Applebee's does not give large-party discounts. So Joaquin called the restaurant's marketing director. He noted his frequent business and his desire to host the party. He noted that restaurants often give discounts for large parties. The marketing director gave him a 50 percent discount on appetizers and desserts. Joaquin, now involved in his family's business in Chile, used linkages, found the decision-maker, and was persistent.

Whenever Daniel Hu asked for a discount for less than a case of wine at his local wine shop, "I was harshly rejected," he said. So one time Daniel sought out the owner, George, and Jessica, the sommelier. He asked their opinions about various wines. He asked about their wine-buying philosophy. They gave him a detailed tour of the store and were pleased to share their knowledge with him. Few people ever ask, they said.

Daniel noted that he often shopped there, although neither George nor Jessica remembered him. So Daniel mentioned some of the wines he had bought. They were impressed. He asked for recommendations, which they gave him. Daniel said he normally buys six bottles at a time, but he buys often. As a result, they gave him the case discount price, 10 percent. Daniel, now a debt specialist in Beijing, said that sharing information and making a personal connection are negotiation tools he uses daily.

Annie Hindley asked the name of the cashier at an Au Bon Pain at the University of Pennsylvania. The cashier said that students never ask her name, that she feels like a servant at an Ivy League school. Annie, now a financial analyst at Disney, got a $3 drink for $1.

"What if everybody did it?" you ask. Well, they don't. Besides, if everybody started being nicer to each other, we'd have a better world, as I've mentioned. Wouldn't you like to see that world?

How do you make a connection with the other person? By asking questions and looking for signals. Shikhil Suri wanted free next-day shipping for his repaired laptop. The customer service clerk said no. Shikhil asked the clerk where he was from. "New Delhi," he said. "So am I," Shikhil said. They talked about New Delhi. "Does the company ever give free next-day shipping?" Shikhil asked. The clerk answered, "Not normally." "Not normally" is a signal that most people miss; it means that free next-day shipping is sometimes provided.

Shikhil, now an attorney at Cromwell & Moring in Washington, D.C., asked if the clerk could fit him into the free-shipping category. No problem. In addition, the clerk gave him a $100 discount on the repair.

It is easier to make a people connection if you prepare. Alexander Gitnik's wife wanted a doula for the birth of their child. Alex researched doulas and found that fees were $500 to $800. A doula he liked wanted $800. He didn't respond to the fee, but instead peppered her with questions, showing respect and appreciation for her background and profession.

"I realized how important mutual trust and respect are. And she was clearly impressed with my competency," said Alex, now an investment professional in Boston. The doula accepted $500.

How much do you notice about those around you? That is, the ordinary people who influence, over time, the resources you have and the sum of your experience?

"I tried to get a discount on a book at the Penn bookstore," said Lital Helman, now a scholar at Columbia Law School. "They don't give discounts unless it's already marked. I noticed the salesperson. He seemed lonely and tired. So I started a conversation with him. I asked if he could help me with a discount. He took my new book and sold it to me for less than the price of a used book."

I sometimes get questions about whether this is fair. My view is, the bookstore got a happier customer and a more motivated employee. What if a billion conversations were different? Would that not have a net positive effect on the entire society?

François Hall wanted to join AT&T long distance. They had a set rate. "I had no history with them," he said. He is from France and speaks with a French accent. He asked the sales rep, "Have you ever been to France?" The rep had, and loved France. They struck up a conversation. Result: hundreds of dollars in annual savings.

"I had little leverage," said François, director of product management for Motorola in Brazil. "I am one customer in millions. But I made a personal connection and it was worth a lot of money."

Sometimes, the affiliation doesn't have to be you. It can be someone you know or an organization you belong to. Stephanie Lyras hoped to get a 15 percent student discount on a suit she bought from J. Crew the year before. This was long after the store's policy allowed.

Stephanie mentioned to the clerk that Wharton Women in Business, to which she belonged, recently had an event at J. Crew. The clerk was interested in WWIB, and the two chatted about it. Stephanie asked the clerk if she would reconsider her request. She did, and Stephanie got the discount. "In-person negotiations make a difference," Stephanie said. "The connection was essential. Attitude is important, too."

Now, this doesn't always work. Some vendors refuse to negotiate, frequent customer or not. But you'll get a discount more often than if you don't try this.

Stacey Brenner made a people connection nonverbally. She wanted a discount on a $130 pair of shoes at Steve Madden, a stylish shoe store. She walked in wearing a pair of Steve Madden shoes. She talked to the sales clerk about the various shoes on display. She was offered 25 percent off everything in the store. What Stacey did was value everyone in the store with her every step.

"This is dangerous!" said Stacey, now a physician in San Francisco. "I *never* expected to get 25 percent off of everything."

It should be evident by now that a combination of tools is often better—and necessary—than relying on one tool alone. Using personal connections as well as standards gives the other party a specific reason to say yes, after they feel good about you.

Rebecca Kolsky wanted to use an expired 20 percent discount certificate to buy yoga shorts from J. Crew online. Rebecca told Sandy, the customer service rep, that she wanted to get the shorts to keep physically fit through yoga. She asked Sandy if she ever did yoga.

Sandy didn't, but said that she had lost 222 pounds. Rebecca, then a med student, was impressed. They chatted for several minutes about what Sandy did: water aerobics, spinning class, medical considerations. Rebecca asked Sandy her career goals; Sandy wanted to go into pediatric health. Rebecca offered her some advice.

Rebecca then said she had missed the deadline for the 20 percent discount, but knew J. Crew's goals of customer excellence. It was a no-brainer for Sandy; in fact, she added free shipping. "Connecting with someone, sharing a bit about myself, and asking more about them, made a HUGE difference," said Rebecca, now a pediatrician in Seattle. "Sandy offered me things that I wasn't even asking for."

TRADING AND LINKAGES

Rebecca did at least three other things of importance in negotiating with Sandy. She traded information, providing career advice. She linked this negotiation with many others. In other words, Rebecca provided things of value back to Sandy—both implicitly and explicitly.

We saw earlier the power of this tool: using intangibles; linking your negotiation to other needs and interests not necessarily part of the deal. This expands the pie and makes it more likely that the parties can reach an agreement. It's especially true when there is a disparity over money. Here are some ways this can be applied in the marketplace.

Every time you buy something, make it a larger deal than just the transaction at hand. A repeat customer is a volume customer. You are buying multiple things at different times. Frame it as such.

Ena Hewitt bought a Nikon digital camera from Ritz Camera in Philadelphia. "While Ritz matches any lower price found in Philadelphia, I could not find a lower price," Ena reported. Otherwise, Ritz does not discount.

Ena told Chad, the manager, that she wanted to learn more about photography and buy more equipment as she got better. What could he do to support this? He gave her, for free, a $200 photography course and a two-year international warranty (instead of the standard one-year U.S. warranty). Ena, who now lives in Pretoria, South Africa, didn't just get a discount on the things she needed: she got them for free.

Even when you buy just two big items, you should ask for a volume discount. Dean Krishna, one of my law students, decided to frame buying two flat-screen TVs at Best Buy as a "volume discount" situation. First, he found the decision-maker, Justin, who managed the department. Then Dean asked how he got to be department manager.

"He was proud of the fact that he had a master's degree," Dean said. "After a few minutes of conversation, I asked him what incentives he could give me to buy two TVs today." Justin used his employee discount to provide an additional 10 percent discount. Dean is now an Iowa tax attorney.

Fresh from his success with T-Mobile, Charles Chen went to Tiffany's to get an engagement ring for his fiancée, Arisa. He asked the sales rep for her opinion on several rings. Charles said he hoped this was the first of many purchases from Tiffany's. He asked for her business card and said he was glad to have a knowledgeable contact there. As a result, he got a 7 percent discount on his ring, worth $770.

Companies will give you discounts in return for longer-term contracts. Pursue this routinely.

Vikas Bansal wanted to enroll his three-year-old daughter, Vani, in a class at The Little Gym. "Who can I talk to about an enrollment discount?" he asked the assistant when he walked in. He was directed to Joseph, the franchise owner. Vikas wanted a discount, but realized it was unfair to ask for one unless he could do something for Joseph. What might that be? It turned out that Joseph had a class that was only 60 percent full. Vikas said he would spread the word to three other families with small children in his condo building. He got a 25 percent discount and two free classes ($40).

You have to try to figure out the pictures in the other person's head in order to create a vision of the longer-term benefits to the other person. Some years ago, Mark McCourt wanted to buy a $4\frac{1}{3}$-octave padauk wood marimba, a percussion instrument related to the xylophone. The list price was $3,200.

The store owner, Dan, would drop the price only a few percent. Mark wanted to show the store manager that he would be a frequent customer. He did research and found out the wholesale price was about $1,600. So Mark offered just over that. But he also offered to give the store $200 more as a credit against future purchases. The store owner sold the marimba for $1,600, a 50 percent discount from the retail price.

Who benefited most? Hard to tell. After the marimba, Mark bought clarinet lessons and drums for his children at the store, as well as guitar straps and strings and other musical items. His son learned the marimba and became a first-chair percussionist at the state high school competition and later a drum line captain at the University of Arizona. "We still have the marimba," eight years later, said Mark, a regional vice president for Oracle.

If you just go through the process, you will often be surprised that you can get much more. Stephane Dufour asked the sales manager at a new hotel for pricing on an events room for his Wharton club. Price: more than $1,000. Stephane then asked what was possible if the club promoted the hotel on campus. Price: free.

These tools work for businesses, too. Igor Cerc, mentioned earlier in this chapter in connection with the wedding clock, saved $600,000 for his company by getting a supplier of raw materials to roll back a price increase for six months. He did this by committing to more volume during that period. The vendor's sales rep was willing to lower the price because the rep's bonus depended as much on volume as price. And the sales rep was right in the middle of the bonus measurement period. "I looked for the behavior drivers of the other party," Igor said.

As a business vendor, you can use your ability to deliver volume to help keep customers. Larry Bowskill was faced with a customer prepared to take its business to a competitor with a lower price. Larry contacted other divisions of his company that also sold to this customer, and negotiated a package that, overall, met the competitor's price. Larry made it a larger deal.

A client complained to Patrick Hennon of Advent Software in San Francisco that the company's pricing was unfairly high. Patrick dug deeper. He found out that there had been relationship issues in the past, including unkept promises about product performance. "The real issues were not price," said Patrick, now a health insurance advisor. "It was about trust." Once Patrick addressed the trust issues, the complaints stopped and sales rose.

In business, people usually care as much or more about job security and career success as they do about raises or bonuses. Dan Streetman, a manager at Amdocs, the telecommunications technology company, was having trouble with a sale. The customer wanted only two of the three products that Dan was selling. The customer didn't see the value of the third. Dan wanted to sell the third product, which was much more expensive, to complete the suite. And he thought the customer would genuinely benefit in the long term.

In thinking more about the negotiation, Dan used role reversal to put himself in the customer's shoes. Dan found out that the customer liked the third product a lot. But the customer was nervous that if he bought it, someone else in his company would use it, benefit from it, and look better than he did.

"So we told him that we would recommend him to the company's CIO [chief information officer] as the project owner," said Dan, now senior director of business development at C3, LLC, a San Francisco energy research and management company. "We also gave him assurances that the project would be owned by him only if it was a success. If it was a failure, we would take responsibility." The customer bought the product, and it turned out to be very successful. Dan had found the real problem and a creative solution.

PERCEPTIONS AND RISK

If you can reduce the other party's perceived risk, you will usually get a better deal. Gene Yoon was trying to hire an investment bank to buy a company for him. The bank wanted a big nonrefundable retainer up front to reduce its risk.

Gene reminded the bank that his group had previously closed two deals with them. He and the bank were "already friends," so were different from the normal case. The bank signed the engagement letter with no retainer. "We used both relationships and standards," said Gene, now a private equity director at Goldman Sachs in New York.

Reducing the other party's perceived risk can be worth millions of dollars. These tools work for businesses, too.

Anytime you confront perception of risk in negotiations, you should immediately think, "Be incremental." By being more incremental, you lower the perceived risk. This means splitting sales into trial periods, and setting up tests and trials.

CARS

Negotiating to buy or sell a car doesn't have to be a drag. Many resources are available. Most of you already know the drill. But here are some things in a negotiation context.

First, anyone who doesn't check the Internet for dealer costs and car values, and use it for negotiation, is likely to be throwing money away. This goes for new and used cars and is necessary preparation. Even my assistant knows about checking the Vehicle Identification Number for the history of an individual used car. Look up "buying a new car" or "buying a used car." There is a lot of great advice.

Aravind Immaneni, the financial services senior vice president, also excels in personal negotiations (good negotiations are process experts for any subject). Aravind wanted to buy a particular used Lexus model. "Only one such car was available in Richmond," where he lived, and was priced at $24,500, he said. "This was $2,000 more than I could afford."

So Aravind did his research. On carmax.com, he found the model in Atlanta for $21,200, or $3,300 less. He saw that the Kelly Blue Book value was $23,000. He faxed all of this information to his Richmond dealer. The result? He didn't even have to make his case in person. The dealer offered the car over the phone for $21,900, a savings of $2,600 for a couple of hours' effort.

Aravind's research also found that the manufacturer offered a three-year, 100,000-mile warranty for $1,500, and that the dealer's cost was about half that. So he suggested that he pay the $21,900 asked by the Richmond dealer, but that the price include the extended warranty at wholesale. Thus, the dealer would match the carmax price ($21,200) and sell the warranty for $700 more. The dealer agreed. "No hassle at all," he said.

For new cars, find out the promotions being offered to existing customers, the "friends and family" rates, and other sales coming up. Dealers will sometimes tell you about these, especially if you create a vision of a relationship or the possibility of referrals.

Ask for the meaning of every term on the invoice and check it. For example, "dealer prep" may involve only a couple of hours' work so would not be worth a few hundred dollars. Shipping costs and licensing fees are often inflated. Demo models are often a terrible buy. Assume the other party may lie; check every statement. The interest rate on leases is often inflated. Higher base prices are used on leases and "0% financing." The information readily available on the Internet is astonishing, and you will eventually wish you had read it beforehand if you haven't.

Whatever standards you get, it is still about the people first. Make the connection, and try to make the negotiation broader. If you don't feel comfortable with the salesperson, don't buy from that person. Ask for someone else. Anytime someone tries to sell you an add-on, ask for its wholesale price, and then check.

Be careful of ploys, such as a buyer criticizing the seller's car to get a cheaper price. This tactic just devalues the seller and makes them defensive. Use standards instead.

All of these methods also work for dealers in their treatment of buyers. You build trust by disclosing information and using fair standards. If someone makes an extreme offer, ask them, in a nice way, to justify it.

Rafael Rosillo bought a car from Ron's Used Cars in an "as is" condition, meaning no guarantees. Within a month, the car needed a $700 transmission repair. Rafael went back to Ron, explaining that his family had a really limited budget. He asked Ron to cover half the repair bill.

"I asked Ron if they had ever covered any part of a major repair in an 'as is' sale if there was a hidden defect before the car was sold," Rafael said. "Not usually," Ron responded. "Not usually" was a signal: it meant "occasionally, under the right circumstances."

Rafael told Ron that he was a Penn Law alumnus and was orienting eighty new students that month. He'd be glad to mention how Ron fixed his used-car problem at 50 percent off. In all, Rafael, now an attorney in New York, used four separate negotiation tools—making a personal connection, being calm, not arguing over who was right, and not asking for too much. The result—Rafael got the $350 he asked for.

It's another instance of human relations trumping the terms of a contract. The two anecdotes here show how the tools of *Getting More* can turn an often uncomfortable transaction into an easier one.

Your checklist should also include these resources:

- Car rental agencies, banks, and loan companies sell used cars. Auctions are usually dominated by professionals, since you need cash and a mechanic on the spot.
- The National Highway Safety Administration has a toll-free number where you can check defects or recalls. The Better Business Bureau (BBB) and state Attorney General often list unresolved complaints against dealers. You can use this to try to negotiate additional warranties.
- Unless you are a car mechanic, it's foolish to buy a used car without having it checked by such an expert.

When you see something you don't like, STOP. Take a break. Regroup and start over. No one is forcing you to do this today. Control the process to get more. Finally, one of the smartest things you can do is hire a car sales rep who has left the business (or dealership) as your "consultant" on buying, or even selling, a car. For a few hours' fee, they can save you thousands. It might not be easy to find such a person. Ask around. You will eventually be rewarded.

CREDIT CARDS

Billions of dollars in extra credit-card interest is paid annually because consumers do not know how to negotiate effectively. Below is a list of things you can do. Do them all, every month, until you are satisfied. Treat it like a part-time job. It will pay as well as one.

- Ask for the best rate they offer customers. When do they give that rate? What if you always pay on time? Not counting promotions, credit card interest varies from 4 percent to 23 percent for on-time payers, according to a 2010 study.

• Key on something the credit card company values. Kenneth Reyes told a Citicard rep, "I've been a loyal customer for more than ten years." He got his interest rate cut from 22 percent to 15 percent, or $500 per year—in a five-minute phone call. American Express promises "world-class service" and "integrity." Discover offers "the most re- warding relationship consumers and businesses have with a financial services company." Use these standards with them.

• Make a human connection. Cleo Zagrean asked Marcy at Citibank where she was from. Marcy said South Dakota. Cleo had visited there recently, and they chatted about it. Marcy gave Cleo 0 percent inter- est for six months. In a sense, it was a payment for treating her like a person.

• Ask if any lower interest rates are available for people in your cat- egory. Call back and talk to someone else if the rep you speak to doesn't offer you a lower rate.

• Ask for the credit card company's *card retention department*. John Vang did so with Bank of America, asking, "Can you help me remain a customer of BofA?" He noted he was getting lower interest rates at other banks. BofA promptly reduced his rate by 3 percent. It saved John, a New York public interest attorney, several hundred dollars per year.

• Read your credit card agreement carefully to ensure they are adher- ing to their standards. Read the Fair Credit Billing Act and the Fair Credit Reporting Act; you can find them online. Use all of this for ne- gotiation. Almost all credit card companies allow reduced payments if you run into trouble.

• Become familiar with "how to file a complaint against credit card companies" (or "credit reporting agencies"). Type these phrases or something similar into an Internet search engine. The Office of the Comptroller of the Currency (COC) and the Federal Reserve, which are U.S. agencies, also work on consumer complaints against banks that issue credit cards.

Sometimes you will not know at the start of a negotiation which tool will work best: being persistent, being incremental, making a human connection, or invoking a standard. Try different approaches. Send the credit card companies copies of all complaints you make to agencies, including local Better Business Bureaus, Consumer Affairs departments, the Federal Trade Commission, and, in Britain, the Financial Ombudsman Service.

Of course, you should do all of this incrementally. After each letter, see if they want to negotiate. And, before going through the effort, quote their service standards to them. At first, it will take some effort to collect the information and set up some files and phone numbers. But once you do it, you will be a prepared negotiator who is getting more at the end of the year: both in money and in satisfaction.

For people who work for credit card companies and their bill collection agencies, here is some advice. If you treat consumers fairly and don't put unreasonable people on the phone, you won't get as many complaints, more people will pay on time, and maybe even Congress will put less pressure on you. The tools of *Getting More* will work for you, too!

REAL ESTATE

Buying or selling a home is usually the biggest deal most people ever make. It is another negotiation most people hate. Home buyers and sellers are often afraid they will be hoodwinked. That won't happen if you use the right negotiation tools.

When Pamela Bates-Christensen filled out her mortgage application, someone at the mortgage company told her the interest rate lock-in period was sixty days. But when she got her approval, the lock-in period specified was only thirty days.

"I had taken notes of all phone calls, personnel, phone numbers, even before there was a problem," said Pamela, now a senior advisor with the U.S. State Department in Paris. She next got the company's mission statement, which listed various standards, including the importance of customer service. When the mortgage company supervisor failed to return several phone calls, Pamela documented that: date, time, message left, etc. She continued to log the company's bad behavior while going up the chain of command at the bank. Within a few days, she got the extra thirty days back.

Do you have to go to these lengths to get what was promised to you? Sometimes, unfortunately, you do. Carry a pen and a notebook with you. If you are nervous about the other side keeping their promises or when the stakes are high, take down details. It may seem excessive, but the first time you need it, you'll realize it was worth all the trouble.

Real estate commissions for brokers across the country vary from 1 percent to 6 percent. People who negotiate with brokers stand to save thousands of dollars. Above 4 percent is considered excessive by most; many think above 2 percent is excessive. Wouldn't you rather have those extra funds in your pocket? On the sale of a house for $300,000, a 2 percentage point lower commission is worth $6,000. That's not chicken feed!

Century 21 offered to sell Jay Chen's home for a 3 percent commission. He did some research on the Internet and found that ziprealty.com charged only 2 percent. Jay, an equity analyst near Philadelphia, preferred to sell his house through Century 21 because they were local, so more accessible. But he would do so only if they dropped their commission. They did, offering to sell it for a 2.5 percent commission. Savings on a $500,000 house: $2,500. Negotiation time: five minutes. Tool used: standards.

If you are worried that your real estate agent won't try as hard if you pay less, try being creative. Offer incentives. Let's say you and your broker have looked at comparable sales and agree your house will sell for about $400,000. So you offer a 2 percent commission for any sale up to $400,000, and 20 percent of everything over $400,000. If the agent sells the house for $450,000, the commission is $8,000 for the first $400,000 and $10,000 for the extra $50,000. The total commission of $18,000 comes to 4 percent overall.

Does the thought of paying the extra money bother you? If so, you *have* to get out of that mind-set. The extra $40,000 net that you received over $400,000 is found money. Think about meeting your goals, not about winning over someone else.

You can pursue other creative options. One is a flat fee. Another is an hourly fee ($75 to $150 usually), with a cap. Each of these needs performance standards; the agent actually has to sell the house.

The more of a personal connection you make with everyone involved, the more likely you are to meet your goals. Try to meet the other party. Make small talk. Find out if they have intangible needs. Introduce your children to their children. This is also important because if anything goes wrong in the sale, the relationship is a cushion to prevent the deal from tanking.

A participant in one of my courses went to look at a house in San Francisco. The place was jammed with potential buyers. When he got a moment with the owner, instead of talking about price, the buyer asked the owner why he was selling, where he was moving, etc. After about twenty minutes, the seller kicked everyone else out and sold the house to this guy for less than the highest offer.

Why? Because trust was established. A lot of people play games when buying or selling things. Others don't keep commitments. In this case, the seller felt comfortable that the deal would actually happen with this one buyer, who made the effort to get to know him.

Often an agent won't let you near the other party. That's because the agent thinks you will go around them and negate the commission. Ask a reluctant agent if that is their fear. Offer to sign a specific non-circumvention agreement that guarantees the commission if the deal goes through.

Even if an agent refuses to let you meet the other party, keep peppering the agent with questions about them. The more you find out, the more likely a connection will surface, even through a third party. Remember, the difference between success and failure is small.

Many states require disclosure statements by the seller. There can be stiff penalties for incompleteness. After reading the statement carefully, insist on getting an inspector to go through the house. If the seller refuses, be suspicious! Ask them how you can pay a lot of money for something that isn't inspected. Any price you offer before the inspection should be subject to the inspection. If the inspector finds major issues, you can negotiate the price downward.

This happened in buying our house. The inspector found a lot of nondisclosed issues. The agent said, "Too bad, the price stays." I said, "What are you going to do with the next buyer?" The agent said she wouldn't change the disclosure statement. I said that she now had knowledge of defects in the house, and if they weren't on the disclosure statement, she could lose her license.

It was a hard-bargainer situation, but we used standards and a vision of the future in order to be successful. I did not threaten the agent directly. I said that we were willing buyers right there, why start over again? We bought the house for 19 percent below the asking price in a strong market.

As a seller, this means you don't want to hide things. Give bad news up front. If the buyers can get past it, you will have a good sale, especially if they trust you. Mention the bad with the good; give them your ideas on how to fix the bad, like a list of local contractors you like. It adds credibility.

FAMILY BUSINESS

No chapter on buying and selling would be complete without looking at family businesses. More than 80 percent of the world's employees work for businesses owned by families. A third of the U.S. Fortune 500—about 170 firms—are owned by families. Family-owned businesses produce more than 65 percent of the U.S. gross national product and more than that internationally.

These are astonishing numbers. Most business schools and economists don't deal much with the dynamics of buying and selling involving family-owned businesses. So many business leaders are ill-equipped to deal with most business enterprises. And most of those in family-owned businesses do not deal well with the dynamics involved, either.

I've *advised* on family-owned business deals; I've *owned* my own business; I've been a *partner* in family-owned businesses; I do cases in class on family-owned businesses, and have written cases on family-owned businesses. So I've experienced the dynamics firsthand as well as studied them. Here are the dynamics of concern in any negotiation involving these kinds of businesses—that is, most of the world's businesses.

FAMILY BUSINESS—SOME TRAITS
- Pride, emotion, strong egos
- People fighting old battles
- Many feel undervalued, unappreciated
- Centralized decision-making
- An organizational structure that may not reflect actual power or influence
- Assets overvalued due to personal effort for decades
- Less shareholder driven
- Personal finances may cloud company finances
- Not so easy to fire people
- Intangibles are very important
- Less reliance on outside expertise
- The "culture" of company is key
- Competence is not necessarily key for job

Clearly, emotion, the enemy of effective negotiations, is much more prevalent in family-owned businesses. Many of those in such businesses

Title: Getting more : how to negotiate to achieve
barcode: 31185011104926

Mitchell Park

M---7349

ex Thu Dec 24 2020

take almost everything personally. They feel undervalued. They fight about yesterday. They do not make decisions based on logic. They do a lot of things that do not result in good deals. They have a harder time meeting their own goals. And their goals are often not just about money.

When one deals with a family-owned business, one has to pay extra attention to whether emotion is driving decisions, to whether intangibles must be provided, and to whether emotional payments must be made. Ask yourself to what extent ego might influence price.

That's true whether you are buying a hand-crafted statue in South America or an entire company in Chicago. It's true whether I'm selling an idea to three brothers in Atlanta or trying to sell someone's coffee plantation in Africa. People who are emotional listen less and often get distracted more easily from their goals.

The tools in *Getting More* will help managers deal effectively with such issues. As with cross-cultural negotiations, it starts with finding and valuing the perceptions of the other party.

Michael Farley, an investment banking partner in the former accounting firm Arthur Andersen, was having a hard time buying an apparel company for a client. "The owner's expectations were altogether unrealistic," Michael said.

Little by little, Michael and his group were able to peel the onion. "It was very emotional for him," said Michael, now a director of a Miami-based real estate acquisition company. "By putting ourselves in his shoes, we found the answer." They found out that the owner wanted to stay on for three years with various perks. He wanted half a percent equity (worth $2 million) in the company. He wanted use of the company jet, particularly to take him to and from his eight weeks of vacation each year. His employees needed to be able to stay on. In return for these intangibles, Michael was able to buy a company worth more than $400 million for only $42 million in cash and a lot of stock.

One buyer had an even more difficult emotional conflict with the seller of a privately held company. One owner wanted to sell. The other owner didn't want to sell. When asked why not, the owner who didn't want to sell said, "I want to die at my desk."

These are the kind of visceral issues for which one must be prepared. To go forward, the buyer created an active and meaningful role for what he called the "die-hard founder." In return, the buyer got the price of the company lowered. "Emotions were much more important than money or anything else," said the buyer.

Finally, from the sublime to . . . Small talk is almost always effective. It makes you more human in the myriad negotiations of your life. And it will get you more.

Josh Alloy went to a deli on Sunday. He wanted the Tuesday special: a turkey hoagie with fries and a drink, half price. No deal. He ordered it anyway—at full price, no complaints. "How about these Phillies?" Josh asked the sandwich maker. Baseball talk ensued. Josh put a $1 tip in the jar. As they chatted, the sandwich and fries grew in size. Then the server gave him the Tuesday deal on Sunday, and a lot of food. "The key was forming a personal connection," said Josh, now an attorney. To everyone else, it was just a conversation at the deli. To Josh it was a negotiation that resulted in *getting more.*

11

Relationships

A manager in one of my classes wanted her mother to live in a nursing home. It would be safer, her mother would get better health care, and she would have more companionship. Her mother agreed that would be the case, but refused to go. "I'm just not ready yet," her mother kept saying.

First her mother said she didn't want to part with her belongings, the treasured artifacts of her life. Finally her daughter was able to articulate her mother's fears: "Once you throw out your stuff, you've thrown out your life; then you're just waiting to die." Her mother cried, and agreed.

So her daughter suggested that her mother take everything with her. They could find a storage space nearby. When her mother was ready, she could go through her things, keep what she wanted, and donate or throw away the rest. Her mother willingly went to the nursing home.

A multibillion-dollar industry has sprouted around fixing relationships—psychiatrists, marriage counselors, mediators, business consultants, family advisors. It is clear from the experiences of those in my courses, however, that most relationship problems do not require professionals. Relationship issues, whether business or personal, generally begin with a simple lack of understanding. Poor communication ensues. Often, this can be fixed, simply and quickly.

Without the proper skills and treatment, a minor injury can become a major disease that requires professional medical help. The same is true of relationships. The way to repair most relationships, before things fester, is to be more direct, offer the other person emotional payments, ask more questions, listen first, and consider the feelings and sensibilities of the other person.

Of course, sometimes professionals are needed. But many people who use the tools in *Getting More* have greatly improved their relationships, as well as saved friendships, marriages, and deals, while also discovering a better way to attract and hold on to those they care about.

In the example above, it should be underscored that the mother was emotional and the daughter addressed those emotional feelings. She understood the perceptions of the mother and used framing to provide an emotional payment.

This chapter will look more closely and specifically at tools that are effective in relationships. Using these tools to solve relationship problems will enable people to get more for both themselves and their partners.

A significant part of relationships comprises emotion, addressed in Chapter 6. But effective relationships require more than emotional intelligence. They require use of the broad range of tools outlined in the first half of *Getting More:* standards, trading items of unequal value, problem-solving, being incremental, and so forth. So here we focus not just on one strategy, but on applying multiple strategies and tools toward improving relationships.

First, it should be crystal-clear to you that you actually *want* to form or hold on to a relationship.

Many people in business pretend that they want to have a relationship with you. In too many cases, however, their real aim is to use your knowledge or connections to get ahead.

This is known as a "confidence game." People pose as friends to gain your confidence. Once they do, they take whatever they can. As mentioned earlier, if people in business do not have the skills or experience to meet their goals fairly, they are more likely to lie, cheat, and manipulate. So any chapter on relationships must start with the premise that you should strive to form a relationship only with people who are trustworthy. With nontrustworthy people, you can still do business, but you need to be more incremental and get commitments.

In relationships, people expose their ideas, their clients, and sometimes their bank account numbers to those they trust to varying degrees. Before you do this, the first rule of thumb is: the less certain you are about the trust relationship, the less information you should release.

The second rule of thumb is: what's the worst that can happen—and have you protected yourself against that? One of my favorite expressions is: "Even paranoid people have real enemies." Even people with the most secure-seeming jobs find themselves outmaneuvered as a result of lies, innuendos, or politics, no matter how qualified they are.

There is much less loyalty in today's organizations. Companies shed people for all sorts of reasons. Even when organizations claim to support "collegiality" and "ethics," it may not be practiced in day-to-day life.

Most companies publicly say they favor diversity. And, as noted, data shows that those organizations with a diversity of ideas end up being more creative and usually more profitable. But just *try* being different in an organization. You may be seen as a pariah. One study found that executives choose new company directors with similar perspectives, "suggesting uniformity of thought." Another study showed that the promise of diversity in organizations often does not approach the reality, where sameness is valued and differences produce social divisions.

My advice in business relationships is to document everything. It sounds paranoid. But I have seen too many instances where people put their careers and their family's security at risk in a business relationship only to fall victim to politics or someone else's personal gain. Keep notes of important meetings, what you did, what they did and said. Think of it as an investment in your future security. Take five or ten minutes every day to write down what you did to add value to the company. Record the details of anything someone did that concerns you.

President Ronald Reagan's famous quote about nuclear arms limitation is good advice in every business relationship: "Trust but verify." Don't just go on faith in a business. Ask yourself what's in it for them. Ask yourself what each of you is giving up. Ask yourself if you are placing yourself in a vulnerable position.

My goal here is to prepare you to negotiate *in the real world, not in an idealized one.*

USING EMOTIONAL PAYMENTS IN RELATIONSHIPS

The strongest basis for a relationship is an attraction based on feelings. This includes personal chemistry, trust, mutual needs, social bonds, shared experiences, and common enemies. The stronger these qualities, the more of a commitment that people make to each other.

One can easily see how a threat can undermine these feelings. A threat is a warning to hurt someone in some way. Threats are, as one researcher put it, "utterly bankrupt as a strategy" in forming relationships. And yet, people do it often, especially in business. Threats push people apart rather than bring them together. They create fear and a desire for retribution.

The strongest way to establish bonds in a relationship is emotional payments. Without them, no relationship can survive.

An emotional payment is something that makes the other party feel better: empathy, an apology, a concession. It can include all sorts of intangible things, such as respect, face-saving, a statement of the other person's value.

An emotional payment is almost always something that provides a solution to an irrational need. It is part of everyday life. Virtually everyone gets nervous, upset, panicky, angry, depressed or sad, and disappointed at some point. We all second-guess ourselves. Your job in a relationship is to help the other person get past it.

You may have to overcome their saying mean, hurtful things to you, which they say not because they mean it but because you are the only one around and they need to vent. If this is the case, you must stay calm and give them what they need. Emotional payments must be specifically tailored to the individuals involved and can include silence as well as talking.

And you MUST take their irrational words or mood at face value and start there. This is because people who need emotional payments are hardly listening. There is only a small window through which they hear things: messages that connect with their emotion. You have to be careful not to upset them further. One wrong word can close the window and hurt the relationship, because you are not providing for their emotional needs.

Dack LaMarque, whom I mentioned before as having negotiated a 41 percent salary increase, also uses his skills on the home front. His wife, Emily, was having a "severe panic attack" over the prospective loss of tens of thousands of dollars from the sale of their Philadelphia house in their move to California. Emily was also upset about leaving her friends and surroundings.

Dack decided his wife did *not* need advice on how to solve her problems or calm down. She needed emotional payments.

So Dack asked his wife questions about her feelings. "For about an hour, I did absolutely no talking," Dack recalled. His wife did all the talking. The whole episode took six hours. A big part of the emotional payment was simply listening to her. Gradually his wife calmed down. When she did, they were able to talk about life in California, and Dack could paint a small positive picture to be continued later.

Valuing people also provides an emotional payment. There are many ways to value people. Too often, however, we lack the skill or inclination to figure out how the other person can be valued. You need to make the effort if you want to get more.

As the chairman of a conference on India, Arjun Madan was trying to convince a high-profile Indian cricket player to be a speaker. The player had a big ego, according to Arjun. The cricket player had demanded first-class airfare and a luxury hotel suite. Arjun's group could only afford economy class. So Arjun and his team thought about how else to value the athlete. They did role reversal, and realized that the player was most concerned about status and publicity.

So while the offer of economy travel remained, they promised to set up interviews with three leading TV channels, create a brochure about the speech, produce a podcast of his visit, and share a "dinner in his honor with cricket-crazy Indian fans." The team noted that some of India's most successful business leaders would be in attendance. (Do I hear "endorsements"?)

The cricket player agreed to come, flew economy class, and stayed in a standard room. "It worked out exactly as planned," said Arjun, a California financial manager.

Emotional payments can also reduce the other person's fears. Fear can paralyze people, making them unable to think clearly. A big part of negotiating in a successful relationship, and strengthening it, is to reduce your partner's fears. To do that, you first have to know what their fears are.

Scott Wilder proposed that he and his wife, Lara, hike the Inca Trail in Peru. She read there were no showers or cabins along the trail. "Absolutely not," she said. But Scott realized that it couldn't really be what was holding her back. Lara had done adventuresome things before. Maybe there was something deeper. He tried to look at the world through her eyes. "Are you afraid of being alone in the Andes?" he said. "Absolutely," she admitted.

So Scott developed contingency plans for cabins, showers, and trains. He gave his wife lots of information about what the trip would be like, and how so many others like themselves had had a great time. He promised never to leave her side for the entire nine days. She agreed to go. He had reduced her underlying fears by both validating them and addressing them. "We had a great time," said Scott, a consultant for Boston Consulting Group in Dallas. Scott had done role reversal to identify his wife's perceptions, and then reduced her perceived risk by providing specific details.

Even if the other person's fears seem ridiculous, they are very real to *them*. Walk them step-by-step from where their fears reside to a perception of safety.

Steve Shokouhi wanted to get a dog for his daughter, Brigitte, but his wife was afraid for their daughter's safety. She also thought dogs were unsanitary. Steve told his wife, Debra, that in many cases she would be absolutely right. This was an emotional payment. Steve then asked if they could get a smaller, cleaner dog for their daughter. It would teach her about responsibility.

Steve took Debra to a friend's house. Their friend had bought a cocker spaniel from a respected breeder. Debra agreed it was a beautiful dog. "I just needed to find out the exact source of her fears so I could make her more comfortable," said Steve, now a principal in his family's New York real estate business. He also was incremental and provided visual details. The family got a cocker spaniel, Benji.

Mark Silverstein and his wife, Stefani, were planning a dream vacation in Europe. His wife insisted on taking the train in Italy. She didn't want them to drive there. "She was afraid of me driving in Italy," he said. But she wasn't afraid in the United States. Why not? The United States has more speed limits, cars with automatic transmissions, bigger cars. All that added up to her perception that driving was less safe in Italy.

Mark pointed out that Italians' driving practices are little different from Americans'. Stefani wasn't persuaded, because her fear wasn't rational. What helped him to persuade her was to deal more directly with his wife's fears. We'll rent a bigger car, said Mark, an attorney in New York. We'll get more insurance on the car. We'll get a GPS navigation system. We won't drive at night. We'll get maps. "And I'll take you to Prada" for a purse or a pair of shoes.

"Prada?" his wife said. "Really?" "Absolutely," said Mark. "Okay, as long as we rent a midsize car and drive through Tuscany." My point? You should keep coming back to the pictures in the other person's head, and try to address their concerns. Here, Mark also traded items of unequal value: Prada and Tuscany.

People in romantic relationships are looking for "unconditional love." That doesn't mean you can't offer constructive criticism. It means that the other person in your relationship wants your love and support no matter what. They want you to love and value them despite their foibles. This contrasts sharply with the traditional, more destructive, action of withholding emotional support as part of a "relationship" negotiation.

Emotional payments also include the notion of "saving face." It's often associated with Asian cultures, although its usage is much broader. It really has to do with helping the other person maintain his or her dignity and sparing embarrassment in the presence of those they care about.

Raluca Banea sent her grandmother a debit card to withdraw money from her account so she could buy medicine. But her grandmother refused to use the card, even though she couldn't afford the medicine herself. "I realized she was trying to save face," Raluca said. So Raluca reframed the situation for her.

"Didn't you raise me for seven years?" Raluca asked. "Didn't you take care of me when I was in the hospital? If I was sick, wouldn't you insist that you should help me?" Raluca said she wanted to give her grandmother a gift in appreciation of all the things she had done for Raluca over the years, and because one's health is one of the most important things in the world. Could she accept the gift? This framing enabled her grandmother to hold on to her dignity and still accept money from her granddaughter.

Resist the temptation to make fun of the other person's perceptions. If you don't take their fears and feelings seriously, they will be angry and resent you for it.

Alan Kessler's fiancée was a vegetarian. She wanted to make a political statement by not serving meat at their wedding. "My friends are carnivores," Alan said. "They are not vegetarians. They'll have a terrible time if we force them to eat wheatgrass."

"I offered to get a free-range, humanely killed cow for the wedding feast," said Alan. "That way our wedding won't support Big Meat." He also told her that if they didn't have meat at the dinner, their guests would likely go out to a fast-food restaurant right after the reception. Fast-food restaurants, he opined, use the least humanely slaughtered cows. Alan's fiancée agreed to have "humanely slaughtered cow" at the wedding feast.

"This would normally have been an impossible argument," Alan admitted. "She is very proud of her political convictions." What did he learn? To value her, whatever her perceptions. "I will do this with her until the day I die," he said. Yes, he took it less seriously than she, but he met her needs and didn't have to change his personality.

BEING INCREMENTAL IN RELATIONSHIPS

An emotional payment is usually only the first in a series of steps you will have to take for others to move from their perceptions to your goals.

Too many people try to get others to change all at once. As we have seen throughout *Getting More,* it's usually too big a step. First, validate their feelings. Next, bring them step-by-step to where you want them to go.

Arjun Somasekhara did not want his wife, Lana, to leave her job at AT&T. Like many entrepreneurial managers, Lana was frustrated with the bureaucracy typical of many large companies. Arjun had a lot of good reasons why Lana should stay at AT&T: flexible working hours, training, a company car, great maternity benefits, and a promise of a transfer to London, where Arjun would be assigned next.

However, Arjun knew if he said all of this to Lana at once, she would feel he wasn't sensitive to her feelings. So he first told Lana that yes, many big companies have burdensome bureaucracies. He was confirming the validity of her feelings.

Next, Arjun told Lana that she could still excel at AT&T because of its training and opportunities, and that the couple would also have a better life in London with two incomes. Meanwhile, Lana could decide her future on her own time frame. When it was explained to her that way, Lana could see the wisdom of Arjun's words, and agreed. Eventually, Lana found a way to use her creativity at AT&T in London and became a productive and happy senior manager there.

Looking for solutions in an incremental way is important in all negotiations. But it is especially important in relationships. Trying to suggest too big a move can feel like a threat to many people. Lin Gan described the relationship between her and her parents as difficult: "We always fight whenever I come home. My house is really cold and I hate going home in the winter."

As a result of what we teach in class, however, she put herself in the shoes of her parents and realized that it hurt them when she complained about their house. She also realized from talking to them that heating is very expensive where they live.

Finally, she realized that showing respect for her parents would offer them an important emotional payment, in line with traditional Chinese cultural values. Instead of accusing her parents of keeping a cold house, Lin praised their thriftiness. Then Lin suggested that they raise the heat in only one room in the house—the room where Lin would sleep and study. Her parents agreed, and everyone was happy. It was a smaller, more incremental solution.

When the subject concerns deeply held beliefs, it is essential to be incremental in your attempts to persuade the other person. In the Caraballo-Garrison household, the subject was religion for the children. Phil was not particularly religious; Jackie was. Phil started with a wise suggestion: "First, whatever we do, we're not going to break the family up over this, right?" In other words, he was saying, Let's keep focused on our main goals.

Second, the couple agreed to some ground rules in dealing with each other: (a) Tone is very important in a discussion like this. (b) We're not going to solve every issue at once. (c) Everyone can't get everything they want all the time. (d) The "I'm right, you're wrong" syndrome doesn't work very well in relationships. (e) Whatever our beliefs are, we each respect the other's beliefs. Finally, (f) if tension develops, STOP! Take a break, come back to it later.

Jackie wanted the kids to have a formal religion—hers—and Phil didn't. Phil wanted to know if the children would eventually be able to decide their religion for themselves. Jackie said yes, but she wanted the children to believe in God. They were able to take these initial thoughts and achieve their first agreement: (a) no Sunday school, in which one religion is force-fed, and (b) Jackie would teach the children about religion—not just one religion, but several religions.

That's as far as they got that week. But it was a start. And their relationship was as strong as ever. Phil was mindful of trading items of unequal value, too. "If I feel very, very strongly about something and Jackie doesn't, what could we trade?" said Phil, now an attorney in New York. "If I get what I want here, what can I give her that she feels strongly about?" He said the negotiation tools are "indispensable" to his professional life, too, in structuring on both the civil and criminal sides. "Life is about give and take," he added. If you demand that you get everything, your relationship is unlikely to survive.

COMMON ENEMIES IN RELATIONSHIPS

Relationships aim to strengthen the bond between people. Emotional payments get people to listen to one another. Valuing the other party causes them to be positive in return. One of the fastest and most powerful ways to bind people together in both new and existing relationships is by establishing common enemies.

A common enemy puts the people in the relationship in the same foxhole together against some third party (an "enemy"). The "enemy" can be a person, a group, a thing, or an idea. Parties that are bound together against someone or something feel closer.

People complain about the weather at the beginning of a conversation. Some people in a negotiation half-jokingly complain about "lawyers" or "bureaucracy." Others yet complain about traffic delays or "miscommunication." All are attempts to find a common enemy, to bring the two parties closer together.

Of course, the use of common enemies is also a favorite tool of demagogues. In one of its basest forms, Adolf Hitler tried to make the Jewish people common enemies to the German people, and his success resulted in the Holocaust. Bigotry in all forms attempts to create common enemies, whether by race, social class, nationality, politics, age, religion, or culture.

Some legitimate common enemies in business relationships are loss of profit, loss of time, failure to retain good people, and inability to capitalize on opportunities. In personal life, they include waste of talent, loneliness, and poor health.

A good way to determine if the "common enemy" employed in a relationship is fair, as opposed to demagoguery, is to ask: Is the "common enemy" a single uniform enemy? If it's diverse, it can't legitimately be a common enemy. For example, religion as a common enemy is blatantly unfair in that "religion" is composed of individuals far too diverse to all be the same. The same is true of "American people," although speakers in U.S. politics use this term regularly. A generalized indictment of doctors, lawyers, accountants, and other groups is, bluntly, prejudiced.

Mothers Against Drunk Driving, on the other hand, stands for opposition to an act that is fairly uniform: driving while under the influence of alcohol. A boss might be a common enemy, at least with respect to certain actions. Herb Brooks helped the members of the 1980 U.S. Olympic hockey team to bond and win the gold medal by deliberately making himself the team's common enemy. Team members in interviews afterward specifically (and admiringly) said his over-the-top criticism and work demands helped bond them together as a "family" capable of championship.

Christopher Yee wanted a friend to send him an accounting of expenses for their recent trip to Ecuador. Months passed without a response, despite many reminders. Chris thought his friend was being lazy but didn't want to alienate him.

So Chris wrote to his friend blaming all the work each of them had in explaining why his friend didn't have the time to do the accounting. Chris, now an attorney in San Francisco, asked when his friend might have the time. He asked how he could help. This also had the effect of letting his friend save face. His friend sent the accounting and their relationship was preserved.

Some people call this "tact" or "diplomacy." There is, to be sure, a bit of tension between being direct (usually good) and allowing someone to save face through indirectness. Effective communication is persuasion. So the starting point should be, What will convince the other party to meet my goals?

Blackstone, the big investment firm, had not scheduled a meeting with Wharton students during a student group's trip to London. One of the student organizers, Florent Moïse, made many unreturned phone calls. Finally he left a voice mail for a partner saying that Wharton had already firmed up meetings with several of Blackstone's competitors. Blackstone had spent a lot of money on campus trying to recruit Wharton students, Florent continued.

"I really want Blackstone to be in there to meet with Wharton students," Florent said. "How can we make sure you are?" He got a phone call back almost immediately, with a commitment for a meeting. Florent, now a partner in a health care consulting firm, didn't blame Blackstone, but he instead focused on a common problem: the enemy was the lack of Blackstone's presence.

Vivian Fong and some of the other editors at *The Journal of Constitutional Law* at Penn Law School had a sharp editing disagreement. Curt emails were exchanged, and tensions rose. So Vivian suggested an in-person meeting, attributing the problem to the coldness of the email process. Everyone seemed to heave a collective sigh. The dispute was solved in fifteen minutes. "Finding a common enemy helped us set aside emotions and work together," said Vivian, now an attorney in Los Angeles.

TRADING THINGS OF UNEQUAL VALUE

All successful relationships depend to a degree on quid pro quo. People do things for one another. Relationships almost always dissolve when one person forces his or her will on another. Trading items of unequal value is one way to solve potential relationship disputes on a daily basis.

Tommy Liu wanted to watch football games with his friends in Philadelphia on Sundays during the football season. His wife, Xiaolin, wanted to visit her parents in New York City on Sundays—with Tommy. After thinking about what their interests really were—Tommy, watching the game; his wife, seeing the parents—they realized that where they met up wasn't really the issue. So they traded off.

"We would buy train tickets for the parents to come down to Philly on weekends," said Tommy, who manages his family's investment business. "We'd go up to New York whenever the Giants had the week off." What made it all work was the couple's attitude of wanting to solve the problem together, so each of them got something.

So many relationship issues have simple solutions if the people involved look for things to trade.

Rory Conway, a product manager at Microsoft, wanted his wife, Pia, to go to India with him for the New Year's holiday. His wife did not want to go. So she said, "Sure, as long as we can stop in Rome over Christmas and see my friends." This is not so hard. Items of unequal value traded.

Okay, here's one a little harder. Aleksandr Hromcenco wanted to buy four museum-quality miniature toy soldiers for his collection. But the cost was $600. "Are you crazy?" his wife said. So Aleksandr looked for something to trade to get his wife's approval. "How about, I do the grocery shopping next time?" Not good enough. "A gift certificate for the spa?" Aleksandr asked. Not good enough.

So Aleksandr offered to (a) do all grocery shopping for the next two weeks, (b) give his wife a trip of her choice, and (c) take their daughter to and from after-school activities for a month. Accepted! Indeed, the mere act of looking for such things to trade can reduce the tension in a relationship. (Maybe Aleksandr can buy the toy soldiers with some of the $13,500 raise he got in Chapter 9.)

Trading items of unequal value is what you do when the other party is already listening. That is, after any necessary emotional payments have been made.

An Asian database vendor was charging $3,999 for its financial information. No exceptions, no complimentary access. Atul Kumar wanted to use the database for a paper at Wharton. He mentioned he was a student with limited resources. The company's answer: No.

Atul noted that the company was trying to enter the U.S. market. He offered to widely distribute its name at Wharton and mention it to his previous employer, which uses a rival. Atul, now the vice president of business development for a Silicon Valley company, also noted he wanted to see only a small part of the database for one project. The database company changed its mind and said yes.

Matthew Dilmaghani had invited his girlfriend to dinner, but an unusual night-out-with-the-guys invitation came up.

He apologized profusely to her and asked her if he could reschedule their dinner. She seemed upset. Was this because they were not spending enough time together? he asked. She told Matthew that she didn't trust that he would reschedule their dinner anytime soon. "I immediately pulled out my cell phone and rescheduled our reservation, to illustrate my commitment," said Matthew, now a director at an investment firm in New York. He thought his cell-phone commitment saved the relationship.

Of course, before dealing with such sensitive issues, it is especially important to prepare. If you are not prepared, it is okay to say to your partner, "I'm not prepared to discuss this. Before we have a disagreement, can I collect my thoughts first? Then we can try to work this through—together."

Cindy Wong-Zarahn wanted to go to a party with a friend of hers on Saturday night. But Cindy's friend didn't want to go. Cindy, thinking about the issue from her friend's point of view, remembered that her friend hated to be alone on the weekend. So Cindy told her friend they could do whatever she wanted on Friday night, if she would go to the party on Saturday. Her friend quickly agreed. "Role reversal is my favorite negotiation tool," says Cindy, a senior manager at American Express. "It's the best way to focus on joint interests and avoid bickering." Here, it helped Cindy find things to trade.

Families sometimes get separated because of work or school. Inevitably, such separations over time cause arguments. But the real need among such families is usually not just face time, but quality time. For example, Keith Antonyshyn was attending school two hours away and traveling back and forth daily. He was exhausted.

So Keith asked his partner if he could get an apartment close to school for three nights a week. In return, he would arrange his schedule so he was home the other four nights, Thursday through Sunday. His partner would have more quality time with him than now. She agreed to the new arrangement. Keith is now a consultant in New York.

Rebecca Schwietz wanted her boyfriend to deep-clean their apartment. He was uninterested. You can just hear the drill: "The place is filthy." "Aww, it's not that bad."

Then Rebecca remembered trading things of unequal value. "If you bring your friends over to clean the apartment, I'll cook you all the best dinner you've had in months," said Rebecca, now vice president of a health insurer. And that was all the incentive her boyfriend needed. She got a clean apartment, and he got to enjoy a terrific dinner at home with his friends.

One of the more creative ways of trading items of unequal value in a relationship was done by Craig Trent. The Trents had a two-year-old, Caroline. Babysitting in their area cost $15 an hour. And the quality of local babysitters wasn't very good. So Craig and his wife, Anastasia, talked to friends who also had a young child, and offered to trade babysitting each other's kids so each couple could have the night off periodically.

They saved a lot of money, got much better-quality babysitting, and were able to set up an instant playdate for their toddler. It also made the relationship between the two couples stronger. "If you're having an issue, look for others in the same situation; solve your problems together," said Craig, a naval officer.

Some people already use their neighborhood as a support group. But not enough people do it in a structured fashion. It's just like expanding your network of relationships in a company. Perhaps you can shop for each other, run errands for each other, or exchange carpool duties. Time is such a valuable commodity in life. Always look for ways to get more time.

KNOWING THEM

The better you know the other person in a relationship, the more you will increase your chances of being persuasive. This is often said and too rarely practiced. Knowing them helps you better figure out how to meet their needs.

Jordan Zaluski fell in love with a young woman, Judith, in Paris. He decided that Judith was the one for him. But Judith wasn't so sure. Judith was religious and Jordan was not. "I wanted to persuade her that I'm the man for her," he said. So he read and learned as much as he could about her religious values.

"I got in touch with people in her life to know more about what she values," he said. He let her know he was doing this. He wanted her to know how motivated he was to understand her better and meet her needs. Done wrong, this could come across as creepy. Done openly, with a clear declaration of good intentions, it is more likely to seem charming.

Judith's hesitation ultimately disappeared and she flew to America to visit him, and they had a romance. It didn't work out for various reasons. But Jordan, an attorney in London, demonstrates clearly how to overcome barriers to a relationship: make it about their needs as much as yours.

Giannina Zanelli's mother wanted her to come back to Peru after graduate school. "I thought she wanted me back to control my life," Giannina said. "She thought I didn't love her as all good daughters should."

So Giannina, a marketing director in San Francisco, put herself in her mother's shoes. Her mother lived alone in Peru. What did her mother really want? For her daughter to live in Peru? Maybe. Or maybe her mother just wanted to be near her daughter. So Giannina asked her mother about this. It was the latter: proximity, not geography. So Giannina suggested an alternative solution: she got a two-bedroom apartment in the United States, and her mother stayed there with her daughter for six months a year.

The point: don't assume you know what the other person is thinking. Ask more questions. You might be very surprised by the answers.

"I'm not moving to New York," John Eckman's wife said to him when he got a job offer there. She told him she just didn't like the city. He couldn't get any more out of her. "Why can't you find a job somewhere else?" she wanted to know.

John did a role reversal exercise with his friend Nick. John played the role of his wife. Nick played John. In the process, John discovered her true feelings. "She wants a house with a yard, doesn't like the high cost of living and the rude people, and is upset at the distance from her family in South Carolina."

So John and Nick came up with solutions to her concerns. One was to live outside the city, in a suburban community with houses and lawns. John agreed to commute into the city. He also agreed not to go to the city on weekends except for job emergencies. And he promised to spend at least one holiday a year with her family in South Carolina. "I shared some of our problem-solving options with my wife," said John, who is president of a medical device company. "She was persuaded."

Too many relationships are hurt because one party doesn't ask enough questions and just assumes the worst. Arguments follow.

So it's important in relationships to set ground rules for tone and in dealing generally with each other. Everyone feels stress sometimes. It's natural to lash out at those nearby when we're upset. But this can damage the relationship with your biggest supporter. So talk about the process: preferably not in the heat of an argument. Take a break first.

As with many of the tools in this book, don't be surprised if you have to help the other party. Especially in emotional situations, they may not be able to help themselves.

Karin Hart-Thompson's seven-year-old daughter would not dress herself quickly enough in the morning, and was constantly missing, or nearly missing, the bus. Threats and punishment had proved useless. So Karin did a role reversal in which Karin played the role of her daughter. What Karin realized was that her daughter needed help in the morning. She wasn't organized enough to get herself out the door on time.

So Karin bought a shiny new clock for her daughter's bedroom. Mommy and daughter had a nice talk the night before about getting her clothes and things ready. (It also gave her daughter more time with Mommy.) At the end, her daughter felt more control over her life. "We reduced the level of emotion and identified the real issues," said Karin, a senior travel manager for Viasat, a satellite communications company in California. Karin explained to her daughter that Mommy had a hard deadline to leave for work to make money for all the fun things the family did. Her daughter began to be ready on time.

STANDARDS

Although standards are best in hard-bargainer situations, they can also be useful in relationships. Be careful how you use them, as they can be perceived as aggressive.

One of my former students had a demanding job, and she wanted her husband to take more responsibility for raising their children. But her husband was reluctant to switch roles. So the wife pointed out that other men, whom her husband respected, provided significant care for their young children. "Do you think people look down on them?" his wife asked.

Essentially, the wife used the standard set by third parties her husband respected. Seeing her point, her husband agreed to provide significant care for the kids. A key point is that this was all done in a loving, collaborative tone.

It is important to first agree on the standard to be used. Just because the first standard doesn't work, it doesn't mean that no standards will work. Julia wanted a journalist she knew to write about her dance show in the local newspaper so they could get free publicity. But journalists can't ethically do that—it's biased promotion.

However, journalists can write about legitimate issues, and in those stories mention the source of a story. So Julia asked her journalist friend if he could write about several dance shows occurring in a close time frame. Yes, he answered. After further discussion, she realized she did have a legitimate story: how nonprofit art organizations are finding it hard to locate reasonably priced theater space in Philadelphia. Her organization was one of them. The journalist agreed to write the article and mention the date and location of Julia's show.

"It showed how important framing is," said Julia, who works for a financial media company in New York. "The article is about a legitimate news issue. But it still achieves my goal of getting publicity for my show." Without compromising her friend.

We met Jason Weidman earlier when he negotiated the fee for music at his wedding across the bay from San Francisco. Before that, he had to negotiate with his mother, Mary Jo. His mother wanted Jason and his fiancée, Colleen, to add some stores in Michigan to their wedding registry. Michigan is about 2,000 miles from San Francisco, where Jason and Colleen live. Mary Jo, however, and some of the other wedding guests live in Michigan. It is the kind of fight that occurs all the time before weddings, and it can make the process hateful.

So Jason used standards to make his case to his mother: "Is it a good idea for us to register at faraway stores where we don't like the merchandise, in order to make it easier for some of the guests?" he asked. His mother said no. Jason then asked if she thought it would be inconvenient for Jason and Colleen to have to handle returns and exchanges remotely. She said yes, it probably would be. Then he asked if there were any specific guests who were not capable of buying gifts online. His mother could not name one.

Finally, Jason said that a local store in Michigan, Marshall Field's, was now owned by Macy's, one of the couple's registry places. And there was a Macy's where Jason and Colleen lived out West. His mother agreed.

Jason figured out during their negotiation that the choice of registry store was not really the issue anyway. "My mother wanted more involvement with wedding details," he said. "The specific registry place was only a manifestation of her frustration." So Jason asked his mother if she would like to be more involved in some of the wedding details. She jumped at the chance. The result—the rest of the wedding planning went smoothly.

I can already hear some of you saying, "But what if she screams and hollers?" "But what if she says, 'I'm your mother, you need to respect my wishes . . .' "

Remember, you have a whole book full of negotiation tools. Pick the right tool for the person you're negotiating with. If your mother screams and hollers, try offering her an emotional payment. Talk to her about common enemies—it's you and me versus the wedding industry, Mom. The reason I am relaying all these stories is not for you to memorize the details. The point is that real people have accomplished uncommon success in myriad situations by picking the right tools for the right situation.

And let's be clear: you will *never* achieve a 100 percent success rate. To repeat, the title of this book is *Getting More,* not *Getting Everything.* But you will get more and will increase the quality of your life when you use the tools and models discussed in this book.

When using standards in relationship situations, tone is very important. That's because standards tend to push people by using their own criteria. A cold or even neutral tone can cause the relationship to fray.

Sharif Atta was planning to go out to dinner with a male friend. His girlfriend thought his friend was "morally suspect" and urged him not to go. She didn't have any specific evidence.

Instead of bridling at this, Sharif, now a hedge-fund partner, asked some standards questions. "Is it okay to pass judgment on someone you don't know well?" he asked, in a caring, collaborative tone. It gave his girlfriend something to think about. "Don't you trust *my* judgment?" he asked, again, in a soft, caring tone. His girlfriend agreed to give the friend the benefit of the doubt, and Sharif went out to dinner without an argument.

Clearly, thinking about how to frame the situation helped Sharif's girlfriend to see that perhaps she was being unfair. But his tone conveyed that he cared deeply about *her* and reduced the emotional content of the conversation.

Many people get unnerved by situations in which someone threatens the entire relationship because of one incident, whether in business or in their personal life. It helps to point out, "Hey, we've been friends for *x* years—over 1,000 or 2,000 days. Do you really want to toss everything out over one bad day?" It helps to put things in perspective.

GOALS AND RELATIONSHIPS

Goals, the be-all and end-all of negotiation, are especially hard in relationships. That's because the currency in most relationships is emotion, and most emotions cloud clarity about goals. The expression "Do your

actions meet your goals?" often just points out the underlying conflict between goals and relationships and makes matters worse if a party is being
emotional.

Successful negotiation in a relationship requires *empathy*—sensitivity
to the other person's feelings and perceptions—as much as it requires
focus on your goals.

Devin Griffin's wife, Sarah (they got married since the last chapter),
wanted a dog. In fact, she had already picked out the dog. Devin thought
this was not a good time to get a dog. His wife was getting ready for her
Ph.D. exam. Devin was unable to care for the dog because of his own
workload. It was a very emotional situation.

The thing Devin decided *not* to do was tell his wife that now was not
the time to get a dog. This would just create more emotion. So Devin told
his wife that getting a dog was a great idea. He asked her how she thought
having a dog then would play out.

Who will walk the dog? Who will play with the dog? Who will train the
dog? Who will feed the dog? Who will care for the dog when we're both at
work or school? If we don't have enough time for the dog right now, is it
fair to the dog? If our goal is to have a well-trained, well-cared-for dog that
we love and have time for, will our actions meet our goals?

As Devin asked his questions, his wife started to get upset. So Devin
said, "Why don't we take a break from this and talk more about it later?"
He wanted to give his wife time to absorb this information and to calm
down. The break was an emotional payment.

When they started talking about getting a dog again, Devin made sure
he reiterated that he really wanted a dog. As for the dog his wife had picked
out, was this the only dog in the world that could make her very happy?
Couldn't they both pick out a dog together, when they were ready? Was
she sure they could not find an even better dog?

Devin eventually suggested that they get a dog eight months later, after
her exams were over and on her birthday. His wife, having a firm date for
getting a dog, agreed to hold off for now.

The negotiation included using the perceptions in the other person's
head, emotional payments, being incremental, standards, commitments,
and questions. In the end, they added up to Devin meeting his goals, making his wife happy, and getting a dog, but not now.

Now, is this manipulative? Well, whom did it hurt? One could argue
that it actually helped his wife in avoiding the stress she would have surely

faced with a dog when the couple couldn't adequately take care of it. To my mind, manipulation is hurting someone in the process of persuading them. Effective negotiation is when you get them to do things that help them. Both manipulation and negotiation get people to do things they might otherwise not do. But that is true of all forms of persuasion. The key is whether or not you are doing it for the right reasons, and the effect on the other party.

You must be careful not to hurt your friends while persuading them. Laura Bagarella, now an attorney in New York, persuaded her friend to go to a rock concert with her after classes ended. Her friend said she had to study for exams instead. Laura reminded her that the previous year they were too tired to study anyway after the last day of classes.

So her friend went to the concert. And, as Laura rightly thought, her friend did fine on the exams. But what if your friend really has to study? Or do something else that might conflict with your plans? It could hurt your relationship if your friend does poorly in something as a result of your persuasiveness. It's something to consider, and is the question that Neil Sethi reflected on after pushing for a free beer in Chapter 4.

Laurent Halimi offered a visiting friend a room in his apartment near the University of Pennsylvania. His friend wanted to rent an apartment in Center City Philadelphia, about twenty blocks east. The friend said he wanted a "real-life experience in the U.S." by being close to restaurants, parks, and shops.

Laurent noted that twenty blocks is very close to Center City and could even be walked. As such, it was well within the parameters of being in "the city." Laurent also said that sharing an apartment would save his friend money, which he could use to travel the U.S. "We've been friends for ten years," said Laurent, now an attorney in New York. "I always want what's best for you."

Essentially, Laurent showed his friend, through framing, that his friend's goals could be met even better by doing things another way. Laurent's credibility increased by invoking their long friendship. His friend agreed.

Here is a business example. The client for a sales manager for a large technology company did not want to show him next year's budget, a private document. Emotion surrounds privacy: fear of misappropriation of something valuable. The sales manager asked his client to describe the company's goals. One was for the manager and his team to provide more specific advice to increase the client's return on investment. The sales manager said he was there to help the client, and invoked their long relationship together. The manager then wanted to know how his client could meet their goals without his examination of the budget. The client showed him the budget. Invoking the relationship was the emotional payment that caused the client to be able to better focus on their goals.

DETAILS AND RELATIONSHIPS

One way to show people how their actions don't, or won't, meet their goals is to put them into the situation mentally. Most people are not visual enough to actually "see" it. If they are able to be open or patient enough to allow a picture to be painted for them, it is a powerful persuasive tool in general, and for relationships in specific.

Melissa Feemster's mother insisted on a videographer at Melissa's wedding. Her parents were paying for the wedding. Melissa did not want a videographer. So she drew her mom a word picture of what videography would be like indoors: the bright, hot strobe lights, the cameras in people's faces, the upstaging of the event itself, the often poor quality compared to a top still photographer.

And didn't the notion of "capturing every moment," as her mother put it, depend less on the type of camera than the eye of the photographer? And, unless there are five or six cameras, every moment wouldn't be captured anyway. Her mother agreed to hire a top still photographer instead. "The pictures were great," said Melissa, Client Services Vice President of LinkShare, a Chicago online marketing company.

Details mean that you need to look at every facet of the negotiation, break it down into its component parts, and review it for the other party. Giannina Zanelli had a roommate who wasn't doing her share of their agreed-upon apartment chores. Rather than make accusations, Giannina walked her roommate through the process.

"Did we agree to share chores?" Giannina asked. "Yes," her roommate answered. "Have you done your share?" "I don't have time."

"Do you think I have time constraints, too?" "Yes." "Do you think I do my share?" "Yes."

"What would you think if I stopped doing my share?" Giannina asked.

"It would be unfair," the roommate responded. "Do you think your not doing your share is unfair?" "Maybe."

The roommate promised to do her share, or hire someone who would. Giannina remained calm and respectful throughout. "The key," she said, "is getting the other person to apply the same principles to themselves that they would apply to others."

You need to review the details without making yourself the issue. The more you challenge their statements, the more documentation you have of their bad behavior, the more you need to treat the other person with care—if you care about the relationship.

Dana Romita-Cox was expecting a baby. When she discussed buying furniture, or the kinds of TV programs they might watch together with the baby with her husband and mother, her mother would say, "Well, you grew up just fine. I did an excellent job raising you!" When Dana bought some innovative new learning toys for her new baby, her mother said, "You grew up just fine. I wasn't a terrible mother."

Dana thought about this for a minute. "Have I ever criticized the way you raised me?" Dana said to her mother in an empathetic tone. "No," her mother said.

"Are you going to yell every time I do something different from what you did?" Dana asked. "No," her mother said. "I was just kidding; can't you take a joke?"

Dana, now the owner of Ajune Day Spa in New York, never got upset or showed annoyance. She just probed, asked questions, and asked for details. Her mother realized for herself that she was being overly controlling, and unfair to her daughter. Dana said that she and her mother have reached a lifelong accommodation.

Working through the details is especially good for disputes over money. "We can't afford it" is a typical refrain in families. Well, have you actually worked through the numbers and figured out what's possible?

Lynn Castle's husband said they couldn't afford a vacation on their budget. Lynn, a consulting firm manager in Atlanta, built a spreadsheet and showed how they could. Carlos Vazquez's wife said they could afford both a trip to Africa and a cruise. Carlos built a spreadsheet and showed how they couldn't. In both cases, the spreadsheets were persuasive. "The details value them," he said. It was a key part of the reframing. If one partner says, "We can't afford a vacation," renovation, car, or membership, ask what "afford" means. How much money are they talking about? Perhaps a cheaper alternative is possible.

I once had an MBA graduate who asked for additional compensation because she couldn't afford to live in New York City otherwise. After being declined, she prepared a spreadsheet of all her expenses, including student loans, and gave it to the hiring partner. An additional signing bonus, bonus advance, and some other funds were provided. It was a business relationship and the student had to be very humble and tactful.

THE RELATIONSHIP ENVIRONMENT

Most of the questions I get on where a negotiation should be held center on how to get power over someone else. This is a bad way of thinking, since making others uncomfortable hurts most relationships (and deals); good negotiators will call out the bad behavior anyway.

A better way is to use location to enhance a deal by getting both parties to feel better. The more a negotiation looks like it's part of a relationship, the more likely the other party is to treat it like one.

For example, you would probably not conduct a negotiation on a sensitive subject with a loved one on opposite sides of an office desk. On the other hand, you would very probably not want to take a colleague to a romantic restaurant to discuss the budget.

Conducting a negotiation in person is always best in a relationship. The more difficult or emotionally fraught the subject, the more important it is for it to be discussed in person. It's always surprising when students ask in emails for big exceptions to things, in work or recreation. Exceptions require a special favor, so the ability to have human contact to engender empathy is usually essential.

George Cheely realized this when he wanted to become involved in a friend's business. The friend had questions about his ability to make major financial decisions because of his lack of experience. He consciously discussed the matter with her face-to-face. As he made his case, he was able to see her reactions to everything he said, including nonverbal cues like nodding or appearing unsure.

It enabled him to be more responsive to her in the conversation. He was able to better adjust his own responses. As a result, she saw him as more thoughtful than she had originally believed: she saw a different side of him than he had showed in their friendship. This led her to agree to bring him into the business—of course, incrementally at first. George, now a resident at Duke University Hospital, plans to use his combined experience for a career in medical management.

Unless you are trying to hurt the other party or the relationship, you want the parties to be as comfortable as possible. People who are uncomfortable get cranky. And cranky is bad for negotiations.

Now let's talk about the psychological setting. Preventing yourself from being emotionally out of control is essential to maintaining a stable long-term relationship. The more you are seen to act out, the less reliable you seem to others—including those who love you. Empathy and passionate romance are lovely. Over the long term, however, people want a safe harbor, not stormy weather, however exciting at the time.

Jessica Tait developed a problem working with another producer of a play at Wharton. She was angry at him for interrupting her repeatedly. She showed her anger. He got angry in return. Their relationship soured.

Jessica realized that as the skilled negotiator, it was up to her to solve the problem. She told him that she had been angry at him for interrupting her. Jessica, now an Internet company associate near Philadelphia, told him that she could have found much more productive ways to solve the problem than getting angry. They then were able to thoughtfully agree to a better process going forward.

A tense setting strains the entire relationship. Informality, humor, a sense of sharing and caring—all part of good relationships—create a much better personal environment. Anna Larsson felt she was doing all the housework and 60 percent of the cooking. She wanted her husband, Peter, to do more of the cooking. Instead of complaining, she used the closeness of their relationship.

"I'm tired of my own cooking," she said. "Can you try your hand at it? Make what you want. I'll help." She offered to look through cookbooks with him and discuss recipes. She recalled some of the great meals he'd made in the past. She suggested they try it for a week. (Be incremental.) If his schedule was too jammed up this week, perhaps he could try it next week. No big deal. And he didn't need to cook all dinners, just some of them.

"He agreed to cook ALL dinners this week," she said. "The first one was yummy." She said that putting herself in his shoes before the negotiation was key. He clearly wanted to be fair. But he didn't want to be hit over the head with it. This is good advice for anyone with whom you'd like to form a relationship. Few people prefer high pressure; low-key is better unless the other party likes pressure cookers. "He still cooks," nine years later, said Anna, a Minneapolis consultant. "We told our friends about this; they do it, too."

THIRD PARTIES AND RELATIONSHIPS

As in all negotiations, using third parties can help. But this cannot be perceived as manipulative in any way, or you risk hurting the relationship. Be up front with the other person if you are going to consult someone else for their valued opinion. Just tell the other person that it's part of your information collection process.

Bernadette Finnican wanted to run a road race in New York City on Thanksgiving Day. "My controlling mother" Pat, as Bernadette put it, wanted everyone at her house all day on Thanksgiving. First Bernadette asked her brother-in-law. He was completely on her side—definitely *not* interested in sitting around and eating all day.

Bernadette passed this information to her mother and said she wanted to find out what others in the family would think of her running a race in the morning, to ensure that the whole family was okay with it. It was presented in such a way that her mother didn't feel offended.

Bernadette's father, Tom, it turned out, wanted to play golf. Her sister, Cathleen, had some things to do at her own house earlier in the day. The grandsons, Craig and Jack, however, were happy to spend the day with Bernadette's mom, their grandmom. Dinner could be set for later, when everyone was finished with their other activities.

Bernadette, a financing manager for IBM, was able to meet her goals with her mom without rancor—and it was the first time ever. Her mother actually thought this was a great process. "Building a coalition, framing, finding interests, and preparation were key," Bernadette said. People often ask me how these tools can be used in emotionally wrought family situations. Well, this was an example.

TRANSACTIONAL RELATIONSHIPS

Transactional relationships are those that have no obvious longer-term element. As you can imagine, they are far weaker than those created by feelings or mutual benefits. Clearly, one should try to make the transaction bigger and the relationship longer when it adds value. Still, many business relationships are transactional, so it's important to see how one can get more from these.

Typically, transactional relationships include "arm's length" agreements. They include agreements between people who don't know each other well, often in marketplace buy-sell situations. They also include situations where at least one party doesn't want to show favoritism (such as with the government or a major company as buyer). They also include situations where money appears to be the only item of importance—commodity sales, financing deals.

Some cultural settings have more of a transactional atmosphere than others. Often, societies that use law instead of relationships to bind people together are more transactional.

The farther one gets from feelings in a relationship, the less committed people are to the relationship. Feelings, including trust, are much stronger levers than contracts. So I would be careful in relying on structural elements, such as contracts or other incentives, to be strong enough to sustain a relationship by themselves. They are okay when times are good. But when times are bad, people have a tendency to break them. As shown earlier, a human connection, even in a transaction, is your best strategy, whether it's with you directly or a third party.

Walter Lin was an emergency room doctor in Philadelphia. ER situations are quite transactional; medical staff focuses on efficient operations, as lives are often at stake. An older patient who did not need emergency care "kept insisting on sharing his life story," Dr. Lin said. After some hours, the staff tried to kick him out of the ER and the patient became aggressive.

Dr. Lin realized that the staff was frustrated and emotional. He suggested that they take a break from this patient and go back to their other duties; he would handle it. Then he put himself mentally in the shoes of the patient. The doctor discovered that the patient just wanted a new regular doctor but couldn't get an appointment for six months. Dr. Lin called a doctor in front of the patient and got an appointment in two weeks.

The patient left the ER within thirty minutes. "He thanked me profusely," Dr. Lin said. He said neither side, staff or patient, was able to solve the problem by themselves. More dispassionate, Dr. Lin focused on a relationship by articulating the needs of each side and getting a solution quickly.

MEDIATION IN RELATIONSHIPS

You will continually find that people important to you in your life will not be able to solve their own problems. But what if more than one person at a time can't solve a problem between them, either professional or personal?

In that case you may well have to solve their problems as a mediator—someone in between them.

For example, a disagreement between two other departments about who should work on your project. Or a family dispute over vacation plans.

So I thought it would be useful to outline some important tools for mediation. Contrary to what many people believe, a mediator must *never* take sides. You are not a judge or referee. If you are perceived by even one side to be taking sides, you will lose all your credibility. One of the parties will accuse you of being unfair.

A mediator is a facilitator who has no power to decide anything. It's your goal to help the others reach an agreement. Even if you think one party is right, it's not your role to be their advocate. You can ask questions, you can ask about standards, but you can't take sides.

As a mediator, you are actually the confidant of each side. They will each tell you things in confidence if they trust you. You can't share this information with the other party until the person disclosing the information to you wants you to. But getting this additional information may help you get at the root cause of the problem. Maybe the parties are still stinging about something that happened years ago.

To gain these confidences, you need to meet with each of the parties separately, probably more than once. You need to walk them through the problem-solving model, ask questions about interests and standards, and take breaks when things get difficult. If you do it right, people will start turning to you as a problem-solver.

Tatiana Toussi's parents were on the verge of separating. "They kept rehashing things that happened twenty-five years ago," said Tatiana, a U.S. pharmaceuticals manager now stationed in Greece. "They were each angry and stubborn." She spoke to each separately, to understand their perceptions. Then she asked each, separately, to imagine the perceptions of the other. "They each wanted respect and understanding from the other." They started to talk again. Ultimately, the marriage was saved.

Meet briefly with both parties together, if possible (to set ground rules), and then meet separately with each. Flip a coin if necessary to decide the order. That way, they can share perspectives with you in private. Always separate the parties, the length of time depending on the state of the relationship. The worse the relationship, the more separation.

Once they're together, at any sign of trouble separate again. Discuss their different perceptions. If an agreement is better, lead them to it using negotiation tools. Because you will become the center of the relationship between the parties, you *must* stay involved after an agreement is reached, until they can deal with each other on their own. You will need to wean them from you.

If the mediation isn't going well or you find that a party is being unfair, *don't take sides!* You will hurt your reputation. Withdraw, or threaten to withdraw, if the parties don't follow the process you have outlined. You are the keeper of the process, so make sure you clearly establish how you will do it, standards, and so forth. Those around you will love you for it.

END OF RELATIONSHIP

Any chapter on negotiating relationships must include when it is not useful to negotiate a relationship. At least not without third parties.

One of my students had a friend whose boyfriend repeatedly beat her. He kept promising to go to couples therapy. This is not a subject for negotiation by the victim. Physical abuse is against the law in most countries. It too often leads to injury or even death. The student should urge her friend to move out and seek professional help; a family doctor and Internet sites are starting points.

The friend should then give the boyfriend one chance to see the therapist and no more chances if another beating occurs. The girlfriend should not move back in until he is rehabilitated, by some standard of agreement by the parties. If this doesn't work, the abused person needs a third party immediately. The Internet has many sites on third parties who can help.

Virtually all of my former students I contacted and who have been involved in abusive or failed personal relationships did not want their names in this book. The situation seemed too emotional and stigmatizing. But here are some general guidelines they provided.

1. Put some distance between you and the cause of the problem, whether at home or at work; physical space increases clarity of thought.
2. Find a professional, *unemotional* third party for some perspective.
3. Do research on the issue you face.
4. Value the other party, to take the emotional temperature down.
5. Provide an emotional payment, such as just keeping a recovering alcoholic company.
6. Use standards, particularly in a job situation, to find out what is fair.

7. Prepare—write down—questions and issues to discuss with the other party or third parties.
8. Take breaks whenever you feel emotion coming on.

You will never make up for yesterday. Trying to inflict pain on the other side just causes them to fight back. If they try this with you, a third party needs to explain this to them. A former student, now an executive in Singapore, was divorcing a sometimes violent husband, who also wanted most of the assets. She invited a fair-minded friend of the husband to a meeting to mediate an agreement. The friend was able to keep the husband in check.

A calm, structured approach leads to a better solution, even for break-ups short of extreme.

Jeff Fuhrman, now the executive director of business and legal affairs for Comcast in Los Angeles, once wanted to change his relationship with a young woman from romantic to friendship when he was a law student. He said the best thing was being honest about his feelings while valuing her. "If they start getting emotional, let them be emotional," as the course teaches, he said. "Appreciate their concerns; at the same time, tell them your limits."

Today, Jeff uses the same tools in negotiating talent deals regularly. As for the young woman, she and he remain friends.

TRUST AND RELATIONSHIPS

The basis for any relationship is trust. That means if you lie to the other party, you are endangering the entire relationship. It also means that you will enhance the relationship if you are straightforward with bad news. This is counterintuitive for many people. But, in fact, people know the world is not perfect. What they hate is when people cover things up or lie to them.

Grace Kim, vice president of a New York investment bank, wanted to change the date of a reunion trip with her best friends from college. The trip had been planned for six months. She was very up front about it with her best friend in the group. "I said she was my best best friend in the whole world, and how I really wanted to go on the trip," Grace said, "but that the timing was turning out to be really bad for me."

Notice that Grace valued her friend at the same time that she gave bad

276 GETTING **MORE**

news. She also made a commitment to going on another trip in the near future. And she asked about the options there might be so that everyone would be happy with the result. Her friend said others in the party had begun to express some doubts about the date, too. So they all decided to reschedule.

Grace did have this negotiation five months before the trip was to take place. It would have been more serious if Grace waited until a week before the trip. However, it would have been better to mention a potential problem from the first moment she thought of it. "There's a really good lesson here in expressing your concerns right away," Grace said. "I knew from the beginning that the date might be a problem. If I had said that, the whole situation could have been avoided."

This is good advice. If you have concerns, express them up front. Holding them back, especially in a relationship, just makes things worse. The problem doesn't go away.

To end the chapter, here are two difficult family negotiations requiring multiple tools and a very keen sense of other people's feelings. The successful negotiations below could easily have turned out poorly if not done right. They start by identifying the *process* that the parties might use to make tough choices and not jeopardize the relationship. The process should seem fair to the parties. It should be clear and simple. It should be done in advance before things get muddied up with details and conflict.

Tamara Kraljic was an attorney in New York City. She wanted to cancel her promised attendance at her annual family reunion in Europe. She had made a commitment to attend, and the whole family was coming. But she was burned out from work, and had more work yet to do. She was afraid, however, that any excuse, including work, would be viewed as putting the family second.

The first thing Tamara did was find the person in the family most likely to support her. In this case, it was her oldest sister. Her oldest sister had missed several family events and had the most experience in the subject. Her sister reminded Tamara of their father's motto, "Work comes first." Tamara had forgotten that. What a standard!

Who was the next person most likely to empathize? Tamara's mother. Tamara telephoned her mother and said how torn she was because of her desire to attend and yet she was exhausted. Now, it is true her mother could have said, "Come over, we'll all make you feel better." Tamara said, however, that she would be no fun for anyone. She'd be jet-lagged, stressed, fielding work calls, tired, and grumpy.

Tamara asked her mother if it was really worth the trip for her under these circumstances. Tamara promised to call during the reunion. She'd even set up telephone videoconferencing. At the same time, Tamara expressed her extreme disappointment in not attending. Tamara's mother agreed with her and said she should stay home, call when she could, and find another time to visit.

Next, Tamara called each and every person who was coming to the reunion and went through the same negotiation. People felt valued that Tamara went out of her way to call. It only took a few minutes per call. She used different tools for each person: standards for her father, empathy with her mother, alliances with her sister.

Her family members began sending text messages saying, "You are doing the right thing." Her relationships were preserved. Tamara, now working in Paris, said she should have started the negotiations earlier, rather than a week before the event. She could have been more incremental and better prepared. Clearly, though, she used the right kinds of tools. The process she used is the hallmark of the best negotiators.

Husbands and wives often have a hard time with newborn babies. The parents get exhausted. Arguments often flare. Bhishma Thakkar, a Wharton student, had an eight-month-old who woke up every two hours. His wife was exhausted from dealing with this. Bhishma wanted to sleep in the guest room during the week, in order to be fresh for his classes. His wife was unhappy about this.

"My wife does not want to be the only one who is sleep-deprived," he said. This was surely an emotional situation: the notion that "misery loves company."

First, Bhishma told his wife that he knew "she had been working very hard with the baby and had every right to insist that I continue to sleep in the same room." This was an emotional payment, necessary for his wife to even want to listen to him.

He next noted that they had a great relationship. "I asked her how we can get sanity back in our lives," he reported. He suggested that instead of both of them being exhausted together, at least for a while, *both* of them could be less exhausted separately. Bhishma said that if he got a good night's sleep in a separate room, he would be less tired when he came home from work. Then he would care for the baby for several hours while she had some time off—to sleep or just to unwind. She agreed.

You might say, "Gee, that's obvious." Well, it's not so obvious to millions of people who fight over such things. The point is that virtually every relationship situation can fail due to emotions or lack of skill—or can succeed due to a structured and systematic use of negotiation tools.

Remember, every relationship in your life except in your family began as a transaction. The more you look for relationships, even in transactional situations, the more possibilities that at least some of them will turn into long-term relationships. And you will get more. With the caveats presented above, look around. Time and energy permitting, start conversations with people. Look in their eyes. Over a lifetime, you will be rewarded. And you will get more.

12

Kids and Parents

An architect's daughter missed the bus to school every single day. Her father had to take her to school. Fifteen minutes there, fifteen minutes back; thirty minutes a day, two and a half hours a week. Nothing he could do could get her up, dressed, and ready on time.

Working on the problem in class, we had a little negotiation in which the father played the role of his preteen daughter. Why did she miss the bus every day? "To spend more time with Daddy," her father realized.

So we worked out a strategy. First, he would say to his daughter, "You know, I take you to school every day. That's two and a half hours a week. Because of that I have to work on Saturday to make up the time to earn money for our family. Money to buy food, to pay for the house, and the other things we need. Wouldn't you rather I spent the time with you on Saturday instead of having to work? We could plan something together on Saturdays. But that can only happen if you save us the time by taking the bus."

The architect used two negotiation tools in his talk with his daughter: trading items of unequal value, and giving the daughter decision power.

This was good. But the architect didn't think this was enough. So he formed a coalition with a third party. He called the mother of one of the daughter's best friends, who lived a few doors down. They arranged for the friend to stop by and pick up his daughter on the way to the school bus. The father figured that his daughter would not want to leave one of her best friends standing at the door and make her miss the bus, too.

His daughter never again missed the bus.

The reason that children are often much better at negotiating than adults is that children do by instinct what *Getting More* makes explicit. Children very carefully watch adults, gauge where adults are coming from—what's going on inside their heads—and then negotiate to push adults' hot buttons. They use words like "Just a little more" (it doesn't cost you much—they are essentially trading items of unequal value); "I love you, Mommy" (offering an emotional payment); or "I'll be a good girl" (satisfying your needs). Children are very focused not just on their own goals but also on the other party.

So in order to do better at negotiation with children, you have to think the way children think and try to understand how they feel. You have to understand their perceptions.

Too much of the published advice and conventional wisdom on negotiating with children is not very useful. It often doesn't achieve the goals of parents, that is, for children to grow up to be well-mannered, caring, and intelligent adults. Some of this advice focuses on what the parents want—not on the pictures in the heads of their children. Other advice tries to manipulate children into doing what the parents want. Children see through this.

Here, we will focus on the language and perceptions of children. The result is more power and less frustration for parents in negotiating with children. But a lot of this depends on your *attitude* in dealing with your kids. Remember, the way you approach a negotiation determines largely what you get from that negotiation.

So if you want your children to listen to you and to meet your goals, the way you treat your children is the biggest determining factor. As such, everything you do with your children is part of the negotiation. How you treat them, what you say, and what you do will shape the trust or mistrust they have in you.

The observations and advice in this chapter draw from psychology, as well as from decades of my observations of how people act, whether they are children or adults. And they come from tens of thousands of journals of students who have tried these tools with people of all ages.

I've included in this chapter the things that work, and why, as well as the things that don't work, and why. We've reviewed a lot of studies; some are consistent with the behavior we've observed, some are not. When there's a conflict, we go with observed behavior.

To get better at this, you'll have to practice, and debrief yourself. Children practice all the time. They are prepared for negotiations with you.

For you to be effective with children, you have to do more than know this material. You have to use it, learn from it, use it again. Remember, there is a big difference between conceptual knowledge and operational knowledge. What you know is good. But your ability to implement what you know is key.

Negotiating with children is not a special skill. With some specific "cultural" differences, mentioned below, negotiating with children is a lot like negotiating with adults. The tools for negotiating with children include valuing them, listening to them, doing role reversal, communicating clearly, focusing on goals, and not being emotional. It also means you can change the behavior of children just as you can change the behavior of adults. As with adults, it's best done incrementally. And with children, there are plenty of things to trade.

Cultural issues aside, children are individuals. *Getting More* has a special chapter on negotiating with children not because treating them differently is a *valid* stereotype, but because it's a stereotype. Actually, a treatise on "how to negotiate with children" is as foolish as one on "how to negotiate with the Japanese." There are millions and millions of different Japanese and billions of different children.

The same is true of saying that there are different ways to negotiate with boys versus girls. It depends on the individuals involved. Cultural averages will give you insight about general questions to ask. But you still must begin with the individual. And every individual is different.

So the first thing you need to do is figure out the pictures in the head of your child. This is more important than anything else you can do. What are they thinking? What are they feeling?

Why is it important to know how to negotiate well with your children? Here's the thing a lot of people miss. Children and parents have a special bond that no one else in the world has. They are, in the deepest sense, part of you. It is the same with adopted children, since parents must overcome many hurdles to adopt.

That means your children are potentially the closest people in the world to you. They are almost the only people who will give you unconditional love. In this risky, often dangerous, often alienating world, children can be your biggest supporters. Parents have an opportunity, unmatched with virtually anyone else, to nurture and cultivate their biggest supporters throughout the parents' lives.

Parents who negotiate poorly with their children can easily miss out on something very special, a bond that can last forever. So getting this right is an amazing opportunity, one that, unfortunately, too many people fritter away. This chapter is intended to reduce the chance of that. And even if you've made mistakes, it's almost always possible to turn things around.

Let's first talk about the three biggest "cultural" differences with children.

First, largely at least until they leave home, children are keenly aware that they have less traditional power than adults. Until their midteens, children are almost always smaller and less physically strong. Until they leave home, they have less money. They depend on their parents for food, shelter, clothing, and almost everything tangible. This makes children insecure. That means if you increase a child's perception of his or her power and security, they are willing to give up a lot for it.

Of course, this is exactly opposite of what most parents do. Too many parents threaten children, making them feel less secure. That's why threats don't work over the long term, or the medium term, or the short term, either. Children just try to find a way around them.

Second, children use crying and tantrums more than adults, often, but not always, because of less developed communication skills. Crying and emotion in adults generally have limited value. But children know that crying often works in getting them what they want, because many parents can't stand to see their children cry. Young children also cry when they get frustrated by not being able to get their needs met or points across.

The smart parent, however, knows that crying is always Plan B for children. It takes energy to cry. Crying is not a happy circumstance. Crying is a sign of frustration. It's physically upsetting. The key is to give children the chance to use Plan A more: giving them more power, more of a sense of control, emotional payments, helping them get their needs met, understanding what they are trying to say.

Third, a child's life is about getting more. Children think mostly in terms of two categories: things they like and things they don't like. So they are constantly negotiating for more of what they like: more ice cream, more TV, more toys, more time with Daddy or Mommy, more time with friends. To get these things, children are often willing to trade. Don't think of it as bribery but as a way to teach children a valuable skill for life.

I knew a lot of this in theory before I had my son Alexander in 2002. But then I got to practice it day in and out, consciously and as a professional, from the time my son was an infant. Our son has turned out to be a great negotiator.

When he was about four, I once asked him to do something for me. He didn't want to do it. I said, "Didn't Daddy buy you ice cream last week?" He nodded yes. I said, "If Daddy bought you ice cream last week, isn't it only right for you to do something for Daddy now?" The result: he did what I asked him to do. I had linked our current negotiation to a past negotiation—and, by implication, to future negotiations.

About a week later, my son asked me for some ice cream. I declined, saying he had had too many sweets already that day. Without skipping a beat, he said, "Didn't I do something for Daddy last week?" I had to hand it to him. I also gave him some ice cream, although we negotiated over the amount.

So let's look more specifically at some of the mechanisms that get children to do what you want—and in a way that meets their needs, too.

The first thing you need is to define your *goals*. Many if not most parents think of short-term goals: do your homework, stop screaming, clean your room. It is very important to think about whether your actions toward your children will meet your long-term goals: having them grow up to be successful, responsible, and loving adults. The tools below are designed to help you do that.

When you probe more deeply, you will often find out that you are not meeting your goals with your child, because something deeper is at work. Linda Kaufman, a sales rep at Comark, the Canadian clothing distributor, said she continually had to negotiate with her preteen on doing homework. We did a role reversal exercise in class where she played the role of her son.

"Homework wasn't the problem," she found out. "I hadn't taken the time necessary to map out a plan with him that was agreeable to both of us." The real problem, she said, was trust. Together, they agreed that her son would do his homework after school, and after that he would have Internet access. And they set up a trial period. "My son wants to keep Internet access," she said. "We proved that we can keep commitments to each other. And I realized I should make sure we solve problems *together*."

Assuming you know your goals, the most important thing you need to understand is *the pictures in the heads of your children*. Otherwise, you don't know where to start. It means asking questions. It means not assuming anything.

Franz Paul's four-year-old son, Henry, had become a picky eater at dinner, and also disruptive. Franz thought about the pictures in Henry's head. Dad realized that he had recently stopped playing with Henry before dinner because of work demands; the family ate as soon as Franz walked in the door. As soon as Franz, a hedge fund manager, started playing with Henry again before dinner, everything returned to normal.

So the right answer to many of your child's fits should be questions. If your child says, "You're mean!" your answer should be "Why?" or "Tell me more." If your child says, "Robert stole my toy!" your answer should be "Why?" or "Tell me about it." If your child says, "I want a cookie now!" you ask, "Why a cookie?" or "Why now?"

Yes, you can certainly guess. But it's not as good as asking your child a direct question.

I've seen advice for parents that says things like "When they say they want a cookie, ask them if they want a banana instead." What? Your child knows the difference between a cookie and a banana. If they wanted a banana, they would ask for a banana! "Why do you want a cookie?" is better. Or "Why do you want a cookie so close to dinnertime?" Or "It's so close to dinnertime, will you take half a cookie?"

Or modify the common advice: "You could have a cookie, but it's not so good for you. Can you satisfy your sweet tooth with a banana instead?" This is very different, because it contains respect.

Rahul Sondhi's three-year-old nephew insisted on eating in his parents' bedroom. Instead of just saying no, Rahul asked his nephew "to show me exactly where he wanted to eat." Whereupon the nephew took his uncle to a corner of the bedroom where there was a stool. The nephew sat on the stool.

"I realized that he wanted to eat like an adult, not in a high chair," Rahul said. "The room was not material. So I took the stool into the dining room and sat him down to eat. He ate there happily." His nephew just wanted to be "big," to be treated more like an adult. "Looking at the problem from his perspective allowed me to solve the problem," said Rahul, now strategy chief for a New York hedge fund.

Cesar Grullon's nine-year-old son, Stefan, wouldn't sleep in his own bed. After questioning him, Cesar, a marketing entrepreneur, got to the root cause: his son thought his bed was a "kiddie" bed. So Cesar offered to go with his son to the store and pick out a big-boy bed if his son would agree to sleep in it. "In situations where power is so lopsided," Cesar said, "it's tempting to flex one's strength and unilaterally decide outcomes. But these outcomes are often short-lived, because root causes are not articulated, understood, and addressed."

In other words, you have to not only understand your children's perceptions but appreciate them. Bill Taylor, a sales rep from BASF, said that his son, a high school senior, wanted to attend music school after graduation. "I want him to get a degree in a field where he can support himself," Taylor told the class. He was willing to pay tuition to study education, business, or science, but not music.

So we did a role reversal exercise, where Bill played the role of his son. "I realized," he said, "that the old dude mistrusts the young buck's judgment. And the young buck thinks the old dude is a dinosaur."

Bill and his colleagues used the exercise to come up with a proposal: the son would go to a state school for a general degree, as well as a special music school. "I needed to appreciate and value him," Bill said.

The key is to *communicate honestly* with your children about the pictures in their heads. Don't try to hoodwink them. Just because they can't express themselves as well as you do, don't think they don't notice things. They probably notice things even more acutely than you do. Watch your child as much as, or more than, your child watches you. What revs him or her up? What calms him down? What are her likes or dislikes? What are the indications of their various moods?

Next, *listen to what they have to say.* Studies show that many parents do this poorly, even though they think they do it well. Think how an adult would react if you treated them the same way. Say your kid is talking to you and you continue to do what you're doing, without real feedback, or even turning around to look at them. It's insulting!

More important, you will be training your children to do the same thing to you. If you wonder why your child doesn't listen to you, think about whether you listen, really listen, to them. You say, Johnny's just a child. Actually, Johnny, or Sara, is a small adult—with a memory. Your kids will grow up, too. They won't forget how you treated them when they were young.

What this means is that if you want your child to stop and listen to you, you have to do the same thing. Unless you are in the middle of something critical, when they call you, STOP and listen to them. Get all the details. The golden rule here is very important; children learn to apply it even before they can articulate it.

In a study done in England and Wales a few years ago, almost 75 percent of teenagers felt that being listened to and understood by their parents was key to their relationship. Only 41 percent of parents thought so. Even from a young age, children who feel listened to and understood by parents gain more self-esteem, are able to think independently, and develop more social competence and decision-making ability.

You may need to be creative. Steve Shokouhi, who got the cocker spaniel for his daughter, Debra, also had a problem with Debra not going to
sleep on her own. She wanted Mommy or Daddy to sleep at the foot of the
bed until she fell asleep. She wouldn't say why. So Daddy set up a puppet
show, and his daughter talked through the puppet. The puppet said Debra
was afraid of the dark. A night-light wasn't enough.

So the parents put all the lights on in her room, and Debra fell asleep.
She was okay with the fact that her parents would turn off the lights later
in the night after she was sound asleep.

What if you bend over backward to listen to them, and they then don't
come when you call them, or don't listen to you? Remind them, *nicely*,
what you do for them. Will this work all the time? Absolutely not. But each
time you use the tools in this book, your success rate will go up.

A related point is to *consult* with your children. Let them into your
decision-making whenever possible. This addresses a key insecurity of
children: that they have no power. It encourages them to trust you more.
They feel included. They feel loved. "What could we have done better for
next time?" you might ask them, for example.

Rod Palmer, a manager at Marathon Petroleum, could not seem to
motivate his nine-year-old daughter to do her homework and participate
in sports. He finally decided to consult her for answers. They came up with
a schedule that worked. Rod let his daughter participate in the decision
process, he said, including setting rewards and consequences. They imple-
mented it incrementally. In the process he found out that his daughter
looked at the world differently, in wanting to feel some control. "Letting
her take ownership made her better at things," he said.

If you want your child to brush her teeth, it's better to put five toothbrushes and five tubes of toothpaste on the bed than simply telling her she
must brush her teeth. Tell your child, you have the *power*. Decide which
one is yours. Discuss the various pros and cons of the toothbrushes—color,
taste, looks, etc. This may take more time than just yelling at them to brush
their teeth, but it is far more effective.

And actually, what you are doing is training your child to make decisions and work collaboratively with you. It translates to all kinds of situations. Ask your children to help you pick restaurants; it will often satisfy
their desire for more control.

John Murray's three-year-old daughter, Kelli, wouldn't brush her teeth
without a fight. He offered her a choice of toothpaste, and he also offered

to read any book she wanted. "It was like flicking a switch," John said. "She was willing to brush her teeth. I gave her a little control; she felt empowered and was willing to meet my goal." Instead of giving something up, they each had something to contribute.

In my opinion, the sentiment "Children should be seen and not heard" is a terrible message to convey to our children. It devalues children, essentially saying that their perceptions are not important. It causes them to stop listening and to look for ways to fight back.

Studies show that children who make more of their own decisions wind up being more self-motivated, creative, healthy, and intelligent and having higher self-esteem.

How would you like it if you were watching your favorite TV program and someone came into the room and just shut it off without asking you? You would be livid. But that's what a lot of parents do to their children. Too often parents assume that what children think, or need, isn't important. Parents resort to the use of raw power. And, eventually, your kids will hate you for it.

People of all ages have been found to have a higher risk of mental and physical health problems when they feel powerless. Having the chance to make choices they feel are meaningful increases people's sense of well-being. It also increases their ability to cope effectively with stress. Such people negotiate with others more calmly and effectively—and that includes children.

Giving people information helps them feel more powerful, as well. Children facing surgery, for example, can be taken on a tour of the hospital beforehand, to let them see what the hospital is like. Allow children to express themselves. Fully answer your children's questions. What parents should be asking is, "What can I give my child control over?" The more you do this, the easier it will be to negotiate with them.

Alan Switzer's son, Brandon, insisted on playing with the new train his dad bought him at Disney World the night before their return home. Alan wanted him to pack it. "Do you want to take the train home with you?" asked Alan, an infotech director. "How do we do that if it's not packed up?" Brandon, given the decision authority, let his dad pack the train.

Children who feel empowered at home are less likely to turn away from their parents when they get more power as teenagers. So many of the problems that parents have with their teenage children are the result of having used poor negotiation skills early on. Research shows that by the time kids are thirteen, those from controlling families are often ready to run away from their parents. The peer group becomes more important than the family group, as a result. Yet this is almost entirely preventable.

Andrew Jensen was teaching a class of ten-year-olds in Sunday school. "They're ten years old, so they are very hyperactive," he said. "Some have little discipline at home, and thus are unruly at school."

Andrew thought back on his experience as a ten-year-old in Sunday school. He remembered how he reacted to his stern teacher—rebelling against her rules. So he decided to be less formal, to provide the children with more incentives, and to consult with them on when and how to do their lessons. He used lesson-based games to demonstrate concepts of reverence. Small treats were given for good behavior now. Pizza was available later.

"The children started bringing their books," Andrew said. "There was no misbehavior. There were many volunteers to answer questions." He learned to think about what made his students tick, what roadblocks there were to learning, and how students might have different perceptions. He realized one must be willing to try new things, without losing focus on one's goals. "This stuff works with anyone!" said Andrew, finance manager of an industrial supply company.

Even two-year-olds. John Valovic's two-year-old was going to bed too late. But he refused to go to bed earlier. "I realized," said John, "that my son wanted to be in control of his schedule." So they had a talk and decided together what to do. For example, they agreed to reduce his son's midday nap from three hours to one hour. "Including children in discussions works," he said.

You will be amazed at the extent to which children will *trade things* of unequal value when you let them. Brian McDevitt, head of retail for a major Internet company, wanted his five-year-old son, Thomas, to talk to his dad when they got up in the morning. Brian thought it was a good habit to get into. So Brian told his son that in exchange for fifteen minutes of conversation in the morning, Thomas could have fifteen extra minutes of coloring. Thomas started talking immediately.

Some of you might think of this as a bribe. I disagree. A bribe is paying someone to do something that (a) they should do for free or (b) is unfair to others, like giving cash to a government official to sway a decision. The trading discussed in *Getting More* is fairer to all, and is a reasonable bargain for both.

Children love to trade. Philip White's three-year-old son, Ethan, didn't want to get out of the bathtub. He wanted to keep playing with his toys. Daddy was in a rush. "I made sure I was empathetic and acknowledged my son's power in having the right to stay in the tub," said Phil, a director at an Internet company in San Antonio. "I convinced him to get out of the tub now in return for having colored water in the tub the next day." His son agreed, and got out of the tub. Even three-year-olds are willing to negotiate.

Soo Jin Kim's five-year-old daughter had trouble getting ready on time for school. Mommy knew her daughter, Min Suh, liked her hair braided. "I proposed to braid her hair every morning if she goes to bed one hour earlier and gets up thirty minutes earlier," said Soo Jin, now a senior counsel for Samsung Electronics in Seoul, Korea.

Notice how easy each of these negotiations was. If you have the right key, children are very willing to negotiate.

Alexandra Levin's friend brought her two-and-a-half-year-old, Sydney, to Alexandra's house. When it was time to go home, the child didn't want to go. She wanted Alexandra to continue reading *Eloise*. Her mother sensed a tantrum coming. So Alexandra used negotiation tools. "I agreed to read her two more pages now," Alexandra said. In other words, she was being incremental. "And I said that next time I'd read the whole book again."

Sydney calmed right down. She understood what "incremental" means.

It was also a great lesson for Sydney, learning to postpone gratification to an appropriate time in the future. Alexandra, who lives in Philadelphia, has since had three kids of her own and the same tools work just fine with them also, she said. As such, you don't need to have your own children to master negotiating with kids.

At 5:30 A.M., Brian Murphy hauled himself out of bed to go downstairs to work out. His three-year-old daughter, Evelyn, woke up early and came to see him. "Daddy, can you keep me company?" she said. She wanted him to sleep on the floor in her room. Who can resist such a request? Brian didn't want his daughter to think Daddy loves exercising more than her. At the same time, Brian knew he really needed to work out, and this was the only time he could do so.

He thought about the things Evelyn really liked. One was her "Little People" toys. Evelyn was not allowed to sleep with them. Brian asked Evelyn if the Little People could keep her company in bed while Daddy worked out to stay healthy. Evelyn agreed, and the problem was solved. Brian later formed a principal investment company and was running for governor of Maryland on the Republican ticket in the fall of 2010. He said the same negotiation tools work in politics as with his daughter: defining what value means to each person and then exchanging items of unequal value.

Jacqueline Sturdivant was babysitting her friend's three-year-old son, Alexander. Alex wanted to play with his cars on her newly reupholstered silk sofa. She wanted Alex to play with the cars on the floor. Instead of ordering him to do so, Jacqui told Alex that playing on the floor was better. The surface was smoother. And there was space for six cars, instead of one or two on the sofa. "We had a car race on the floor so I could show him," she said. "He won two of three races."

"Telling my friend's son not to play on the sofa because it messes up the fabric has no meaning to him; he does not care about fabric," said Jacqueline, who directs a translation service in New York. "But he does want his cars to go faster. And hard flat surfaces make cars go faster. Therefore, it was a simple sell to get him to change."

This means framing things in terms of the child's needs.

Poorvi Chothani wanted her teenage daughter Chadni to take typing lessons. "She hates typing," Poorvi said. This was compounded by peer pressure. The parents of two of Chadni's friends did not think it was a useful skill. Using two fingers on their BlackBerries worked just fine.

So Poorvi focused on her daughter's needs. "She wants to be a journalist," Poorvi said. "I showed her studies that showed how much faster you can write with touch typing." Poorvi also told her daughter that instant messaging would be more efficient with better typing skills. Poorvi said she understood peer pressure, but this was for her daughter's career. She added that her daughter could choose the days of the week to take classes.

"Role reversal made me sensitive to her feelings," said Poorvi, founder and managing partner of a law firm in Mumbai, India. "Focusing on her interests made her feel I was on her side. Pointing out third parties' studies made me less of her enemy. Being incremental—taking classes part-time—made it easier to start. Giving her the power to choose which days she took classes was persuasive." Chadni took the typing course and became a writer, her mother said.

As you can see, it often takes several tools to achieve a successful negotiation. As long as you are listening to your kids and valuing them, it doesn't really matter which tool you start with. You will discover your own favorites with practice.

Mary Gross's four-year-old daughter, Eleanor, made a scene every time Mommy had to go on a business trip. "I thought about her interests and needs," Mary recalled. The first thing that Mary said to her daughter might seem so obvious that most adults don't say it. But it's very meaningful when you look at the world through a child's eyes. "Doesn't Mommy always come back?" Mary said to her daughter. She wanted to ease her daughter's fears.

Next, she asked, what could her daughter do that she enjoys when Mommy is away? They put together a list. Finally, Mommy promised to bring back a "surprise" for her daughter. "I was able to leave with a big hug and kiss instead of tears and tugging on my coat," said Mary, a career services counselor at Wharton. "I had acknowledged and validated her feelings." And there is nothing wrong with bringing home a "surprise" from such a trip. After all, how many spouses bring back presents after a business trip? Not fair to have double standards for children.

REWARDS

Ying Liu wanted to stop his six-year-old son, Jing, from watching so much TV. He also wanted to encourage Jing to play the piano and do more math. The first thing Ying did was prepare. He made a list of his son's interests. They included, in addition to watching TV, playing with Legos and going to the zoo.

He then suggested to his son that he could trade TV time, piano time, and study time for Legos and visits to the zoo. They established a point system. So whenever he watched less TV, he got points. Whenever he studied math or played the piano, he got more points. Dad and son monitored the process together. As Jing got points, he felt valued and good about himself. He spent quality time with Dad.

Ying, now a McKinsey associate in New Jersey, also used standards to negotiate with his son. He noted that a classmate and a cousin were each limited to thirty minutes of TV per day. Ying's son watched hours of TV per day. All three of them said they wanted to go to Harvard. Ying next asked his son which of the three he thought would be going to Harvard, and why. Jing told his dad whichever of them worked the hardest. And that became his goal. The process worked.

Some parents might object to trading TV time for homework, but I see nothing wrong with this. Kids watch TV anyway. Parents should get something for it! And more often than not, eventually the kids will come to like the activity they are being encouraged to do, so you won't have to trade them things to do it.

Some experts declare that a system of rewards and punishment decreases motivation over time. Based on experience, in the *real world,* I beg to differ. Rewards and consequences work just fine, *if* (a) the child has a hand in choosing the rewards and consequences, (b) the process seems fair to all, and (c) it creates the right incentives. It's also a great idea to keep a record: a colorful spreadsheet, a journal—something that parents and kids can share. They can discuss how to make continual improvement.

Julie Haniger told me she has never been successful in getting her children to keep up their responsibilities around the house. "They sometimes let me think they have agreed, but then they do not follow through," she said.

So Julie had a meeting with her kids. She wanted to know if the family members would agree to make a commitment to help each other. They said yes. So they all came up with a reward system (a weekly allowance). There was a schedule for chores, provided with some flexibility. There were penalties for inaction. They also created a chart with stars to record their performance. And finally, the family agreed to monthly meetings. "It worked better than I thought possible," she said.

By now it should be clear that the willingness of children to meet your goals as parents has a lot to do with how you treat them. *Treating children with respect* trains them to treat you with respect. That doesn't mean you have to approve of everything they do. But it means you need to give them reasons when you say no, just like you do with adults.

And it needs to be done in a way that doesn't undermine your child's sense of security. The best security of all for a child is the love of their parent or parents. I find it amazing how many parents undermine their children's sense of security and confidence by withholding love. Or by threatening it in some way.

The *trust* relationship between parent and child is absolutely critical. If you lose or harm it, everything else will be affected. That means if you have a problem with your child, you need to sit down and *communicate* with each other. Talk about trust, and anything else your child has on his or her mind.

When children are young, trust is built with face time: doing projects together (art, scrapbooks, Legos), sharing things together (games, sports, educational TV, reading, counting water towers or different states' license plates on cars along the highway). All of this affects the child's attitude toward negotiating with you on a wide range of things that both of you care about. Everything is related.

Some parents sit with their children at dinnertime and the whole family talks about the best and worst things that happened to them that day. At my house each member of the family also has to bring up three other items of interest. When children communicate and are listened to this way, trust is built. So when I want my child to do something important for me, he is usually much more willing to give me the benefit of the doubt. It's a backdrop that affects the entire parent-child relationship.

When you do projects together, children are less likely to be demanding in general. When your child does not want to be left at day care, start a project with the youngster with the teacher's help. Ask them to show it to you when you get back. You can check on their progress with them by phone during the day.

If you were to ask about the kinds of things that people value most from their loved ones, high on the list is "unconditional love." That doesn't mean that the other party can't criticize you. It means that the other party loves you despite your weaknesses and faults.

When you emotionally undermine your child, the pictures in your child's head are often "Mommy doesn't love me" or "Daddy doesn't love me." What it also means is that the child, without knowing the term, thinks you are withholding your love. If you do that, don't expect to get their love in return.

Blaming adults causes them to shut down and not listen. It is even more pronounced with children, because kids are insecure and dependent on you. Whenever there is a problem in which I'm involved, I first think it must be my fault. After all, I have the most control over myself. If my son broke something, my first thought is, Why didn't I train him better?

It doesn't mean that you should go around praising your children all day long. Children can detect manipulation probably even better than adults can. Studies show that specific praise is better. "You're a good boy" is not as good as "That was a great piano recital."

Remember, you've lived longer and have more experience and skills. It's *your* job to teach your child—and teach until he or she gets it. If you don't follow this advice, you won't meet your goals. And we have thousands of journals and twenty years of study to back it up.

So tell your child, "I love you with all my heart and soul. But you can ask for more ice cream all day and I'll still say no. And here's the reason . . ." They need to make sure that your love is unconditional. If they still don't get it, you might say, "I've lived longer than you have and I've seen more things. And here's what I found out." Even a four-year-old understands that. Touch them on the arm while saying it. How many of you show your children affection as an *absolute prerequisite* to criticizing them? It makes a world of difference.

It's also key to *set priorities*. Don't sweat the small stuff. Safety, health, laws, ethics, and manners are nonnegotiable. Everything else we can learn incrementally and twin it with responsibility. Humor is great with kids. If your son spills flour all over the floor, you might say, "Whoops! Are you baking a cake on the floor?" Then add, "I guess we have to clean it up."

And we clean it up together. Adults drop things, too. Your child will already feel bad about it. Don't make it into a comment about his or her entire personality or self-worth. It's not fair, and they know it. You'll just teach them to be unfair.

Paint them a picture. "You need to brush your teeth or we'll soon have to go to the dentist, and no one thinks that's fun!" It's just how adults would frame it to themselves.

How you *frame things* to children (and others) is key to how they will respond. Walk them through the process. Give them the courtesy and respect of working through the problem with them. *Give them the details.* Maryann Wanner's seven-year-old daughter, Aimee, would not wear knee and elbow pads while riding her bike because they weren't "cool." "We then did an inventory of her many, many bruises and I asked her to pick out the coolest," said Maryann, a finance manager. "She grimaced and put on the pads."

David Luzzi needed to negotiate with his twin eleven-year-old boys to play fewer video games. David's goal was to cut video game time to half of total playtime instead of almost 100 percent.

The first thing David did was talk to his wife, Marla. As all parents know, kids often try to play parents off against each other. David and his wife made sure they were on the same page. And they would also all do the negotiation together.

The second thing David did was figure out the setting for the negotiation. He didn't want the boys to run off to some other activity. So they had the discussion over a forty-minute drive on the Pennsylvania Turnpike.

Then he needed to get his boys to realize for themselves that video gaming was only one part of a full life. That if they played too much video, they would be depriving themselves of other activities they liked. So David asked his sons for a list of fun activities that they liked. They named a long list of activities that his wife wrote down. Video gaming was only one of the many items on the list.

Then Mom mentioned studies by scientists that said too much video gaming was not good for kids. Well-balanced play was better. The two eleven-year-olds, Colin and Marcus, had of course taken science class and were always "educating" Mom and Dad on things they learned in school. Authoritative studies by scientists were respected in the Luzzi household.

David's son Colin was no dummy. He could see where this negotiation was going. He started to become upset. David was ready for this. He knew from studying emotion in class that many negotiations are not rational. Emotional payments must be given. So David asked Colin why he was getting so upset.

Colin said he likes video games and "hardly ever gets to play them." David, now the dean of engineering at Northeastern University, did not argue with Colin about this. Being right didn't matter here. Instead, David and Marla said that half the total playtime in video games seemed fair, didn't it? The rest of their time would be spread among all the fun activities the kids had mentioned. Everyone was thrilled. The boys came away from the discussion with a new sense of responsibility and family decision-making.

The part that takes parents some getting used to is slowing down and being incremental. Asking the children about their dreams and fears. Making an emotional payment.

At the beginning of chapter 6, we saw the example of a mother getting her daughter willingly to go to the hospital to get stitches on her forehead. Incremental, emotional payments are effective. Children think in terms of being *incremental*. They ask for some cookies, and you say no. So they ask for one cookie. Why can't you do the same thing? When they ask for cookies, you say, "How about one cookie?" Or "You can have half a cookie now, and half a cookie later."

Michael Johnson's three-year-old daughter, Anne, rolled up in a ball on the soccer field, crying and noncommunicative. It was her first soccer game. This is not unusual, but most parents just don't know what to do in this situation. Michael got her to start communicating by telling Anne that she didn't have to do anything, that Daddy loved her, that Daddy was here for her.

Anne finally confided that she was afraid of all the parents watching her and seeing her make mistakes. No problem at all, her father said. He suggested they go to the next field, where no parents were watching, and "play our own game." Anne loved it. They did that for a while, as Anne became increasingly confident. Finally, she was willing to join the other kids for the last few minutes of the game. Anne even scored a goal. "She had a great time and is now confident," said Michael, a private equity manager outside Philadelphia.

Bob Evans's son, four, refused to take swimming lessons. "I'd rather ride my scooter," he said. Bob realized that his son, Michael, might be afraid of the water. He told his son it was okay if he was afraid of the water. Bob, a financial services executive, said that when he was a little boy he was afraid of the water, too.

So Bob and his wife first gave his son a lot of baths. Then they took him and his friends to the shallow end of the pool where the son could stand up, "just like in the bathtub." Later, they put water wings on him; he tried deeper water. Then they took him and his friends to a swimming class. Afterward they all got pizza. The process was very incremental, dealing with the child's fears and eventually meeting the parents' goals. Peers and pizza of course helped. The process got Michael to love the water; he later swam in the Marin County championship in California.

Yucong Li needed to transfer her daughter to another school that was closer to their home and Yucong's work. Her daughter was sad about this and opposed the transfer. So Yucong encouraged her daughter to talk about all of her concerns. She said she would miss her friends. And she was afraid of an unfamiliar new place.

So Yucong gave her daughter plenty of time to get used to the new school. They visited the teachers there, who were nice. Yucong helped her daughter write good-bye letters to all her friends at her present school, and made sure everyone exchanged phone numbers. Plans were made for playdates with her friends. The next time they visited the new school her daughter was more interested. Finally she agreed.

"Negotiation skills can be useful in all kinds of situations," Yucong said. "Appreciate your child's concerns. Take breaks. Help your child find workable solutions."

Children are very good at watching adults, but they are less skilled at putting themselves in the roles of adults. It is important for children to understand what adults have to deal with. If you can get your child to play along, try a *role reversal* with them. Children love to play-act, so it will usually not be a problem.

The five-year-old daughter of William Song was constantly whining and not paying attention. He thought it might have something to do with jealousy over the extra attention that her parents paid to her twenty-two-month-old brother, Joshua. So the father and the daughter, Sophia, did a thirty-minute role reversal. The father played the daughter and the daughter played the father.

In the role reversal, Sophia had the power, and she was trying to get her father to pay attention to her and to do some things together. William, an attorney in New York, responded with exaggerated whining and not paying attention. Sophia soon saw the unattractiveness of her own behavior as demonstrated by her father, and the frustration that it was causing. This helped them get to the root of exactly what was bothering her: not feeling she had enough of her parents' attention. So they put in place some guidelines that helped everyone.

Mike Vertal had a similar problem with his five-year-old son, Liam. Liam had become increasingly defiant over the previous months, ignoring his father's requests. Their interactions often led to yelling.

So Mike asked Liam to "play me" for fun, and he would "play" his son. I've found most kids can't resist such games. The father, playing his son, said, "Why do you get mad at me when I don't listen?" This forced Liam to think about why he should listen to his daddy more. It was a big aha moment for the son.

Mike also needed a commitment. So he asked Liam what they should do in the future when one of them doesn't listen to the other. Here, Mike included himself in the equation. He told Liam, "Maybe Daddy should listen more, too." Liam said they should remind each other of this conversation. In the future, this is exactly what they did. Mike, founder of an information technology company, said such role-reversal experiences have helped his son think things through better, especially in science.

Giving children extra responsibility is key to success in dealing effectively with them. In fact, it's a cornerstone of all human behavior. It's just more pronounced with children because in general they feel a lack of power much more deeply. The mere act of getting children to "play" their parents empowers children to think like big people (with power) for a few minutes. Children usually remember the insights they get from such a role reversal.

Putting yourself in your child's shoes is also a good way for parents to gain insight into why children do what they do. Is your child ornery? Ever think maybe they just had a bad day? Aren't adults ornery at times? What, you think your child never feels any stress? So what if they want fast-food French fries? Or if they want to play computer games for an hour or two? Don't adults use stress relievers, as well—watching TV or having a drink at the end of a hard day? Which is worse?

It's important to be sensitive to your kids' need to relieve stress. If you aren't, they may later turn to things you like a lot less—smoking, alcohol, illegal drugs. Sometimes my son wants to watch TV just to "chill out." Maybe he doesn't want to do his homework just then, he's too keyed up. As long as we can discuss when he will do his homework and why he's watching TV, it's fine. Maybe your child just wants to spend some time alone.

Everything that your kids do is not just about you. They're not out to get you. They're trying to live their own lives. Parents often find out that *they* are the problem, rather than their kids.

Humor is wonderfully effective with kids. Take some time out of *your own day* and show them funny cartoons. Whenever I went on a business trip, I would get my son a funny hat. I got him so many hats that one day, with a smile, he told me to stop getting him hats. Then I got him T-shirts. Sometimes I draw him funny pictures. It's like the small talk I mentioned earlier in the book. It gets him in a better frame of mind when we're talking or he's negotiating about anything and everything.

Let's look at some more difficult cases. Some children scream and cry and refuse to cooperate. They are hard bargainers, just like adults. With them, it's okay to use *standards*. But they need to be used carefully and tactfully, as this is a relationship situation.

Brian Garrison decided that his son's tantrums were unacceptable. So he waited until his three-year-old son, Connor, was calm enough to talk. Waiting for his son to be ready was itself an emotional payment. Brian asked his son whether kicking and screaming and rolling around on the floor was a good thing to do. This is a "be extreme or come to me" question. His son grudgingly admitted it was not okay. Even three-year-olds know this.

So Brian asked his son what they should do when this happens. Consultation is another emotional payment. The father suggested that the son may need a "time-out," that is, some quiet time by himself to calm down. They decided together that three minutes in the son's room was enough time to calm down. It was a decision that the son participated in.

He would first get a warning before a time-out was called. And it worked. Connor realized he could no longer use Plan B, manipulating the situation with bad behavior. "He became much better behaved," said Brian, now a Navy commander.

"Even at three," Brian said, "my son understands the consequences of his actions. Our earlier attempts to negotiate with Connor based on reason had somehow conveyed the impression that he could manipulate situations by misbehaving. By establishing standards and enforcing them consistently, we have redefined our daily negotiations."

Ideally, you should establish the process with your child before an actual event happens. This may not be possible in every case. But each time something happens that the parents or the child don't like, they should have a discussion to prevent the next time. This fixes the process, not just the problem. And it is important to find out the real cause of the temper tantrum.

That's what Charles Gallagher did with his three-year-old daughter, Nicola. After one particularly bad outburst at the home of friends, Mommy, Daddy, and daughter sat down after things calmed down and talked through what happened. Their daughter promised to be good and discuss any issues she had later with her parents in private.

Lo and behold, Charles got a call between classes from his wife. Their daughter was acting out again at his in-laws' house. Could he talk to her on the phone? "I said that we had all agreed on the rules about acting up," said Charles, now a financial officer in New York. "And that it was not acceptable within our family's standards."

Then, without explicitly threatening her, her father said that it was not in her best interest to act out. "You like to go stay with different people, and if you don't behave when you're there, other people won't want you to come over." He added, "She listened to my arguments, and immediately decided on her own to tell her mother she was sorry and would be a good girl."

Showing that their actions don't meet their goals is a powerful tool that can be used to stop arguments. Eric Schneider called home one evening to find that his wife was having a problem with their seven-year-old daughter. The wife and daughter had made an agreement that the daughter could play outside with her friends after school as long as she came inside before dinner to do her homework.

"Unfortunately, when it came time to do her homework, my daughter said the agreement was unfair," Eric said. "When I called, my daughter and my wife were in the middle of an argument." Eric asked to speak to his daughter on the phone.

"I asked her what was wrong," Eric said. "She said she wanted to continue playing outside. I asked when she would do her homework. She said she would do it later while watching TV." Eric and his wife didn't allow that. He asked his daughter whether she could do her homework faster with the TV on or off. "Off," his daughter said.

His daughter quickly saw that if she just did her homework first, she would have more time to watch TV. Eric then asked if his daughter thought it was okay if Mommy and Daddy made promises to her and then broke them. "No," his daughter said. He stopped the negotiation at that point. It was incremental enough. The rest could be handled in person. The argument was over; his daughter did her homework and came away with a greater sense of commitment.

It is important for parents not to lose their cool, or their temper, in negotiating with children. It just encourages children to do the same thing. Parents screaming at their children is good for neither party.

Remember, emotion begets more emotion. And more emotion means less listening, and less of an ability to meet your goals and interests. Screaming is almost useless except to get someone's attention in a dangerous situation. You must be calm to bring up your kids to be calm.

If they throw food across the room, you might say, "That's interesting." You could add that if it hits the wall and leaves a mark, "we'll have to get the room repainted. And then there will be less money for toys and vacations. And if we waste food that we could eat, the extra food we will have to buy will cost money and I'll have to work harder. And that means I won't be home with you as much."

This trains children to understand actions and reactions. If you do get upset, apologizing for being upset or rude to them is okay as an emotional payment. But understand that you are apologizing for your own bad behavior, which should have not occurred in the first place. Instead, try empathy: focus on their feelings and how you can deal with them. Your own uncontrolled emotion is bad for everyone.

Patrick Gallagher discovered that his college-aged son had charged $156 on Patrick's credit card for several recreational items without Dad's approval. This despite an explicit agreement that the credit card was to be used only for books and emergencies. Patrick calmly called up his son and said he "wanted to help, but the respect has to be mutual."

His son agreed that he had violated the pact. Dad asked his son how he proposed to repay the money. The son suggested paying it back in two installments, and agreed to keep to their agreement in the future. "Call your children on unacceptable actions," said Patrick, a pharmaceutical industry executive. "But do it calmly. They respect you more and learn better how to deal with conflicts. I wanted him to see I could address his behavior without attacking him personally." Everything worked out fine, he said.

Many kids like lists, just as many adults do. It represents a sense of order in a disordered world. Making lists together to solve problems is a good activity for parents to do with their children. It improves the relationship and increases commitments.

Abigail Andrews, the eleven-year-old daughter of friends of ours, fought with her mother, Heather, over responsibilities around the house. Finally, they came to an agreement. Abigail was perfectly willing to take care of her responsibilities as long as Mom kept her end of the bargain.

So Abigail wrote up and printed out a "contract" on the computer, complete with artwork on the cover, with the terms inside. Abigail signed it and left it on the dinner table for her mother to sign.

Many parents think it's hard to get their kids to keep commitments. Actually, many kids are thinking the same thing about parents. So talking explicitly about commitments is key. That includes talking about what happens if someone breaks the commitment.

What Abigail did, and what you and your children can do, is to develop a list of standards that you set for yourselves that will govern how you treat each other and what you do for each other. People find it almost impossible to disagree with their own standards, which they themselves set. So the key is to have both children and parents develop their own set of standards. It enforces a sense of responsibility to one another.

You can also let kids discover things for themselves, instead of forcing them to do—or not do—something. If our son wants to stay up late, sometimes we let him. We warn him he will be tired the next day. Then we make sure we wake him up on time. And he is tired and miserable for the day.

His growth won't be stunted for not getting enough sleep for a day. But he gets a good lesson in life: actions have results. It took a few times before he got it. Many kids like to stay up. But now, when we say it's getting late, he remembers what the next day feels like if he doesn't go to bed. It's much better than screaming at him to go to bed.

There is a limit to how far we will take this, and we could have used standards instead, or trading. But the approach is the same: instilling children with a greater sense of responsibility.

I am sure there are many things you can think of that offer good lessons for your kids. Think of yourself as the head teacher of a school with one, or two, or three, or however many children you have in it.

You can go even further and have your children turn the tables. What can your child teach *you*? Children often know more about computers than many parents. Children have entire social networks through their phones. For many adults, this is a mystery. A great way to improve your relationship with your children is to ask them to teach you what they know. This is not to check up on them, and it shouldn't be framed that way. It is to share things with them.

This way, when children reach their teenage years and naturally start turning to their peers for support and advice, you can be included as a peer. Almost every negotiation will seem easier. The mere fact of asking your children for help values them. And they will value you in return.

If you are having trouble negotiating with your children, third parties can often help. That includes grandparents, uncles, aunts, siblings, and even their friends and friends' parents. Relations can get strained between parent and child. You may need a kind of mediator to help sort it out. Too often, parents forget about this avenue.

Why not share this chapter with your child or children? You can help each other settle disputes in your family. You can advise one another. Maybe your child won't agree with everything in this chapter. If so, that's good insight, too. All feedback is in the service of building the kind of relationship necessary to negotiate everything better.

Jon Rogers's four-year-old and two-year-old sons, Patrick and Andrew, were constantly fighting with each other. He sat them down and asked why they weren't buddies. "I told them they should have the responsibility to monitor themselves. Tattling to me on each other—big boys didn't do that." Jon told them they should be watching out for each other. From that point on, he said, they played games together. They began looking out for each other, and they still do, eight years later, said Jon, now a managing director for Citigroup in New York.

It would not be fitting to complete this chapter without saying a few words about using force against children—physical violence and emotional violence. In a sense, it's just bullying, isn't it? A parent takes advantage of their own size and resources to beat down a child who cannot defend himself or herself. The child responds by being extreme.

Let's put this in perspective. You know the expression "That child is a terror"? Well, if it's true, you should more appropriately say, "That child is a terrorist." What you have done is beaten up the child in such a way that they resort to extreme behavior. Coercion just teaches kids that might makes right.

Dozens of studies show that hitting (or spanking) children increases aggression and behavioral problems on the part of the child. One study showed physical attacks by children on other children in kindergarten occurred twice as often in children whose mothers hit them. Another study showed a relationship between corporal punishment for boys and, later, physical assaults on their girlfriends.

Studies show it can also lower his or her I.Q. as much as five points. Children are so distracted by having been beaten that they can't focus as much in school. They suffer more depression. Language development is delayed. The conventional wisdom about spanking or otherwise hitting children is simply wrong.

So you say your parents did that to you? Well, most of you still remember it with distaste. Why not stop the cycle of abuse? Even in cultures where children are more accepting of spankings, is this really what we want to teach? Or is it just the actions of parents who don't know the other tools to use?

In the United States, *more than 50 percent of parents still hit their children regularly.* More than 90 percent hit children under four at least once a year. Given the negative impact (including lack of trust) and the better alternatives, these are astounding numbers. Some people compare hitting children to smoking: it's really bad, but lots of people still do it.

It's not enough for your kids to just accept what you tell them. Get your kids to be active participants in their upbringing. The tools are here.

But to be successful, you need to use the tools every day, and you need to prepare with them. If you do this right, your children will pass the tools down to their children, and a better way of raising kids will begin.

13

Travel

A participant in one of my executive programs took his wife to one of the finest hotels in San Diego for the weekend. He awoke on Saturday morning to the shrieks of his wife. There were ants all over the bathroom floor. Rather than just call up and complain to the management or whoever else would listen, he decided to use negotiation tools from class.

He went down to find the manager, and asked, "Is this one of the finest hotels in San Diego?" Of course the manager said yes. "Does this hotel pride itself on the highest level of service?" Of course the manager said yes. "Does this service include ants in the bathroom?"

The executive said you never saw an upgrade to a suite so fast in your life, as well as a complimentary dinner and champagne. The key is using a conscious, structured negotiation approach that will get you more of what you want than if you shoot from the hip.

Much has been said and written about negotiating travel arrangements. Almost all of it focuses on price. With the tools in *Getting More*, price is clearly one thing that people can learn to negotiate better. But there are many other things to negotiate: just in terms of lodging, there are late check-outs, upgrades, room availability, personalized attention, better locations, more services, disputes over bills or facilities.

In negotiating travel arrangements, you need to know a few things. First, almost all travel professionals are used to negotiating. If you don't negotiate everything in sight, it's like taking the first price you are offered at a bazaar: you will likely overpay.

Second, the squeaky wheel really does get the grease. You don't have to be a jerk about it. But if you say nothing, you will get nothing. As the stories in this chapter will show, persistence is *very* important in getting more. The first or second or fifth "No" should leave you, well, undeterred.

In fact, being loud and a jerk actually gets you less overall. Airline and hotel people write notes about you in their computers. It's there forever. Over time, you get less. The more you value the other person, the more they will value you, and you will get more.

People at every level of the travel business usually have a great deal of discretion to give things to customers. It depends upon how they feel about you. If they like you, they will give you more.

It is also true that some people in the travel industry seem to be in a perennial bad mood and won't do anything special for you. This is why, in addition to having skills in relationships and interests, you have to be skilled in finding and using the other person's standards. What are their policies? What are the exceptions to their policies? Bring their written standards with you. Show them their standards.

But *never* make yourself the issue. If they behave badly, well, you can use that to get more!

As in most negotiations, you need to use several tools to get what you want. Making small talk—developing a relationship—is important to use along with standards. When you use their standards, don't make the other person so angry that they won't do anything for you no matter what. And after you've used their standards to get what you want, you may have to focus on their needs to close the deal. Practice with these tools, prepare beforehand, debrief yourself afterward. Over time, you will get better and better at it.

Given the importance of standards in the travel industry, framing is very important. "Does this service include ants in the bathroom?" is framing. "Is it your goal to make your customers happy?" is framing. It's a standard embedded in a question. The best standards questions emphasize the difference between what is promised and what is delivered. It gives the other party a choice of whether to do something reasonable for you or be unreasonable—with a whole set of risks, including complaints to third parties.

Remember, no one size fits all. This is situational negotiation: ask yourself what your goals are, who the other person is, what it will take to persuade them. Every negotiation is different, even with the same airline on the same day with different people. That's one of the great things about negotiating travel arrangements: there is a wide selection of people on the other side to choose from. If one treats you poorly, find another. Look for decision-makers. Don't waste your time on people who can't or won't help you.

AIRLINES AND STANDARDS

As you know, things are a lot tighter and tougher than they were some years ago, especially since the September 11, 2001, terrorist attacks. But there are still millions of opportunities to negotiate.

Arjun Madan's father missed his flight from London to the U.S. Arjun did not want to pay the $200 change fee. Two Virgin Air supervisors said that the only exception is for hospitalization.

"After talking to two stone-hearted supervisors," Arjun said, he reached a third. "I asked her how she was doing. I told her about the good weather I had in the Maldives, where I recently went. It turned out she was planning her honeymoon, and the Maldives was on her list. I spent ten minutes suggesting honeymoon destinations."

Arjun then said that he, his father, mother, sister, brother, and their children all fly Virgin Air. "We wouldn't think of flying another airline," he said. He said his father missed the flight. "My dad is old and unwell," Arjun said. "Can you help us out?"

The customer service rep agreed to push his case with the London office. "Old and unwell," that's almost hospitalized, isn't it? Arjun was a frequent flier. All good framing. Arjun got the exception. He also made a friend at Virgin. "Persistence is key," Arjun said. "Never quit. Take the time to get to know the other person."

Here's another important negotiation tool that Arjun used: details provide credibility. The more details you provide to the other party, the more real your problem seems, and the more they will want to help you.

Many students say that they have called up an airline representative who quotes them a price and makes a reservation for them under their name, or waives a fee, and the next day, no reservation is to be found, and the price has jumped. Or the fee waiver disappears. I say, "Who did you speak to?" The student says, "I don't know." Not very persuasive.

What if, instead, when you called back and were denied, you said: "Well, let's see, I spoke to Tina in Tulsa yesterday, it was about three minutes after noon. Tina said I didn't need a reservation number, that it would be under my name. She asked me to spell my name, twice, so she could be sure to get it right."

Sound more persuasive? It's all in the details. Phillip Kang, who now works for a medical equipment company in Pennsylvania, wanted a discount on a bus ride from Philadelphia to New York City. On his last bus ride, there was a mechanical problem and he was late for an appointment.

The cashier and supervisor were not friendly at the bus line's ticket offices. Then Phil pulled a stack of ticket stubs from his pocket from past bus rides and riffled through them like a deck of cards. "I've been your customer for a while," he said. He had the evidence to show that he was a valuable, long-term customer. He got a free trip to New York.

The details Phil provided were visual. They were understandable in any language. No, you don't have to lug satchels of boarding passes to the airport. But you should think consciously about details. Watch, listen, be creative. Bring up some news you read or heard about the airline. Wear a hat from their organization.

Aisha Henry's flight from Detroit to Washington was canceled due to mechanical failure. She got hotel and meal vouchers for one night in Detroit from Northwest. Then her flight the next day was canceled due to bad weather, so she had to stay another night. Northwest's standard is not to provide vouchers due to weather delays.

Other passengers trying to get on that flight were waiting at the gate when the flight was canceled. Aisha, an attorney in Washington, started asking people if they had been scheduled for the previous day's flight, too. Some had. She asked how many nights' vouchers they got. Some said two. Armed with this information, Aisha went to the Northwest representative and got another night's hotel and meal vouchers.

We often see people victimized in travel snafus. Too often, people sit there passively. You must be proactive. Ali Behbahani was denied a hotel room voucher by US Airways even though he missed the last flight out of Charlotte to Philadelphia because the incoming US Air flight was late. The gate agent said the missed flight was weather-related.

"Was that the only reason?" Ali said. "Was the crew delayed? Was there a mechanical problem? If it was delayed for some other reason, as well, could US Air pay for my room?" The answer was yes. He checked with the airline—the crew was also late; this contributed to the delay. The result? Ali, a Washington, D.C., health care investor, was given a free room. "You've *got* to ask the questions," he said.

While she was filling out the paperwork to rent a car, Tanya Louneva overheard the branch manager at Enterprise Rent-A-Car in San Diego explain to another patron how important customer service was to the company. She had waited in line for an hour, so she brought up this issue with the service rep, very nicely. And she was upgraded to a premium car.

Speaking of standards, airlines and other travel companies have all kinds of categories of discounts and perks: (a) children, (b) teenagers, (c) partner's customer, (d) company, (e) senior citizen, (f) location traveled to or from, (g) number of people, (h) organization, (i) birthday, (j) special occasions. Call a travel agent, or the airlines, or hotels and rental car companies, and get all the categories of discounts. Go down the list. As you will discover, there is also a "stranded traveler" rate at some hotels. Robert Hodgen, vice president of a grain business, got such a discount from $159 to $59 when his flight was canceled. All he had to do was ask about it.

Find out the occupancy rates of hotels at various times of the year. They charge less when occupancy is low. Are there special tourism promos? Are there two-for-one deals? In addition to price breaks, there are likely extra services: spa treatments or diving lessons. What incentive packages do they have? Are any upgrades available? Ask what they do for repeat customers.

Some managers get intangibles for their conference groups from hotels where no discounts are available: a round of golf, reduced rates on drinks, sailing lessons, and so forth. They say the hardest part is actually identifying their own group's intangibles so they can then negotiate with the hotel.

Ask for exceptions to policies—it should become second nature. "When do you make exceptions?" should be one of your most common questions.

You have a lot of persuasive ability. Use it or become a victim. In the United States, airlines can no longer force you to sit on the tarmac for more than three hours. Get the new regulations. I did, and several of the passengers got US Airways to take us back to the gate after two and a half hours on the tarmac. No overflowing toilets for us. In 2009, a $180 million drop in United Airlines' stock price was attributed to a clever complaint song posted on YouTube. United probably made some changes after that.

MAKING THE CONNECTION

People in customer service positions generally have a dreadful time. So lighten up with them. Give them something to smile about. They will be grateful and give you things in return. Think of the world from their viewpoint.

Nathan Slack wanted to get a free upgrade to a suite at the Westin Hotel in Cincinnati. "The desk person told me there were no suites available," he said. "She seemed to be in a bad mood."

So Nathan did *exactly* what a great negotiator is supposed to do. "I've just had a really long flight," Nathan said. "How was your day?" She said, "I just dealt with a jerk." Nathan sympathized. "You don't need that," he said. He then asked if they get a lot of repeat customers, because he was one. She checked her computer, and found it was true. He said he really liked the hotel. He asked if they ever provide unused suites to their repeat customers.

"She gave me an upgrade to a corner suite for free," said Nathan, who heads an investment team for JPMorgan Singapore. "She also made a nota-tion in the computer to do it in the future if one was available."

It often doesn't take much. John Duncanson wanted to get a free up-grade from Thrifty car rental for a week in Los Angeles. The saleswoman was young, he said, "so I asked her where she was from, how long she had lived in L.A., whether she liked L.A., where she went to school. Then *she* asked *me* if I would like an upgrade."

John said he'd love a convertible but couldn't afford to pay for one. No problem. He got the convertible at no extra charge. "Simply being friendly and asking for things works more than you can imagine," said John, now an attorney in New York.

What's key is that you have to be sincere. The other person can tell the difference between sincere and insincere feeling. If you can't do this, don't try. Get a traveling companion to do it if you have one. Attitude is the key. Have a talk with yourself beforehand. Do you want to meet your goals or not?

Again, travel reps usually have a lot of discretion and give things to people they like. Dana Guo wanted to get on a Southwest Airlines flight for Chicago through the standby list, without having to buy a full-fare ticket. She commiserated with the gate agent on how stressful it must be deal-ing with flights in bad weather. She mentioned that she'd miss her friend's birthday dinner at home if she didn't get on the flight.

"During the conversation, I told her that I understood they have poli-cies to follow, but they also have the power to make adjustments to those policies on a case-by-case basis," Dana said. She acknowledged the em-ployee's power and also showed her own knowledge of how things work. Dana got on the plane without extra charge.

The major difference here between the way most of my students act and the way most people act is that my students learn to think about others first. Not to give away more but as a means to get more. Most people in problem situations go up to the service rep and start talking about their own problems. It is better to talk about the other person's problems. They will see you as a person more worthy of help.

Annie Martinez wanted to get a new room or a free room at the Divi Southwinds Beach Resort in Barbados because her existing room was near a loud discotheque. It was 2:00 A.M. There was only one manager on duty. Earlier, a friend of hers was told there were no other rooms.

Annie went to the front desk in person to see Tadea, the manager. Annie mentioned the loud music. She said it must be disturbing Tadea, too. Annie noted it was not Tadea's fault. Then Annie brought up, tactfully, that in the hotel's customer brochure, "customer satisfaction" was mentioned explicitly. "How do you normally resolve situations like this, with relocation or compensation?" Annie asked sweetly.

Annie told the manager that she realized the manager couldn't do this, but if she wanted, Annie could call the police for both of them to complain about the noise next door. Anne made it a common problem. And she did all of this in a helpful tone. Annie offered to write a thank-you note to Tadea's superiors if she helped Annie out of a difficult situation.

Tadea moved Annie, a labor lawyer in Philadelphia, to a penthouse at no extra charge. Annie's friend, in a nearby room, had gone to the same manager earlier in the evening. The friend started screaming, blaming the manager and hotel, and demanded a new room. He got nothing. This happens a lot. One person uses the tools in this book and meets his or her goals. Another person does not, and does not.

The more you look at things from their viewpoint, the more they realize you are trying to understand things from their perspective. You're not being unreasonable. And in a world where most people look at travel reps as a means to an end, the more grateful they will be. When you call up for an airline reservation, the airline rep has a script that must be followed. It includes date, itinerary, time, number of passengers, fare class, and so forth. If you interrupt them, if you get annoyed, you will just make them unfriendly. Their computer screen demands they input certain information in a certain way. If you ask, "In what order would you like information from me?" they realize you care about making their job easier. It's little things like this that matter a lot.

Most people don't think about offering to send letters for an employee's personnel file. But such letters can mean a lot to a sales clerk or customer rep. A candygram is an unexpected, nice way to thank an employee—

completely discretionary. Candygrams are great for representatives in the travel industry, especially in a time of layoffs and economic trouble. For airline workers, a candygram from a customer can mean the difference between being furloughed and having a job. Or being kept on part-time versus full-time.

David Chao missed a connection to Cartagena, Colombia, after his Continental Airlines flight was delayed by a mechanical problem. It was Thanksgiving weekend. There were ten other passengers with the same issue. When it was his turn to talk to Florence, the airline rep, he told her, calmly and sympathetically, that if she could help him out of his problem he'd be sure to commend her, in writing.

David, now a consultant in Taiwan, got an overnight stay in Bogotá, with a free hotel, free dinner, and free breakfast, as well as seats on flights to Bogotá and Cartegena. How many times have you had trouble getting a fraction of this?

Remember Aliza Zaida, the student who got a better seat and a free meal on a plane by being nice to the gate agent? When I mention these things in class, other people try them. And guess what. They work!

Aliza also gave advice to her aunt, who lost her job soon after spending $2,000 for nonrefundable tickets on United. Aliza urged her aunt to call up a ticket agent, talk about being laid off, and mention how so many people, including airline employees, are feeling the pain of that. The ticket agent had United send Aliza's aunt the $2,000 back in cash.

The more you put a positive attitude toward your problem, the more help you will get. One student found out that after she and a friend bought tickets for a Carnival Cruise Lines trip, the price was lowered by $120 per person. Most people would scream about the unfairness. Not her. After finding out that the company's customer representative couldn't do anything to help her, she asked for a supervisor. "Supervisors deal with aggravated customers all day long," said the student. "I wasn't going to be one of them." She approached the issue as a positive thing. "I'm thrilled about the decrease," she told the supervisor. She asked the supervisor what options there were for rebates or remedies for those who had already committed to the cruise line by purchasing early.

The supervisor was so thrilled at the way the student approached this that she and her friend got $350 in on-board credits—almost 50 percent more than she had asked for.

Even when you use standards, it helps to have created a relationship, as well—or the vision of a future relationship.

Richard Adewunmi wanted to move his vacation dates by four days at the Casa Alta Vista guesthouse in Vieques, Puerto Rico. He paid a discounted rate for a stay during spring break. A gruff manager told him that any change would mean forfeiture of the entire payment, and he wouldn't get a room. Most people would get really annoyed at this. Richard saw it as an opportunity.

Without responding directly to the manager's curtness, Richard congratulated the manager on his promotion. "When I met you four years ago, you were a booking agent," Richard, a pharmaceutical company in-house counsel, reminded him. Richard mentioned he had also hosted his best friend's wedding at the hotel in 2004. And that Richard's brother and his wife had stayed at Casa Alta Vista for their honeymoon on Richard's recommendation.

Finally, Richard noted that the hotel's website says it provides services that will "surely bring you back to our island home." Now, Richard asked, "Is this the way to treat old friends?" Was there even a question that Richard would get the change? "I related to the hotel manager like family, professionally and personally," Richard said. He added that bringing up the hotel's standard was essential in confirming that.

The best negotiators are calm, but they are completely focused on their goals. They negotiate in a structured and prepared way.

In transactional situations, look for opportunities to establish relationships. As an MBA student, Ken Ades befriended a Club Med employee, Richard, when Ken went on a Club Med trip. He kept up the relationship. Two years later Ken wanted to go to the Turkoise Club, the most popular Club Med in the Western Hemisphere, with friends.

He was told several times by Club Med reservations that (a) the Turkoise Club was booked and (b) there were no discounts available. So Ken, now vice president of a trading firm in New York, called Richard. Richard got Ken (a) a reservation and (b) a discount. Result: $1,320 in savings, plus one great vacation.

John Burke was 200 miles short of an American Airlines free travel voucher on the second-to-last day of the year. It would have been difficult to find an inexpensive flight to get the necessary miles. American Airlines reps told him that the company is very strict about this standard. If you don't have the miles, you don't get the voucher.

John decided to frame it differently. He got the name and phone number of one of the AA reps' supervisors so he could call later and discuss what he might do further, including scheduling a flight. He called the supervisor, represented himself (truthfully) as a 200,000-mile American Airlines flier. He asked if she could do something consistent with the airline's high standards for customer service.

"Do we have to argue over two hundred miles on the last day of the year when I'm such a good customer?" said John, now senior vice president of a private equity group involved in energy. Point made. She waived the mileage requirement. "Framing is so important," he said.

FRAMING

Olympic Air, Greece's national airline, erroneously canceled a flight from Crete to Athens on Joshua and Anne Morris' honeymoon. Then the airline declined to give Joshua a refund when the couple decided to take another carrier. He asked the customer service representative, "Is your airline's behavior indicative of the hospitality of the country of Greece?" He got a refund immediately. He used framing and standards.

When you get good at this, a single sentence can end a negotiation in your favor. Rajan Amin wanted to change his United flight without paying a penalty. He wasn't getting anywhere using loyalty and standards. One reason he wanted to change his flight was that the time of his departure had changed four times during the space of two hours. He got four separate emails from the airline changing the departure time.

He contacted a supervisor and said, "Why is it fair for United to change the time of my flight four times without compensating me, when I have to pay when I do it only once?" Brilliant! The United rep was so impressed at Rajan's way of framing the world that he got the ·change at no charge. Rajan had a firm grasp of the obvious and framed it as such. A worthwhile exercise is to practice finding contradictions, and then finding ways to articulate them.

Sometimes an inherent tension exists between two different company standards. For example, Southwest Airlines prides itself on customer service. It also has a policy that changing your flight costs $100. Elisabeth Leiderman recognized this tension when she asked the service rep to put her on an earlier flight at no extra charge. Of course, she first asked for the manager on duty—the decision-maker—and Thomas came over.

Elisabeth mentioned that bad weather was coming in, and there was some chance the later flight she was on could be canceled. Did Thomas agree? He did. "Well, if you put me on the earlier flight, where there are plenty of seats, it might be one less person you have to deal with later,"

Elisabeth said. "And you will have one happy customer." He saw the logic of her reasoning, and agreed. Here, Elisabeth, who works as an associate in the health care field in New York, tipped the balance by making it in the airline's interests and standards to reschedule her flight. She had thought about both in advance.

Madhavan Gopalan recognized the tension between Avis's slogan "We try harder" and its policy that late returns pay extra. He noticed the "Cars Available" sign in the corner of the Avis counter. He wanted to know if Avis in the past had waived two hours of late fees if it didn't cost the company anything because cars were available. He also noted there was very heavy traffic on the road to the airport. Was that ever factored into a decision to waive a late fee?

The answer to both: yes. And his late fee was waived. Avis remained true to its customer service standard, trying harder. "I did it again many times after that," said Madhavan, a Boston consultant.

Alexandra Munteanu was told she had to pay a $100 penalty and a $40 ticket-price increase to reschedule her plane ticket from Philadelphia to Abilene, Kansas. She had already gotten a one-year extension on the ticket.

She called the airline and asked to speak to the person in charge of decisions regarding the rescheduling of plane tickets. Again, find the decision-maker. She framed the one-year extension as an example of what the airline has done for her in the past because she was such a good customer. Instead of the airline supervisor thinking, "We've already done her a favor once," he or she would think, "Here's a very good customer."

The company's policy was that the fee had to be paid, the airline supervisor said. "Has there ever been an exception for longtime clients?" Alexandra asked. Yes, the airline had made some exceptions, the airline supervisor said. Result: a rescheduled ticket at no charge.

"Framing is great, but you have to be careful how you use it," said Alexandra, now an attorney for a U.S. law firm in Romania. "Some representatives get aggressive when they understand where I want to go with it." The key is to let the other person know where you want to go with it as soon as you can. If they get mad, ask them what's wrong with what you are saying. Ask for criticism. Say what's going on. Ask them whether they can blame you for trying to save money.

The notion of reframing to change their perceptions is especially important when dealing with jaded people. Airline reps deal with thousands of people each week, and say most people are awful to them. So it stands to reason that you will get the benefit of the doubt if you act nicely. You have to find a way to *differentiate* yourself. Show that you are different from the crowd. One way is to be nice to them; another is to provide details. What you are doing is changing their perceptions of you.

Min Kim hadn't flown American Airlines very often in the past year or so. The airline sent her a letter saying her gold status would be revoked unless she paid a fee of $258. Min said to herself, "What perception do people at the airline have of me?" It has to be that she's not a very loyal customer.

So Min called up the airline's number and talked to a customer service representative. "The reason I haven't flown very often," she said, "is that I've been in business school. But I will soon fly often. It will be a job requirement."

So now she has changed the airline's perception. But she has just gotten back to even. She wants to positively persuade them. "I told her that I love Texas and that I am moving to Dallas after graduation," Min said. "That's where American Airlines is located, of course." And she reiterated what a loyal customer she's been. She asked if AA had ever made an exception and extended its gold status for a few more months.

So Min got to keep her gold status without charge. But be careful; all that information is being entered into a computer. If Min doesn't fly much on American the next year, her gold status would be revoked, and she would have to earn back every mile of it. They *will* check. This was no problem for Min. As a project leader for Boston Consulting Group, she would travel a lot.

Framing includes painting a vision of the future. Iman Lordgooei didn't want to pay the $25-per-day fee for under-twenty-five customers renting cars in Miami. He said on the phone to the reservation clerk, "I will probably spend $50,000 to $100,000 on car rentals for business travel alone in my lifetime. Can we make an investment in each other?"

Great framing! The reservation clerk offered him a $15-per-day waiver. Had Iman, a Silicon Valley attorney, done this in person, my guess is that he would have gotten the full $25. Finding a way to make the negotiation seem a lot bigger will cause people to do more for you in the present.

PREPARATION

One of the best things you can do for yourself is start to make a list of the standards used by airlines and other travel companies and groups. Bring the list with you. It will help you frame things. Under federal law, for example, an airline has to pay at least $200 if it bumps you. Yet many people accept as little as $50.

It's not hard to find this information. Just call up customer service and say you want to find out the airline's rules for travelers. In theory, people know to do this, but too few people take the time. Invest a couple of hours. It will save you many, many times that much in time, expense, and aggravation. Look up the airlines' standards and the government's rules, such as those of the U.S. Department of Transportation.

Michael Magkov, a consultant in New York, wanted his $150 fee waived for making a change to his ticket. "We don't waive change fees," said Juanita, the airline's customer service rep he spoke with. "Yes, you do," Michael said, "if I make the change the same day that I buy the ticket." How persuasive that information makes you! And just for a small investment of time.

Nicholas Mak was afraid to put his camera film through the security machine at the San Francisco International Airport. The TSA officer said he *had* to, since his film was under ASA 800. "The officer pointed to a security sign saying the X-ray machine is film-safe," said Nicholas, a lawyer in Hong Kong. So, should he have backed down? No! "I told him that the Transportation Security Administration website says travelers can request hand inspection, and that Chicago and Philadelphia honored my request without question," Nick said.

The officer actually tried to put the film back into the machine while Nick was talking. "Please stop," he said. And the officer did.

Are you afraid? Isn't it a fundamental responsibility in a democracy for citizens to know their rights? Nick's film was priceless.

When my students don't use these tools, it shows. Either it's harder to meet their goals or they don't meet them at all. One of my students was told by an airline rep that his price was "locked in." The next day, when he tried to buy the ticket, it was $25 more. He thought it wasn't fair. He finally found a manager, and asked him if the airline valued its promises. Eventually, he got the $25 back. "But was it worth the hour I spent?" he asked.

Well, maybe not. But he didn't have to spend the hour. The problem was, he didn't get the name of the person who told him the price was locked in. He didn't get the location. He didn't get any of the relevant details. So he had to work much harder to get his money back. This is the price of not doing it right. Sometimes you won't succeed at all. If you do it right, you *will* get one extra hit every nine games. At least.

HOTELS

Avery Sheffield was a Starwood Preferred Guest. As part of the program, when you have a bad stay you get 500 points usable toward hotel rooms, airline tickets, etc. Matter of factly, Avery told the manager that someone else's hair was in her shower. She saved it for the hotel if they were interested. On check-in, she also hadn't been able to get the promised upgrade despite her Platinum status. Other things were not up to snuff.

"I paid $400 for this room," she told the manager. "I could have stayed elsewhere for $200. But I've always gotten such great service at Starwood. It's always been just great." No threats were involved.

The manager gave Avery 20,000 points, equivalent to a U.S. round-trip airline ticket. Avery felt she could have done better. "I could have asked her about her day," she said. "I could have offered to send a note to her supervisor about what great service she provided." In other words, every negotiation, even a success, is a learning experience for the next one.

As with most things in life, the more you use a business, the more they will give you. What you should *not* do is threaten them with ending the relationship unless they do such and such. It's like threatening your spouse with divorce every time you have an argument. After a while they don't believe you. Instead, talk about your *investment* in the relationship.

Jacqueline Sturdivant stayed at the Hilton whenever she could. She wanted to go to Hawaii and stay at the Hilton there. But it was during the black-out period, where using points for rooms was prohibited, even though Jacqui had enough points for a three-week stay. "I just wanted to use my points for two out of the fourteen nights," Jacqui said. "The reservation clerk would still get credit for twelve nights." Jacqui told the clerk she was celebrating her own graduation from business school, after years of hard work.

The clerk thought about this and offered her *six* free nights. Jacqui used several negotiation tools here: She was incremental. She shared details and she made her long-term relationship with the hotel clear. She thought about the reservation clerk's own bonus. "And, I was upgraded to a premier Aloha suite," Jacqui added.

Even if you don't have an existing relationship with a hotel, hotels like to start them. It's the vision of loyalty that matters. Salman Al-Ansari made a ten-day reservation for his uncle at a Sheraton Hotel in Philadelphia.

At the last minute, his uncle got sick. It was an online booking. The hotel manager, Mr. Mark, told Salman that he'd be charged whether his uncle stayed there or not. Online bookings are not refundable. No exceptions.

Salman asked if he could move the reservation to graduation week and have his family and friends stay there. The total number of days would be larger. This was a statement of loyalty, and it provided more business for the hotel. He was trading items of unequal value. And Mr. Mark approved it. Salman, now an attorney at his family's law firm in Qatar, had to do all the suggesting. But that's what you will often have to do.

Every traveler has "war stories." The difference with *Getting More* is you become very conscious of the fact that you are in a negotiation. It makes things more precise, focused, and successful because you can more easily replicate what you are doing from one negotiation to the next. One of my graduates wanted to stay at a hotel in McLean, Virginia, next to his employer, SAIC. The travel agent said the hotel was fully booked and would not even call the hotel for him. The hotel's central reservation office reported the same thing.

So the graduate called the hotel himself. He noted to the front desk that he worked for SAIC, whose visitors stay at the hotel a lot. He also noted that many hotels have "reserve" rooms available for last-minute emergencies. "Could you use one of those reserve rooms for me?" he asked. Persistence, standards, and linkages got him a room at the hotel. " 'No' doesn't always mean 'No,' " he said.

Elaine Boxer booked rooms at the Flamingo, a hotel in Las Vegas. She tried to get upgrades on two rooms: for her friend, and for her and her partner. But when she called and asked about upgrades, none were available. She asked a reservations clerk behind the counter before checking in, as well. Same answer: none were available. She thought about it briefly, then got in line again to talk to someone at the front desk.

When it was her turn, she addressed the person by name and said hi. She said they were in Vegas to celebrate her friend's full recovery from an injury in Las Vegas last fall. And they chose the Flamingo to celebrate. "Isn't that nice," the clerk said. Elaine asked, "Have you ever given upgrades for special occasions? This sure is one for us!" They got two upgrades, with king beds, on a high floor overlooking the Strip. Value: $280. Persistence and framing.

Thomas Greer wanted to cancel his reservation at the Fairmont Copley Plaza hotel without cancellation charges. The reservation office told him there would be a charge since he was within the twenty-four-hour cancellation period. It was 4:00 P.M. on Sunday. "I am providing twenty-four hours' notice," Thomas said. "I don't plan to check into the hotel until six P.M. tomorrow night."

The reservations clerk said the hotel's cancellation policy assumes a 3:00 P.M. check-in. "Isn't that the earliest possible check-in?" Thomas asked. "What percentage of the guests check in at the first moment that check-in is available? Couldn't this all be misinterpreted by a well-intentioned customer?" He was polite the entire time. Cancellation fee waived. Great example of reframing.

This kind of reframing works often. Atul Kumar wanted a very late checkout (7:00 P.M.) without penalty at the Starwood Palace Hotel in San Francisco. As you can imagine, this was hours after the regular checkout time of 2:00 P.M. Atul was a frequent guest at Starwood, but this clearly wasn't enough by itself.

So Atul asked if the hotel was 100 percent booked. It was not. In other words, the room was not needed. He noted that he checked in at 11:30 P.M. the previous night. So even if he checked out at 7:00 P.M., he would have been at the hotel less than twenty hours—less than a full day. He asked if the cleaning staff worked at night. They did. "So another late check-in can get my room," he said. He added that if it turned out that the hotel really needed the room, he'd be ready by 5:00 P.M. and could leave then.

And the hotel agreed! Atul reframed the situation, keyed on the relationship, used the fact that it wouldn't cost the hotel anything, and offered to be helpful if things changed. His whole attitude was helpful and calm.

When you want a late checkout, you can ask when the last room is going to be cleaned. For hotels without night shifts, it's usually about 5:00 P.M. You can ask that your room be cleaned last, or at least later. If you are a frequent guest and you have a good reason, you will often succeed. You can also ask, "When do you need the room for another guest?"

I know, you're going to ask, "What if everybody did this?" Well, everybody doesn't do this. Second, this is a high-class problem for a hotel. It will increase customer service. Hotels will better be able to match guests with their needs. Not every guest needs a late checkout.

Jason Cummings went to Lexington Park, Maryland, to participate in a triathlon, only to find hotels booked. He went to one of the hotels and struck up a conversation with the desk clerk.

Where was she from? How long has she lived there? He had come for the triathlon, he said, and didn't realize the hotels would all be booked.

He told her he was in the military, and that's how he'd gotten interested in triathlons. The clerk told him there was a nearby Navy post. She called someone she knew there and found a room for $15 per night for Jason, a former West Point instructor and now a lieutenant colonel.

THE LAW

Of course, not all organizations you might deal with in travel situations are customer-service-oriented. Take the police, for example. Or, more specifically, the U.S. Customs Service at JFK International Airport in New York. Marsha Lazareva was searched on an incoming flight by a senior customs officer, who found undeclared merchandise—enough for a $2,500 fine and who knows what else.

"There were four trainees in the room," Marsha said. "It was clear that the customs officer intended to make an example out of my case."

The first thing Marsha did was apologize. As the customs official, Officer Connolly, berated her, "I kept thanking her for doing her job," Marsha said. "For educating me about the regulations, for keeping me from bigger troubles in the future." Marsha confessed that she didn't have a good reason, either: "The lines were very long," she told Officer Connolly. "I guess that was really stupid. Thanks again for picking me out."

Marsha kept acknowledging that the customs official had the power to "throw the book at me."

In the end, Marsha was fined a mere $33. "You are the first person," Officer Connolly told her, "who ever appreciated me and my job."

The negotiation tools Marsha used included (a) recognizing the fact that she was in a negotiation situation, (b) remaining calm, (c) focusing on the other person, (d) recognizing the role of third parties, (e) being direct and honest, and (f) providing emotional payments, including apologizing and valuing them.

As a result, she went home instead of facing fines and possible confinement. What is the value of *that*? Marsha is now vice chairman and managing director of KGL Investment Company, an emerging-markets private equity fund.

Let's stick with Marsha for a moment. She seems to have it down in dealing with the bureaucracy. Most bureaucrats and officers of the law are underpaid, sometimes overworked, and often unhappy and unappreciated. This is a very good insight to have if you find yourself in a situation where you have to negotiate with them.

Marsha needed a visa within three days at one point, in order to take a last-minute trip to France. The allotted time to get a visa is fourteen days. Call volume was high, making it difficult to reach a visa officer. The secretary who answered the phone was "unwelcoming." Marsha remained friendly and cheerful; she apologized for the secretary being so busy. Before long, she was connected to a consulate officer. Again, acknowledging the other person's power is an effective negotiation tool.

The visa officer located her file. "I involved Officer Colin in small talk," Marsha said. "I made him laugh. I apologized for the inconvenience." Twelve minutes into the conversation, he approved her visa. She could pick it up in three days.

Okay, so you think Marsha was too assertive. Well, did she make the consulate officer's day better? She did. And you know, she went to France, and, I suspect, a lot of other people who didn't use such tools, didn't. And Marsha does something that most people miss: she remains focused on the other party. After all, they almost always have what you want.

GROUND CONNECTIONS

Even when you are right, it is important to make the other person feel important and appreciated. Many people think it's a drag, especially those who already feel important, are successful, and have enough money. But most of the world does not fall into this category. And we live in a society where, for better or worse, people of all sorts depend on one another—whether they like it or not.

So before you call that moron a moron, you'd better make sure you don't need them for something! As someone I know once said, "Don't laugh at the crocodile until you've crossed the river."

Fatih Ozluturk was charged $470 for returning a rental car to Boston instead of to his rental location. A repeat customer, he had never been charged before. What's more, the car agency's website said he could return it to Boston without an extra charge. "The clerk at the desk refused to consider my request," Fatih said. "He was actually rude."

What would be your first reaction in that situation? Righteous indignation? It shouldn't be. The clerk is not the decision-maker. Don't waste any time on him. Fatih asked for the manager. "When the manager came out, I immediately acknowledged his power as the decision-maker," Fatih said.

Fatih said the company's website had the wrong information and suggested that the manager check it then and there. He did. "Instead of my writing the corporate office, why don't you?" said Fatih, vice president of a wireless company. "You can get credit for fixing this." Fatih mentioned to the manager that the incident was very stressful. The manager thanked him and "reduced my bill by more than 50 percent," in addition to waiving the $470 return charge, Fatih said. The key, he said, was helping other people fix their problems instead of blaming them.

If the other person is in a bad mood, offer to do something for them. Ajay Bijoor saw that the Hertz rental car agent was upset from a previous customer. Without saying a word, he just stepped back from the counter and gave her a moment to catch her breath. The manager noticed and appreciated the gesture. People are always rushing at travel service providers. Give them a chance to breathe.

When she was ready to deal with him, he said hi and was pleasant to her. He said he was hoping to get an upgrade from his economy car. And he wanted to know if he could do anything for her. "I've always been pleased with Hertz's service," he said. "Could I fill out one of the surveys you have here?"

Ajay, a restructuring vice president in New York, didn't get one upgrade. He got upgraded three levels, to an SUV. Did he manipulate the situation? How, by making the manager feel better? By giving her a chance to catch her breath? By allowing her to make him an especially loyal customer for the future?

You say, "I don't live in a world like that!" Yes, you do. Only now, you don't see it as clearly as you will when you start trying these tools. There's a saying, "The harder you work, the luckier you get." The more you use these tools, the nicer people will be to you and the more you will meet your goals.

It should be clear by now that different kinds of people mean different kinds of negotiations. Just because a tool doesn't work with one person doesn't mean it won't work with someone else on the same issue with the same organization. Jessica Weiss missed the 5:05 P.M. train from New York to Philadelphia because the ticket machine was broken. Her ticket on the 5:17 was $79, compared to the $60 she would have paid for the 5:05 train.

The ticket agent changed the ticket for her but would not reimburse Jessica for the price difference. Jessica said, "Is it Amtrak's policy to charge customers for its own errors?" To which the ticket agent responded, "Honey, you can either haggle with me or you can get on that train."

Jessica said she was tempted to just take the loss. The world isn't fair. But isn't it the hundreds of small insults each week that detract from life?

So she called Amtrak customer service, and spoke to Floyd. She explained the problem. Floyd was reluctant to give the credit to her. So Jessica, now an attorney in New York, again asked, "Is it Amtrak's policy to charge customers for its own errors?" Floyd said, "No, absolutely no." Floyd sent her a $20 train voucher. That is the importance of using standards and exercising persistence.

Fiona Cox always asks travel professionals where they're from. She often makes lasting connections. Once, the cheapest fare she could find home to New Zealand was $1,900, according to the sales rep. Fiona asked the sales rep where she was from. New Zealand. The sales rep spent the extra time to find Fiona a $1,500 flight. "I do this all the time now," said Fiona, now a finance manager at a global bank in Florida.

Mike Leskinen was taking a hired car from Midtown Manhattan to Newark. It was $65 plus tolls. Mike told the driver he often used a car service to the airports. "It would be nice to have a driver to call first," Mike said. The driver told Mike that if he called him directly, he would save the 30 percent fee to the dispatch company, or $20. So Mike offered $50 plus tolls for the ride. And he got the driver's business card.

Mike learned how to eliminate the middleman. It is something thousands of businesses have learned: dealing directly with the vendor, either for better service or better deals.

Here are two extraordinary examples of framing, one with Amtrak, one with Avis. They will give you a sense of what some real pros do with these tools, almost effortlessly, every day. First is Al Jurgela, who operates companies for private equity owners. Al bought a ticket on the Metroliner from New York to Philadelphia. He got to the train station very early, so he tried to take an earlier Northeast Express. It was sold out, as the ticket agent told him and about ten people ahead of him.

So Al found a train conductor and asked, "What does 'sold out' mean?" He was told it meant every seat was paid for. "Do people sometimes not show up for their train even if they bought a ticket?" Al asked. Yes, the conductor said, there are almost always seats. "So can I have one of the seats someone is not going to show up for?" Al asked. He was let on the train— and at a $30 savings. His colleagues waited another hour at Penn Station for the next Metroliner. Standards, framing, and asking for definitions.

The other example involves a student who rented a car from Avis in Albuquerque, New Mexico, for spring break week. When he got 100 miles from the lot, he realized that he paid for a car one class higher than he got. Rather than go all the way back, he drove the car for a week and asked for a credit upon his return. He was refused. The customer service rep told him that the contract says you pay for the car you signed for when you leave the lot. And she turned over the contract with the provision and his signature.

You think that's conclusive? Think again. There is negotiation to do. As you know, most rental car contracts are printed in tiny, light gray type on light pink paper, very hard to read. So the student said, "It's not my responsibility to read this contract." "Why not?" the Avis rep asked. "Look at this contract," the student said. "You can hardly read it. Why, if it was my responsibility to read this contract, your slogan would not be 'We Try Harder.' It would be 'You Try Harder.'" He got the credit.

TRAVEL ORGANIZING

Clearly, the more you effectively prepare for a trip, the less unpleasantness. As travel is expensive, you should enjoy every moment.

Dr. Jeff Stanley's goal, as he put it, was to "resolve conflicting summer vacation dreams" among his elderly parents in Virginia, his sister's family in California, and his own family. His parents were too tired to travel, his brother had a conflict around a school trip, and his sister felt guilty about not coming home.

So Jeff stepped back and said to himself, "What is really going on here?" One, hardly anyone was in the mood for a vacation. Two, only one sibling needed to see their parents. Three, no one had done any real planning. Four, trying to sort this out in a conference call would only make it worse.

So Jeff talked to each party separately, to find out hopes, dreams, and fears. After collecting the information, he proposed a delay till Christmas. "We have six months to get our act together," he told the others. "We'll put down an inviolate date. Everyone gets a task." Jeff committed to see his parents over the summer. And his brother saved $1,500 on plane tickets. "The key was managing the process," he said.

What do we learn from this? First, there should be *one* coordinator: the calmest person. Second, information should be collected incrementally, from one person at a time. Third, the coordinator should collate agreement and disagreement points, and then propose a better solution.

Marco Antonio and some friends were on vacation in South Beach, the trendy part of Miami. They wanted to get into the Mynt Lounge on Columbus Day weekend, but it was a hard club to get into.

So they did some research beforehand. They were permitted into the club in their hotel, the Whitelaw. And Whitelaw and Mynt shared lists of

VIPs, they discovered, and referred people to one another. "Wouldn't refusing entry to one of your partner's club members be bad for business?" Marco asked the Mynt gatekeeper. Marco was prepared, asked questions, used third parties, found out about interests, and identified the pictures in their heads. And got in.

Justin Bagdady, a Washington, D.C., attorney, improved all of his family's holiday gatherings by developing a planning process. His fiancée, Kayte, wanted to spend Christmas with her family in Boston. Justin wanted to spend Christmas with his family in Michigan. So Justin immediately expanded the size of the negotiation. He asked Kayte which holiday her parents in Boston liked better, Thanksgiving or Christmas. Answer: Thanksgiving. Issue solved.

He would have kept expanding the pie until he found a trade. There is New Year's, birthdays, summer vacation, Easter—the list goes on. This is what the best negotiators do.

BRINGING BACK THE PLANE—A REPRISE

As those I've taught hear of the successes, similar results appear repeatedly. The anecdotes mentioned here are not one-time events, but can be reproduced if you learn the tools. So I wanted to end this chapter with another story of someone who was able to bring a plane back to the gate so he could board. This was a business situation.

A young manager from Johnson & Johnson was scheduled to make a presentation to his company's board of directors on a six-month project. It was the most important business meeting of his life. The plane on the first leg of his trip was late, and he was about to miss the connecting flight to get him to the meeting.

The next plane did not depart for six hours. He would miss the board meeting and his career would take a big step backward.

The young manager was beside himself; the gate agent felt bad for him. So she led him, running, down the Jetway to try to make the plane. But when they got to the end of the Jetway the plane had already pulled away. It was stopped about twenty feet from the Jetway. The pilots were doing their preflight checks.

The gate agent tried desperately to get the pilot to bring back the plane, gesticulating with her arms. But it wasn't working.

Then the young manager remembered one of the tools from my course. Why are people about to be shot by a firing squad blindfolded? Because it's hard to shoot someone when you are looking them in the eye. When you are let onto a freeway during heavy traffic, it's after you make eye contact.

So the student took his bags, walked to the very edge of the Jetway, looked up at the pilot, and stretched out his arms, wide apart, as in the gesture "Shoot me." He just stood there, waiting to be shot.

The pilot brought back the plane.

It just took a minute, with very little inconvenience. But it had a dramatic, positive impact on that young manager's life.

The young manager had conducted a negotiation, to be sure. A business negotiation. A travel negotiation. Completely nonverbal. But the negotiation was conscious, structured, and it used a negotiation tool that is invisible to those who don't know it.

As you travel through life, through airports, roadways, hallways, other countries, no matter where you go, if you use these tools, you *will* get more.

14

Getting More Around Town

It was pouring rain, and Chuck McCall had forgotten his umbrella. His office was four blocks away, and he had an important meeting in thirty minutes.

He spotted someone getting off the same train who worked in a building a block away. He didn't know her, but he'd seen her on the train before. "Hi," he said, "I work a block away from you and I forgot my umbrella. Can I buy you a bagel and coffee on the way if you walk me to work? I know it's a block out of your way." She sort of stared at him. "I'm Chuck," he continued. He looked up at the sky. "It's *wet*. Maybe I can return the favor someday."

They walked to work under her big umbrella. He bought each of them coffee and a bagel. When they arrived, she told Chuck she felt good about doing this. They had each made a new friend for the train. "What I've learned the most," said Chuck, now the CEO of Astoria Energy, a big energy provider to New York City, "is that being candid about what you want is a key to success in business and in life in general."

In a world that sometimes seems full of muggers and other threats, we still have to get through the day. We have dozens of small interactions from the time we get up to the time we go to sleep. Together they can spell a life of frustration, or one of mastery and joy. Using the tools in *Getting More*, you will have a greater consciousness about the world immediately around you in a million different ways.

These include conversations with others on any number of subjects, driving down the street (yes, negotiation is involved), talking to a police officer who's just stopped you for a traffic infraction, getting into the gym when you forgot your I.D. card, getting better service at a restaurant, getting family members to be on time, talking effectively to neighbors whose child has just bullied yours, not losing your cool after a car accident.

This chapter will show how ordinary people master ordinary situations, resulting in more control over their lives and better mental health over the short and long term. The chapter will be organized both by individual negotiation tools and by subjects (apartments, dry cleaner). Each negotiation will use multiple tools.

Getting off the train, Chuck first decided to negotiate. Then he traded items of unequal value (a bagel in return for shelter). He invoked common enemies (the rain). He linked the negotiation to the future (I'll return the favor if I can). He focused on people (I'm Chuck). He reduced the perceived risk (I work nearby). He also made a new friend.

THE PICTURES IN THEIR HEADS

Let's start with the dry cleaner. Not a very big subject. But it gets people exercised the world over. So many of the participants in my courses write me about problems with their dry cleaner! And it's really representative of small family-owned businesses that you deal with daily in your town.

The first thing to recognize is that people in many dry cleaners are treated badly by many customers. In the U.S., at least, many are foreign-born and don't speak English well. So you should think about valuing dry cleaners. They are proud of what they do.

Many dry cleaners must think, "If I don't say no to everything, soon I'll be out of business." And they've seen too many people make up bogus claims for clothing that was already damaged when they received it. And then there's that stained shirt that the customer says cost $300.

But there are dry-cleaner standards, and you can use them. And there is the notion of repeat business and referral business.

Let's start with something simple. Raghu Kota, a strategy and analytics manager for a large Internet firm, was looking for a new dry cleaner. He told a prospective dry cleaner he'd have clothes to dry clean every week. He offered to recommend other people where he lives and works. Does the dry cleaner give discounts for that sort of thing? Yes, he was told, 10 percent. This seems like the standard discount if you make *any* collaborative overture. Many people don't ask for it. Think of reducing a lot of your costs by 10 percent, off the bat. And that's after-tax income.

Justin Baier's shirt was ruined with grease stains when he got it back from the dry cleaner. The shirt was not brought in with grease stains. "Not our fault," he was told. It seemed to be a standard response. Instead of going ballistic, Justin told the dry cleaner, Sojung, "I am sure the shirt didn't come in with grease stains. But why argue over it? Can you reclean it at no charge?" Yes. He offered the dry cleaner face-saving. Of course the dry cleaner knew he was blowing smoke.

The shirt came back with spots, however. "Sojung," Justin said, "I've been coming here for almost two years. I've recommended you to friends. What is your policy on customer satisfaction?" Sojung told him it was to try hard for customers to be satisfied. "Do you ever give refunds for damaged items?"

"Yes, when it's our mistake." "Well," said Justin, "I'd like to be a satisfied customer and there is some question here." At that point, Sojung offered him $50.

"How about free dry cleaning instead?" said Justin. So Sojung gave him $100 worth of free dry cleaning.

Justin, who works for Boston Consulting Group in Chicago, never raised his voice, never said anything arrogant; he just kept looking for a solution that didn't blame anyone. Note: this example is a surrogate for the camera store, the shoe repair shop, the local clothing store, the nail or beauty salon, and so forth.

Ben Chaykin's suit had a tear. He didn't know if it happened at the dry cleaner or not. "Our dry cleaners place a lot of value on loyalty and customer satisfaction" was the slogan on the wall. He thought about how the dry cleaner, from another culture, might view a U.S. attorney. Ben, a U.S. Labor Department attorney, said he couldn't be sure it happened at the dry cleaner. But he'd been a regular customer; could the dry cleaner help him out? They fixed it at no charge.

How far will the other person go? How far do you want to go? Sebastian Rubens y Rojo needed his dress shirt from the dry cleaner for an important interview. The shirt was not ready. He referred to the printed slogan, "We love our customers." Anger would have led to a dead end, he realized. So Sebastian gave the dry cleaner details about the importance of the interview, how he didn't have time to wash and iron another shirt and didn't have the money to buy a new one. "Do you have *any* shirt that could fit me?" he asked.

Without skipping a beat, the dry cleaner went to the rack, eyed Sebastian for size, and picked out someone else's clean white shirt hanging on the rack. He gave Sebastian the shirt. Sebastian tried it on, feeling the cool elegance of the newly cleaned shirt. He adjusted his tie, slipped on his suit jacket, and went to the interview.

Sebastian had given the problem away to the dry cleaner. But before he did that, he gave enough details so the other party felt it was a problem worth taking on. He got the other party personally involved. The more visual the picture you create, the better. Some people will have a problem with this. If you do, don't do it.

APARTMENT LIVING

Apartment living can be a hassle. So many people in close spaces. So many managers that look at any expense as a loss of profit. But it is possible to enjoy fixing problems. It doesn't have to be all about aggravation, threats, and non-responsiveness. Just use some of these negotiation tools.

Here are four examples of the same problem, with different outcomes based on the use of negotiation tools.

Jana Meron, a digital brand marketer in Brooklyn, told the manager of her apartment building that there were holes in her walls where mice could get in. "The super just gave me traps and said the exterminator was coming," she said. "The exterminator never came and the holes stayed there."

David Weinstock also had mice in his apartment, told the manager about it, and nothing happened. Instead of accepting traps and the promise of an exterminator who never showed, David found the head of facilities. David quoted the apartment building's motto: "Our staff has been trained to appropriately respond to emergencies, and assist residents in resolving concerns." The exterminator came the next day.

Shawn Rodriguez, a law student and future attorney, went farther. He told his landlord that there were holes and mice in his apartment, that it was a health risk, and that medical and reputational effects could result. He called the local Health Department and got the codes regarding mice. He looked up the diseases one can get from mice. He got pictures of diseased mice. He sent all of this to the landlord. The holes were plastered the same day. The exterminator came and laid traps personally.

"For many people," said Shawn, "you have to paint them a picture. This is a key negotiation tool." In other words, create a picture in their heads. Indeed, Jana Meron soon figured this out. She finally called up the apartment super and said her two-year-old was pointing at the mice and saying, "Look, Mommy!" They came immediately and plugged the holes.

Vlado Spasov did the same thing as Shawn when Vlado found mouse holes in his apartment. "They completely redid the kitchen," he said. "They replaced all the pipes. They replaced the cabinets and the stove. Maintenance personnel worked extra to finish on the same day." He added: "You've got to frame this right. You have to start with the pictures in their heads and find out what's important to them."

These tools work for other repairs, too. Lital Helman needed five different repairs in her apartment. Many requests to the building office, she said, were ignored. Some of the repairs were going to be expensive. She got the name of the maintenance manager. She waited until she could catch up with him.

"Hi," she said. "I'm happy to meet the person who makes everything work around here." What a standard! He seemed a little uncomfortable. "I appreciate your time," she added.

Lital told the maintenance manager that she knew their standard was to fix problems swiftly and completely, and that this was just a one-time oversight. "He agreed and apologized," she said. All the fixes were made. The key was finding the person who could actually fix the problem, citing the standard, and letting them save face.

Service people often feel they are viewed as part of the infrastructure, like furniture or soda machines. If you put yourself in their shoes, you can get ideas on how to make them feel better. Doug Goldstein needed the ceiling of his apartment fixed. He was not high on the repair list, the office said. He found the maintenance guy, told him how much he appreciated the work the guy was doing, and wondered if "one small item" might be squeezed in.

"He fixed the ceiling and, while he was there, all sorts of other things," Doug said. "It took only two minutes beforehand to consider his perceptions."

That also means empathizing with them. Vinh-tuan Ngo needed his bathroom repaired. The apartment plumber was just about to leave for the weekend, and was in a foul mood.

"I'm sorry you've had a bad day," Vinh-tuan said. "Is there anything I can do to help?" The plumber fixed the toilet. Luckily, the plumber didn't say, "Get your bathroom fixed on Monday." But a good response to that would have been, "Any way you can fix it today without being mad at me? I'm just a guy trying to use the toilet." Framing. Vinh-tuan's now research director for a hedge fund in Paris.

Let's talk about rent. Tamara Kraljic wanted to stay in her apartment for two months beyond her lease at the old rent. Before she met with the land-lord, she Googled him. She asked him about various things she learned about him. "He told me a lot of business stories," Tamara said. Tamara also brought a friend, who was interested in another apartment in the building. "I know a lot of other international students," Tamara said.

Tamara got the extension at lower rent, saving $400. And she was told she would be paid $150 for each referral who rented an apartment. She had traded items of unequal value. Everyone was happy.

As with other negotiations, the other person saying no often has a lot to do with their perceived risk. Kumar Dhuvur wanted to sublet his apart-ment. The landlord said no, as did the terms of Kumar's lease. He tried to find out why. "They had a bad experience with subletting before," Kumar said. "They had to evict the tenant for nonpayment of rent."

Of course, Kumar was not the other tenant. But people do stereotype entire groups. In its worst form, it's bigotry. At best, it's likely some sort of coping mechanism. People tend to solve the problem by creating rules to protect them from an entire class of people, even some who are no prob-lem at all.

To solve the perceived rent risk, Kumar offered to pay the entire rent up front for the sublet period. He also got references from credible business-people: "good guy," "prompt on rent," etc. And he offered to promote the apartment by putting up notices at strategic places at Wharton, where he was a student. Landlords could go on campus themselves, but they don't know the high-traffic places. Result: Kumar, who is now a consultant, was permitted to sublet his apartment.

Another frequent problem in apartment buildings is noise. Neighbors often make noise. People argue over it. Tempers flare. The police sometimes get called. Jean-Pierre Latrille was in that position. He and his neighbor were no longer on speaking terms, Jean-Pierre had complained so much. Then Jean-Pierre took my negotiation course and tried something differ-ent. He first asked two apartment board members who the decision-maker was in the neighbor's family. It was the neighbor's wife.

Jean-Pierre contacted the woman during the day. "I apologized if I was being unreasonable before and I thanked her for her efforts to date," said Jean-Pierre, now a trader at Barclay's Capital. He wanted to know if he could be helpful in reducing the noise even further without upsetting their lifestyle. The two of them brainstormed. The neighbors agreed to put felt pads under their chair and table legs and padding underneath their rugs. Jean-Pierre offered to pay half the cost. She insisted it was not necessary.

Getting More will help you deal with crazy people, too. Just stay calm, provide details, call in third-party advisors, provide emotional payments, and gently name bad behavior. *Don't* tell them they're crazy.

STANDARDS AND FRAMING

Standards, by now our old standby, will help you solve negotiation problems quickly and easily around town. Often it will take only a turn of phrase, that is, good framing. Below are a variety of examples among thousands from my students. They were accomplished calmly, effortlessly, as a part of the day.

The movers did a bad job transporting Brian Egras's household stuff. Brian, a director at an electronics firm outside Philadelphia, had already paid them. Brian: "Have you ever given a discount to a customer?" Moving company official: "Occasionally." Brian: "Should I expect movers to leave behind materials and mislabel boxes?" Official: "No." Brian: "I would like to use your company in the future." Official: "Great." Brian: "What's an hour of time worth, for my cleaning up the mess and finding the right things?" Result: $100 discount. Standards, questions, being incremental, being calm.

Ana Lucia Marquez needed her hair straightened for a wedding to which she had to travel that night. Charlotte, at the hair salon, was uninterested: the process was too involved. "Isn't the policy of this beauty salon to provide the hair care services that customers want?" asked Ana, now an attorney in Panama. Result: Charlotte enlisted two other hairstylists and together they got it done.

The bouncer at a popular dance club refused to admit Chris Seay because "the fire marshal says the club is full." Chris was on the VIP list. He watched and waited. Soon the bouncer let in five people. Chris went back up to the bouncer. "Is it the policy of this club to lie to VIP customers?" he asked. Aghast, the bouncer apologized profusely, implored Chris not to make an issue of it with his boss, and bought Chris and friends a round of drinks. Chris, now a commercial real estate investor in New York City, says he names bad behavior "on a regular basis."

Meng Zhang wanted to park a friend's car in his apartment's lot for eight days. Fee: $12 a day ($96), or $200 a month. "Ever make exceptions?"

Meng asked the building manager. Answer: "Rarely." "What are those rare situations?" Meng asked, picking up the signal. Answer: "Snow." "It snowed last weekend," said Meng, now CEO of a New Jersey medical services firm. Fee: $40 for the eight days, a discount of more than 50 percent.

Here are some more serious things. Al Taj's father, Mefleh, was in the hospital after back surgery. He was in pain. His attending doctor was in a meeting and unavailable. The nurse said she couldn't give Al's father morphine without another doctor's approval. The nurse found another doctor, but the doctor declined to give the shot.

"Is it the hospital's policy to leave patients in pain when the attending doctor is unavailable?" Al asked the doctor. The doctor stopped, took the time to look over the father's chart, and ordered the morphine shot. "It would have been easy for me to get emotional," said Al, a lawyer at Skadden Arps in New York. "I saw my father in a lot of pain." Instead, he kept a cool head and used standards and framing to get the painkillers his father needed.

One wonders why people don't just do the right thing to begin with. But we're dealing with the real world, not the world that should be. Brendan Cahill parked his car at the curb of a hospital while he went inside to get his wife and their newborn baby. "You can't leave that car here; security reasons," the valet claimed. Of course, the valet wanted to be paid the high price to park the car.

"You expect me to leave my wife with a newborn out in cold weather while I get the car?" Brendan asked. The valet didn't care. But Brendan went to his supervisor, who sure did. Yes, security is a concern these days. But Brendan provided details of his wife, Ann, newborn baby, Alessandra, and the doctor's name. Brendan, now the vice president and publisher of Open Road Integrated Media, an electronic publisher, could have tipped the valet to hold the car there for a couple of minutes. But the valet hadn't been very nice. The more you practice framing and standards, the more you will be able to use them at a moment's notice.

FINANCIAL INSTITUTIONS

Stephen Bondi was paying 1.45 percentage points above prime for his home equity line of credit. He saw a promotional rate for new customers at the same bank for 3.75 percentage points less. On a $300,000 loan, that's $11,250 less a year. So he asked a bank rep about the promotional rate. On three separate occasions, a bank rep promised to get back to Stephen and never did.

Stephen finally reached a manager. "Is it the bank's practice to treat existing clients worse than new clients?" Stephen asked. Clearly, that wasn't fair. So the bank manager offered him a 0.5 point discount from where he was. Better, but not good enough, and Stephen said so. He was told that customers can receive only one "bargain rate" during the life of the loan. Stephen had received the best rate when he first got his loan.

"Have there ever been any exceptions?" asked Stephen, now the chief operating officer of van Biema Value Partners, a New York hedge fund. She replied that she didn't know. "Well, I know of one," Stephen said. "Me." He had received a better rate as interest rates dropped after his initial loan. So there was a precedent. "Besides," Stephen said, "representatives of your bank failed to call me back three times in the past week."

Naming bad behavior and asking standards questions showed the manager that Stephen deserved something. And Stephen had a good option ready. "Put the loan in my wife's name," Stephen said. "That will make it a new loan, won't it? Then give my wife the new low rate." Done. He was persistent; he prepared; he didn't make himself the issue. He used standards and framing. The framing was especially good: instead of accepting that previous discounts did not entitle him to more, Stephen said previous discounts formed a precedent.

Javier Olivares was rejected for a Bank of America credit card because of a negative credit report by Comcast. He asked: "Do you think I'm a credit risk because Comcast did not pick up my modem for two months?" He continued: "Isn't my credit report perfect except for the modem?" It puts things in perspective. And he got the card four days later.

The key is finding these banks' standards and to keep asking questions. In my experience, most financial institutions are not prepared to continue unfair practices in the face of persistent, intelligent, standards-based questions from consumers. But they know well how to name bad behavior when consumers get angry, so the real issues don't have to be addressed. Take this as a negotiation lesson.

RESTAURANTS

A big part of the difference in price between making a meal yourself and paying higher prices at a restaurant is that the restaurant is supposed to be less hassle. They make the meal, they serve it to you, they provide a nice atmosphere. If they don't, you are not getting what you paid for.

John Gachora and some friends went to Jillian's Restaurant in Philadelphia. The restaurant would not seat the party because one person was wearing jeans. It was against the restaurant's dress code, they were told. "So we recited for them the message we had received regarding their dress code, on an earlier call," John said. "It didn't say anything about jeans." John had written the message down. They were seated. As noted before, if you are concerned about fairness, document it. It wasn't so hard. John is now a managing director of Barclay's Capital in South Africa.

You get to a restaurant. You have a reservation. The table is not ready. They say, "We're really busy." You ask, "Is this your first night in business? Haven't you been busy before?" They say, "We're especially busy tonight." Ask for the manager, as Varun Gupta did at Tinto Restaurant in Philadelphia.

"What do you imply when you give someone a reservation at your restaurant?" Varun wanted to know. "What is your definition of customer service?" Varun told them that he had introduced at least ten people to the restaurant. Varun and his group were given 50 percent off the bill, excluding alcohol. Now a consultant at Booz & Company in New York, Varun had used both standards and linkages. "The negotiation tools help me to structure any conversation," he said.

How much do you ask for? There isn't one right answer. Although extreme requests kill deals, asking for too little makes you feel bad, maybe even ripped off. You will learn from practice. The more you do this, the more you will develop an instinct for what most people would ask for, and what you should ask for.

This won't always work, of course. But it will work much more, and better, if you use the negotiation tools in this book. Sometimes Babe Ruth struck out. But he's in the Hall of Fame.

Again, the more of a personal connection you make, the more the other person will do what you want. Even if the restaurant makes a mistake, such as overcharging your credit card, be nice about it and ask what they do for customers when mistakes are made. It's an open-ended, nonthreatening question that will usually get you more. Sometimes people make innocent mistakes.

A fine local restaurant was sold out the day after Thanksgiving. Jeff Gorris, an attorney in Delaware, wanted to take his family there for dinner. "Do you ever make exceptions, try to squeeze people in?" he asked. "In extraordinary circumstances," the reservations head said. Great standard. "My family is visiting from the West Coast and I want to take them to one of the best restaurants in town," Jeff said. "Is that an extraordinary circumstance?" It was.

DAY IN AND DAY OUT

What do you do around town day to day? You run errands. You go from store to store—getting groceries, buying stamps, getting your car repaired. All of these are full of opportunities to negotiate to get more in your life.

Greg Dracon went to Eastern Mountain Sports in Arlington, Virginia, to buy some mountain-climbing gear. He asked James, the store manager, what his favorite outdoor sport was. James didn't have a favorite, but mountain climbing was a passion, too. Greg was going to Tanzania to climb Kilimanjaro, the highest mountain in Africa.

"James got really excited," said Greg, a venture capitalist in Boston. "He gave me lots of tips. He went over all the equipment, piece by piece." He also gave Greg a 20 percent discount, worth $250.

Fusun Sevgen wanted a rebate from Taylor Fuel when it failed to deliver promised gas to her house. Before she called the company, she did some research. "I called and talked to Bill, the owner," Fusun said. "I told him I was new to the area and I understand his is a family business started by his father fifty years ago." Fusun said she prefers local business, but she wondered about the service and was hoping for some insight.

"As soon as I said 'local business,' he offered a five percent rebate," Fusun said. "After further discussion, he agreed to a ten percent rebate." Fusun, a director at a major pharmaceutical firm in Delaware, said she resisted the time-worn instinct to threaten to change to another supplier. "Amazingly, the softer approach of 'providing feedback' instead of 'complaining' worked wonderfully." Five years later, she's still getting great service and the discount, Fusun said.

Jeremy Delinsky thought his electric bills were high. He thought the electric heat pump unit was malfunctioning. Rather than just ask his landlord's property management company for a new one, he decided to prepare. He called the electric company and got a history of his energy consumption. Then he showed the history to the management company and mentioned its national motto of "legendary service." A new heat pump, costing more than $1,000, was installed within a week. "Just claiming the heat pump was inefficient wasn't a very strong argument, because it was working," said Jeremy, now a health care executive in Massachusetts. "I learned the importance of preparation to frame the negotiation."

This sort of thing should become routine if you want a big annual raise in your net disposable income. Max Mettenheim wanted his car repaired the same day at AAA Keystone in southeast Philadelphia. Max found out that the owner, John, had served in the army. "I asked about his experiences." Max said he was in the Pennsylvania National Guard and had been a German army officer before coming to the United States. John was fascinated.

"The car was done immediately," Max reported. "Army discount."

What is the value of a contract? Lawyers say it's a foundation of our legal system. But the origin of contracts has little to do with holding people to commitments. Contracts were developed because most people couldn't read and write. The contract was a memory aid to help people remember what they agreed to. If they weren't sure, they got the scribe to read it to them.

Shan He had a leak in her apartment, costing a little less than $100 to fix. "The landlord insisted that fixing costs below $100 was not her obligation," Shan said. "But that's not what it said in the contract. The landlord was responsible.

"I told the landlord that I've been living in her apartment for more than one and a half years," Shan said. "We had a peaceful, friendly landlord-tenant relationship. Can't we keep it that way?" She said the cold water leak was really bad for the apartment. The landlord agreed to hire her own plumber.

Should Shan, now an attorney in Beijing, have waved the contract in the landlord's face? "A binding contract is not always the core of the negotiation," Shan said. "The transaction costs are high. Kindness and commitment to a relationship are often better."

Sometimes people are looking for a way to help you, but feel constrained by their job or position. You need to give them a reason. Katy Chen arrived at the parking booth ten minutes after the ninety-minute free parking period had expired. The attendant insisted that she pay. First she used standards. "Have you ever made an exception?" No, he told her. So she blamed a third party. "The medical spa started its appointment with me forty minutes late," Katy said. He shrugged, uninterested.

"You know," Katy said. "It's Thanksgiving weekend. Can't you give me a break?" The attendant said okay. But she had to write on the ticket that she needed the extra time to get it validated. In other words, he needed a reason to override the time clock. But he wouldn't have told her that if Katy's manner had not improved his mood.

People you hire are not commodities. They have feelings. If they like you, and something goes wrong, they will try harder to fix it for you. It's a big key to *getting more.*

Ask people their opinion. It values them. Each adult has lived a lot of years. They've seen things you haven't. Each one of them has something to teach you if you pay attention.

THE LAW

Many people talk about the police as if they are all unfair and overreactive. The news is peppered with such stories. This can become a self-fulfilling prophecy. You devalue someone and they become emotional. It doesn't have to be that way.

Carlos Cherubin was driving 51 miles per hour in a 25-mile-per-hour zone in Westerville, Ohio. A police officer pulled him over. Of course Carlos was wrong—why deny it? "I acknowledged her power by apologizing," he said. "I said I was not paying attention as I should have been." Carlos, a senior vice president at a major apparel company, said the officer looked uncomfortable. It was a hot day. "I asked her if she felt okay. It turned out she was pregnant. I asked her when she was due, and congratulated her."

Carlos did not get a ticket. The police officer asked him to be more careful in the future. And undoubtedly he will be. The question is, What percentage of drivers would have noticed the police officer enough to ask if they are okay? Very few.

"I always used to argue," Carlos said. "This is the first time in fifteen years I didn't. I used the negotiation tools. And it's the first time in fifteen years a cop let me go." That's because Carlos stopped thinking just about himself, and thought about the other person.

Jean-Pierre Latrille was stopped by a New Jersey state trooper for going 68 miles per hour in a 50-mph zone. Jean's first thought was to be angry, since he was going as fast as the other traffic. But he remembered it wasn't about being right, but meeting one's goals.

Jean-Pierre apologized, listened attentively to the officer's comments, thanked the officer, and gave details about visiting New Jersey for the weekend. No speeding ticket, no points on the license, no car insurance payment increase; just $43 for not having insurance papers available. "I just tried to connect with him," Jean-Pierre said. Does this work all the time? Absolutely not. But you will get an extra hit every nine games.

It's hard to apologize if you're not wrong, of course. I'm not suggesting that you do that. But too many people don't even apologize when they should. As Carlos Cherubin said, "Don't get macho—it won't meet your goals."

Details of your predicament can be persuasive. But (a) you have to mean what you say, (b) it has to be the truth, and (c) they can't have heard it a million times already. The purpose is not to hoodwink the other person or make an excuse, but to make a connection with them.

Any gatekeeper is going to get jaded hearing excuses. You should be prepared for their being ornery. "Why can't people just do what they're supposed to do?" they say to themselves.

Nikhil Raghavan wanted to get into the gym but forgot his I.D. card. "The security guard was gruff," he said. "No I.D. card, no entrance." Is anyone allowed to let me in? he wanted to know. The manager. Nikhil asked the guard to get the manager. He then asked the manager to look him up, and verified various personal details. The purpose of security, of course, was to verify who he was, not to check I.D.'s. The identification card was only one *method* of validation.

Nikhil, now a manager at Bain Capital in Mumbai, India, introduced himself to the manager, and also to the locker room attendant. They had a nice conversation about squash, which Nikhil was there to play. They both said that if Nikhil forgets his I.D. card again, just ask the security guard to call for one of them. The whole thing was about establishing an infrastructure on which the parties could rely in the future.

We often think of government employees as "the (hated) bureaucracy." However, we are not negotiating with "the bureaucracy." We are negotiating with individuals. These individuals may feel even more burdened by rules, regulations, and delays than you do. After all, they have to live with them every day. So give such people a break, and they'll often give you one. Ask their advice. Commiserate with them. So you're mad at the world. Do you want to meet your goals or not?

Jonathan Schulman got a $65 fine for leaving his garbage out too long for collection. Actually, Jonathan didn't do it—his subtenant did, during the summer. So in court, Jonathan apologized, said it was his subtenant who had broken the ordinance, gave the subtenant's name, and told the judge that he (Jonathan) had given explicit instructions that the subtenant had disobeyed. "Don't all of us have a hard time getting people to listen to us?" Jonathan said. His fine was reduced to $25. Again, it is about getting more in each situation.

TRADING ITEMS OF UNEQUAL VALUE

Even in daily transactions, you can find items to trade, the same as in billion-dollar deals. Sometimes it might be just the respect and conversation you offer to someone who is usually treated as a faceless service provider.

Ron Schachter wanted to park his motorcycle in a garage, but didn't want to pay $120 a month. The attendant said the garage doesn't make exceptions. "I needed to find something intangible that would cause him to let me park the bike," Ron said. "So I asked him, 'Do you ride a motorcycle?' " "No," the attendant said. "But I'd love to learn."

Bingo! "I agreed to teach him how to ride a motorcycle (not mine)," said Ron, now a partner and portfolio manager in a Hong Kong hedge fund, Nine Masts. The result: no fee. Trading items of unequal value.

Justin Baier wanted to eliminate various bank fees on his checking and savings accounts at Citibank. The bank representative was uninterested in helping him do so. Although Citi's competitors have fewer fees, the employee said, Citibank is a better bank.

"I engaged him in small talk," Justin said. "I asked what his career goals were. He said he wanted to get an MBA. I told him I was currently an MBA student and I'd be happy to write down some resources that he would find useful." Fees eliminated.

"He actually had to go into the system and MANUALLY remove the fees," Justin said. Did the representative steal from the bank? Well, will Justin remain a loyal customer? Do you think that *some* customers at Citibank don't pay fees? They don't. So (a) there is precedent and (b) the bank benefits through Justin's continued patronage.

Jaimie Chen, a UPenn law student, had a bad back but couldn't afford $50 an hour for therapeutic massages. Jaimie offered to put the therapist's card up around the law school and promote him to her friends. They got to talking. He was involved in a legal dispute. Jaimie offered free legal research for him. "I got free massages the whole time I was in Philly," said Jaimie, now an attorney in Washington with a much-improved back.

Learning more about how the other person thinks, of course, helps you find items to trade. Carolina Dorson wanted to rent the upstairs of Haru, a restaurant and bar, for a party. The manager wanted $300 for the DJ. Carolina asked around. She learned that other venues did not charge for a DJ if the customer guarantees a minimum bar charge.

Carolina offered $2,000 for bar and food. She committed to paying immediately by credit card. Done. The actual tab turned out to be $3,000. The DJ was free. Carolina, a private equity recruiter in New York, used standards and reduced the other party's perceived risk.

Bernadette Finnican needed to get a required bone scan so she could run in a marathon the next day. No appointments were available at the radiologist covered by her insurance. The receptionists were not helpful.

Bernadette asked if the radiologist was in, and where his office was. She waited for him to appear. "I told him I was going to run a marathon and needed a bone scan," she said. She asked if he ever worked with marathon runners. He did, and was proud of it. They talked about his work. Then he personally escorted her into the room and did the scan immediately.

Have a problem getting through the gatekeepers? Be creative about making the connection. Nana Murugesan wanted to use a highly rated San Francisco doctor, Prasanna Menon, for his wife's pregnancy. But the doctor's schedule was full for most of her pregnancy period, and his gatekeepers weren't letting Nana even talk to the doctor. Nana had done his homework. Dr. Menon spoke the same Indian dialect as his wife, Charu, and went to the same med school in India as his sister, Shree.

Nana wrote down on a piece of paper "Kannada" and "Karnatak University." He asked the receptionist to hand the paper to the doctor. The doctor came out himself to sign up Nana's wife. The connection itself was of value to him.

Of course, these tools don't work perfectly all the time. Michele Michaelis wanted her condo's management company to pay $3,000 in legal fees she incurred as a condo board member to defend a tenant complaint over maintenance. The management company finally admitted it was at fault.

The management company, however, would pay only $500. "I even offered to give him a good reference," Michele said. They didn't care about the reference. "Using the negotiation tools doesn't guarantee complete success," noted Michele, a consultant. "But it does make success more likely and it does get you more." She accepted the $500 and vowed to get better commitments up front next time.

COALITIONS

You don't have to do the negotiation by yourself. Local vendors, buyers, and officials depend on their local reputations. Goodwill is very important. So if you ally with others, you will have more persuasive power.

A group of people who frequent a restaurant, store, or dry cleaner can make a lot of difference in what you get, as you represent more volume. Some existing groups are ready-made for such negotiation coalitions: homeowners associations, PTAs, civic clubs, scouts.

If a police officer is unfair, you can all complain. If the garbage is not picked up properly, you have a larger pressure group. You can rotate coordinators, or develop or use a website.

As Chuck McCall did at the start of this chapter, look for others to help you. Here is a story that occurred in China, but it is very appropriate here.

In Beijing, Alan Baer was in a store trying to negotiate for an expensive carved ivory elephant. The store was full of people. The person behind the counter refused to negotiate on the price.

"Why should I give you a discount?" she said. "I've got a store full of people." She gestured at the group milling around. Alan, now the president of Ocean World Lines, a freight company based on Long Island, New York, turned around and looked at the group. Then he turned back to the store owner. "See all those people in this store?" he said. Pause. "They're with me." They were his classmates. He got the discount.

15

Public Issues

Public issues, almost by definition, represent the failure of negotiation. So often because of conflicts or poor processes, a problem becomes so large, costly, or worrisome that it involves a lot of people. Even if it's a natural disaster, like a hurricane or a tsunami, the matter becomes a public issue only when people get in harm's way.

Wars, abortion, global warming, energy, health care, the local school controversy—one can trace each of these issues to the failure of people or governments to solve their problems effectively. Hurricane Katrina's damage was greatly magnified by poor planning and follow-up, and by conflicts among various constituencies. The 2004 Indian Ocean tsunami, killing more than 250,000 people, was greatly worsened by the lack of an adequate warning system: essentially a communication and planning issue.

Getting More is essentially a book for individuals. I've included a chapter on public issues because they are individual issues writ large. When people's children die in wars, that's an issue that affects individuals, isn't it? So is tax money that is being used to fund an activity that provides little value, when the funds could be freed for something more worthwhile, whether education or health care.

When terrorism worldwide causes someone to try to blow up a bomb in the middle of Times Square, that's an issue that affects individuals. As a result, the government has to spend money on police and security instead of business tax credits or subsidized housing.

And when the possible extinction of the human race becomes an ordinary conversation topic and the subject of many TV documentaries, it is probably time for ordinary individuals to take stock of what's going on. Are we using the most effective processes to avoid calamity? Do we even have the right people negotiating on our behalf?

By better understanding the people or process failures that cause public issues, we are better prepared to do something *more* about it, with our votes, in our daily conversations, and in countless other ways through which a change in a collective psyche can affect business and political leaders. This same sentiment helped to end the Vietnam War, prompted the civil rights movement, and helped to overcome gender discrimination. At a certain point, when a lot of people won't tolerate the status quo, it changes.

Even when better negotiation would not completely solve a problem, better processes can lessen the negative impact of many public issues.

Remember, *less than 10 percent* of the reason agreements occur or fail has to do with the substance of the matter. *More than 90 percent* has to do with the people and the process. As such, public problems can be lessened through the use of better people skills—trust, valuing others, understanding their perceptions, forming relationships. They can be further lessened by using better communication, uncovering needs, standards, trading items of unequal value, framing, and commitments.

It is my intention in this chapter to look at public issues through the lens of how successful the participants are in solving that 90 percent of a problem—the part that involves people and process. I do not address every public issue or intend to propose a specific solution to any specific problem. But I believe this chapter can create a template for examining any public issue. It will enable you to assess how well the parties are doing in trying to solve an issue that has become large enough, costly enough, or worrisome enough to affect you.

I'm going to use the Middle East (Israel, Palestine, Iran, Iraq) as a proxy for public issues, since it's almost become synonymous with unresolvable conflict. I'll mention some other issues, too, including North Korea, piracy, race, and abortion. Clearly, public issues are much more complex than, say, negotiating over a ruined shirt at the dry cleaner or negotiating for a job: there are more constituencies, more people, more emotions. But they are still amenable to analysis with the same people and process tools.

Lest you think this is a pipe dream, these tools have already begun to be used successfully. For example, Jim Vopelius, a former Wharton student who later became chief engineer on a nuclear submarine, said he taught the tools from my course to some of his military colleagues who went to

Afghanistan. Today they are making personal connections and trading items of unequal value to gain support of local tribal leaders against the Taliban. Instead of using the traditional threats, he said, the Americans have started to observe the ceremonial fasts with the tribal leaders. The soldiers also give notebooks and pens to the tribal children.

"Even in difficult military operations, they can form an organizing principle to achieve your goals," he said.

He also used course tools to resolve conflicts among Navy SEALS and submarine command on training exercises. Quickly finding out the pictures in people's heads has proved essential in military situations where internal conflict must be quickly fixed, he told me. Clearly, issues in the military qualify as a public issue, since poor military processes reduce the effectiveness of our troops.

An Israeli who was vice president of strategy for Merck, the pharmaceutical firm, told me that he and a team went to Saudi Arabia and negotiated a pharmaceutical deal with the Saudis. It didn't matter to the Saudis that he was Israeli and Jewish. The deal he struck was an important economic agreement that benefited everyone. As such, there is a precedent for trading items of unequal value between Arabs and Jews in significant deals in the Middle East.

There are a significant number of joint businesses and peace groups among Israelis and Palestinians in the Middle East. And in Somalia, community leaders have begun finding legitimate jobs for pirate crews as an alternative to hijacking.

The Parents Circle is composed of several hundred Israelis and Palestinians who have lost loved ones in the conflict and share one another's pain. Combatants for Peace contends that violence is not an acceptable way to resolve the conflict. Israeli and Palestinian Bereaved Families proclaims that "under our feet is an ever-growing kingdom of dead children." Joint Arab-Jewish groups have included sports clubs, language instruction, theater, and even a circus.

The real question to be confronted now, of course, is scalability. How do we get more people to use these tools so that eventually there will be a critical mass? One way is to teach people, to publicize these tools, and to show where they have worked.

So, here are some of the major questions that you should be asking when evaulating how well people are doing in solving a public issue—whether on the local planning board or halfway around the world. The answers will tell you whether you have the right people and the right process.

- How effective is the *communication* between parties? Does it exist at all?
- Do the parties find, understand, and consider one another's *perceptions*?
- Is the *attitude* one of forcing the other party's will or of *collaboration*?
- Do the parties *blame* others for yesterday, or *value* them for tomorrow? Who is the right *negotiator* to convey this message?
- Are the respective *needs* of each party uncovered and *traded*?
- Is the action *incremental,* or do parties try to do everything at once?
- Are the parties taking actions that meet their *goals*?
- How high is the *emotional* level? Do the parties try to be *dispassionate*?
- Do the parties use one another's *standards* in reaching a decision?
- Is there a *problem-solving* process in which *differences* are *valued*?

COMMUNICATION

A major theme of *Getting More* is that if the parties don't talk effectively to each other, a sustainable agreement is not possible. A lack of communication means the parties don't value each other enough to chat. Poor communication risks misperception and can result in no deal. So, the first question to ask is, Are the parties talking? If they are not and it's a local issue, push to start a dialogue. Anyone who won't do so should be replaced, as they are more interested in inflicting pain than creating opportunity.

Let's look at some very public issues and see how the parties are doing. As a negotiation expert, I find that the lack of communication, and the poor communication, among people in charge of solving public issues worldwide is shameful. It causes conflicts and costs lives.

In the Israel-Palestine conflict, the parties have not talked directly for years. In Israel, individual Israelis and Palestinians have millions of conversations daily with each other on the street, but the leaders who represent them can't bring it upon themselves to meet face-to-face. Don't they eat lunch? Could they not start by talking about sports or children? Formality is not necessary. Without communication, persuasion cannot occur. As this book went to press, the parties were considering restarting negotiations. That doesn't inspire confidence. It should be a no-brainer.

As noted earlier, establishing preconditions to negotiating just adds a layer of debate that thwarts the process. The parties seem to think that when they meet, they have to discuss substantive issues right away. But substantive issues should come at the end of the process, after the parties begin to establish trust and develop a way to talk to each other. Whatever side one is on, whatever their position on any individual issue, a failure to talk is self-defeating, unless one welcomes war.

As a result of terrorist killings of tourists in Mumbai (Bombay) in November 2008 by some Pakistanis, the Indians broke off peace talks with the Pakistani government. Why? The terror in Mumbai should have been a reason to *start* talking, not to stop talking! They didn't decide to resume official talks until February 2010, fifteen months later. There is some indication that some informal private talks were held before then, but not announced because each side didn't want to further inflame their constituents.

If true, this is another example of poor communication by the respective governments. If millions of people think communication with the other side is bad, the government should be trying to change that perception. The governments should find a way to frame the issue more cleverly. For example, "Whatever we think about the other side, it is in our interests to know what they are thinking. So we are going to hear what they have to say and ask them questions."

This is what the United States should have done with Saddam Hussein before invading Iraq. One doesn't have to legitimize the other side by collecting information. If the other side is extreme, quote them verbatim; it will help to build a coalition against them.

If a country rebuffs our overtures to talk, we should keep trying, and publicize that we are trying. Countries that don't talk will appear unreasonable. Let them make themselves the issue. It is skill in framing the issues that makes one appear strong.

For example: "We have contacted Iran every day for a hundred days to talk, and they have turned down a hundred such requests. They are really not interested in peace, just in making excuses." Contrary to being weak, it is aggressive in a positive way. "We are aggressive for peace."

Again, if a party demands concessions as a condition to talk, we should say it's a subject for the negotiating table. This keeps the focus entirely on opening communication.

In 2010 there were allegations by South Korea and others that North Korea blew up a South Korean military ship. North Korea has denied this. There was tough talk about war and sanctions. Why didn't the parties immediately start talking about this face-to-face? Instead of threats and accusations, the only refrain should have been, "When do we talk?"

For more than eight years, North Korea's president has said how interested his country is in joining the international trade community. He almost came right out and said he'd trade his nuclear program if he could join international trade groups. Not only did we not trade him, we wouldn't even hold direct talks.

Of course, North Korea did go back on its pledge to permit international inspectors to see its nuclear facilities. Recall my discussion of commitments from Chapter 3. Korea's commitment wasn't based on mutual respect. It wasn't the result of a relationship. North Korea very likely didn't consider its pledge binding. We needed to get a commitment from Korea in the way that *they* make commitments: with relationships, not contracts. Indeed, in many Korean circles a contract is considered a nonbinding memo of understanding, to become a commitment only through work together.

And yet, the president of North Korea, Kim Jong-il, released two journalists after former president Bill Clinton came over and had his picture taken with him, showing the Korean president respect. North Korea again allowed the restart of reunions with family members in South Korea. North Korea paid its respects, in person, after the death of former South Korean president Kim Dae Jung in 2009. Year after year, North Korea has asked for bilateral talks with the United States, but the United States has insisted on multination talks. Whatever one's position on North Korea, it is not defensible, from a process viewpoint, to refuse to talk.

In 2009, the head of Hamas said his group was ready to talk to the United States. We or our allies should take them up on it, even if it means sitting in silence or listening to speeches or accusations. If they say something more collaborative, we can use it in negotiations with them. If they say something extreme, public opinion will turn against them. If they refuse to talk without concessions, they can be portrayed as not being serious about peace.

This also means engaging in talks with terrorist sympathizers. Except for the few terrorists who want to kill for its own sake, most terrorist sympathizers appear to go along because of the lack of meaningful alternatives. It's clear, however, that such groups are not monolithic. Many mothers of Arabs don't want their children to blow themselves up. There are a lot of moderates who have been willing to listen to talk of détente, or who could be persuaded.

There is a precedent for this. In Sri Lanka, the government defeated the Tamil rebels by first offering blanket amnesty. Many rebels laid down their arms and came back into the fold. Some of these people then told the government where the other, extremist rebels were so that the government could go after them.

It was proclaimed a military victory by some. But it was really the result of a negotiation with moderates who had sympathized with terrorists but then converted. One of them, leader Karuna Amman, the second most powerful figure of the rebel Tamil Tigers, actually was permitted to join Sri Lanka's government. The government had offered amnesty and job training to any rebel who came back to the fold. It was a great example of looking forward and improving the future.

Something similar occurred with M-19, a rebel group in Colombia, in the 1980s. So many people came back to the fold that there was no M-19 organization left to go after, according to Agustin Velez, a government consultant retained to find economic opportunities, including jobs, for those who returned.

Of course, an important element here is part of the communication tool kit: not fighting over yesterday, not getting involved in the assignment of blame. It takes discipline to do this. And leadership. And a focus on goals.

What it also means is that if alliances are forged with moderates, they will become allies against extremists. It requires understanding that the parties are not monolithic. And it requires effective communication with moderates: to value them and create a vision they can buy into.

PERCEPTIONS

Once communication starts, one has to understand the other side's perceptions. Unless you understand the pictures in their heads, you don't know where to start to persuade them. I have stressed this point throughout *Getting More.* Whether their perceptions are accurate or not, we have to understand and deal with them if we want to meet our goals.

In other words, the other side has to *want* to reach an agreement. And that will happen only if they feel understood. That means that in any public issue, the extent to which another party wants to understand your viewpoint actually is a measure of your persuasiveness.

So the key questions are: Do we understand the other side's perceptions? Can we articulate them? Have we discussed them with the other side? If not, you will not get more.

This is a particular problem for the United States in a post-9/11 world. There is substantial residual resentment against the United States in much of the developing world for perceived market and economic exploitation, toxic-substance proliferation, internal interference in other nations, and a general arrogant attitude. Fair or not, it is important to understand the basis for some of these perceptions as a precursor for gaining the support of much of the world's population in combating the United States' dispersed enemies.

For example: in December 1984, an estimated 3,000 people were killed in Bhopal, India, from a chemical leak at a factory designed by Union Carbide, a U.S.-based chemical firm. Thousands more died from after-effects. An investigation I did with another *New York Times* reporter found a dozen violations of the company's own manual by the company's factory workers there. The company had known about the violations and did little of consequence. Its chairman has declined to ever come to India to face the country's legal system.

The number of people who died at Bhopal exceeds the 2,985 people killed by terrorists on September 11, 2001, at the World Trade Center and other U.S. locations. Much of the developing world sees no material difference between Bhopal and the World Trade Center. One was a deliberate act of terrorism. The other was what India believed were deliberate decisions to leave a lethal process in place.

Unless and until the United States and other developed countries understand such perceptions, they will *never* be able to achieve rapprochement with much of the world. This means it will continue to be difficult to gain broader cooperation against those who try to develop weapons of mass destruction. "Each time we fail to live up to our values," said a critique in 2009 by the chairman of the Joint Chiefs of Staff, "we look more and more like the arrogant Americans the enemy claims we are."

Much has been written about the United States' reputation as an arrogant country. Incidents like the mistreatment of prisoners of war in Iraq have long-term negative implications for our ability to persuade others. This does not for a moment excuse violence against Americans. But if we want to reduce violent efforts against us, we need more support.

Not all of the grievances by others are preposterous, just as not all of our demands are realistic. We need to hear all of them. Then we need to articulate them, discuss them, and find something mutually beneficial. The easiest ones we should fix quickly. The hard ones we should consider and work on. The preposterous ones we should publicize to isolate extremists.

Such a process became a basis for the 1998 peace settlement between Ireland and Northern Ireland. Once the two sides finally sat down and started talking with one another, they shared their perceptions. They realized that most people didn't want to keep fighting, that they had a lot of the same values, and that they could all do better independent of British rule, noted Dr. Teo Dagi, a former student who is now a Harvard Medical School lecturer and has been involved in the peace process as chair of a medical advisory panel. Although at times the peace has been uneasy, he said, the open lines of communication and the frank discussions of perceptions have been a safety valve against continued war.

In the Middle East, research shows that many on each side have no clue of the other side's perceptions. Daniel Lubetzky, an entrepreneur who has started various businesses employing both Arabs and Jews since 1993, more recently gauged how the perceptions of each side differed. He figured that if each side understood the other side better, there would be a better basis for peace and, as such, economic prosperity.

He collected 150,000 questionnaires of ordinary people and found diametrically opposed perceptions on the two biggest issues: the use of Jerusalem and the return of refugees. Both sides claimed that their possession of East Jerusalem was nonnegotiable. Palestinian refugees wanted their specific lands back, even if they had already been converted to other uses.

Lubetzky, the founder of PeaceWorks, said he has begun to show each side's perceptions to the other side—and they were astonished. "Unless each side is flexible, no agreement would ever be possible," he said. He said that this perception is helping each side be more creative in developing solutions: for example, Palestinians having a part of Jerusalem for their capital, and refugees getting land for themselves, even if it is not the exact same land they once had.

Kenji Price was a military officer in Iraq before attending the University of Pennsylvania Law School and becoming editor of the law review. Had he taken the negotiation course before his tour of duty in Iraq, he said, he would have considered the perceptions of the locals much more. "It is easy to dismiss the local police as corrupt or uneducated," he said. "But they really know the country. They could have made our job easier."

In general, he added, whether in the United States or abroad, military and police often get into an "enforcement mentality." They are so busy trying to keep the peace that they don't listen enough and miss key signals that could resolve a situation. He mentioned the national uproar regarding black Harvard professor Henry Louis Gates Jr., arrested by a white police officer as Gates was trying to break into his own house after losing his keys. It was a perception and communication issue: easily fixed with effective focus on communication and perception.

ATTITUDE

I have repeatedly emphasized in *Getting More* that if you come to a nego-tiation with a confrontational attitude, you will get less: in fact, 75 percent less over the long-term. So the next questions are: How do the parties treat each other? Do they blame each other? Do they threaten each other? Do they try to hurt each other? Or do they try to work collaboratively toward a solution that meets the needs of all?

If your needs are not met, you will not give things to the other side. This is a fact of human nature. Usually, if someone tries to hurt you, you will try to hurt them back.

Part of the problem in too many public issues is that there is not a collaborative process. Instead, it's winner takes all. This is the first of four definitions of negotiation presented in Chapter 1—getting the other party to do what you *will* them to do. It is the most expensive and least effective form of negotiation.

For the parties to have a sustainable agreement, they have to want to meet each other's needs. At least, they have to try hard to meet each other's needs.

Let's measure this against some public issues of recent years. Former U.S. president George W. Bush called North Korea part of an "axis of evil" in 2002. And he said the United States would feel free to attack any country that the United States perceived as threatening us. Then the United States attacked Iraq, part of the same "axis of evil" as North Korea.

If you were the North Korean president, what would you do? You'd try to develop nuclear weapons to protect your country. Essentially, the nego-tiation strategy of the United States encouraged North Korea to continue developing a program of nuclear weapons. When people feel threatened, they fight back.

Let's look at sanctions, which are, essentially, threats of economic harm. It's a perennial negotiation strategy for public issues. In principle, sanctions are designed to break a government's resolve to continue its current behavior.

A legion of studies shows that, historically, sanctions have not worked well. They tend to unite a country against the nations trying to force their will. They cause the target to be inventive in building its own coalitions or trying to find ways around sanctions. It's hard to hold a coalition of na-tions together in imposing sanctions for very long. Sanctions are hard to enforce. The black market is inventive.

At best, sanctions are a long and arduous road. They haven't worked with Cuba in fifty years. The people largely hurt from embargoes are already victims, those at the bottom of the economic scale. The leaders of all countries live well.

Sanctions work best when the target has few other options (Yugoslavia), when there is powerful internal dissent (South Africa, Rhodesia), or when the relief sought is limited (Libya in the return of two terrorists).

Iran, with its big nuclear program and lots of oil, strong military dictatorship, and multiple allies, doesn't fit these conditions very well. North Korea, more economically disadvantaged and politically isolated, fits them somewhat more and occasionally shows some response to sanctions.

It is estimated that sanctions cost the United States up to $20 billion a year in lost exports. Even if you can make an argument for their use, there are usually better negotiation options using the kinds of tools I have discussed in this book.

Let's look at some. First, the opposite of sanctions: flooding the market. One reason the former Soviet Union fell was the increasing internal demand for foreign culture, representing a better life. From blue jeans to computers, movies to magazines, Western goods and services have proven to be a powerful door opener. They are harder to resist.

Lifting the trade embargo to Cuba would expose the country to the kind of capitalism—such as teenage culture—that extreme societies would find it difficult to combat. Indeed, hip-hop and rap, the U.S. music inventions, are spreading messages of individuality to teenagers worldwide. It's not fancy, but it's more of a foreign policy opportunity than many people realize. It is a communication opener. Similarly, promoting the Internet is a strong negotiation strategy.

Why equivocate about whether Cuba should join the Organization of American States? Invite them to join everything! It's not a reward. In fact, it's just the opposite. It will make it harder for Cuban political leaders to maintain the status quo, and it opens communication. It makes the other party more persuadable.

In 2008, Iran bought wheat from the United States for the first time in twenty-seven years. The more than a million tons of winter wheat are a basis for economic cooperation. The best way to persuade people to do something for you is to provide benefits, not to threaten them. China is making money exporting goods to Iran. Why isn't the United States, with its cash-strapped economy, doing the same? Iran imported about $57 billion in goods and services in 2009. In other words, the maxim "Hold your friends close and your enemies closer" is good advice for persuasion. Holding them closer means getting more information and having more influence. It may seem counterintuitive to many people, but it is far more effective in meeting goals.

"If there was more communication with Iran, the United States would know more about the Iranians as people and would have a better idea of how to persuade the leaders to keep their treaties," said Asa Mohammadi, an Iranian attorney and a graduate of Penn Law School. She said that many Americans, after meeting her, said they didn't like Iranians until they met her. She also said she was usually the first Iranian they had met.

YESTERDAY VERSUS TOMORROW: THE RIGHT NEGOTIATORS

This was mentioned above, but is worth giving it its own category because it is a major criteria of successful versus unsuccessful negotiations.

The questions to ask are: Are the parties fighting over yesterday? Are the parties blaming each other for yesterday? Or are they focused on improving tomorrow? If a local town council or school board candidate is more interested in casting blame than creating opportunity, it is a big clue that they are less interested in adding value, the key to successful negotiations.

In the Middle East, the parties seem mostly to be fighting over yesterday. No matter how many treaties and envoys there are, someone will always try to take revenge on someone else for something that happened yesterday. Peace is not possible under those circumstances; the process is poor.

It also raises the question of who the right negotiating parties should be. If the process is poor because the people can't get past yesterday, then the individuals involved are the wrong negotiators. So the style and identity of the negotiators are key.

For example, the mere presence of the United States is a radicalizing influence in much of the world. As such, a reduced overt presence by the U.S. would not only be cheaper and safer; it would be more effective in negotiation. Again, the U.S. military forming an alliance with tribal leaders is a highly effective negotiation strategy.

Various reports indicate that the defeat of the Taliban in Afghanistan in 2001 was spearheaded on the ground by, at most, a few dozen U.S. special forces operatives who trained many local tribespeople. The tribespeople knew the countryside, where the Taliban were, and how to recruit their own fighters. This is clearly an effective way to achieve our goals: persuading the locals to fight their own war.

Within each public issue, the clearest division is between moderates and extremists. As such, the right third parties in a negotiation are moderates. They, more than extremists, are focused on building a better way of life (tomorrow), whereas most extremists are focused on tearing things down as a penalty for yesterday.

That means, in the Middle East, the right people to go after Jewish extremists are Jewish moderates. The right people to go after Arab extremists are Arab moderates. Why look for terrorists ourselves when others are better equipped to do so? In all public issues, the choice of negotiator is key.

UNCOVERING AND TRADING NEEDS

Ultimately, to be successful at negotiating, you need to meet the needs of the other party. Communicating effectively, understanding their perceptions, having the right attitude, and having the right negotiators just bring you to the place where you are ready to talk effectively. Now you need to determine what needs of each party can be met and how they can be traded. This is the currency of the negotiation.

This currency for most people in the world is basic human needs. Whether a negotiation involves the victims of Hurricane Katrina or Palestinian refugees, addressing the basic necessities of life is a starting point. So, negotiating for a solution to public issues has to begin with those needs.

In that context, psychologist Abraham Maslow's hierarchy of needs is a good basis for the negotiation of major public issues.

People's most basic needs involve food, water, stability, security, employment, the safety of their families, health, and property, as well as

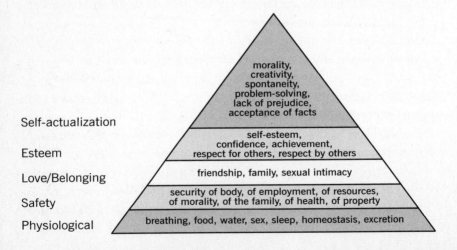

various bodily functions. They need enough to eat, clean drinking water, shelter, and freedom from bodily harm.

Notwithstanding this, issues and things that are less important to most of humanity occupy much of the time of the media and politicians in major public issues: morality, prejudice, politics, achievement. In many big disputes around the world, policy makers start from the top: peace, democracy, various ideals.

Yet few people are interested in even listening to an appeal to their ideals before their basic needs are met. Right now, people who need basic things like enough food are being radicalized daily for lack of them.

Ideology is not the only reason that extremist groups like Hamas have so many supporters, although the Hamas political line says so. Hamas feeds Arabs without enough to eat. Hamas also provides medical services and even matchmaking services. People whose basic needs are met are more apt to repeat the organization's party line.

Conversely, there is much evidence that hunger begets violence and social unrest: we have seen that in Egypt, Haiti, Senegal, Burkina Faso, Niger, Malaysia, Thailand, Mexico, Uzbekistan, and other places. "If you're hungry you get angry quicker," said Arif Husain, deputy chief of food security at the World Food Program. Studies show this is even more pronounced with children, and can cause severe emotional problems. The cycle of violence starts young.

If the United States and other countries want to win the hearts and minds of hundreds of millions of people, something similar must occur to what the United States did with the former Soviet Union in the arms race: bankrupt the other side. If Hamas provides bread, the United States, the U.N., or other allies should provide bread and meat. If Hamas provides 1,000 calories a day, the people wanting to stop Hamas should provide 2,000 calories a day.

As such, if Israel wants to start building a coalition with Arabs, it needs to start providing basic needs for more people. By and large, Israel has not done that. Sending missiles to blow up things in Gaza just creates more Hamas sympathizers. Instead, the Israelis should be throwing *food* at them. "Israel bombed Gaza today with fifty tons of bread and meat!" Some people will ridicule this. Hungry people won't.

After that, provide the moderates with something they won't want to lose—food, housing, education, medical care, health care, security. The moderates will then find the extremists and turn them in—or eliminate them. It is a basic human principle: bread works better than bombs at long-term persuasion. Building on the existing Arab-Israeli peace groups is a negotiation process that would add moderates.

If you are skeptical, try living in the desert for six months without much food, water, medical care, education, air conditioning, or the other niceties of life. Then get fed by some people who say your misery was caused by the United States. See how you feel. You will agree with much of what your providers tell you. In other words, we must provide terrorist sympathizers with a *meaningful choice* for a better life in order to persuade them to follow a different path.

Some policy experts claim that the notion of terrorism arising from poverty has been disproved. They point to a few rich people financing or carrying out terrorism. True, there are a few rich ideologues. But they derive much of their power and support from the tens of millions of the destitute. This is about persuasion of those who are *persuadable.*

I came upon this subject in 1981, after Israel bombed and destroyed a nuclear power plant being built in Iraq. As a journalist, I was doing a story on the technology to prevent the spread of nuclear weapons. Israel thought Iraq was trying to gather material for bombs from the reactor. So I called all of the scientists I could find who had worked on the Manhattan Project to build the atomic bomb for the United States during World War II.

Most of them were in their eighties and retired from places like MIT, Caltech, and other of the best engineering schools in the country. I asked each of them the same question: what technologies existed to prevent the spread of nuclear weapons?

Unprompted, they all gave me almost exactly the same answer. Each said something like, "Wrong question. If you want to prevent the spread of nuclear weapons, feed people, give them medical care, clothing, education, shelter, and jobs."

An Arab businessman once told me about which side he thought had the best arguments. He said, "I'm on the 'I feed my family' side. I'm on the 'Good medical care' side." It is about Maslow's needs pyramid first. And after that, it is about prosperity.

In Syria, even businesspeople without any love for Israel think economic cooperation is a good idea. It would help Syria's economy. In Lebanon, dialogues are occurring at the community level between Western and Islamic professionals. It is the basis for joint business.

After the fall of the Soviet Union, Ukraine, at the request of the United

States, sent its nuclear warheads to Moscow. In return, Ukraine got various economic benefits. There is a precedent for trading economic benefits for a nuclear program.

North Korea has had to ration food. Food-growing technology as well as food itself could be provided to North Korea in exchange for nuclear forbearance. This is not intended to provide a specific solution for North Korea. It is intended to show there is a road not taken here, one that taps into fundamental human needs.

This is not to say that politics has no importance in resolving public issues. But government can be used to support the economic growth that provides for basic needs. The negotiation reason for doing so is that when people are deprived, they are emotional. When they are emotional, they are less persuadable; they respond to the people who provide them with emotional payments: that is, the basic necessities of life.

This negotiation strategy has not been pursued as vigorously as it could be. In fact, the history of the Middle East peace process has been a quest for *ceremonial* peace—pronouncements by envoys, and formal treaties. Instead, to gain supporters, one needs *operational* peace. That is, peace on the ground, where people live.

Instead of operational peace, the United States has also pursued technological peace: increasingly sophisticated technology and expensive infrastructure to contain terrorism. I am not suggesting we stop this; however, ultimately, we will not be able to stop terrorism this way. As Albert Einstein said after the atomic bomb was dropped on Hiroshima, "There is no secret, and there is no defense." Every time we find a solution to a terrorist action, terrorists will find a new method. After 9/11, there was a shoe bomb on a plane. After shoes were checked, there were plastic explosives in someone's underwear. After men were profiled and separated, young women started blowing up themselves and others.

U.S. intelligence agencies have been criticized for not "connecting the dots" with the hundreds of bits of information buried among trillions that would show terrorism in planning. But there are different dots each time. The human mind is inventive. Human institutions will never be able to cull the constantly changing pieces of information from smart people bent on hiding things—as Einstein said. The logical extreme is nuclear and chemical terrorism weapons in cities. If the United States and other countries want to succeed at stopping mass terror, we should start providing food, clothing, jobs, housing, and medical care to the people who can find the terrorists. In other words, many more people on the other side have to *want* to stop the path we are on. We can't make them.

Some years ago in South Africa, oceanographers found a dead whale on the beach outside Cape Town. They towed it out to Seal Island, a famous habitat of great white sharks that sometimes leap from the water in snagging birds and seals. For hours the sharks gorged themselves on the whale, so much so that they could hardly move. They just floated in the water as if drunk.

Divers went into the cages, right next to the sharks. Instead of the usual attacking and bumping, the sharks had no interest in the divers. This is a great analogy: when people get their needs met, they are generally much less interested in fighting.

There is nothing intrinsic about Arabs and Jews that causes them to be enemies. Hundreds of thousands of Arabs live in Israel; surveys show most are happy with their environment. A basis for successful negotiation is a coalition of diverse people built around collective interests: the necessities of life.

This is not intended to provide a substantive answer to the Middle East or any other public controversy. How settlements and refugees are located, the precise location of land uses, these can all be figured out by experts. The point of this chapter is how to use better negotiation tools so that agreements are possible.

BEING INCREMENTAL

Throughout *Getting More,* one theme I've repeated is to be incremental in bridging large differences between parties. In public issues, where differences are often the largest, the parties are often the least incremental. Trying to move from complete disagreement to complete agreement in one step rarely if ever works.

All of the processes noted in this chapter depend on incremental action. It is not necessary to fix everything at once. It is only necessary to start somewhere. Smaller steps mean less perceived risk. More people will go along with them.

Are the parties involved moving incrementally toward agreement? Or is one party demanding everything at once? If so, they are the wrong people to be negotiating on their party's behalf. In most public issues, there are too many constituencies, there is too much money, and there are too many conflicts to solve everything at one time.

Starting somewhere and achieving a success gives people a model, the confidence to go on, more trust, and a more collaborative working relationship. A small, scalable project is better than a grand effort that is difficult to achieve.

So let's look at the Middle East again as an example, particularly Israel-Palestine. What have the parties been trying to do for decades? Solve everything at once. It's no wonder there's no deal. Instead, let me pose a hypothetical idea, not a specific proposal, but an example of what being incremental looks like.

Let's say you start with one small factory, somewhere on the West Bank. Half the workers would be Israelis, the other half Palestinians, both previously unemployed or underemployed. Financed with government or World Bank funds, perhaps private equity. You would need at most a few hundred workers.

The factory would do something that already works in the region. A good possibility is pharmaceuticals. There are already some pharma factories in Jordan. And Israeli companies are geniuses at making and selling generic drugs.

The factory would support nearby housing, medical care, a school, and a supermarket. The workers would be required to live together. Each would get profit sharing, equity, and a better life for themselves and their families.

You would get someone to publicize it, so that everyone could see that it works. Pretty soon, the workers would be saying, "Hey, I'm feeding, clothing, and sheltering my family. We have education, health care, and good food. How about that?" The Palestinian workers would have more in common with the Israeli workers—schools, neighborhoods, standard of living, etc.—than with extremists in Hamas, and the Israeli workers would also more closely associate with their neighbors than with extremists in Israel. They would build a sense of combined purpose and fraternity among former combatants that would serve as a model for other conflict areas.

Scaling up, it could take a generation, twenty years, to reach a self-sustaining critical mass. People will hear this and say, "That's too long!" I first proposed this in 1981, twenty-eight years ago. I proposed it again nine years ago, on September 23, 2001, twelve days after the World Trade Center destruction, in an article that appeared in *The Philadelphia Inquirer* and elsewhere. The article spelled out the basic principles of this chapter. I repeated it in more detail the following year, and again in 2006. The point is, we have to get under way sometime—why not now?

Besides pharmaceuticals, one could easily see businesses centered around agricultural products, using Israeli low-water-use technology. Or mining minerals from the Dead Sea.

The development of a new State of Palestine could, incrementally, become a proving ground for entrepreneurs to try new ventures. One could envision alternative energy development: solar, biomass, and wind, both for power and for desalinating plants to provide drinking or crop water. And there is almost a clean slate for creating new housing and infrastructure.

The Saudis and Kuwaitis are clearly interested in regional peace. One could see them investing in Palestinian projects in return for equity. Many well-to-do Arabs and Jews living outside the Middle East are itching to help achieve peace. They might buy stock in bona fide projects to promote peace. Projects could qualify for pro bono work for associates at law firms to set up the deal structures.

Instead of building West Bank settlements only for Israelis, Israel could start giving away settlement residences to Arabs in return for work and support. I think there would be some takers. And it would be a model for others.

The more that Israel gives Palestinian moderates, the more likely Israel will gain supporters. For example, Israel has declined to permit more cellphone networks in Palestinian areas it controls and has made access to capital difficult. Israel says that it won't change this policy until it is confident of its own security. But by declining to provide the incentives needed to make itself more secure, Israel is actually preventing its security from being enhanced. In other words, helping Palestinians economically would *promote* Israeli security by collecting more friends among those with more to lose.

What does this have to do with negotiation? You are persuading people to do things differently, to perceive things differently, in order to meet their goals. You are persuading them to deal in a better way with those who are different. You are showing them how to solve public issues. The extent to which government and private enterprise gets behind this would affect the time it takes to implement.

Another global issue that would benefit from supporting incremental steps is climate change. There is much controversy over the right steps to reduce carbon dioxide pollution, which leads to global warming. Some parties want incremental action; others want global consensus. Much time is taken debating individual plans, such as a consumer tax based on pollution, or the trading by companies of the right to pollute.

Instead of searching for the one right answer, from a negotiation viewpoint it would be more effective to embrace incremental steps whenever we can. If someone can reduce net pollution, why not do so? We should do the best we can with the people and the process we can muster at the moment.

And while people are selling or taxing pollution and helping to slow global warming, governments should be actively working to find better processes. When we find one, we will be farther down the path to solving the problem.

The subtle but important difference would be a change in attitude from conflict over the "right" method to incremental action with all methods as an interim step. It would be useful to view the many methods being employed as a laboratory for study of the most effective methods. Governments could support objective studies to continually contrast, compare, and suggest better incremental steps. Protests at international climate meetings are a symptom of the problem. Idea generation, as noted throughout this book, is more effective when it's inclusive, not exclusive.

GOALS

As I've noted often in *Getting More*, the more important a negotiation is to the parties, the more emotional it becomes, the more irrationality comes into play—and the harder it is to meet one's goals. Another key question to ask in public issues is, Are our actions meeting our goals?

Let's look again at the war on terrorism. The primary response to terrorism by developed countries has been violence and threats of violence: in other words, an "in-kind" response. After 9/11, former U.S. defense secretary Donald Rumsfeld said the task the United States had with terrorists was "to find them and to capture them or kill them." After the 2010 Moscow subway bombing, the Russian president said something similar. The "war on terror" continues to have violence at its core.

Violence has always been expensive and time-consuming as a persuasive device. But today there is increasing evidence that violence is working even less well in persuading others.

Historically, if you killed or threatened enough people, the target country or group would give up. Today, however, people—especially ideologues and those with little to lose—are not nearly as persuadable. Suicide bombers are not frightened by the threat of death.

To stop them, you would have to kill them all—a practical impossibility. And many military actions inevitably kill innocent people, whether by accident or not. Such actions create more terrorists and sympathizers.

Moreover, the more we destroy people's land and homes through war, the more people are left with little or nothing, making it easier for terrorist ideologues to recruit them, or at least get their acquiescence.

A few suicide bombers can kill a lot of people and cause millions or billions of dollars in damage. Not only are they not afraid of violence, they seem to embrace it. It is virtually impossible to win a war of violence against a group that welcomes death. And this has become a worldwide phenomenon.

Finally, cultural dispersion has made it much more difficult to find the enemy. The enemy doesn't live in one place, have similar habits or looks, act the same, or speak the same language. That means broadscale attacks are apt to kill innocents and miss terrorists, thus helping to create more terrorists. The United States has found, to its frustration, that even home-grown residents can be terrorists.

Israeli officials were quoted as saying they wanted "to destroy the terrorist infrastructure of Hamas." But it is impossible for Israelis to do this, because they will keep creating enemies as people are killed. It's a goal that can *never* be achieved through violence, technology, organization, or infrastructure.

Every so often a terrorist leader is captured or killed. But there are hundreds of replacements. In Iraq, an eight-year-old Iraqi girl was killed by what the United States said was "an accidental discharge of a weapon." In Gaza, a Palestinian doctor dedicated to peace, who worked with Israeli doctors, saw three of his daughters killed by Israeli fire outside a U.N. school. Each of those who died has a family, perhaps a large family. The result? Hundreds more people who hate the nation that did it and are willing to consider messages against that nation.

Focusing on meeting the needs of moderates, instead of finding and killing the extremists, is a negotiation strategy that appears cheaper, and with a higher chance of success.

Another public issue in which the parties appear not to have met their goals is abortion. After forty years, there is still a bitter struggle. Every once in a while, a doctor who performs abortions is killed. Sometimes, someone is arrested and goes to jail. Does this stop abortions? No. Does this stop the killing of abortion doctors? No. Protests occur, court cases are filed, laws are passed and repealed. And no one meets their goals.

This is clearly not a rational issue. Both sides have framed their arguments in terms that leave no room for negotiation: the killing of fetuses versus a woman's right to choose. Most interesting, however, is that while this struggle continues, abortions continue by the millions. Even if abortions were banned in the United States, people would just find a way to go to other countries, or seek out a black market.

In terms of negotiation tools, therefore, one must look more deeply to find the underlying problem, and then change the goal. The real problem is that there are too many unwanted pregnancies. The second real problem is that each side sees this as all or nothing; neither side's position provides for incremental improvement. The third problem is that the parties are not even talking much to each other about finding common ground and improving the situation.

To be more successful at finding a negotiated solution, I believe the choice should be reframed from right to life versus right to choose to more abortions versus fewer abortions. The current situation means more abortions. Focusing on incremental steps will lead to fewer abortions, something both sides would agree is a good thing.

Thousands of would-be U.S. parents travel the globe looking for babies to adopt. Hundreds of thousands of Americans say they would adopt if they could. A natural question that arises is what are the people on both sides of the abortion issue doing to match pregnant women who have unwanted fetuses with would-be parents who want to adopt? The answer is, clearly, *not enough*. At least *some* of the women who initially didn't want their babies might have them to term instead of aborting them if there were more of a benefit for them, the baby, or both.

If the goal were to prevent unwanted pregnancies, then options such as birth control would become more prominent and supported, making the problem incrementally smaller.

Again, I do not mean to provide specific, substantive answers to the abortion issue. The point is, the process that currently exists does not meet either party's goals.

Any solution needs to start with the notion that no solution is possible unless both parties agree. It begins with respecting each other's perceptions and looking for workable solutions to make the problem smaller. We need calm, empathetic communications. As long as extreme positions dominate, the problem will go on indefinitely.

EMOTION

Both the abortion issue and the reliance on violence come from emotional responses. As a result, people don't meet their goals. I am making the topic of emotion a separate section in this chapter because it is almost always a negotiation problem on its own.

To the extent that an issue becomes emotional, the parties are not listening to each other and effective negotiation is not occurring. In evaluating public issues, one should therefore ask if the parties are emotional or dispassionate.

To continue with our Middle East example, it's not just the violence and the focus on yesterday that cause emotional distractions. Many other issues distract the parties from meeting their goals of peace and a better life.

One obvious distraction in the Middle East is the Israeli settlements being built on the West Bank. Absent emotion, this might be seen as a nonissue. Even though they house more than 300,000 Israelis, these settlements constitute about 5 percent of the land area of the West Bank. Arguing over them takes time away from discussing a new Palestinian state. Land swaps, land carve-outs, compensation, and other solutions are standard in real estate, are known to the parties, and could be approached in a straightforward way as part of a statehood discussion.

In fact, the Palestinian response to almost everything Israel does should be, "When do we talk about a Palestinian state?" This is also true with the debate over East Jerusalem as the Palestinian capital. The Palestinians keep losing sight of their goals, because they get emotional about the settlements. This is a negotiation process failure.

And the Israelis are not offering compensating emotional payments to the Palestinians, such as offering some of the housing for Arabs, or making concessions elsewhere. The point is not whether they *have* to. The point is whether the Israelis want to reduce violence or not.

Another distraction from achieving goals in the Middle East is the continual war of words. Whether or not there was a Holocaust, whether someone should apologize for a given event, alleged corruption in one country or another: these are all important subjects, at least to those involved. But every time they are raised, hot buttons are pushed, and leaders and ordinary citizens get emotional. They stop focusing on peace and economic growth—issues that both sides say are important—and focus on yesterday.

Whatever the issue in whatever country, every time someone else tries to distract the other side with insults or other subjects, the response should be, "Okay, so when do we talk?" It takes discipline to do this. Leaders and media could assist in maintaining focus on goals by pointing out whenever the distractions occur.

Emotional payments reduce the intensity of emotions, and thus distractions. In war-torn areas, one important cause of intense emotion is an inability to fully grieve. The loss of a loved one at the hands of others almost always produces a desire for retribution.

Let's look at the Middle East in this context. There is no effective system to assign and enforce blame on the perpetrators of violence. Often the individuals responsible can't even be found. Without an outlet for grief, people resort to stereotyping. They seek retribution against anyone who seems similar to those behind the violence, even if they had nothing to do with the tragedy. And so the cycle repeats itself.

We've seen this in other countries, too, including the United States, when, for example, African Americans rioted in 1992 in Los Angeles after four police officers were acquitted in the merciless beating of Rodney King. Or retaliation and restrictive action against people from the Middle East living in the United States after the World Trade Center tragedy.

Emotional payments, which can help to avoid distraction from goals, include apologies—both in general and to specific, targeted groups and individuals—as well as respect for other parties and their pain and perceptions. Monuments erected to those who were killed can help surviving friends, family, and relatives to come to terms with their grief and their loss, and reduce emotion.

The Vietnam Memorial in Washington lists the name of every American soldier killed, offering a permanent record of those who died. It is the most visited monument in Washington, often attracting 15,000 visitors a day. It is considered an eloquent, emotional, and powerful source of comfort. It offers family, comrades, and friends an emotional payment by paying respect to those who gave their lives in the war.

There is no such major monument in the Middle East, although various minor monuments have been erected. In fact, there has been opposition by each side to monuments recognizing victims from the other side. Some of the monuments that do exist have been defaced. The lack of a proper monument postpones both sides' ability to come to terms with their losses. It postpones an emotional payment and makes negotiation harder.

A combined Arab-Jewish Middle East memorial, listing all names from whatever date seems right, could convey a sense of common history, consistent with two of the meanings of *monere*, the Latin word for "monument"—"to remind" and "to instruct." It would key on the negotiation tool of finding common enemies, in this case, war, as well as on bonds of similarity among those who have shared a tragic loss.

Similarly, multidenominational grieving centers, open to those who have lost loved ones, would promote common bonds as a common distaste for war. As long as people from all sides were permitted to grieve together (for example, wearing visible pictures of departed loved ones), this would offer both sides another large emotional payment. Without such emotional payments and a resulting drop in the emotional temperature, effective negotiation will continue to be very difficult.

STANDARDS

The concept of fairness is especially important in public issues, where the process and results are visible to a lot of people. From a negotiation standpoint, the best way to ensure the perception of fairness is to use standards that the parties can accept. So the first question to ask is, do the parties accept the notion of using standards? The second is, what standards have parties used in the past? Third is, what standards would the parties accept for this negotiation?

It is best to start with the most general or easily acceptable standards. As noted earlier, for the Middle East, it could be something like, "Do we want dead children?" Anyone who says yes would be perceived as extreme, so this is a good way to separate the bigger group of moderates from the smaller group of extremists. Another might be, "Should refugees eventually have a decent place to live?" Yet another might be, "Should we accept violence that kills civilians?" Or "Should people have enough to eat? Medical care when they're sick? Clean drinking water?"

At the local level, including the school board or planning board, one could ask: "Should government include key voter (or resident) groups before making a decision that affects them?" In all these cases, framing is key. The better or more prepared the party negotiating, the more persuasive the framing will be.

Eventually, standards can become more specific, as in, "Should a State of Palestine be created in exchange for nonviolence?" Or "Should police ask questions to determine if someone is truly threatening?" The questions themselves make the party asking them seem more persuasive. The more people who ask questions with standards embedded, the more persuasive your side will be in any public issue.

PROBLEM-SOLVING

In the 1960s and 1970s, the phrase "Think globally, act locally" became the watchword of the environmental movement. A generation believed that the way to solve the world's problems was to start at the community level, with action by individuals. Somehow, this message got lost in the decades that followed.

Today, the idea is reemerging. It is one of the central ideas of *Getting More*. You, acting alone or with friends or colleagues, can make a substantial difference in the world, and in your life, by using the negotiation tools in this book. All you need to start is the right attitude and an organized process for dealing with others.

So it comes back to this: Ask, "What are my goals? Who are they (the other side)? What will it take to persuade them?" Use the supporting tools of perception, standards, framing, needs, incentives, trading items of unequal value, and losing the emotion. It's not rocket science. It's not perfect. But it will get you that one extra hit every nine games. It might get some people talking who are not now doing so. It might even solve some longstanding problems. The point is to ask whether the parties are interested in using a problem-solving model. A number of my former students are now working in areas of major public concern. They found that the tools have been working as just described.

Sachin Pilot is now the Minister of Telecommunications, Information Technology and Posts in India. He says that the tools of valuing differences have proved indispensable in getting agreements from constituencies in a country with hundreds of distinct cultures. It has been a significant cause of the recent improvements in telecommunications in India, he said.

Meredith Dalton is now the country head for the Peace Corps in Azerbaijan. She has to persuade highly educated Peace Corps volunteers that the right thing to do is learn to knit, learn to cook local dishes, just spend some time with the local people, and talk about their kids. A good grassroots model worthy of replication. The solution, she said, is to take very small steps, "one cup of tea at a time," to paraphrase a popular book title.

Every public issue can be examined in these ten steps to determine whether a successful process is occurring, whether the right people are involved, and how to make things better. The result is not getting everything. But it will get more.

16

How to Do It

Now that you have all this stuff, what do you do with it? How do you start the negotiation? Who should make the first offer? How do you know when the other person is ready to walk away? How do you close the negotiation?

Answers to these questions have been sprinkled throughout *Getting More*, but a summary chapter might be useful.

So here are some thoughts on how to actually do the negotiation—after you've learned the tools, understand your goals, and think you understand the other party. While every situation is different, this chapter should be viewed as a kind of template.

ATTITUDE

If you are nervous, afraid, angry, or distracted, you are more likely to do poorly. Morale is important. The other side will know if you are nervous.

Think about the worst thing that could happen to you in a negotiation. If you can withstand it, you will be more confident. If you can't, this is probably a bad negotiation for you to attempt. Find someone else to conduct the negotiation: prepare more, change the perceived risk, or examine opportunities elsewhere. Get yourself more mentally ready.

If you feel intimidated by the other person or party, imagine them in the most embarrassing position you can think of. Let your imagination run wild.

Lower your expectations about their good faith. Be prepared for anything they might pull. You will be less rattled if they do pull something, and you will be surprised far less. Be incremental. Don't think you have to do everything today. Chill out! Unless your life is on the line, there's always a tomorrow.

Your ability to meet your goals, and your confidence level, is often in your mind. As Henry Ford once said, "Whether you think you can or you can't, you're right."

PREPARATION

A big confidence builder in doing a negotiation is preparation. The more prepared you are, the less nervous and more effective you will be. You won't be busy trying to remember what you're supposed to do next. You won't be as worried about what you don't know.

WHERE AND WHEN TO HAVE THE NEGOTIATION

Short answer: it doesn't matter, as long as you are comfortable, and as long as they are comfortable. If the other side does something that makes you uncomfortable, say, "This will make me uncomfortable." Or "I'm not ready to negotiate yet."

If they say, "Tough," say, "So you'd like me to negotiate unprepared?" Or "Can I get back to you with a more complete answer?" Students sometimes ask, What if it's a job interview? Let me tell you, the interview is the nicest a future employer will ever be to you. If they are unkind to you in the interview, run! If you have to take the job to eat and pay the rent, start planning your exit immediately.

Negotiating on their turf doesn't have to give you less power. It depends on how you frame it. You might say, "Okay, so you'll serve lunch?" Or "Can you send a car for me?" I once was so obnoxious that I sat down in their conference room, leaned back in my chair, and put my feet up on their conference table. My message: "I'm right at home."

This doesn't mean you shouldn't negotiate over where and when a negotiation should take place. It just means that every situation is different. Where and when would be the best place to hold the negotiation to meet your goals?

From time immemorial, men proposed marriage to women in the most romantic place the men could find, at just the right moment. Labor and management might start their negotiation where the company was founded. Disputes among combatants might be settled on hallowed ground. This is not necessary, but might be considered under "nice to have."

GET TO KNOW EACH OTHER

It's not a dance. There are no magic incantations. I tend to be informal. I might say, "Hi." Or "What's going on?" You might be more formal, depending on your comfort level and how well you know them. Find common enemies: complain about the weather or the traffic. Compliment the other person on a suit, dress, or watch. The only thing is, *you have to mean it*. Again, people can spot phonies a mile away.

I've been in negotiations where the other party has said, "How's your family?" And when I started to talk about my wife and son, they appeared to be hardly listening. To me, this was a manipulative person who read about small talk somewhere, but doesn't really care about me.

Think about the other person's perceptions. They put their pants on the same way you do. They get hungry and thirsty and tired and sometimes overwhelmed. They are human, too. Make a human connection.

You may not have time for small talk. But you can still make a human connection. Rayenne Chen at the opening of the book made eye contact in bringing back the plane.

Small talk is big talk in a negotiation. It helps to make a human connection. And humans are social beings, with few exceptions. People like to make connections with each other. Even discussing differences is a connection. It's an act of interacting. Studies have shown that humor (if they recognize it as such), small gifts ("Want a mint?"), or a comment about something interesting that happened today are all key in setting a more collaborative tone.

If you are not interested in the other person, don't conduct the negotiation if you can help it. Your lack of interest will come across. You will seem bored, distant, rude. The best negotiators are curious. They want to know about other people. They want to make a connection.

That does not mean you need to be a social butterfly. But there must be *something* about the other person that's interesting. Something you can learn. The act of being curious about others, by itself, is persuasive.

How can you make yourself and others more comfortable? This is exactly the opposite of what people often do, which is try to make others less comfortable.

Of course, if the other person or party is pressed for time, don't waste their time. Ask them how much time they have. It's another way to make the connection. It shows that you value them, and their time.

The best "small talk" I ever experienced took place during a factory tour. It was the first time I went to Dnepropetrovsk, Ukraine, to tour the sprawling factory complex of Yuzhmash, which I was representing.

After a brief meeting in a conference room, they escorted me to the factory floor, and brought me right up to a huge nuclear missile lying on its side. It must have been as long as a football field.

The nuclear warhead, of course, had been removed. But there were the guidance systems, exposed and being worked on. There were the huge exhaust cones. I could reach out and touch things, and I did. The technicians with their work overalls said hi. One guy told me, proudly, that his target had been Minneapolis. Now that's what I call getting familiar.

GETTING STARTED

Even in a short negotiation, you should know *specifically* what you are going to talk about. That is, what subjects will be covered, and in what order. Get an agenda that both parties agree to. This will help the parties get back on track if they get lost. It will also help organize things.

Karine Adalian, a consultant in California, said she started going into meetings with a one-page written agenda. "The first time, I appeared to be the most prepared person at the table of much more senior people, including thirty percent lawyers," she said. No one else had an agenda or an organized list of issues. So she had copies of her agenda made for everyone. And she got everything she wanted.

If several people bring agendas, it's that much better! Now you have surfaced most of the issues to discuss.

How long will the negotiation take? Sometimes circumstances dictate this. Other times, have a discussion about this. It's often best to break a negotiation incrementally into smaller pieces. Every time you get new information that can affect the negotiation, consider taking a break to think about it, and then resume.

Start with the easy things. It gives the parties a sense of accomplishment and progress as they agree on them. Tell people as soon as you can in the negotiation what you can't agree to. That way, people don't waste their time. If you wait until the end to mention your dealbreaker, one of three things usually happens: (a) the deal falls apart, (b) you lose trust and get a worse deal, or (c) they ask for much more to compensate them for what you are now asking them to give up.

As noted earlier in the book, try to set a time limit on issues. For example, anything you can't solve in fifteen minutes, go on to the next issue. That way, you get as many issues out of the way as you can. Also, try never to commit to any one thing until you see the entire package of points to be negotiated. In lieu of that, make conditional, or tentative, commitments.

THE NEGOTIATION DYNAMIC

You need to discuss the other person's perceptions every time you confront an issue. Through your preparation and role reversal before the negotiation, you should already have ideas about this that you can share. If you want to persuade them, their perceptions are the starting point.

If something surprises you, take a break immediately. My team once took five breaks in the first hour of a merger negotiation where we were presented with a bunch of surprises.

If you have a disagreement on your own team, stifle it while you are in front of the other party. You risk others exploiting the disagreement to play people off against one another. It's okay if more than one person from each side talks, as long as it's not confusing and you are in agreement. That is, if people have assigned roles or you are brainstorming.

If a contradiction emerges, call for a break. Tell the other side something like, "When we figure out what we really mean, we'll let you know." People don't expect you to be perfect. They do expect you to be real.

Decades of studies have shown that time pressure at the end of a negotiation produces: (a) worse deals, (b) less ability to process information, (c) less value added, (d) neglect of important information, (e) bad judgments, (f) more emotion, (g) fewer options, (h) more raw use of power, (i) more stereotyping of the other side, and (j) more stress. It can fray relationships and kill the deal entirely.

If you realize you don't have enough time to cover everything, don't. Get a couple of things done very well, rather than a lot of things done poorly. Use all the time you have.

Time pressure can be real or imagined, internal or external. It's all the same in its harm to negotiations. If you are stressed out by deadlines, make adjustments. Try to allot more time. Or decide you won't negotiate in pressure situations. Whether buying a car or a house, you can tell the other party at the start that if they set a deadline on something, you won't consider buying it. It trains people to behave.

HOW YOU TREAT EACH OTHER

In negotiation classes, we often ask students to rate how they treated each other in a case. Those teams that treated each other poorly almost always did much worse. What do I mean by treating people poorly? Using threats, insults, or sarcasm; interrupting, blaming the other person, devaluing the other side, failing to communicate effectively, not having an agenda, and other people-and-process-related failures. In big cases, the differences in outcomes often mean millions of dollars.

Negotiations are very sensitive to the exact words used. For example, you could issue a veiled threat, such as, "If we don't reach an agreement, it will hurt your reputation." Or you could say instead, "How can we help you use this deal to enhance your reputation?" The latter is a "collaborative threat," as noted earlier. The other party understands what the flip side looks like. But the way you say it—putting a positive spin on it—makes it easier for the other side to hear.

There are many ways to do that. Instead of saying "We don't trust you," why not try "How do we start to trust one another?" Instead of saying "You aren't answering my phone calls," how about "Did you get our calls? We'd love to talk to you about things." You will get better at this with practice.

Is an emotional payment needed? Being nice to them in a hostile situation will make the negotiation better. Focus on what each of you can achieve together—a sense of vision. Let them talk. Let them explain their side of things.

It is usually helpful to appoint one person on your side, at least, as the observer of the other team and process. Whenever this person sees something getting out of whack, they can either ask for a break or say something tactful or diplomatic to keep things on track.

HOW YOU DISCLOSE INFORMATION

Most people are afraid to give too much information up front. My guideline is, give out information that tends to bring you closer to your goals. Don't give out information that tends to bring you farther from your goals.

So if your goal is to buy a car or a company for the least amount possible, it's probably not a good idea to tell the other party how much you can afford, at least not at the start of the negotiation.

However, at the end of the negotiation, if they are asking for more money than you can afford to pay, you might as well tell them that, and let them know what your top price is. That might get them to come down into your range.

Of course, you can also try to bridge the gap with intangibles. But go ahead and reveal your bottom line if (a) you have tried everything else, (b) they are still outside your bargaining range, and (c) it looks like you're at the end of the negotiation.

The same is true with telling them your interests and needs. If you think they will take advantage of you, then don't tell them how much you want something. However, you do need to tell them *something,* or you might not get what you want. The danger of lying about your needs is that they might give you what you don't want. That will turn out to be a mess.

Be incremental if you're not sure about how much good faith the other side is exhibiting. You should say, "I'm interested in this painting," as opposed to "I absolutely adore this painting."

You are not required to disclose information in a negotiation. You are not on the witness stand in court. But you shouldn't be coy about hiding something, either. If you don't feel comfortable answering, you can say, "I don't feel comfortable answering that question."

If someone asks you if you have other offers, ask yourself, "Now why would they ask me that?" The obvious reason is that they want to know if you are desperate, and if you would therefore take less. Instead, ask why that's important. You might say, "Will you pay more if I have other offers?" or "Will you charge more if I don't have other offers?" That's a bit obnoxious. But you should tell people if you think they are playing games. You could ask more tactfully, "What effect do you think this might have on our discussion?"

In a job situation, reframe this and say that you have a lot of "opportunities." You could also say, "Are you trying to find out the (or my) market value?" Then you can suggest using standards.

Who makes the first offer? This answer is actually much easier than you might think. If you have a lot of information about the negotiation, you should make the first offer. That would include price, value, terms, what they know, competitors, and so forth. That is because you are "anchoring" the negotiation, setting expectations if you will, within a narrow range.

So if you know the car prices and details, you should make an offer. In general, you do 3 to 5 percent better if you make the first offer under those circumstances.

If the bargaining range is broad or uncertain, don't make the first offer. You are likely to negotiate against yourself. Their expectations may be a lot different than you think.

A young manager in the Columbia University Executive MBA Program, Charlie Smith, went to buy a kitchen table and chairs with his wife. The set was priced at $3,000. Charlie understood that the store rarely discounted, maybe $50 or so. But he wasn't sure. So he asked the salesman if the store could discount the $3,000 set if they bought it today, and also since they were starting to furnish their new home.

"How about $300 off?" the salesman said. Charlie was so flabbergasted that he just stood there, unable to speak.

"Okay, what about $500 off?" the salesman said, filling the silence. Charlie started to regain his voice. "Well, uh . . ."

"And I'll throw in free delivery and eat the sales tax," the salesman said. Total discount: $800. The point: don't make the first offer if you don't know the bargaining range. You *will* negotiate against yourself. "It's happened again and again since then," said Charlie, now managing director and head of corporate finance at Loughlin-Meghi Company in New York. "It's a good lesson that one's perceptions might not be a complete picture of the situation."

Now that doesn't mean you can never make the first offer if the bargaining range is wide or uncertain. You can narrow the bargaining range by asking questions. Why is the other person here to discuss this matter? You can find out their needs. People will often tell you a lot if you ask them.

But the rule of thumb is not to make the first offer unless you have a lot of information about them, the bargaining range, and the situation. Always try to find out.

EXTREME OFFERS

Extreme offers kill deals. The other party usually feels insulted. If it's too low, it devalues the other party. If it's too high, often the other party gives up. It risks your credibility. If you make an extreme offer and then quickly back off it, the other party thinks you were trying to take advantage of them. Mistrust ensues.

An extreme offer is an offer upon which no reasonable standard or information is based, as perceived by the *other* party. Not you, but the other party. Even a madman thinks his offer is reasonable. You need to look into the head of the other party and figure out what they think. As such, the tactic of asking for a lot to give yourself negotiating room will too often backfire.

What if an extreme offer is made to you? The antidotes are (a) not reacting emotionally, (b) asking questions, and (c) using standards. Maybe they're not trying to take advantage of you. Maybe they don't know how to negotiate effectively. Maybe someone taught them to do this. So ask them how they got to this offer. Did they pick it out of a hat? Do they have some data? Also, you can say that the offer is out of line with what you've seen elsewhere. So where did they get their information?

Extreme offers also violate one of the fundamental principles of the book: being incremental. Almost by definition, an extreme offer is the opposite of incremental. So the chances of the other party accepting it are much less. In a meeting, if someone is extreme, you might turn to the other members of that person's team and say something like, "Do you all agree with each and every word that was just said?" If there is any hesitation, ask for a break. Maybe they can talk some sense into the person being extreme.

Check and test everything. If you are buying a car and they tell you a particular option costs more, check it on the Internet. *The Wall Street Journal* once did an article in which a dealer added $2,000 to the purchase price for high-end tires and rims. The buyer did an Internet search right there on his cell phone and found that the wheels were actually less expensive than the standard ones, which came with the car at no extra charge.

THE POWER DYNAMIC

As noted throughout this book, be careful of overusing power. Just use enough to meet your goals but not more. Lessening the misuse of power by the other side is important only if it enhances your ability to meet your goals.

It should be clear by now that the notion of power in and of itself is irrelevant. It is relevant largely in relation to your goals. Traditional ideas that size equates with power are simply not true. First, small parties can be very powerful. A single well-prepared advocate such as Martin Luther King Jr. or Mahatma Gandhi can inspire millions and bring governments and other power interests to their knees. The young man who stood in front of a line of tanks at Tiananmen Square in the 1989 uprising changed the power balance. Though he never said a word to the public, his standard apparently was, "In China, it's not right to use violence against individuals expressing themselves." He made a human connection with his countrymen, the operators of the tanks. They were unwilling to run him down under those circumstances. At the same time, large parties can be weak, or become weak. Consider Enron, which lost all its power quickly amid a financial scandal.

Who has more power, General Motors, which essentially went bankrupt, or a highly profitable, medium-size technology firm? GM had a lot of expenses and debts. But the smaller firm probably had much more control over its goals and its destiny. And it likely has a lot more credibility.

In the 1970s and 1980s, the multibillion-dollar nuclear power construction industry in the United States was all but destroyed by a loose-knit coalition of people who had been ridiculed and deemed powerless by utility companies. Those people included college-educated housewives, retired people who went to the library, various journalists, activist attorneys, and public interest groups whose members were in college or recently graduated. This collection of people formed a coalition, did research, and found safety issues, including the hazards of what to do with nuclear waste and how to evacuate the surrounding area in the case of an accident. They persuaded lawmakers to pass more stringent regulatory requirements, and the economics of nuclear power went out the window.

In a 1987 treatise by Martin K. Starr and John E. Ullman titled "The Myth of U.S. Industrial Supremacy," a line has stuck with me. I hope it sticks with you: "There is no institution, enterprise, society or human achievement of any sort, no matter how strongly established and esteemed, that cannot be ruined." Good comment on the misuse of power: with your kids, your company, your counterparts, or even your competitors.

As you negotiate, don't throw your weight around. It may well come back to bite you. And if they throw their weight around, make sure you document every unreasonable action.

If they have a lot more raw power than you do, they can certainly beat you up. In such a case, you should acknowledge their power, giving them an emotional payment. And you should ask them, just because they can beat you up, should they? For example, if an opera house can beat down a star performer in negotiations, how will that performer feel? Will he or she be as motivated to give a great performance, thus benefiting the opera house? If you can beat up employees, will they work less hard for you?

Better to focus on meeting needs and expanding the pie by using the tools in this book. And feel free to have a frank discussion about power with your counterparts. Feel free to educate them, tactfully, if they are mis-guided. Remember, though, they might be emotional about their power, so they may need emotional payments.

WHAT ARE OUR NEEDS?

After you become comfortable with one another, the parties need to figure out what to negotiate about. Goal-setting will help this. So will agenda-setting. Now you need to go more deeply into what your needs are. Not just in the negotiation itself, but in life. That's because you can trade items of unequal value. What can you trade off in the negotiation, on any subject?

WHAT CRITERIA SHOULD WE USE TO EVALUATE OPTIONS?

For things that you cannot trade off, you should be looking for standards (criteria) to help you decide the best criteria. What are their standards? What criterion should you use to decide? Is it prices of comparable houses? Is it past practice?

WHAT CAN WE DO NOW? MEDIUM TERM? LONG TERM?

It is empowering to figure out what the parties can do now. A lot of people get lost in negotiations because they argue over things they have no control over. Even if the other items on your agenda are really important, if you can't do them now, who cares?

That doesn't mean you shouldn't have a strategy for long-term gains. But the more stuff you get done now, the more all the parties will feel a sense of accomplishment. And the more likely they will keep trying to agree on things.

As noted earlier, prioritize the issues based on what is easiest and fast-est. Easiest is a subset of fastest in most cases. You should do all the things now that you can do now. Then tackle the medium-term things. And then the long-term things.

If the parties can't decide anything, can they recommend something? Can they decide when to meet next? Can they figure out what parties should be involved next time? Can they get to know each other better? Can they explore creative options that will make each look better to their own third parties back at home or the office?

This is all part of being incremental. A lot of people want to do the whole thing at once. This takes so much up-front planning, cost, and organization. We live in a rapidly changing world. If you plan out every detail of a long, long campaign, and the world changes (which it usually does), then you've wasted all this time, effort, and expense.

WHOM DO WE NEED TO HELP US?

Almost everyone needs third parties to help them complete things. Even when negotiating with a contractor. Do you need to get something at the hardware store? Do you need permission from the town? Is there some electric or water hook-up that needs to be dealt with?

A really good task for the parties in a negotiation is to figure out the third parties and other resources that are needed.

HOW CAN WE MAKE A COMMITMENT THAT STICKS?

As I pointed out earlier in the book, just because two parties say, "I agree," or sign a contract, doesn't mean you have a commitment. You need a commitment from them in the way *they* make commitments. This should be explicitly discussed as part of the negotiation.

They will want to know, also, whether you've made a commitment. Third parties can both strengthen *and* weaken commitments. Boards of directors, bosses, bankruptcy officials, an economic recession, or other kinds of new information could scuttle the deal. If there is a ratification process on each side, what does that look like? Which third parties or incentives can hold the other party to its commitments?

The making of a commitment also needs a deadline and a time frame. This needs to be explicit. If there are any conditions that will cause the other party (or you) to be able to get out of the commitment, spell them out.

Finally, what happens if a party breaks its commitment? Will anything be owed to the other party? Best to get all this settled up front. The other party might say, "We won't break the commitment! Don't you trust us?" You should answer, "What if you leave the company? What will the next owner or management team do? What if you get hit by a truck?"

If they say there is no chance they will break the commitment, ask for strong penalties, since it carries no risk for them, but "It will make me and my team feel a lot better." Test people. Be careful of taking on more risk.

Risk should be discussed explicitly in negotiations. This ranges from key employees leaving to third-party interference (friends, lovers, regulators) to a noncollaborative person. Clearly, the more risk one takes, the more one is entitled to be compensated in some way. So a key thing to do in a negotiation is to understand the other party's risk profile. Then try to minimize their perceived risk. If you reduce their perceived risk, they will pay you more if you are a seller, or take less if you are a buyer.

This is why people who start new businesses try to get seasoned businesspeople on their board of directors or their advisory board: financiers will think there is less risk.

You can argue with the other side about actual risk all day. This is not as important as figuring out their *perceived* risk and reducing it. All of these things should be *specifically* discussed in the negotiation.

Some negotiators try to *increase* the other party's perception that they are risky, in order to exact more in the negotiation. This is what happens when lenders lower your credit score based too often on some spurious example of a credit problem. Consistent with the advice in *Getting More*, ask for details and evidence. Get the standards.

More effective is a *joint* effort to reduce perceived risk. Make risk a common problem. That way, you are working on it together. If they don't want to help you, assume they are trying to manufacture perceived risk in order to charge you more (for example, a bank or credit card agency). Be suspicious.

WHO DOES WHAT BEFORE OUR NEXT MEETING?

You've all had this experience. You leave a really great discussion. Then you think about it and you are not sure who does what: spouse, kid, friends, colleagues, counterparts. "Now who was going to get the tickets to the game? Who was going to call about the airline schedules? And was the person who called going to buy the tickets, too?"

So when the moment of truth comes to put everything together, a key thing has not been done. Everything is ruined. Everybody blames everybody else. Or it is blamed on "miscommunication."

But the real culprit was the lack of tying things down. So at the end of each negotiation, develop a task list, with a timetable and individual responsibility.

If something goes wrong, who contacts whom? Is there a sort of emergency lever that anyone can pull? Who does your job if you get sick?

Does each person have a back-up plan if their first choice doesn't pan

out? Does each person have a range within which to make a decision before consulting others? Sit down and think of all this stuff. Take a pen and
a piece of paper and five, ten, fifteen, or thirty minutes. It will save days of
time, lots of money, and tons of aggravation.

FROM PICTURES TO GOALS

I want to come back to the summary of my course: what are my goals, who
are they, what will it take to persuade them. I just want to make sure you
have the picture in your head. Here is the model in a nutshell.

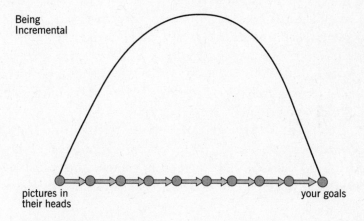

Being
Incremental

pictures in
their heads

your goals

First, the big arc is what people usually try to do: go in one step from
the pictures in their heads to your goals. It's too big a step for most people.
Instead, go back until you find the pictures in their heads. Then ask them
questions that confirm those pictures. Do you want to reach an agreement? Do you want to have a meeting? Once you get them to confirm it,
move one small step at a time toward your goals.

So, your goals are at the right, who they are is at the left, and what it will
take to persuade them is the step-by-step, incremental process that you
will use to get them there.

Yeah, yeah, yeah. Don't need to repeat it. You know all this. But it's not
enough to know all this. You actually have to *do it*. Which, of course, is the
title of this chapter. And the way to get more. Which, of course, is the title
of this book.

You're ready! Go out there and *get more!*

Acknowledgments

It would have been impossible to do this book without the twenty years of contributions by the thousands of students and other participants in my courses. They submitted hundreds of thousands of pages of their personal and professional negotiating problems and insights in journals and shared them in class. Several hundred of these negotiators agreed to have their names, often their company names and what amounts to competitive or personal information, shared with others. This is a remarkable endorsement of their commitment to the tools and teachings of *Getting More* and their desire to make the world a better place. Their real-life stories pushed me to clarify and focus the new negotiation ideas that form the basis of this book, and to integrate and contrast them with traditional ways of thinking.

I'd especially like to recognize Merrill Perlman, former copy chief of the *New York Times* and a former colleague there. Merrill served as my outside editor on this project, and she was marvelous in honing the material, asking tough questions, sharpening my focus, and in general making it a better book.

Two outside readers, who are friends and colleagues, deserve particular thanks for taking an enormous amount of their own time to carefully review the manuscript. They are Susan Brandwayn, an economist at the U.N. Conference on Trade and Development in New York, and Christopher Arfaa, an attorney in private practice in Radnor, Pennsylvania. Their comments made the public-issues sections, in particular, much better, and I am indebted to them.

Jennifer Rudolph Walsh, co-head of the worldwide literary department for WME (William Morris Endeavor) in New York, was my agent on this project and an early supporter. It was she, as a participant in an executive program I taught at Wharton, who first recognized the importance of this work as being much different from the conventional wisdom, and believed it could be a book. She shepherded the entire process and found just the right publishing partners.

The team at Random House, coordinated by my editor there, Roger Scholl, patiently worked through many drafts and thousands of changes so *Getting More* had the right tone, content, and story for the North American market. The team at Penguin, coordinated by editor Joel Rickett, was enthusiastic and helpful in understanding what I was trying to do, and in establishing sales in the United Kingdom, India, Australia, and other parts of the British Commonwealth.

My staff in Philadelphia has been little short of astonishing in helping to research and complete the book—working nights, weekends, and holidays, making constructive suggestions, and in general doing whatever it took. They include Mara Cutler Katsikis, Amy Federman, Ahsiya Shiffrin, Sabura Shiffrin, and Julie Fallin. Among the students who worked part-time to help contribute were Livingston Miller, David Slifka, Rachel Brenner, Zoe Zuo, Tanya Louneva, and Karthik Jayashankar.

Every new perspective in human evolution builds on the work that precedes it. I am grateful to The Wharton School, Penn Law School, and the colleagues with whom I interfaced for the time and opportunities that enabled me to practice my craft while learning from it. So, too, my corporate and government clients and business partners have provided insight and experience hard to develop elsewhere.

Finally, my wife and partner of thirty-six years, Kimberly Greer, has been on this project every step of the way, lending her considerable professional skills and putting up with personal challenges morning, noon, and night. This book would never have been possible without her. My eight-year-old son, Alexander, exhibited patience far beyond his years.

For anyone I have omitted, I apologize; as the book says, there is always tomorrow.

Index

About the Author

STUART DIAMOND has taught and advised on negotiation to corporate and government leaders in more than forty countries. He teaches at The Wharton School, often ranked as the world's leading business school, where his negotiation course has been the most popular for thirteen years in the student course auction.

He has also taught at Columbia, NYU, USC, Berkeley, Oxford, and Penn Law School, where he is currently an adjunct professor. He holds a law degree from Harvard and an MBA from Wharton, and is a former associate director of the Harvard Negotiation Project. He has won numerous teaching awards.

Diamond advises companies and governments on more effective negotiation, and has owned or managed businesses in a variety of countries, from an airline to medical services to finance deals for multiple constituencies. He has provided negotiation advice and training to attorneys and to managers and executives for half the Global 100 companies and a quarter of the Global 500 companies. His clients have included JPMorgan Chase, Citibank, General Electric, Johnson & Johnson, Google, Yahoo!, Merck, Microsoft, BASF, Prudential, the World Bank, the Government of Colombia, a $16 billion petrochemical company in China, a $4 billion foreign dealership network in Russia, scientists in Ukraine, entrepreneurs in South Africa, and pharmaceutical companies in the Middle East.

He has consulted extensively for the United Nations. He once persuaded three thousand farmers in the jungles of Bolivia to stop growing illicit coca and start growing bananas for export to Argentina. In 2008, he provided the process that enabled the Writers Guild to settle their dispute with the studios in Hollywood. And he has taught parents how to get their kids to go to bed on time and brush their teeth with a minimum of hassle.

In a prior career, Diamond was a journalist at the *New York Times*, where he won the Pulitzer Prize as part of a team investigating the crash of the space shuttle *Challenger* in 1986. He has written two previous books, two documentary films, and more than two thousand newspaper and magazine articles.

There is a more extensive bio at www.gettingmore.com.